Essential Figures
in the Talmud

Essential Figures in the Talmud

Ronald L. Eisenberg

Jason Aronson
Lanham • Boulder • New York • Toronto • Plymouth, UK

Published by Jason Aronson
A wholly owned subsidiary of The Rowman & Littlefield Publishing Group, Inc.
4501 Forbes Boulevard, Suite 200, Lanham, Maryland 20706
www.rowman.com

10 Thornbury Road, Plymouth PL6 7PP, United Kingdom

British Library Cataloguing in Publication Information Available

Library of Congress Cataloging-in-Publication Data

Eisenberg, Ronald L.
  Essential figures in the Talmud / Ronald L. Eisenberg.
p. cm.
  Includes bibliographical references.
  ISBN 978-0-7657-0941-7 (cloth : alk. paper) — ISBN 978-0-7657-0942-4 (ebook)
  1. Talmud—Biography—Dictionaries. I. Title.
BM501.15.E37 2013
2009.2'2—dc23

2012021308

Printed in the United States of America

To Zina Leah, Avlana Kinneret, and Cherina Carmel, who beautify, nurture, and uplift my life's journey and joyously share in my love of Torah.

Contents

Preface

Searching for information about Talmudic figures can be a difficult task. In my own studies, I have found that the available sources provide either brief identification of the more than 2,000 Rabbis mentioned in the text or detailed descriptions of a small number of individuals. In response to what I perceived as a gap in existing reference works, I decided to develop *Essential Figures in the Talmud* to present manageable amounts of information about the more than 250 Rabbis that I found to be most important to an understanding of the text. The goal was to make the book sufficiently comprehensive, yet efficient and accessible. Written in a narrative style and taking material from the vast expanse of the Talmud and Midrash, each entry contains biographical information with illustrative quotations from the Talmud and cross-references to other entries in the book.

In addition to interpretations of the biblical commandments and legal issues, the Talmudic rabbis were deeply involved in all aspects of life, from scientific speculations in medicine, astronomy, and biology, to moral and ethical teachings, folklore and legends, and profound observations on all phases of human experience. Since these elements of the Talmud could be of interest to anyone who wants to learn more about Jewish life and history, I wanted to make sure that my discussion of them was accessible to everyone, not just the rabbinic scholar. Consequently, I have added material in parentheses to improve the flow in English of the often terse Talmudic writing, also inserting additional explanations to clarify the text.

Besides an introduction to the various components of the Talmud, several appendices are included to aid the reader. One table provides a timeline of the individuals in the book, which extends from the fourth century B.C.E. to the sixth century C.E. There is also a list of the abbreviations of the biblical and rabbinic works cited in the text, as well as a glossary of terms that includes a brief synopsis of the tractates of the Mishnah and other rabbinic writings. Two maps illustrate the geographic locations of the major Talmudic academies in Babylonia and the Land of Israel.

The individuals described in the book developed the rabbinic Judaism that persists to the current day. Therefore, *Essential Figures in the Talmud* is designed to appeal not only to a broad Jewish audience, but also to educated general readers of diverse cultural backgrounds who want to learn more about the development of traditional Jewish thought during its formative period.

—

Acknowledgments

In preparing the English translations from the Bible and rabbinic literature, I consulted several superb references I would like to acknowledge. These include the Jewish Publication Society Tanach, the CD-version of the Soncino edition of the Babylonian Talmud (Davka), and the Schottenstein editions of the Babylonian Talmud and Jerusalem Talmud (Mesorah).

I also want to express special thanks to my wife, Zina Schiff, for her continual encouragement and constant enthusiasm in reading and thoughtfully editing my writing, which were so vital to the publication of this book.

Introduction

The destruction of the Second Temple in Jerusalem by the Romans in 70 C.E. ended the sacrificial system and convinced the Rabbis that the survival of the Jewish people depended on an intensified dedication to Torah. In addition to the Five Books of Moses, the Written Law, this required a focus on the Oral Law, the body of rabbinic discussions, expositions, and commentaries on the Torah that deals with all aspects of existence from the most trivial to the sublime. Consisting of two major divisions—*halachah* (legal) and *aggadah* (nonlegal)—the Oral Law was traditionally considered part of the Revelation given to Moses and subsequently transmitted faithfully by the leaders of each generation to their successors.

In about 220, Judah ha-Nasi (Judah the Prince) wrote the Mishnah, the earliest rabbinic book, which contained a summary of the large number of legal opinions of the *tannaim* (literally, "repeaters" who acted as "living books") that had developed over the centuries in the academies of learning, primarily in the Land of Israel. This book describes those Rabbis living in the Land of Israel, then and later, as "Palestinian." This reflects the term that was applied to the country during the rabbinic period by the Romans, who refused to use the Jewish word "Judah" (or even the Roman adaptation "Judea") for the land.

The Mishnah is divided into six sections, known as *sedarim* (orders): Zera'im (seeds), dealing with the laws of agriculture; Mo'ed (appointed seasons), dealing with the laws of the Sabbath and holidays; Nashim (women), dealing with the laws of marriage and divorce; Nezikin (damages), dealing with civil and criminal law; Kodashim (holy things), dealing with ritual slaughter, the dietary laws, and sacrifices; and Tohorot (purities), dealing with various aspects of ritual purity. Each order is divided into *massechot* (tractates), which are generally arranged according to their length. The first order, though primarily dealing with agricultural tithes, first fruits, and similar topics, opens with tractate Berachot (Blessings), presumably because this seemed to be the most appropriate way to begin this compendium of the Divine will (Holtz, 132). Written in Hebrew, the Mishnah records disagreements among the various sages and schools and frequently does not conclusively determine the *halachah*, yet it provides a uniformly recognized basis for the subsequent deliberations of centuries of scholars and commentators.

The Tosefta (supplement) is a collection of *baraitot*, which are legal, historic, or *aggadic* traditions that were not included in the Mishnah of Judah ha-Nasi. From an Aramaic word meaning "outside," the *baraitot* are attributed to rabbinic teachers who lived in the Land of Israel at or before the time of the Mishnah. The Tosefta is arranged according to the order of the Mishnah, but is about four times larger.

The Gemara (Aramaic for "study") refers to the extensive legal and ethical discussions and interpretations on the Mishnah in the great academies of learning that were compiled over several centuries by the *amoraim* (those who discuss). The combination of the Mishnah and Gemara constitutes the Talmud. In general use, the term "Talmud" refers to the Babylonian Talmud, though there is also a much smaller Jerusalem Talmud, which actually was compiled in the Galilee. The Babylonian Talmud, a monumental work of almost 6,000 folio pages, is the authoritative text of rabbinic Judaism.

Abbreviations

Ar.	Arachin
ARN	Avot d'Rabbi Nathan
Av. Zar.	Avodah Zarah
Avot	Pirkei Avot
BB	Bava Batra
B.C.E.	Before the Common Era
Bek.	Bechorot
Ber.	Berachot
Betz.	Beitzah
Bik.	Bikurim
BK	Bava Kama
BM	Bava Metzia
C.E.	Common Era
Chron.	Chronicles
Dem.	Demai
Deut.	Deuteronomy
Deut. R.	Deuteronomy Rabbah
Eccles.	Ecclesiastes
Eccles. R.	Ecclesiastes Rabbah
Eduy.	Eduyot
Er.	Eruvin
Esth.	Esther
Esth. R.	Esther Rabbah
Exod.	Exodus
Exod. R.	Exodus Rabbah
Ezek.	Ezekiel
Gen.	Genesis
Gen. R.	Genesis Rabbah
Git.	Gittin
Hab.	Habbakuk
Hag.	Haggai
Hag.	Hagigah
Hal.	Hallah

Hor.	Horayot
Hos.	Hosea
Hul.	Hullin
Isa.	Isaiah
Jer.	Jeremiah
Jon.	Jonah
Josh.	Joshua
JT	Jerusalem Talmud
Judg.	Judges
Ker.	Keritot
Ket.	Ketubot
Kid.	Kiddushin
Kil.	Kilayim
Lam.	Lamentations
Lam. R.	Lamentations Rabbah
Lev.	Leviticus
Lev. R.	Leviticus Rabbah
Mak.	Makot
Mal.	Malachi
Mech.	Mechilta
Meg.	Megillah
Me'il.	Me'ilah
Men.	Menachot
Mic.	Micah
Mid. Ps.	Midrash Psalms
Mik.	Mikva'ot
MK	Mo'ed Katan
Nah.	Nahum
Naz.	Nazir
Ned.	Nedarim
Nid.	Niddah
Num.	Numbers
Num. R.	Numbers Rabbah
Obad.	Obadiah
PdRE	Pirkei de-Rabbi Eliezer
PdRK	Pesikta de-Rabbi Kahana
Pes.	Pesachim
Pes. Rab.	Pesikta Rabbati
Prov.	Proverbs
Ps.	Psalms
RH	Rosh Hashanah
Ruth R.	Ruth Rabbah

Sam.	Samuel
Sanh.	Sanhedrin
Sem.	Semachot
Shab.	Shabbat
Shek.	Shekalim
Shev.	Shevuot
Song R.	Song of Songs Rabbah
Soph.	Sopherim
Sot.	Sotah
Suk.	Sukkah
Taan.	Ta'anit
Tam.	Tamid
Tanh.	Tanhuma
Ter.	Terumot
Tosef.	Tosefta
Uk.	Uktzin
Yad.	Yadayim
Yev.	Yevamot
Zech.	Zechariah
Zeph.	Zephaniah
Zev.	Zevachim

Rabbis Cited without Patronymics

Eleazar	Eleazar ben Shammua (Mishnah)
	Eleazar ben Pedat (Gemara)
Eliezer	Eliezer ben Hyrcanus
Isaac	Isaac Nappacha
Ishmael	Ishmael ben Elisha
Jacob	Jacob ben Korshai
Jeremiah	Jeremiah bar Abba
Jonathan	Jonathan ben Eleazar or Jonathan ben Joseph
Jose	Jose ben Halafta
Joseph	Joseph bar Hiyya
Joshua	Joshua ben Hananiah
Judah	Judah bar Ezekiel or Judah ben Ilai
Nachman	Nachman bar Jacob
Rabbah	Rabbah bar Nachmani
Rabbi	Judah ha-Nasi
Rav	Abba bar Aivu
Rava	Abba bar Joseph bar Hama
Samuel	Samuel ben Abba ha-Kohen
Yochanan	Yochanan bar Nappacha

A

Abba bar Abba, Babylonian *amora* (second/third century).

Known primarily through his son, Samuel, the illustrious head of the academy at Nehardea, Abba bar Abba is generally cited in the Talmud as "Samuel's father." Although living in Babylonia, Abba bar Abba traveled to the Land of Israel and became friends with Judah ha-Nasi. Abba bar Abba was distinguished for his piety, learning, and honesty. On one occasion, "the father of Samuel found some donkeys in a desert. He returned them to their owner after twelve months, going beyond the requirements of the law [i.e., he could have kept them]" (BM 24b). He also was described as having been entrusted with protecting money belonging to orphans. However, Abba bar Abba died suddenly when Samuel was away from home, and the latter had no idea where the money was hidden. Desperate to find the savings of these poor unfortunates, Samuel went to the cemetery where Abba bar Abba was buried and asked the spirits how to contact him. When the spirit of his father appeared, Samuel asked where he had secreted the money of the orphans. "It is all in the shed of the millstones. The upper and lower layers of money belong to you, and the middle layer belongs to the orphans." When the incredulous Samuel asked the reason for this seemingly bizarre system, Abba bar Abba replied: "If thieves came they would steal the top layer [before running away, and the loss would be ours alone]. If the soil rotted away and destroyed the bottom layer, [again the loss would only be ours]." In either case, the money of the orphans in the middle layer would be preserved (Ber. 18b).

Abba bar Abba declared, "One may not enter into a business partnership with a heathen, lest the latter be obliged to take an oath [in connection with a business dispute] and swear by his idol" (Sanh. 63b).

Abba bar Kahana, Palestinian *amora* (third century).

Emigrating to the Land of Israel from Babylonia, Abba bar Kahana brought with him many *aggadic* interpretations that he repeated in the name of his teacher, Rav. Discussing the verse, "The sun rises and the sun sets" (Eccles. 1:5), Abba bar Kahana explained that it showed how God precisely arranged the world: "Before the sun of Moses set, the sun of Joshua rose; the sun of Samuel rose before the sun of Eli set, and on the day that R. Akiva died,

1

Judah ha-Nasi was born" (Gen. R. 58:2; Eccles. R. 1:10). He interpreted the verse, "The end of the matter, all having been heard: revere God, and observe His commandments; for this is the whole duty of humankind" (Eccles. 12:13), as meaning that a single person "is equal in value to the whole world" (Ber. 6b). Abba bar Kahana stressed the importance of every commandment in the Torah, noting that the easiest to fulfill (sending the mother bird away from the nest when the fledglings are taken so she not suffer the anguish of seeing them killed) and the hardest to perform (honoring one's father and mother) have the same reward of long life (JT Pe'ah 1:1).

Other *aggadic* statements of Abba bar Kahana include: "Such is the way of the righteous; they say little and do much" (Deut. R. 1:11); "No serpent ever bites below unless it is incited from above . . . nor does a government persecute a man unless it is incited from above" (Eccles. R. 10:11); and "If you see the student benches in the Land of Israel filled with Babylonians [interpreted by some as 'every day'], look forward to the approaching steps of the Messiah" (Lam. R. 1:41).

Abba bar Zavda, Palestinian *amora* (third/fourth century).

A student of Rav and R. Huna in Babylonia, Abba bar Zavda returned to the Land of Israel and became one of the leading scholars at the academy in Tiberias. He was given the honor of introducing the lecture that R. Ammi and R. Assi concluded (JT Sanh. 1:4). When the Rabbis urged him to "take a wife and sire children," Abba bar Zavda replied, "Had I been worthy I would have had them from my first wife." However, as the Talmud states, "He was merely evading the Rabbis, for in fact Abba ben Zavda became impotent [sitting] through the long discourses of R. Huna" (Yev. 64b).

The famous expression "A Jew, even though he sins, remains a Jew" comes from a comment by Abba bar Zavda: "Even though [the people] have sinned, they are still [called] 'Israel' [the name of honor for the people when they are faithful to God]." He made an analogy to "a myrtle, [which] though it stands among reeds, still is [and is called] a myrtle" (Sanh. 44a). Delivering a sermon on a public fast day, Abba bar Zavda exhorted those wishing to repent to correct their evil ways. "A man who holds an unclean reptile in his hand can never become clean, even though he bathes in the waters of Shiloah or in the waters of Creation" (JT Taan. 2:1). The Babylonian Talmud has a similar quotation, attributed to Abba bar Ahavah, who stated that confession without true repentance was a worthless endeavor. He compared it to a man who immersed himself in the purifying waters of the *mikveh* (ritual bath) while still grasping in his hand a defiling reptile (Taan. 16a).

On several occasions, Abba bar Zavda quoted Rav: "A mourner is bound by all the commandments of the Torah with the sole exception of *tefillin*, since the word 'beauty' is applied to them [Ezek. 24:17]"; and "A mourner is bound by the obligation of Sukkah . . . [as are] a bridegroom, best man, and all the guests at the wedding festivities" (Suk. 25b).

Abba Benjamin, Palestinian *tanna* (second century).

Abba Benjamin taught that "a man's prayer is heard [by God] only in the synagogue" (Ber. 6a). This was based on the verse, "Turn to the song and to the prayer [of your servant]" (1 Kings 8:28), implying that "the prayer is to be recited where there is song [i.e., that of the community and the *hazzan*]." He added, "When two people enter [a synagogue] to pray, and one of them finishes his prayer first and leaves without waiting for the other [the synagogue being outside the town and it was dangerous to remain alone], his prayer is rejected [lit., 'torn up before his face']" (Ber. 5b). Giving voice to his superstitions, Abba Benjamin observed: "If the eye had the power to see demons, no creature could endure the sight of them" (Ber. 6a). He added, "All my life I took great pains about two things: that my prayer should be near my bed [i.e., he prayed immediately after rising] and that my bed should be placed north and south [a position said to increase the number of male children]" (Ber. 5b).

Abba Benjamin has been identified as "Benjamin the Righteous," who was a supervisor of the charity fund. Once when there was no money in the fund, he supported a hungry woman and her seven children out of his own pocket. Later he became dangerously ill and on the brink of death. The angels addressed God: "You have said that he who saves one soul of Israel is considered as if he had saved the whole world. Shall Benjamin the Righteous, who has saved a woman and her seven children, die so young?" Immediately, the heavenly decree against him was torn up and twenty-two years were added to his life (BB 11a).

Abba Gurion of Sidon, Palestinian *tanna* (second century).

Quoting his teacher, R. Abba Guria, Abba Gurion of Sidon listed several occupations that a father should urge his son to avoid: "donkey-driver, camel-driver, waggoner [elsewhere translated as 'barber'], sailor, shepherd, and shopkeeper, because such professions are those of robbers [i.e., they tend to overcharge for their services]" (Kid. 4:14). Drivers, because when sent on long journeys they hire themselves out to others to work during time that is not rightfully their own; shepherds, because they lead their flocks into the fields of others; shopkeepers, because it is easy for them to supply adulterated goods.

Midrash Abba Gurion, which contains explanations of more than fifty verses in the Book of Esther, is named based on the opening of the work, which quotes several Aramaic passages attributed to this Palestinian *tanna*.

Abba Hilkiah, Palestinian *amora* (first century C.E.).

Like his celebrated grandfather, Honi the Circle Drawer, Abba Hilkiah also was known as a saint whose prayers for rain were answered. However, he would only pray for rain together with his wife, since he deemed her more worthy than himself; she could fix a meal to feed the hungry immediately, while he could only give them money that would provide nourishment later (Taan. 23a–b).

Abba Hilkiah was considered a paragon of righteousness. Once when there was an urgent need for rain, several scholars sent to fetch Abba Hilkiah found him hoeing in the fields. They greeted him, but he took no heed of them. He continued working and then returned home. When they later asked the reason for his bizarre behavior, Abba Hilkiah replied: "I was a laborer hired by the day and I did not wish to waste my employer's time." Why did he carry wood on one shoulder and a cloak on the other? "It was a borrowed cloak; I borrowed it for one purpose [to wear] and not for any other." When they inquired why he went barefoot throughout the whole journey but put his shoes on when reaching a stream, Abba Hilkiah responded: "What was on the road I could see, but not what was in the water." Explaining his reason for lifting up the hem of his coat whenever he walked through thorns and thistles, Abba Hilkiah observed: "This [the torn skin of the body] heals itself, but the other [the clothes] does not." The conversation continued: "Why did your wife come all dressed up to meet you when you entered the city?" "So that I might not look at any other woman." "Why did she enter [the house] first, then you, and finally we?" "Because I did not know your character [and thus could not leave my wife unprotected]." "Why did you not invite us to join you in the meal?" "Because there was not sufficient food [for all]." "Why did you give one portion to the older son and two portions to the younger?" "Because the one stays at home and the other is away at school [the whole day]" (Taan. 23a–b).

Abba Jose ben Simai, Palestinian *tanna* (second century).

Abba Jose ben Simai once traveled with two scholars on a ship that sank. Although the men were presumed to have drowned, no witnesses could attest to this fact. This would have resulted in their wives becoming *agunot*—unable to remarry because there was insufficient evidence of their husbands' deaths. In this case, Judah ha-Nasi permitted the women to give evidence and then allowed them to marry again. The Rabbis questioned this decision, since when a man was presumed drowned in waters without a visible end, his wife was forbidden to remarry since he may have been able to save himself and leave the water beyond the horizon. They concluded that the women who gave evidence must have testified that the bodies of the drowned men had been brought out of the water "in our presence," and that there must have been some independent evidence of their deaths (Yev. 115a–b).

Abba Saul, Palestinian *tanna* (second century).

Earning his living at various times as a gravedigger (Ned. 24b), a shop-keeper (Betz. 29a), and a baker (Pes. 34a), and offering several anecdotes about his experiences, Abba Saul was deemed to be the tallest man of his generation (Nid. 24b). Interpreting the last half of the verse from the Song at the Sea—"This is my God and I shall honor him" (Exod. 15:2)—Abba Saul read the single word *aneihu* used for "honor" as two words (*ani hu*), meaning "I and He [have to act alike]," implying that "just as God is gracious and compassionate, so you must be gracious and compassionate" (Shab. 133b). He also believed that "morality is greater than learning" (Sem. 11), and "discord in the school causes general corruption" (Derech Eretz Zuta 9). Abba Saul declared, "If a *levir* [man whose married brother died without fathering any children] wedded his sister-in-law on account of her beauty, or in order to gratify his sexual desires, or with any other ulterior motive, it was as if he had infringed [the law against] incest; and I am even inclined to think that the child [from such a union] is a *mamzer*" (Yev. 109a).

A paragon of ethical dealing in business (Betz. 29a), Abba Saul said: "It is forbidden to paint human beings [sold as slaves], animals, and utensils to make them seem younger or improve their appearance and thus fetch a higher price" (BM 4:12).

Abba Sikra (first century C.E.).

Abba Sikra devised the plan to spirit his uncle R. Yochanan ben Zakkai, out of Jerusalem during the Roman siege. His name literally meant "Father of the Sicarii," the Jewish zealots who fought against both the Roman government of Judea and those Jews who collaborated with it. According to the Talmud, Yochanan ben Zakkai requested that Abba Sikra spread the word that the sage was seriously ill. One day he placed a dead rodent on Yochanan ben Zakkai's bed, which produced an evil smell that convinced everyone that the sage had died. Abba Sikra insisted that R. Eliezer ben Hyrcanus and R. Joshua ben Hananiah, disciples of Yochanan ben Zakkai, carry the coffin because they were among the few who knew the truth and would not wonder why it was so light (the Talmud states that a living person weighs less than a corpse). Abba Sikra escorted the coffin outside the walls of Jerusalem, for as a zealot leader he could convince the guards at the gates not to pierce the coffin with their swords or even to shake it to test whether Yochanan ben Zakkai was really dead, arguing that they would be shamed by jostling their sainted Rabbi

(Git. 56a). Thus, Yochanan ben Zakkai was able to come before Vespasian, gaining permission to establish an academy for Jewish learning at Yavneh.

Abbahu (Avahu) of Caesarea, Palestinian *amora* (third century).

Born and living in Caesarea, the center of Roman rule and Christianity in the Land of Israel, Abbahu was a disciple of R. Yochanan and a colleague of R. Shimon ben Lakish and R. Eleazar ben Pedat. Abbahu was known for his exceptional beauty, which was compared to that of the patriarch Jacob, who was traditionally the most handsome man of his generation (BM 84a). He also was lauded for his tremendous physical strength, which was said to have enabled Abbahu to have miraculously saved the lives of 101 men by supporting the collapsing roof of the bathhouse with one arm (Ber. 60a).

After the death of R. Yochanan, his fellow scholars voted to appoint Abbahu head of the academy in Tiberias. However, when Abbahu saw that R. Abba of Acre was extremely poor and heavily in debt, he graciously urged them to select Abba instead (Sot. 40a). Later chosen as head of the academy in Caesarea, Abbahu became wealthy by trading in women's jewelry, but remained a humble and modest man. When lecturing on *aggadah* in the same city where R. Hiyya bar Abba was teaching *halachah*, virtually everyone went to hear Abbahu. He consoled his distraught colleague with a parable comparing two merchants, one who was selling precious jewels and the other inexpensive trinkets. "To whom would the people run? Would it not be to the seller of cheaper goods?" (Sot. 40a)

Interpreting the verse, "You only have I loved of all the families of the earth; therefore I will visit upon you all your iniquities" (Amos 5:2), Abbahu offered a parable: "A creditor was once owed money by two debtors, one a close friend and the other a personal enemy. From his friend he demanded regular payments [small sums that did not cause a financial strain], but from his enemy he required a single payment of the entire amount at one time. Thus God punishes Israel only intermittently" (Av. Zar. 4a).

Abbahu sent his son Hanina to study at Tiberias. When he learned that Hanina was engaging in community work, he wrote to his son: "Was there no good to be done in Caesarea, your native town, that I sent you to Tiberias? Did we not decide that learning takes precedence [over performing *mitzvot*]?" The other Rabbis of Caesarea said, "Learning takes precedence only if there are others to perform works of kindness; but if there is no other, doing comes first" (JT Pes. 3).

A story involving Abbahu illustrated that not only sages could pray successfully for rain. During a drought, Abbahu heard a voice in a dream declare, "Let Pentakaka [a person who commits five sins a day] pray and the rain will fall and the drought will end." So Pentakaka prayed and the rains came.

Amazed, Abbahu summoned the man before him: "What kind of work do you do?" "I commit five sins a day," Pentakaka answered. "I hire prostitutes; I am an attendant at the theater; I take the prostitutes' clothes to the bathhouse; I dance and perform before them; and I beat the drum." "And what good deeds have you performed?" asked Abbahu. The man explained: "Once when I was cleaning the theater, a woman came and stood behind a post and wept. When I asked her what was wrong, she answered: 'My husband is in prison. I came here to hire myself out as a prostitute to get enough money to set him free.' Hearing that, I sold everything I had, including my bed and bedding. I gave her the money and told her to go redeem her husband and keep herself free of sin." Abbahu said, "You deserve to have your prayers for rain answered!" (JT Taan. 1:4).

The relationship between Jews and non-Jews in the Land of Israel was tense at that time, and mutual polemics flourished. Referring to Christianity, Abbahu said: "If a man tells you, 'I am God,' he is lying; 'I am the son of man,' he will eventually regret it; 'I shall go up to heaven,' he promises but will not fulfill" (JT Taan. 2:1). Similarly, he explained the biblical verse in Isaiah (44:6), "I am the first and I am the last, and there is no god but Me," as follows: "I am the first" means "I have no father"; "I am the last" means "I have no son"; "and there is no god but Me" means "I have no brother" (Exod. R. 29:5). Abbahu ordered that the Samaritans in his town be regarded as gentiles in all ritual matters. When challenged by their priests, "Your fathers found our food and wine acceptable, why not you?" Abbahu replied: "Your fathers did not corrupt their ways, but you have [corrupted] yours" (JT Av. Zar. 5:4).

Abbahu related that the sages ordained that the phrase after the *Shema*, "Blessed be the Name of His glorious kingdom for ever and ever," be recited in a loud voice, lest sectarians falsely charge that the Jews were saying something improper in a low voice. However, the Talmud immediately notes that this was not the case in Nehardea in Babylonia, where there were no heretics and thus the phrase could safely be recited quietly (Pes. 56a). According to Abbahu, "Jerusalem was destroyed only because the morning and evening readings of the *Shema* were neglected" (Shab. 119b).

A guiding principle of Abbahu was: "A man should always strive to be among the persecuted rather than among the persecutors [oppressors]. For among birds none are more persecuted than doves and pigeons, yet only these were declared by Scripture as acceptable [as sacrifices] on the Altar [Lev. 1:14]" (BK 93a). Other ethical teachings of Abbahu include: "In the place where penitents stand, even the wholly righteous cannot stand" (Ber. 34); "One should not terrorize his household [rule it by fear]" (Git. 7a); "The world exists on account of [the merit of] the man who abases himself [humbly makes himself as if he were nonexistent]" (Hul. 89a); and "Three types of sin are never forgiven by God—overreaching [deception], robbery, and idol worship" (BM 59a).

Abbahu prescribed the order of the sounds in the ritual blowing the shofar on Rosh Hashanah that is still used today (RH 34a). Explaining why *Hallel* is not recited on Rosh Hashanah, Abbahu offered a *midrash* in which God replied to the angels: "Is it possible that the King should be sitting on the Throne of Judgment with the books of life and death open before Him, and Israel should sing hymns of praise?" (RH 32b).

Abbahu's scholarship extended to secular studies. Well versed in Greek literature, he insisted that his daughter learn Greek. He was so highly respected by Roman officials that the Talmud relates: "When Abbahu came from the academy to the court of the emperor, handmaids [or matrons] from the imperial house went out and sang before him, 'Prince of his people, leader of his nation, shining light, blessed be your coming in peace!'" (Ket. 17a). Although attacked by his colleagues for associating with Romans and other non-Jews, Abbahu's connections enabled him to have some anti-Jewish decrees annulled. According to the Talmud, when Abbahu died, "the columns at Caesarea ran with tears" (MK 25b). *See also* Hiyya bar Abba; Shimon ben Lakish.

Abbaye, Babylonian *amora* (third/fourth century).

Born into a priestly family, Abbaye's father died when he was conceived and his mother died in childbirth (Kid. 31b). The orphaned baby was adopted by his father's brother, Rabbah bar Nachmani, a teacher and later head of the prestigious academy at Pumbedita where Abbaye received his formal education. His foster mother took such loving care of Abbaye that she "trained a lamb to go with him to the privy," either as a protection against evil spirits or so that he would not be afraid (Ber. 62a). Devoted in turn to his adoptive mother, Abbaye quoted about twenty of her pithy sayings, many related to food, as if they had been the teachings of a prominent sage. He also remarked about the importance of parental influence: "The talk of a child in the marketplace is from his father and mother" (Suk. 56b), meaning that it was a repetition of words he heard at home.

At the academy, Abbaye's closest friend and study partner was Rava. They engaged in spirited legal debates, which constitute a substantial part of the Babylonian Talmud. They often dealt with hypothetical cases and developed the characteristic dialectical method of analyzing *halachah*. Rava appeared to have been the superior scholar since, with only six exceptions, his opinion was accepted as law (Kid. 52a). Nevertheless, when Rabbah bar Nachmani retired after twenty-two years as head of the academy, Abbaye succeeded him. (R. Joseph bar Hiyya served as interim head for two and a half years before Abbaye; Rava was Abbaye's successor.) Abbaye was devoted to his students and hosted a festive celebration for all the scholars whenever one of his disciples finished a tractate of the Mishnah (Shab. 118b).

Abbaye is quoted more than 3,500 times in the Babylonian Talmud. He urged Rabbis making *halachic* decisions to "go and see what the people are doing" (Er. 14b), thus taking into account popular custom. Abbaye stressed the importance of interpersonal relations: "Be mild in speech, suppress your anger, and always strive to be on the best terms with your relatives and all men, even with the heathen [stranger] in the street [marketplace], so that you may be beloved above [by God] and well-liked below and be acceptable to your fellow creatures" (Ber. 17a). Because it was customary to rise as a sage passed by, whenever Abbaye saw a group of people sitting by the path, he would take a circuitous route rather than inconvenience them (Kid. 33a). Agreeing with R. Huna's statement, "When a man leaves the synagogue he should not take large steps," Abbaye added: "But when one goes to the synagogue it is a pious deed to run," based on the verse in Hosea (6:3), "Let us run to know the Lord" (Ber. 6b). As he observed, "The world never has less than thirty-six righteous men who are privileged to see the *Shechinah* every day" (Suk. 45b). Among the proverbs that Abbaye often included in his lectures were: "The poor man is hungry and does not know it [until food is actually set before him]"; and "If a countryman [peasant] becomes a king, he does not take his basket off his neck [so that one can always determine from where he came]" (Meg. 7b).

The Rabbis noted the importance of personal appearance. Abbaye said, "Overpay for your back, but pay only the exact worth for your stomach [i.e., a person may spend as much as necessary for fine clothing to appear well groomed, but no more than necessary for food to sustain himself]" (BM 52a).

Abbaye calculated that the sun began a new cycle once every twenty-eight years, at the vernal equinox early on the first Tuesday of the month of Nisan. The Rabbis taught: "He who sees the sun at its turning point, the moon in its power, the planets in their orbits, and the signs of the zodiac in their orderly progress, should say: 'Blessed be He who has wrought the work of Creation'" (Ber. 59b). Today, traditional Jews recite *Birkat ha-Hama* (Blessing of the Sun), a service thanking God for the sun and its continued blessings. It also expresses the hope of being privileged to live until the coming of the Messiah, to witness the fulfillment of the prophecy of Isaiah (30:26): "And the light of the sun shall become sevenfold, like the light of the seven days [of Creation]."

Abbaye interpreted the verse "And you shall love the Lord your God" (Deut. 6:5) as meaning: "That the Name of Heaven be loved on account of you. If one studies Bible and Mishnah and attends to the disciples of the wise [is apprenticed to a sage], is honest in business, and speaks pleasantly to everyone, what do people say about him? 'Happy are the father and teacher who taught him Torah; woe to people who have not studied Torah. This man has studied Torah—look how fine are his ways, how righteous his deeds!' . . . But if someone studies Scripture and Mishnah and attends to the disciples of the wise, but is dishonest in business and discourteous in his relations with everyone, what do people say about him? 'Woe to him who studied Torah, and to his father and teacher who taught him Torah! This man studied the Torah—look how corrupt are his deeds, how ugly his ways'" (Yoma 86a).

In the debate regarding whether a person should devote his time to Torah study, to the exclusion of everything else (according to R. Shimon bar Yochai), or should study as well as live a productive life (according to R. Ishmael ben Elisha), Abbaye concurred with the latter (Ber. 35b). *See also* Aha bar Jacob; Dimi; Isaac bar Joseph; Rava; Shimi bar Ashi; Ulla bar Rav.

Abtolmus (Avtilos) ben Reuben, Palestinian *tanna* (second century).

The Talmud notes that Abtolmus, similar to the family of Rabban Gamaliel II but unlike any other Jews, "was permitted to cut his hair in the gentile fashion [leaving a fringe on the forehead and letting curls hang down on the temples] because he was in close contact with the [Roman] government" (BK 83a). The next sentence observes that this relationship with the authorities also allowed the members of the family of Rabban Gamaliel to discuss "Grecian Wisdom."

Adda bar Ahava, Babylonian *amora* (third century).

Adda bar Ahava was said to have been born on the day that Judah ha-Nasi died (Kid. 72a–b; Gen. R. 58). An esteemed student of Rav, Adda bar Ahava twice rent his garments in mourning for his teacher, once when hearing of Rav's death and then a second time when he realized that there was now no authority to consult on vexing *halachic* matters (Ber. 42b–43a). Adda bar Ahava was a prominent teacher at the academy of Pumbedita and attracted many pupils, whom he sometimes taught in the public thoroughfares (Yev. 110b).

The Talmud cites Adda bar Ahava's explanation for living to a ripe old age: "I have never displayed any impatience in my house, walked in front of any man greater than myself, meditated [over the words of the Torah] in dirty alleys, walked four cubits without [musing over] the Torah or without [wearing] *tefillin*, fallen asleep in the study hall even for a moment, rejoiced at the disgrace of my friends, or called my neighbor by a disparaging nickname" (Taan. 20b). However, Adda bar Ahava could be impatient and even reckless when the glory of heaven was concerned. One day he "saw a heathen woman wearing a red headdress [mantle] in the street. Thinking that she was an Israelite woman [dressed immodestly], he rose and tore it from her [and violently rebuked her]." Unfortunately, the woman was a Samaritan, and his attack on her resulted in a stiff fine (Ber. 20a).

Adda bar Ahava was renowned for his piety. According to legend, he was so favored by heaven that his every request was granted. During a severe drought, when he pulled off one shoe in preparation for prayer, an abundance of rain descended; had he pulled off the other, the world would have been flooded. Adda bar Ahava seemed surrounded by a protective shield. One day when walking with Rav and Samuel, they approached a ruin that threatened to collapse. Samuel urged that they "walk around it," but Rav replied: "This precaution is not necessary now because Adda bar Ahava is with us; his merit is great, and therefore I do not fear" (Taan. 20b). Similarly, when R. Huna wanted to take out some wine stored in a dilapidated house on the verge of collapse, he invited Adda bar Ahava into the building and began an intense *halachic* discussion until laborers could safely remove the bottles. As soon as the Rabbis left the premises, the walls fell down. However, Adda ben Ahava was "offended," because of the rule that it was forbidden "to stand in a place of danger and declare, 'A miracle will occur for me'" (Taan. 20b).

One of Adda bar Ahava's most famous statements was: "One who has sinned and confessed his sin but does not repent may be compared to a man holding a dead [defiling] reptile in his hand. Although he may immerse himself in all the waters of the world, the bath would not restore him to cleanness. He becomes clean only when he drops it [throws it away] from his hand and bathes himself in forty *se'ahs* of water [the minimum requirement for ritual immersion]" (Taan. 16a).

The Written Torah encompasses the twenty-four books of the Hebrew Bible, which is divided into three sections: Torah, Nevi'im (Prophets), and Ketuvim (Writings). Reflecting this, Adda bar Ahavah "would review his mishnaic text twenty-four times, and only then would he come [to his teacher] to study Gemara" (Taan. 8a)

Adda of Jaffa, Palestinian *amora* (third century).

Adda of Jaffa is best known for explaining that, when reading the Megillah (the Book of Esther) on Purim, the names of the ten sons of Haman are recited in one breath "because they were hanged together" (Meg. 16b).

Admon ben Gaddai, Palestinian *tanna* (first century B.C.E.).

One of the few civil law judges in Jerusalem whose name is mentioned in Talmudic literature, it was reported that Admon ben Gaddai "laid down seven rulings" (Ket. 108b–110a). Although the sages frequently appeared to have disagreed with him, on several occasions Rabban Gamaliel I said, "Admon's view has my approval."

In late Second Temple times, judges adjudicated disputes and awarded damages for injuries, as well as punished those whom they found guilty of robbery. They were usually elected by the community, which paid their salaries to avoid a judge being bribed by one of the contending parties. Their verdicts were final and they were granted the authority to enforce them. The Jerusalem Talmud referred to these judges, such as Admon ben Gaddai, as *dayanei gezelot* (robbery judges), while the Babylonian Talmud called them *dayanei gezerot* (decree judges). This difference in terminology was probably merely a reflection of the interchangeability of the Hebrew letters *lamed* and *resh* and in these two words.

Aha bar Bizna, Babylonian *amora* (third/fourth century).

Aha bar Bizna cited a legend offered by Shimon ha-Tzadik concerning the harp that hung over King David's bed. "As soon as midnight arrived, a northerly wind blew upon its strings and caused it to play of its own accord. David would immediately arise and begin studying Torah, continuing until the first light of dawn appeared in the sky," when the sages of Israel entered and said to him: "Our Sovereign King, your people Israel need sustenance." David replied, "Go and support yourselves by mutual trading [lit., 'one from another']." The sages said, "But a handful does not satisfy the lion, nor can a pit be filled with its own clods [i.e., a community cannot live on its own resources]." Whereupon David said to them: "Go out with a troop [of soldiers; i.e., invade a foreign territory and attack the enemy for plunder]" (Ber. 3b). This interchange was used as the basis for the mishnaic ruling that the permission of the Sanhedrin was required for the proclamation of war.

Aha bar Jacob, Babylonian *amora* (third/fourth century).

Termed "a man of great distinction" (Er. 63a), Aha bar Jacob was a disciple of R. Huna. His study of mysticism and philosophy, in addition to Torah learning, may have led to his certainty in the power of demons. Waving the *lulav* to and fro on Sukkot, he would say: "This [the performance of one of God's commandments] is an arrow in the eye of Satan [whose aim is the seduction of man]" (Suk. 38a).

A demon was playing havoc with the students in R. Abbaye's academy, attacking them even when they were walking in a group during the day, but no one could remove it. Learning that Aha bar Jacob was coming to visit Pumbedita, R. Abbaye made certain that "no man offer him hospitality." Without a place to lodge, Aha bar Jacob would be compelled to spend the night in the academy, where he might expel the demon ("perhaps a miracle will happen [in his merit]"). During the night, the demon appeared to Aha bar Jacob "in the guise of a seven-headed dragon. Every time he [the Rabbi] fell on his knees [in prayer], one head [of the dragon] fell off." However, the next day Aha bar Jacob rebuked R. Abbaye: "Had not a miracle occurred, you would have endangered my life" (Kid. 29b).

Aha ben Adda, Babylonian *amora* (fourth century).

Moving to Babylonia from the Land of Israel, Aha ben Adda often cited decisions of his Palestinian teachers. His most famous saying is: "Even the casual [lit., 'profane'] conversation of scholars is worthy of study" (Suk. 21b). He derived this from the verse, "And whose leaf does not wither" (Ps. 1:3), analogizing the righteous man to a tree and his casual talk to a leaf, the least important part of the tree.

As Aha ben Adda aged, his hands shook. The Talmud reports that a forger once signed the names of Rava and Aha ben Adda to a deed. After the suspect was arrested and confessed, Rava said: "I can well understand how you forged my signature, but how could you manage that of Aha ben Adda, whose hand trembles?" The forger replied, "[When forging his signature] I put my hand on a rope-bridge [which vibrates at the slightest touch, causing the hand to shake]." Another explanation was that the forger "stood on a hose [causing all his limbs to shake] and wrote" (BB 167a).

Ahai ben Josiah, Palestinian *tanna* (second century).

A teacher who dealt with moral issues, Ahai ben Josiah warned: "He who gazes at a woman eventually comes to sin; and he who looks even at a woman's heel will sire degenerate [unworthy] children" (Ned. 20a). He also noted, "As long as a man eats at his own table [i.e., supports himself] his mind is at rest; but if he eats not at his own table [i.e., is dependent on others], even at the table of his parents or children, he has no peace of mind; still less so when he depends on strangers." Moreover, "He who buys grain in the marketplace is like an infant whose mother has died. Although he is taken from one wet nurse to another, he is never satisfied. . . . But he who eats of his own produce is [as much at ease] as an infant raised at his mother's breast" (ARN 30).

In a legend demonstrating the continuing consciousness of the dead, the Talmud relates that men "were digging in ground belonging to R. Nachman [bar Jacob] when the ghost of Ahai ben Josiah snorted at them." After hearing of this strange occurrence, R. Nachman went to the site and the following dialogue ensued: "Who are you?" "I am Ahai ben Josiah." "But did not R. Mari say that even the [bodies of the] righteous are fated to be dust?" "But who is R. Mari, I do not know him." "But there is a verse in the Bible [Eccles.

12:7], 'and the dust shall return to the earth as it was.'" "He who taught you Ecclesiastes did not teach you [the Book of] Proverbs, where it is written [14:30]: 'A sound heart is the life of the flesh: but envy the rottenness of the bones.'" When R. Nachman reached out and touched the apparition, he felt that it contained some substance. He said, "Let my master arise and come to my house." The ghost of Ahai ben Josiah answered, "You have shown that you have not even studied the prophets, for there it is written [Ezek. 37:13]: 'You shall know that I am the Lord when I open your graves [which only the Lord can do].'" When R. Nachman cited the biblical verse (Gen. 3:19), "For dust you are and to dust you shall return," the ghost of Ahai ben Josiah replied: "That will come to pass one hour before the resurrection of the dead" (Shab. 152b).

Akabiah ben Mahalalel, Palestinian *tanna* (first/second century).

When Shammai died, Akabiah ben Mahalalel was offered the position of *av bet din* (president of the Sanhedrin). However, this was on the condition that he withdraw opinions that contradicted those of the majority of his colleagues concerning four specific issues: special cases of leprosy; a woman who had a bloody issue; wool shed by a clean firstborn animal that was crippled; and a proselyte or freed woman suspected of adultery. Akabiah ben Mahalalel adamantly refused: "It is better for me to be called a fool [for refusing the offer] all my days than become for [even] one hour a wicked man [by denying what I deem the truth] in the sight of God [i.e., that he betray his convictions in order to obtain a high position]" (Eduy. 5:6–7). Consequently, his colleagues placed Akabiah ben Mahalalel under the ban. When he died, the court stoned his coffin. R. Judah criticized the Rabbis for their actions: "The [Temple] court never closed on a man of Israel as wise and sin-fearing as Akabiah ben Mahalalel."

Ironically, just before he died, Akabiah ben Mehalalel urged his son to "reverse your opinion about the four controversial laws which I taught you." When his son asked why he himself had not done so, his father answered: "Because I learned that view from the majority of my teachers, I held fast to what they taught me. But you have heard both sides debated and have heard the minority view [my own] and the majority view [my colleagues]. It is proper for you to leave the minority opinion and to follow the majority."

Akabiah ben Mehalalel's most famous Talmudic saying is: "Keep three things in mind and you will not succumb to the power of sin. Know where you came from, where you are going, and before Whom you will eventually have to give an account and reckoning. From where did you come?—from a putrid drop [of semen]. Where are you going?—to a place of dust, worms, and maggots. Before Whom are you destined to give an account and reckoning? Before the King of the kings of kings, the Holy One, Blessed is He!" (Avot 3:1).

Akiva, Palestinian *tanna* (first/second century).

An outstanding Talmudic scholar, patriot, and martyr, R. Akiva exerted a profound influence on the development of the *halachah* and is regarded as the father of rabbinic Judaism. According to tradition, the thirty-year-old Akiva was an uneducated shepherd who did not even know the alphabet. Rachel, the beautiful daughter of a rich Jerusalemite, fell in love with Akiva and promised to become his wife if he would agree to devote himself to learning. When her father heard that his daughter had secretly betrothed herself to one far beneath her station, he vowed to disinherit her (Ket. 62b; Ned. 50a). Nevertheless, they married and lived in poverty (ARN 6).

Although Rachel's ardent wish was that Akiva study Jewish law, he doubted his ability to learn until one day he chanced to see how water dripping from above had hollowed out a heavy stone. "If water, which is soft, could wear away a hard stone, surely the words of Torah, which are as hard as iron, can hollow out [make an impression on] my soft heart" (ARN 6). So at age forty, Akiva left his wife and eight children for the academy of Lydda. Exceedingly poor, Akiva earned his living by gathering a bundle of wood each day, selling half and using the rest to light the house where he studied.

The Talmud relates that after twelve years of study, Akiva finally returned home followed by 12,000 disciples. When his students, not knowing who she was, wanted to turn the poorly clad Rachel away, Akiva rebuked them: "Let her be. Your wisdom, as well as mine, is due to her" (Ket. 62b). In another version, the returning Akiva heard a neighbor asking Rachel, "How much longer will you lead the life of a living widowhood?" His wife replied that she would happily wait another twelve years as long as she knew that her husband was devoting his life to learning. Taking this as permission, Akiva went back to the academy to study for another twelve years before finally returning to Rachel, now accompanied by 24,000 disciples (Ned. 50a). When her father heard that one of the most prominent Jewish scholars had arrived, he was shocked to see that it was his son-in-law. He begged for forgiveness and pleaded that Akiva release him from the vow to disinherit his daughter. When Akiva gave permission, his father-in-law gave him half of his wealth (Ket. 63a). Returning with his family to Lydda, Akiva became head of the academy where he had studied and later established a new center of learning at Bnei Brak. Appointed to the Sanhedrin, it was said that Akiva was so highly respected that no major dispute was ever resolved without his participation.

Akiva's brilliant and penetrating mind was revealed in his profound interpretations of Jewish law. He believed that the Written Torah was complete, with nothing missing or extra. Every letter and dot had some special significance and could yield profound meanings. If a word in the Torah seemed superfluous, it was only because the person had insufficient intelligence to understand its significance. In one classic legend, when Moses ascended into heaven, he saw God affixing tiny crowns to the letters of the Torah. When he asked about their meaning, God replied: "There will come a man, Akiva ben Joseph by name, who will deduce *halachot* from every little curve and crown of the letters of the Law" (Men. 29b). Indeed, Akiva assembled and edited the teachings of previous scholars, arranging them by subject and thus laying the foundation for the editing of the Mishnah. Moses said, "You have shown me his Torah, now show me his reward." Turning around in response to a Divine command, Moses saw Akiva dying a cruel death as a martyr during the Hadrianic persecutions, with merchants "weighing out his flesh at the market-stalls." Appalled, Moses cried out, "Lord of the Universe, so much Torah, and this is his reward?!" God replied, "Be silent, for such is My decree [i.e., even Moses was not privy to the Divine plan]" (Men. 29b).

A great Jewish patriot, Akiva joined Bar Kochba (whom he saw as the promised Messiah; JT Taan. 4:6) in inspiring the Jews to rebel against the oppressive Roman rule. The decision to enter into armed struggle was made at the seder meeting of leading sages in Bnei Brak. According to the Passover Haggadah, all night they discussed the Exodus from Egypt, for the presence of informers made it impossible to openly refer to Rome and their current situation. As the debate droned on throughout the night, their impatient disciples waited outside. Finally, they opened the doors and announced, "The time for the morning *Shema* has arrived," indicating that a decision must be made. The sages and their disciples began to intone a hymn of vengeance: "Pour out Your wrath upon the nations that have not known You," and the die was cast.

Initially, the Jews defeated the Romans and established their own government. However, the might of Rome eventually proved overwhelming. Casualties of the unsuccessful rebellion were thought to be the underlying cause of the "plague," which the Talmud relates killed 24,000 of Akiva's disciples between Passover and Shavuot (Yev. 62b). This period is now observed as a time of semi-mourning. According to tradition, the "plague" ceased on Lag ba-Omer, the thirty-third day of the counting of the Omer. This may be an allusion to the recapture of Jerusalem, which was said to have occurred on that date.

Eventually, the besieged fortress of Betar fell and thousands of Jews were killed. Hadrian prohibited the observance and study of Jewish law under penalty of death, but Akiva defied the emperor's decree. One of the Ten Martyrs, Akiva was taken for execution at the time for reciting the morning *Shema*.

They tore his flesh with iron combs, but he continued reciting the *Shema*. As Akiva explained to his disciples, he had always wondered how to fulfill the commandment "to love the Lord your God with all your soul" (Deut. 6:5), which he interpreted as "even if He takes your soul." "Now that the opportunity of fulfilling it has come, should I not do so?" Consequently, with his dying breath Akiva pronounced the affirmation of faith, the *Shema*, timing it so that the final word he uttered was *Echad* (One). "A heavenly voice [*bat kol*] proclaimed, 'Happy are you, Akiva, that your soul has departed with the word *echad* [proclaiming the unity of God] . . . for you are destined for the life of the World to Come'" (Ber. 61b).

As the Mishnah notes, with the death of Akiva, "the glory of the Torah ceased . . . [and] the fountains of wisdom were stopped up" (Sot. 49a–b). Nevertheless, the death of Akiva was the first event in a rabbinic tradition that "a righteous man does not depart from the world until [another] righteous man like himself is born," based on the biblical verse, "The sun rises and the sun sets" (Eccles. 1:5). Thus, "When Akiva died, Judah ha-Nasi [Rabbi] was born; when Rabbi died, R. Judah was born; when R. Judah died, Rava was born; when Rava died, R. Ashi was born [i.e., in all these cases, the death of one sage and the birth of another occurred on the exact same day]" (Kid. 7a–b).

According to legend, of the four sages who entered Paradise, only Akiva had sufficient intellectual strength to absorb the mystical doctrines and emerge intact (Hag. 14b). The Talmud ascribes the origin of the *Avinu Melkeinu* prayer to Akiva. During a severe drought, he exclaimed before the ark, "Our Father, our King, have mercy upon us for Your own sake!" whereupon the rain fell (Taan. 25b).

Of all the books of the Bible, the most difficult to gain acceptance was the Song of Songs. Some Rabbis argued that is was merely a love idyll, while others viewed it as an allegory of the love between God and Israel. Akiva sided with the latter camp and had the last word: "The whole world is not as worthy as the day on which the Song of Songs was given to Israel. All the Writings are holy, but the Song of Songs is the Holy of Holies" (Yad. 3:5).

Akiva exemplified the rabbinic distinction between the styles of private and public prayer. "When Akiva prayed with the congregation, he used to cut it short and finish quickly in order not to inconvenience the congregation [by detaining them, since they would not resume the service until the sage had finished his *Tefillah*]. But if he prayed alone, he would pray long with many bowings [generally discouraged at the beginning and ending of each blessing as an excessive display of piety]." Indeed, the Talmud notes that when Akiva prayed privately, his repeated "genuflexions and prostrations" were so vigorous that he would begin in one part of the room and finish in another

(Ber. 31a). When R. Joshua ben Hananiah held that an abbreviated version of the *Amidah* was sufficient, Akiva argued that it should be used only by one who did not know the entire prayer (Ber. 4:3). In the debate concerning when a person may recite the morning *Shema*, Akiva said that it was permissible from the time one can distinguish "between a regular donkey and a wild donkey." Others said, "From the time that you can recognize your friend at a distance of four cubits" (Ber. 9b). Although work is not forbidden on Tisha b'Av, traditionally it is minimized as much as possible in accordance with the observation of Akiva: "Anyone who does work on the Ninth of Av will never see in his work any sign of blessing" (Taan. 30b).

According to Akiva, a person should always say, "Whatever the All-Merciful does is for good." Akiva once came to a certain town and looked for lodging, but was everywhere refused. Consequently, "He went and spent the night in the open field. He had with him a rooster, a donkey, and a lamp. A gust of wind blew out the lamp, a weasel ate the rooster, and a lion ate the donkey." When Akiva later learned that on the same night some robbers came and carried off the inhabitants of the town, he realized that the lamp, rooster, and donkey would have alerted them to his presence! (Ber. 60b).

Akiva taught his son, R. Joshua, seven basic rules of life: "Do not sit and study at the busiest point of the town [many pass there and they will disturb your studies]; do not live in a town whose leaders are scholars [they will be so busy with their studies that they will neglect the affairs of the town]; do not enter your own house suddenly, and especially not the house of your neighbor [people may be doing something you should not see]; do not go barefoot on the street [it is improper behavior]; arise and eat early in summer because of the sun [heat] and in winter on account of the cold; treat your Sabbath like a weekday rather than be dependent on any man [i.e., do not borrow money to buy special foods to make the day festive]; and strive to be on good terms with successful men [lit., 'the man upon whom the fortune of the hour smiles']" (Pes. 112a).

In response to the question posed in Pirkei Avot (4:1), "Who is rich?" Akiva spoke from personal experience: "One who has a wife beautiful in deeds" (since his wife was a devoted woman who made it possible for him to achieve great scholarship). As he noted, "When husband and wife are worthy, the *Shechinah* abides with them; when they are not worthy, fire consumes them" (Sot. 17a). Nevertheless, Akiva realized that some marriages were not as fortunate as his. The Jewish law of divorce is based on the verse: "A man takes a wife and possesses her. If she fails to please him because he finds *ervat davar* [something obnoxious or a matter of indecency] about her, he writes her a bill of divorcement, hands it to her, and sends her away from his house" (Deut. 24:1). The precise meaning of the term "*ervat davar*" was the subject of a Talmudic dispute (Git. 90a–b). The school of Shammai argued that it meant adultery, so that the only proper grounds for divorce was sexual impropriety. The school of Hillel disagreed, maintaining that "something obnoxious" might refer to any act that made the husband unhappy, even something as minor as his wife's cooking. Akiva took a different approach, interpreting the biblical verse as including two separate statements regarding the grounds for divorce. For him, the exact nature of *ervat davar* was immaterial, for the first part of the clause ("she fails to please him") was an independent justification. Thus a man was permitted to divorce his wife "if she spoils his food" or "if he finds another woman more beautiful than she is."

An Israelite named Zunin once said to Akiva: "We both know in our heart that idols have no power. Nevertheless we see men enter [an idolatrous shrine] crippled and come out cured. What is the reason?" Akiva replied: "I will answer you with a parable: Once there was trustworthy man with whom all his townsmen used to deposit their money without witnesses. One man, however, only deposited his money in the presence of witnesses. On one occasion, he forgot and made his deposit without witnesses. The wife [of the trustworthy man] said to [her husband], 'Come, let us deny it.' Her husband replied, 'Because this fool acted in an unworthy manner, shall I destroy my reputation for trustworthiness!' It is similar with an affliction [disease, pain]. When it is sent to distress a person, it is given an oath: 'You shall not afflict so-and-so except on a specific day, at a specific hour, and in a specific way, and you shall not depart from him except at a specific time and through a specific remedy.' When the [preordained] time arrived for the affliction to depart, the man chanced to go to an idolatrous shrine. The affliction pleaded, 'It is right that we should not leave him and depart; but because this fool acts in an unworthy way, shall my oath be broken?'" (Av. Zar. 55a). Thus the ailment left the afflicted man, who mistakenly believed that it was the work of the idol.

Among the statements of Akiva found in Pirkei Avot are: "Mockery and levity accustom a person to immorality; tradition is a [protective] fence around the Torah; tithes are a fence for wealth; vows are a fence to self-restraint; a fence for wisdom is silence" (3:17); "Beloved is man, for he was created in the image of God. . . . Beloved are the people Israel, for a cherished utensil [the Torah] was given to them" (3:18); and "Everything is foreseen [by God], yet the freedom of choice is given [to every person]" (3:19). He warned, "He who eats foods that do not agree with him violates three commandments: he has despised himself, despised the foods, and recited a blessing improperly" (ARN 26). Akiva declared that a person "who does not visit the sick is like a shedder of blood" (Ned. 40a). With R. Tarfon, he asserted: "Were we members of a Sanhedrin, no person would ever be put to death"

(Mak. 7a). *See also* Ben Azzai; Ben Peturah; Eliezer ben Hyrcanus; Elisha ben Abuyah; Helbo; Ishmael ben Elisha; Judah ben Bathyra; Pappus ben Judah; Tarfon; Yochanan the Sandalmaker.

Alexandri, Palestinian *amora* (third century).

A leading *aggadist*, Alexandri said: "One who studies the Torah for its own sake [the love of learning, without ulterior motives] makes peace in the Upper Family [angels] and the Lower Family [human beings]" (Sanh. 99b). On concluding his prayers, Alexandri added the words: "May it be Your will, O Lord our God, to station us in an illumined corner and not in a darkened one, and let not our heart be sick nor our eyes darkened!" According to another version, his words were the following: "Sovereign of the Universe, You know full well that we wish to perform Your will, but what prevents us? The yeast in the dough [evil impulse, which causes a 'ferment' in the heart] and the subjection to foreign powers. May it be Your will to deliver us from their hand, so that we may return to perform the statutes of Your will with a perfect heart!" (Ber. 17a).

Alexandri related the following tale concerning friendship: "Two donkey drivers who hated each other were walking on a road when the donkey of one lay down under its burden. Although his companion saw what had occurred, he initially just continued on his way. But remembering the biblical verse, 'If you see your enemy's donkey lying down under its burden and would refrain from raising it, you nevertheless are required to raise it with him' (Exod. 23:5), he returned and lent a hand. As they talked to each other about how best to accomplish their mutual task, peace arose between them. The driver of the overloaded donkey said, 'Did I not suppose that he hated me? But look how compassionate he has been.' [Finishing their task,] the two entered an inn and ate and drank together, and they soon became fast friends" (Tanh. Mishpatim 1).

The Talmud relates that Alexandri once entered the marketplace and called out, "Who wants life, who wants life?" When everyone gathered around him and asked how to get it, he quoted verses from Psalms (34:13–15): "Who is the man who desires life? . . . Keep your tongue from evil and your lips from speaking guile, depart from evil and do good, seek peace and pursue it" (Av. Zar. 19b).

Alexandri said, "Every person in whom there is haughtiness of spirit will be disturbed by even the slightest wind [i.e., the smallest disappointment is liable to upset him]" (Sot. 5a). Sorrowfully remembering his beloved spouse, Alexandri noted: "The world is darkened for one whose wife has died in his lifetime" (Sanh. 22a).

Among the maxims that Alexandri cited in the name of other sages were: "Thunder was created only to straighten out the crookedness of the heart"

(Ber. 59a); and "A sick man does not recover from his illness until all his sins are forgiven" (Ned. 41a).

Amemar, Babylonian *amora* (fourth/fifth century).

Amemar restored the academy at Nehardea to its former prominence and headed it for more than thirty years (390–422). Amemar also served as president of the court at Nehardea, where he introduced several changes in the ritual (RH 31b; Suk. 55a; BB 31a), and as head of the revitalized *yeshivah* in Machoza. On royal festivals, Amemar joined R. Ashi and Mar Zutra as the official representatives of the Jews at the court (Ket. 61a). On one occasion, Amemar and Mar Zutra were carried on the shoulders of their students when they came to the synagogue to address the congregation on the Sabbath preceding Sukkot, when it was customary for them to lecture on the festival laws. Although some attributed this action to the esteem in which they were held by their students, others maintained that it was to prevent "troubling the public" (who otherwise would have been forced to stand up and wait until these teachers made their way slowly through the crowd to the platform) (Betz. 25a).

The Talmud relates that Amemar rent his garment (*keriah*) as a sign of mourning on the death of his grandson. When "he recollected that he had done it while sitting; he rose and tore [his garment again] standing" (MK 20b). When asked by R. Ashi, "Where do we derive that the rending [of a garment] is [to be done] standing?" Amemar replied that it was from the Book of Job (1:20): "Then Job rose and tore his robe."

Amemar said, "A wise man [sage] is superior to a prophet" (BB 12a).

Ammi, Palestinian *amora* (third/fourth century).

Born in Babylonia, Ammi was a lifelong friend of R. Assi. Since both were referred to as "son of Nathan" and of priestly descent, they may have been blood brothers with the same father. Arriving in the Land of Israel, both were pupils of the illustrious R. Yochanan, at whose death they mourned as if he were a close relative (MK 25b). Both later succeeded him as head of the academy in Tiberias. The names of Ammi and Assi appear together in numerous Talmudic passages, either as being of the same opinion or as opposed to each other. They were highly respected by their Babylonian colleagues, among whom Ammi and Assi were known as "the Palestinian judges" or as "the distinguished priests of Palestine" (Git. 59b; Sanh. 17b).

The Rabbis discussed the devotion of Ammi and Assi to the Land of Israel. According to the Talmud, they "used to rise from the seats where they delivered their discourses to move from the sun to the shade [in the heat of the summer] and from the shade to the sun [in the cold days of winter to prevent them from finding any fault with the weather of the Land of Israel]" (Ket. 112a–b). Ammi and Assi, like other renowned scholars, did not feel constrained to worship in a synagogue, even though they had thirteen synagogues in Tiberias from which to choose (Ber. 8a).

The Rabbis were convinced that a favorite haunt of demons were latrines, leading to the Talmudic statement: "Whoever behaves modestly in a privy is delivered from three things: from snakes, from scorpions, and from evil spirits. There was a certain privy in Tiberias that when two would enter it together, even in the daytime, they would be harmed. [But] Ammi and Assi used to enter it separately, and they suffered no harm" (Ber. 62a).

Ammi often attempted to decrease the stringency of the laws, though at least twice (regarding his permitting the participation of Jews in pagan festivals to maintain peace with their neighbors; and permitting a slave to testify concerning a bill of divorce for a Jewish woman) he was forced to retract his opinion when he was informed of a contrary decision by R. Hiyya (JT Demai 4:3; JT Git. 2:6). Nevertheless, Ammi was a strict moralist, warning: "He who excites himself by lustful thoughts will not be allowed in the presence of the Holy One, Blessed be He" (Nid. 13b). When "it was rumored of a certain disciple that he revealed a matter stated [as a secret] in the study hall twenty-two years previously, Ammi expelled him from the study hall saying, 'This man cannot keep secrets'" (Sanh. 31a). According to Ammi, if a husband stated that he intended taking another wife to sire children (lit., "to test his potency"), he must give his wife a divorce if she desired it and pay her the amount stipulated in her *ketubah* (Yev. 65a). Ammi believed that "Torah should not be taught to an idolater" (Hul. 13a), lest the material found within it be misinterpreted and unscrupulously used against Jews. He also said, "Rain is withheld only because of the sin of violent robbery" (Taan. 7b), and "Rain falls only for the sake of people who are honest in their business dealings" (Taan. 8a).

In the Bible, God described the Israelites as a "stiff-necked people" (Exod. 32:9). According to Ammi, this term was not used disparagingly but rather referred to a praiseworthy characteristic that enabled Jews to be undaunted by failure or opposition during centuries of persecution. As the *aggadah* notes: "Three are undaunted—among the beasts it is the dog, among birds it is the cock, and among the nations it is Israel" (Exod. R. 42:9).

When Ammi was about to die, his nephew found him weeping bitterly: "Uncle and teacher, why do you weep? Is there any Torah you have not learned and taught? Is there any form of kindness that you have not practiced? And above all else, you never accepted a public office or sat in judgment." Ammi sadly answered, "It is for this very reason that I weep. I was granted the ability to establish peace between disputants in Israel and I have not acted upon it" (Tanh. Mishpatim). *See also* Assi (third/fourth century).

Amram Hasida, Babylonian *amora* (fourth century).

Amram Hasida received his surname, "the pious," from an incident in which "certain [redeemed] captive women" were lodged in the upper chamber of his house "and the ladder removed from under them. As one passed by, a light fell on the skylight [separating the two stories and revealing her beauty], whereupon Amram seized the ladder, which ten men could not raise, and he alone set it up and proceeded to ascend." Halfway up the ladder and realizing that he was about to succumb to temptation, to save himself from sin he cried out, "A fire at Amram's!" When his colleagues reproved Amram for causing them to put him to shame by revealing his burning passion, he replied: "Better that you shame Amram in this world than you be ashamed of him in the next." According to legend, "Amram then conjured it [the Tempter] to depart from him, and it came forth in the shape of a fiery column." Exulting in his victory over transgression, Amram said: "See you are fire and I am [merely] flesh, yet I am stronger than you" (Kid. 81a).

Amram was so pious that he "attached fringes [*tzitzit*] to the aprons of the women of his house" (Suk. 11a). His extreme piety led him to impose stringent restrictions on the behavior of the exilarch and his family. Consequently, they seized every opportunity to make fun of him. "One day they made him lie down in the snow. The next day they said, 'What would your honor like us to bring you?' Amram knew that whatever he told them they would do the reverse, so he requested 'lean meat broiled on the coals and wine much diluted.' They brought him fat meat broiled on the coals and undiluted wine." Seeing that the brutal treatment inflicted by her family had made Amram seriously ill, Yalta (daughter of the exilarch) cured him: "She took him in to the bath, and they kept him there until the water turned to the color of blood [from the perspiration] and his flesh was covered with bright spots" (Git. 67b).

Anan, Babylonian *amora* (third century).

Although renowned as a teacher of civil and ritual law, Anan also engaged in esoteric speculations. According to the Talmud, Elijah the prophet frequently visited Anan and instructed him in Seder Eliyahu (lit., "Order of Elijah"), a mysterious rabbinic work of uncertain origin and authorship. However, this relationship ceased as a result of an incident in which Anan allowed himself to be the unconscious tool of a man who cunningly bribed him. After Anan fasted and prayed for Divine mercy, Elijah resumed his visits. However, because Anan greatly feared the prophet, he made a box in which he sat while Elijah was teaching him the rest of Seder Eliyahu. This was the *aggadic* explanation for why the work was divided into two parts: the larger Seder Eliyahu Rabbah (lit., "major"), which Elijah taught Anan directly face to face, and the smaller Seder Eliyahu Zuta (lit., "minor"), written when Anan was sitting in the box (Ket. 106a).

When criticizing one of Anan's arguments, R. Nachman remarked: "When you were at Mar Samuel's academy you wasted your time playing chess" (Kid. 21b). Nevertheless, elsewhere it is evident that R. Nachman respected Anan highly by calling him Mar (Master) (Hul. 56a).

Antigonus of Sokho, early sage (third century B.C.E.).

Antigonus of Sokho was the link in the chain of tradition between his teacher Shimon ha-Tzadik (Simeon the Just) and the *zugot* (pairs). His Greek name indicated the extent of Hellenistic influence during this period. The only preserved statement of Antigonus of Sokho is: "Be not like servants who minister to their master in order to receive a reward, but be like servants who minister to their master not in order to receive a reward; and let the fear of Heaven be upon you" (Avot 1:3). According to rabbinic tradition, Antigonus did not intend this as denying the concept of a future reward in the World to Come, but it was misinterpreted in that way by his pupil Zadok, the founder of the Sadducees.

Aquila (second century).

Aquila was a scholar in the Land of Israel who translated the Bible from Hebrew into Greek. Born a gentile in Pontus and briefly a member of the Christian community, Aquila later became a convert to Judaism. According to tradition, Aquila was the nephew of Hadrian. He was appointed to an office dealing with the rebuilding of Jerusalem as the Roman city "Aelia Capitolina," fifty years after the Jewish capital had been destroyed. As Aquila learned more about its history and ethical values, he became increasingly attracted to Judaism and studied with R. Akiva, R. Eliezer ben Hyrcanus, and R. Joshua ben Hananiah. When Aquila finally summoned the courage to confess his embrace of Judaism to the emperor, Hadrian replied that his nephew could study Torah but should not become circumcised. In response, Aquila answered that he could only learn Torah by entering the Abrahamic covenant, for just as no soldier could draw his pay without bearing arms, no one could study the Torah thoroughly without obeying the Jewish laws (Tanh. Mishpatim 3, 5). *See also* Onkelos.

Ashi, Babylonian *amora* (fourth/fifth century).

Ashi reestablished the academy at Sura and is generally considered to be the first editor of the Babylonian Talmud. According to tradition, the birth of Ashi coincided with the death of Rava, the great teacher at the academy of Machoza (Kid. 72b). As a brilliant scholar coming from a wealthy family, Ashi used his fortune to rebuild the Sura academy, which had been closed since the death of R. Hisda in 309. During his more than fifty years as its head, Ashi restored the academy to its former glory. As the Talmud notes, "From the days of Rabbi [Judah ha-Nasi] until Ashi, we do not find learning [Torah] and high office [social distinction] combined in the same person" (Sanh. 36a). Just as the former compiled and edited the Mishnah, Ashi devoted his life's work to editing the Gemara (the explanations of the Mishnah that had been handed down in the Babylonian academies since the days of Rav, together with all the discussions, *aggadah*, and *halachic* decisions). This task was vitally important, because after so many years numerous interpretations had been forgotten. The Talmud relates that Ashi revised the work twice (BB 157b), and the entire project was not completed until two generations later under Ravina II, who died around 500.

As the Talmud observes, "Blessing comes only on those things that are hidden from sight" (Taan. 8b). In one classic tale, Ashi shocked the guests at his son's wedding when he deliberately smashed expensive glassware to reduce the excessive gaiety of those Rabbis in attendance (Ber. 31a). This action, possibly related to the ancient belief that it was wise to temper joy to prevent disaster, may have been the source of the custom of breaking a glass at a wedding ceremony. The meaning of this practice was later said to be a somber remembrance of the destruction of Jerusalem and the Temple.

Ashi taught, "Whoever is proud of spirit [haughty] will ultimately be brought low," observing that God plucks out the arrogant like "a man who goes out into his fields and gleans the tallest ears of corn" (Sot. 5a). "Only a part of a man's praise should be said in his presence [lest he become arrogant], but all of it may be spoken in his absence" (Er. 18b). Ashi also said, "Any scholar who is not as hard as iron is not a scholar" (Taan. 4a).

The death of Ashi, and his colleague Ravina, brought to a close the period of the *amoraim* and marked the conclusion of the Talmudic era. However, the final editing of the Talmud was probably completed in the middle of the sixth century by the *Savoraim* (the disciples of the last *amoraim* and their immediate successors), who appended some additional commentary and notes to the work. *See also* Isaac bar Mesharsheya.

Assi, the name of two prominent *amoraim*.

The earlier Assi (third century) was a Babylonian contemporary of Rav, to whom the sage addressed a series of famous maxims: "Do not dwell in a town in which no horses neigh or dogs bark [i.e., these animals guard the town, with dogs raising the alarm and robbers chased on horseback]; do not dwell in a town where the leader of the community is a physician [perhaps because he would be so busy treating patients that he would not have time to properly attend to communal matters]; and do not marry two [women, lest they scheme against you, but] if you do marry two, marry a third [who will reveal their designs]" (Pes. 113a).

The later Assi (third/fourth century) was born in Babylonia but moved to the Land of Israel where he was a lifelong friend of R. Ammi. Both were referred to as "son of Nathan" and of priestly descent, indicating that they may have been blood brothers with the same father. A student of R. Yochanan, Assi later succeeded him as head of the academy in Tiberias. The names of Ammi and Assi appear together in numerous Talmudic passages, either as being of the same opinion or opposed to each other, and their views were often introduced by the words "both said." They were highly respected by their Babylonian colleagues, among whom Ammi and Assi were known as "the Palestinian judges" or as "the distinguished priests of Palestine" (Git. 59b; Sanh. 17b).

Assi's most famous statement is: "Charity is equivalent to all the other commandments [*mitzvot* in the Torah] combined" (BB 9a). To provide for children, he urged that one "should always eat and drink less than his means allow, clothe himself according to his means, and honor his wife and children beyond his means, because they are dependent upon him, and he is dependent upon the One who spoke and the world came into being" (Hul. 84b). Addressing the question why children were taught the chapters on the priesthood (Leviticus) before Genesis, Assi explained that, since both sacrifices and children are pure, "it is fitting that the pure [children] should begin their studies with the pure [i.e., the laws of purity]" (Lev. R. 7:3). He described the evil inclination as "at first [fragile] like a spider web, but ultimately [if one continues to yield to temptation] it becomes like [strong] cart ropes" (Suk. 52a), based on the verse, "Woe unto them that haul sin with cords of falsehood, and iniquity as with cart ropes" (Isa. 5:18).

A *midrash* relates that as Assi was about to die, his nephew entered his room and found him crying. He asked why Assi was weeping, for he had learned the entire Torah, had numerous disciples, had observed all the *mitzvot*, and had never sullied his noble traits by acting as a judge or allowing himself to be appointed to public office. Assi replied that the last point was the source of his weeping: "Perhaps I shall be required to answer for being able to administer justice and not doing so," citing the verse (Prov. 29:4), "The king by justice establishes the land; but a fraudulent man tears it down" (Tanh. Mishpatim 2).

Assi was so highly regarded that, upon his death, it was said that "the gates of Tiberias collapsed" (JT Av. Zar. 3:1) and "all the cedars were uprooted" (MK 25b). *See also* Ammi; Judah bar Shila.

Avdimi bar Hama, Palestinian *amora* who moved to Babylonia (fourth century).

Avdimi bar Hama is best known for his *aggadic* interpretation of the verse, "They [the Israelites] stood *under* the mountain [prior to the Revelation at

Sinai]" (Exod. 19:17). Although generally translated as "at the base of," Avdimi bar Hama took the phrase literally, explaining that God "suspended the mountain over Israel like an inverted dome [or vault], saying: 'If you accept the Torah, all will be well with you; but if not, this will be your burial place'" (Shab. 88a; Av. Zar. 2b).

Commenting on the verses, "This commandment is not in heaven . . . neither is it beyond the sea" (Deut. 30:11–13), Avdimi bar Hama observed: "If it were in heaven, it would be a person's duty to ascend to obtain it; if were it beyond the seas, one would be obliged to cross them in quest of it" (Er. 55a). Avdimi bar Hama also stated: "He who occupies himself with Torah study will have his desires granted by God" (Av. Zar. 19a).

Avdimi of Haifa, Palestinian *amora* (third/fourth century).

A recognized authority in *halachic* matters, Avdimi of Haifa also stressed proper etiquette toward the intellectual leaders of the community: "When a *hacham* [scholar] passes, one must rise in his honor within a distance of four cubits [six feet], and remain standing until he has passed a like distance; in honor of an *av bet din* [head of the religious court and vice president of the Sanhedrin], one must rise as soon as he comes into sight and remain standing until he has passed a distance of four cubits; but when the *nasi* [president of the Sanhedrin] passes [to take his seat at the academy], one must rise as soon as one observes him approaching, and must not sit down until he takes his seat." He based this on the verse (Exod. 33:8): "[And all the people stood . . .] and looked after Moses, until he had entered the tent" (Kid. 33b). Avdimi of Haifa also stated: "Since the day the Temple was destroyed, prophecy has been taken away from the prophets and given to the wise [sages]" (BB 12a); and "Before a man eats and drinks he has two hearts [i.e., he finds it hard to make up his mind], but after he has eaten and drunk he has only one" (BB 12b).

Aviya, Babylonian *amora* (fourth century).

Also known as Avia, he was a disciple of R. Joseph bar Hiyya at Pumbedita and strict in ritual observances. "Aviya was once ill and did not go to hear the lecture of R. Joseph [who used to speak every Sabbath morning before the *musaf* prayer]." The next day R. Joseph asked, "Why did your honor not come to the lecture yesterday?" Aviya responded: "I felt weak and was not able." In response to R. Joseph's question, "Why did you not take some food and come?" Aviya noted that R. Huna had said, "It is forbidden for a man to taste anything until he has said the *musaf Amidah*." When R. Joseph suggested that he should have said the prayer privately and then eaten and come, Aviya quoted the words of R. Yochanan: "It is forbidden for a man to say his *Amidah* before the congregation says it" (Ber. 28b).

Once when Aviya visited Rava's home, "his boots were muddied with clay, [yet] he sat down on a bed before Rava. [Thereupon] Rava was annoyed and wished to vex him." Rava proposed a series of difficult questions, hoping to embarrass Aviya if he did not know how to answer them, but the latter gave the correct response to each. Finally, R. Nachman declared, "Praised be the All-Merciful that Rava did not succeed in putting Aviya to shame" (Shab. 46a–b).

Aviya was married to the sister of R. Rami bar Hama. When her *ketubah* became lost, they appeared before R. Joseph for a ruling whether they could still live together. The decision was it was necessary for a new *ketubah* to be written before they could resume living as husband and wife (Ket. 56b–57a).

Avtalyon, *tanna* colleague of Shemaiah (first century B.C.E.).

One of the fourth of the *zugot* (pairs), Avtalyon was the *av bet din* (head of the rabbinic court) while Shemaiah served as *nasi* (president of the Sanhedrin). Although said to be offspring of proselytes ["the descendants of Sennacherib"; Sanh. 96b], the Talmud considered Avtalyon and Shemaiah to be superior to the high priest, "the two great men of their generation" (Pes. 66a) and "great sages and interpreters" (Pes. 70b).

Possibly to prevent overcrowding, the academy of Avtalyon and Shemaiah was not free to everyone. Those who sought entrance paid a daily admission fee of half a *tropaik* (a few cents) to the gatekeeper, an amount equivalent to the wages for a half day of work. One Friday afternoon in winter when he could not afford entry, Hillel "climbed up and sat on the window [an aperture in the roof looking down to the ground floor] to hear the words of the living God" from these famed scholars. At one point they "looked up and saw the figure of a man in the window. They went up and found him covered by three cubits of snow. They removed the snow from him, and bathed and anointed him. As they seated Hillel in front of an open fire, they said: 'This man deserves that the Sabbath be profaned on his behalf' [i.e., to save a human life]" (Yoma 35b).

Avtalyon's most famous saying is: "Wise scholars, be careful with your words [ambiguous teachings capable of misinterpretation], lest you be condemned to exile and be banished to a place of evil waters [heretical teachings], from which the disciples who come after you drink and die [resulting in desecration of the Name of Heaven]" (Avot 1:11). This probably reflected political events of the time, when many scholars were forced to seek refuge in Egypt, forcing their disciples to be exposed to many new ideas opposed to those in the Land of Israel. *See also* Hillel; Shemaiah.

B

Bana'ah, Palestinian *tanna* (third century).

The most famous statement of Bana'ah is: "Whoever studies Torah for its own sake, his learning becomes an elixir of life to him [based on the verse, 'It is a tree of life to them that hold fast to it'; Prov. 3:8]. . . . But for one who studies Torah not for its own sake [for any other reason], it becomes a deadly poison" (Taan. 7a). As an indication that dreams were considered significant during his time, Bana'ah reported that "there were twenty-four interpreters of dreams in Jerusalem." However, when he dutifully visited them all after having a dream, "they all gave different interpretations" (Av. Zar. 5b).

According to a Talmudic legend, Bana'ah placed marks over the caves where dead bodies were buried, lest people mistakenly walk over them and become ritually unclean. One day, Bana'ah arrived at the tomb of Abraham at the Cave of Machpelah and found Eliezer, the servant of the patriarch, standing at the entrance. When the Rabbi asked, "What is Abraham doing?" Eliezer replied, "He is sleeping in the arms of Sarah, and she is looking fondly at his head." Bana'ah ordered Eliezer to tell his master, "Bana'ah is standing at the entrance," and Abraham replied: "'Let him enter, for it is well known that there is no passion in this world [and therefore there could be no objection to his seeing Abraham sleeping with Sarah].' So Bana'ah went in, surveyed the cave, and came out again. When he came to the cave of Adam [who according to tradition was also buried at Machpelah, either in an inner or lower cave], a *bat kol* [heavenly voice] said: 'You have seen the likeness of my likeness [Abraham, who was the likeness of Adam], but my likeness itself you may not behold [Adam, who was created in the likeness of God, was like a monkey to a human being].'" Bana'ah replied that all he wanted was to mark out the cave; the response was that all he needed to do was to measure the outer cave, since the inner one was the same size, or the upper one, since the lower one was of identical proportions. Bana'ah then related what he had learned from this experience: "Adam's two heels were like two orbs of the sun. Compared with Sarah, all other people are like a monkey to a human being; compared with Eve, Sarah was like a monkey to a human being; compared with Adam, Eve was like a monkey to a human being; and compared with the *Shechinah* [Divine Presence], Adam was like a monkey to a human being" (BB 58a).

Bar Hedya, Palestinian *amora* (fourth century).

"Bar Hedya was an interpreter of dreams [but had a cynical view of his profession]. To one who paid him he used to give a favorable interpretation, and to one who did not pay him he gave an unfavorable interpretation [of the same dream]" (Ber. 56a). Once when Bar Hedya was traveling with Rava in a boat, he wondered why he should "accompany a man to whom a miracle will happen [i.e., he will be saved but I will not]." As Bar Hedya was disembarking, he dropped a book on which Rava saw written, "All dreams follow the interpretation." Thereupon, Rava exclaimed, "Wretch! It all depended on you and you gave me all this pain! I forgive you everything except [what you said about] the daughter of R. Hisda [Rava's wife, whose death Bar Hedya had foretold]. May it be God's will that this fellow be delivered up to the Government, and that they have no mercy on him!" Bar Hedya was frightened, realizing that if an undeserved curse from any sage would come to pass, how much more since this was a deserved curse from the eminent Rava. Consequently, Bar Hedya decided to go into exile, which according to a sage "makes atonement for iniquity." Fleeing to the Romans, Bar Hedya sat at the door of the keeper of the king's wardrobe. The latter related a dream of a needle piercing his finger, and Bar Hedya demanded a *zuz* [small coin] to interpret it. When the official refused, Bar Hedya "would not say a word to him." This same scenario was repeated when the official dreamt that "a worm fell between two of my fingers." Finally, the keeper of the king's wardrobe dreamed that "a worm filled the whole of my hand" and that "worms have been spoiling all the silk garments." When this became known throughout the palace and the keeper of the wardrobe was about to be killed, he complained: "Why execute me? Bring the man who knew and would not tell." So they brought Bar Hedya and said to him: "Because of your *zuz*, the king's silken garments have been ruined" (Ber. 56a).

Bar Hedya visited Babylonia to establish the date of Sukkot (i.e., to fix the date of the beginning of the month so that the seventh day of the festival [Hoshana Rabba, when congregants beat willow branches against the ground or a chair to symbolically cast away their sins] never coincides with the Sabbath) (Suk. 43b).

Bar Kappara, Palestinian *tanna* (third century).

The father of Ben Kappara bore the same name, and some of the elder's teachings may have been ascribed to his more illustrious son, who established an academy at Caesarea. Some scholars have argued that Bar Kappara and

Eleazar Hakapar were the same person, while others maintained that they were two different contemporaries of Judah ha-Nasi.

Although recognized as an outstanding *halachist*, Bar Kappara's views were far more liberal than his contemporaries. With regard to secular knowledge, "He who knows how to calculate the cycles and movements of the planets [i.e., understands astronomy], but does not [i.e., fails to pay attention to these things], to him may be applied the verse, 'They regard not the work of the Lord, nor the operation of His hands' [Isa. 5:12]" (Shab. 75a). Bar Kappara was an admirer of "Greek learning" and Hellenic love of beauty. He interpreted the biblical verse, "May God enlarge Japheth and let him dwell in the tents of Shem" (Gen. 9:27), as meaning: "The words of the Torah shall be recited in the speech of Japheth [Greek] in the tents of Shem [in the synagogues and schools]" (Gen. R. 36:8). Opposed to mystical speculation, he urged his students to "seek to know only of those days that followed the Creation, but not what went before" (Gen. R. 1:10).

Among Bar Kappara's words of practical advice are: "When goods are cheap, [hurry to] collect [money] and buy" (Ber. 63a); "A man should always teach his son a clean and easy trade" (Ber. 63a); and "A bad-tempered man gains nothing but [the ill effect of] his temper [which adversely affects the health of his body], but a good man is fed with the fruit of his deeds" (Kid. 40b–41a). He declared, "The work of the righteous [pious] is greater than the work [Creation] of heaven and earth" (Ket. 5a); and "If one sheds tears for a worthy man [who has died], God counts them and stores them up in His treasury" (Shab. 105b).

Bava ben Buta, Palestinian *tanna* (first century B.C.E.).

According to *aggadic* tradition, it was Bava ben Buta, who had been deprived of his eyesight by Herod, who advised the latter to rebuild the Temple in expiation of his great crimes. Herod once appeared incognito before Bava ben Buta, complaining about the actions of "this wicked slave [Herod]" and asking the blind teacher to curse the ruler. When Bava ben Buta refused even after extensive urging, Herod identified himself and exclaimed: "Had I known that the Rabbis were so discreet, I should not have put all of them to death. Now what can I do to make amends?" Bava ben Buta replied, "As you have extinguished the light of the world [i.e., the Rabbis, based on the verse, 'For the commandment is a lamp and the Law a light'; Prov. 6:23], go now and attend to the light of the world [i.e., the Temple, based on the verse, 'and all the nations become enlightened by it'; Isa. 2:2]." When Herod said that he feared the government, Bava ben Buta advised him to send an envoy to Rome, who would stay a year in the capital and take a year to travel each way, "and in the meantime you can pull down the Temple and rebuild it." Herod took Bava ben Buta's advice and received the following message from Rome: "If you have not yet pulled it [the Temple] down, do not do so; if you have pulled it down, do not rebuild it; if you have pulled it down and already rebuilt it, you are one of those bad servants who do first and ask permission afterwards" (BB 3b–4a). Bava ben Buta was so pious in his religious observances that, fearing he might have committed a serious transgression, he brought a daily guilt offering, except on the day after Yom Kippur (Ker. 18a).

Bava ben Buta was willing to overlook an insult to himself in order to make peace between husband and wife. As the Talmud relates, a certain Babylonian went up to the Land of Israel and married, but his wife appeared to have problems understanding his words. When he ordered her to boil two cow's feet, she boiled him two lentils, which infuriated her husband. According to Rashi, this was because she misunderstood his Babylonian pronunciation and mistook *telafe* (feet) for *telaf* (lentil). In another version, instead of boiling him "two" lentils, which meant "some," she took her husband literally and boiled just two. The next day her husband told her to "boil me a *giwa*," a large measure of lentils. Thinking that she had intentionally boiled only two the previous day through laziness or meanness, he asked for an extraordinary large quantity, believing that she would scale it down. However, his wife did precisely as he had requested. Her husband then asked her to bring him *bezuni* (which could mean melons or candles). She dutifully returned with two candles, which he ordered her to "break on the head of the *bava* (threshold)." Unfortunately, the wife misunderstood and broke them on the head of Bava ben Buta, who happened to be sitting on the threshold engaged in judging a lawsuit. When the astonished sage asked the reason for her action, she naively replied, "This is what my husband ordered me to do." Bava ben Buta said, "You have performed your husband's will; may the Almighty bring forth from you two sons like Bava ben Buta!" (Ned. 66b).

Bebai, Babylonian *amora* (fourth century).

Also known as Bibi, he had a "dark-skinned daughter" and "applied an unguent [depilatory] one limb at a time and this brought her a husband with 400 *zuzim* [as a dowry]." A pagan neighbor tried the same experiment with his daughter, but it produced fatal results. He exclaimed, "Bebai has killed my daughter!" Hearing of the case, R. Nachman observed: "Bebai drinks beer [at his meals, a luxury rarely indulged in by Babylonian Jews and said by Rashi to produce obesity and growth of hair], and that is why his daughter required unguents [skin-improving pastes]. We who do not drink beer, our daughters do not need such treatments [i.e., the skin of the children of those who abstain from strong drink is white and smooth]" (Shab. 80b; MK 9b).

Bebai stated, "Three classes of women may use an absorbent [contraception] in their marital intercourse: a minor, an expectant mother, and a nursing mother. The minor, because otherwise she might become pregnant and die. An expectant mother, because otherwise she might cause her fetus to degenerate into a sandal [lit., a 'flat-fish-shaped' abortion]. A nursing mother, because otherwise she might have to wean her child prematurely [because a second conception would cause her breast milk to deteriorate] and this would result in its death." Bebai then defined a "minor" as a girl "from the age of eleven years and one day to the age of twelve years and one day," explaining that before this age conception was impossible, whereas after it conception incurred no danger (Nid. 45a).

Ben Azzai, Palestinian *tanna* (second century).

A student of R. Joshua ben Hananiah and residing in Tiberias, Ben Azzai is best known as one of the four "who entered the Garden [*pardes*]," meaning that they engaged in esoteric speculation. It was reported that "he caught a glimpse and died," implying that he was led astray by mystical teaching (Hag. 14b). However, the Talmud immediately adds that Ben Azzai was the subject of a verse from Psalms (116:15), "Precious in the sight of the Lord is the death of His faithful ones," an indication of his great piety.

The Talmud states that Ben Azzai was wed to R. Akiva's daughter. Like her mother, she made it a condition of marriage that her husband devote himself to the study of Torah (Ket. 63a.). Consequently, Ben Azzai never had children. When R. Eliezer ben Hyrcanus said, "One who does not engage in the propagation of the race is like someone who has shed blood," Ben Azzai added that one who was childless diminishes the image of God. He was immediately branded a hypocrite by the other Rabbis for his own failure to have children: "Some preach well and act well; others act well but do not preach well. You, however, preach well but do not act well." In his defense, Ben Azzai replied: "But what can I do if my soul is in love with the Torah? The world can be carried on by others!" (Yev. 63b).

Among his most famous statements are: "Run to perform even a 'minor' [easy] mitzvah and flee from sin; for one mitzvah leads to another mitzvah, and one sin leads to another sin" (Avot 4:2); and "Do not despise any man and do not consider anything impossible; for there is no man who does not have his hour, and there is nothing that does not have its place" (Avot 4:3). Ben Azzai stressed the importance of the Torah as the foundation of Judaism: "One who allows himself to be humiliated for the honor of the Torah will be honored in the end; one who degrades himself for the sake of the words of the Torah will be elevated in the end" (ARN 11). He recommended, "When you seek a place to sit, choose one a few steps lower than what you think you deserve, for it is better to be told to go up rather than to descend" (ARN 25). Unlike the view of a large majority of the Rabbis, Ben Azzai said: "A man has an obligation to teach his daughter Torah" (Sot. 20a).

Ben Azzai once took the concept of learning from one's teacher to an extreme. "Once I went in after R. Akiva to a privy. I learned three things from his behavior: one does not evacuate east and west but only north and south; one evacuates sitting and not standing [for reasons of modesty]; and it is proper to wipe with the left hand and not with the right." When Judah ha-Nasi asked how he could act so brazenly in investigating such intimate details of R. Akiva's personal behavior, Ben Azzai replied simply: "It was a matter of Torah, and I needed to learn" (Ber. 62a).

After R. Akiva declared the commandment to love your neighbor as yourself (Lev. 19:18) to be "the fundamental principle of the Torah," Ben Azzai stressed that the verse "This is the book of the generations of man" (Gen. 5:1) contained the even greater principle of the common origin and brotherhood of humankind (Sifra Kedoshim 7:4).

Ben Azzai offered a fascinating interpretation of the first word of the Book of Lamentations (*Eichah*). He argued that the numerical value of the four letters of the word "*eichah*" (*aleph* = 1; *yud* = 10; *haf* = 20; *hei* = 5) indicated that the Israelites did not go into exile until after they had denied the one God; the Ten Commandments; the law of circumcision given to the twentieth generation after Adam; and the Five Books of Moses (Lam. R. 1:1).

According to the Talmud, "One who sees Ben Azzai in his dream may look forward to piety" (Ber. 57b); and "With the passing of Ben Azzai, diligent scholars passed from the earth" (Sot. 9:15).

Ben Bag Bag, Palestinian *tanna* (first century C.E.).

Ben Bag Bag was a student of Hillel and, according to some accounts, a convert or son of a convert. When discussing whether a person was entitled to take the law into his own hands, Ben Bag Bag said: "Do not enter [stealthily] the courtyard of another without permission, even to take back something that belongs to you, lest he think you are a thief. But if he is reluctant to return your property, you may break his teeth [give him a hard blow] and say, 'I am taking possession of what is mine'" (BK 27b). Ben Bag Bag is best known for his maxim in Pirkei Avot (5:26): "Delve in it [the Torah] and continue to delve in it [lit., 'turn over in it'—study the Torah from all sides], for everything [all the wisdom in the world] is [contained] within it. Grow old and gray in it, and do not stir from it, for you can have no better portion than it."

Ben Bava, Palestinian *tanna* and one of the Ten Martyrs (second century).

During the Hadrianic persecutions, it was decreed that anyone who issued or received rabbinic ordination would be put to death, and the city where such an ordination took place would be demolished. Judah ben Bava went to a site between two mountains, between the cities of Usha and Shefaram (so that neither city would suffer). There he ordained five of the leading pupils of the martyred R. Akiva—R. Meir, R. Judah, R. Shimon, R. Jose, and R. Eliezer ben Shammua—to carry on the rabbinic tradition. When discovered by the Romans, Ben Bava urged them to flee while he lay down on the ground pretending to be dead. The approaching soldiers, wanting to make certain that the body was dead, "drove 300 iron spear-heads [lances] into his body until it was riddled like a sieve" (Sanh. 14a). Sympathetic to the plight of the *agunah*, Ben Bava permitted evidence of a husband's death based on the testimony of a single witness so as to allow the wife to remarry (Ber. 27a).

"It was said of Judah ben Bava that all his actions were for the sake of Heaven," except for one: he transgressed the injunction against the rearing of small cattle. Ben Bava suffered from a painful and protracted illness, for which doctors declared that the only remedy was to drink warm milk from a small goat. They bought him a goat, which he kept in his house. When Ben Bava eventually died, apparently from this same illness, the sages determined that this was in fact his only sin (BK 80a). As a result of this piety, the Talmud states: "When the phrase 'it once happened to a certain pious man' occurs, it refers either to Judah ben Bava or to Judah ben Ilai" (BK 103b).

Ben Dama, Palestinian *tanna* (second century).

Eleazar Ben Dama was attracted to Hellenism and the Judeo-Christians. He asked his uncle, R. Ishmael ben Elisha, "May one such as I, who has studied the whole of the Torah, learn Greek wisdom [philosophy]?" In reply, the latter cited the verse: "This Book of the Law shall not depart out of your mouth, but you shall meditate on it day and night" (Josh. 1:8). R. Ishmael ben Elisha continued, "Find a time that is neither day nor night and then learn Greek wisdom!" (Men. 99b).

After Ben Dama had been bitten by a snake, a Judeo-Christian wanted to heal him by using a formula in the name of Jesus. However, R. Ishmael ben Elisha did not believe in such charms and refused the Judeo-Christian entry. As Ben Dama was beginning to cite a verse from the Torah to prove that this would not be against Jewish law, "his soul departed and he died." R. Ishmael ben Elisha considered that God had been merciful in allowing Ben Dama to die in peace: "Happy are you, for you were pure in body and your soul likewise left you in purity; nor did you transgress the law of the sages" (Av. Zar. 27b). In this way, R. Ishmael ben Elisha believed that his nephew would avoid punishments after death and enjoy a full measure of happiness in the World to Come.

Ben Hei Hei, Palestinian *tanna* (first century B.C.E.).

Like Ben Bag Bag, Ben Hei Hei was a convert and a disciple of Hillel (some even believe they were the same person). His name was said to reflect the status as a proselyte who, when converted to Judaism, becomes known as *ben* (son of) Abraham and Sarah. According to the biblical narrative (Gen. 17:5, 15), the Hebrew letter *hei* was added to the end of both of their names (Tosef. to Hag. 9b).

In Pirkei Avot (5:26), Ben Hei Hei is quoted as saying: "The reward is in proportion to the exertion," referring to the degree of energy and labor necessary to study Torah and fulfill the Divine commandments.

Ben Peturah, Palestinian *tanna* (second century).

The Talmud discusses the problem of an individual faced with the choice of saving his own life or that of his companion. It raises the hypothetical situation of two men in the desert, with only one of them possessing a small amount of water. If he drinks it, he will reach civilization and be saved; but if the two of them share it, both will die. Ben Peturah advocated that they should share the water rather than have one attempt to save his own life at the expense of the other: "It is better that both drink and die, rather than one behold his companion's death." However, the prevailing opinion was that of R. Akiva, who argued that the person in possession of the water should save his own life and not share the water, for he could not justify that two die when only one death was necessary. R. Akiva based this view on an interpretation of the biblical verse, "that your brother may live with you" (Lev. 25:36), as meaning that your life takes precedence. He observed that if the Torah had meant that a person was required to love his neighbor to the extent of always sacrificing his life for him, the commandment would have been phrased to love your neighbor "more than" yourself (BM 62a). Only when faced with a choice between death and committing idolatry, unlawful sexual intercourse, or murder is martyrdom preferred (Sanh. 74a–b). In addition, one must sacrifice one's life rather than submit to what onlookers would assume was a renunciation of faith through the public violation of any religious law.

Ben Zoma, Palestinian *tanna* (second century).

A disciple of R. Joshua ben Hananiah, Shimon Ben Zoma was a brilliant *halachist*: "Whoever sees Ben Zoma in his dream may hope for wisdom [i.e., is assured of scholarship]" (Ber. 57b). A master interpreter of the Bible, it was said that "with Ben Zoma died the last of the exegetes [*darshanim*]" (Sot. 9:15). Ben Zoma was obsessed with the story of Creation. On one occasion, Ben Zoma was so preoccupied with his mystical speculations that he did not acknowledge his teacher. As he later explained: "I was gazing between the upper and lower waters [Gen. 1:6–7] and I discovered that the space between them is no more than the breadth of three fingers" (Hag. 15a). When speaking to his disciples, R. Joshua ben Hananiah said, "Ben Zoma is outside," meaning that he had passed beyond the limit of permitted research. Indeed, Ben Zoma was one of the four men who "entered the garden" (of esoteric knowledge)—"he looked and became demented [lit., 'stricken' with mental illness]" (Hag. 14b) and died soon thereafter.

Ben Zoma believed that the Torah scholar was the "crown of Creation" (Tosefta Ber. 6:2). Seeing a crowd on the steps of the Temple Mount, Ben Zoma marveled at human progress: "Blessed is He who has created all these to serve me. What labors Adam had to carry out before he obtained bread to eat! He had to plow the field, sow the seed, harvest the grain, bind and thresh and winnow, and select the grains. After that he ground the wheat and kneaded the dough and baked it, and only then could he eat bread. But I rise in the morning and find it all prepared and ready for my use." Ben Zoma continued, "And how many labors Adam had to carry out before he obtained a garment to wear! He had to shear and wash the wool, comb, spin, and weave it, and only then did he obtain a garment to wear. But all kinds of craftsmen [tradesmen] do these tasks and then come early to the door of my house, so that when I rise in the morning all these are ready for me" (Ber. 58a).

Ben Zoma recommended that a proper guest should say: "How much trouble my host has taken for me! How much meat, wine, and cakes he has set before me! And all this effort was only for my sake!" Conversely, a bad guest says: "How much after all has my host put himself out? I have eaten one piece of bread and one slice of meat, and I have drunk one cup of wine! All the trouble which my host has taken was only for the sake of his wife and his children!" (Ber. 58a). Ben Zoma noted that the Bible said of a good guest, "Remember to magnify His works, of which men have sung" (Job 36:24), whereas of a bad guest it is written, "Men do therefore fear him [whom none of the wise can perceive]" (Job 37:24).

Ben Zoma explained that as long as the blessing over bread was made before a meal, no other foods need to be subsequently blessed, except for wine (when used for the purpose of sanctification, as in the *Kiddush*, but not if merely drunk as a beverage) (Ber. 41b–42a). He also gave a reason for mentioning the Exodus from Egypt in the evening recitation of the *Shema*. The biblical text stated that one must "remember the day of your departure from the land of Egypt *all* the days of your life" (Deut. 16:3). "[Had the text said] 'the days of your life,' it would have meant [only] the days; but 'all the days of your life' includes the nights as well" (Ber. 12b).

Ben Zoma's most famous saying is in Pirkei Avot (4:1). "Who is wise? One who learns from every person, as it was said, 'From all my teachers I grew wise' [Ps. 119:99]. Who is strong? One who subdues his personal inclination, as it is said, 'He who is slow to anger is better than the strong man, and a master of his passions is better than a conqueror of a city' [Prov. 16:32]. Who is rich? One who is happy with his lot, as it is said, 'When you eat the labor of your hands you are happy [in this world] and all is well with you [in the World to Come]' [Ps. 128:2]. Who is honored? One who honors others, as it is said, 'I honor those who honor Me, but those who scorn Me shall be dishonored' [1 Sam. 2:30]."

Berechiah, Palestinian *amora* (fourth century).

A master of *aggadah*, most of Berechiah's teachings are found in the Jerusalem Talmud and in *midrashim* from the Land of Israel. Commenting on the well-known verse, "There is a time to be born and a time to die" (Eccles. 3:2), Berechiah said: "Happy is the person who at the hour of his death is as pure and innocent as at the hour of his birth" (JT Ber. 2:4). On the phrase, "Do not overdo wickedness" (Eccles. 7:17), he noted that the Bible did not mean to teach that it is permitted to "be a little wicked"; instead, it means that if you did sin a little, do not say that since God is angry at me for a small sin, I cannot be any worse off for sinning more" (Eccles. R. 7:17). Berechiah interpreted the verse from Psalms (32:1), "Happy is he whose transgression is forgiven," as meaning: "Happy is he who is master over his evil inclination, rather than allows it to master him" (Gen. R. 22:6).

Beroka Hoza'ah, uncertain chronology.

"Beroka Hoza'ah came to a Babylonian market where Elijah often appeared to him. Once in answer to his question, 'Is there anyone in this market who has a share in the world to come?' the prophet said 'No.' Meanwhile Elijah saw a man wearing black shoes but no thread of blue on the corners of his garment (Num. 15:38) and he exclaimed, 'This man has a share in the World to Come. Beroka ran after the man and asked, 'What is your occupation?' The man replied, 'Go away and come back tomorrow.'

"The next day, Beroka repeated his question. The man replied, 'I am a jailer and I keep the men and women separate, and I place my bed between them so that they may not come to sin. When I see a Jewish girl upon whom the gentiles cast their eyes, I risk my life and save her. . . . [Once] I took red wine and put it on her skirt and told them that she was unclean [in this place the laws of menstruation were rigorously enforced].' Beroka then asked the man, 'Why have you no fringes and why do you wear black shoes [distinguishing marks between gentiles and Jews]?' The man replied, 'So that the gentiles should not know that I am a Jew. In this way, when a harsh decree is made [against the Jews], I inform the Rabbis and they pray [to God] and the decree is annulled.' Beroka then asked the man, 'When I asked you about your occupation, why did you tell me to go away now and come back tomorrow?' The man answered, 'They had just issued a harsh decree and I was going first to tell the Rabbis about it so that they might pray to God.'

"Meanwhile, two men passed by and Elijah remarked, 'These two have a share in the World to Come.' Beroka asked them, 'What is your occupation?' They answered, 'We are jesters, and when we see people who are depressed we cheer them up; also, when we see two people quarrelling we try to make peace between them'" (Taan. 22a).

Beruriah (second century).

Daughter of the martyred R. Hananiah ben Teradion, Beruriah (also spelled Bruria) was the wife and spiritual support of the illustrious R. Meir. Living in Tiberias after the Hadrianic persecutions, Beruriah was famous as the only woman in Talmudic literature whose views on *halachic* and secular matters were seriously considered by the sages of her time. The Talmud relates that she could master "300 laws from 300 teachers in one day" (Pes. 62b).

Many anecdotes depict Beruriah's piety, compassion, and wit. A classic *midrash* poignantly illustrates the rabbinic concept that children were a precious loan from God. One Sabbath, while R. Meir was delivering his weekly afternoon lecture in the synagogue, his two sons suddenly died. Beruriah carried them to her room and covered them with a sheet. When R. Meir returned home following evening services and asked for the boys, she replied that they had gone to the house of study. Then she handed him the cup of wine for Havdalah, which marks the end of the Sabbath day. Only after R. Meir had eaten his meal did Beruriah raise the subject: "Some time ago something was left to me for safekeeping. Now the owner has come to reclaim it. Must I return it?" After R. Meir replied in the affirmative, shocked that his brilliant wife could be unaware of such a basic law, Beruriah showed him their dead sons. When R. Meir began to weep uncontrollably, she reminded him of his answer: "Did you not tell me that we must give back what God entrusted to our care?" Then she added the verse from Job (1:21), "The Lord has given, and the Lord has taken away" (Mid. Prov. 31:1).

Several Talmudic anecdotes show how Beruriah corrected the behavior of various sages. Jose the Galilean was once on a journey when he met Beruriah. He asked her, "By what road do we go to Lydda?" "Foolish Galilean," she replied, "Did the sages not say, 'Do not speak at length with a woman' (Avot 1:5)? You should have only asked, 'Which way Lydda?'" Beruriah once came upon a student who was repeating his lessons in an undertone. She rebuked him, exclaiming: "Is it not written, 'Ordered in all things and secure?' [2 Sam. 23:5]. If it [Torah learning] is ordered in your 248 members [bones and organs of the male body, and also the number of positive commandments], it will be secure [in your memory]. But if not, it will not be secure" (Er. 54a).

Although inconsistent with the characters of Beruriah or her husband, the Talmud (Kid. 80b) relates a disturbing legend about Beruriah's death. When she ridiculed the familiar rabbinic saying, "Women are light-minded," R. Meir warned that one day her own deeds might testify to the truth of these words. Beruriah insisted that an educated and highly principled woman would never be led astray. To put her virtue to the test, R. Meir persuaded one of his disciples to attempt to seduce her. After repeated efforts, Beruriah proved too weak to resist. Beruriah then committed suicide, either driven by the shame of her actions or out of mortification when she discovered that her own husband had been the source of what transpired. Tortured by remorse and shame, R. Meir then fled to Babylonia. *See also* Meir.

D

Dimi, Palestinian *amora* (third/fourth century).

Termed "Avdimi Nechuta" (lit., "one who goes down") in the Jerusalem Talmud, Dimi traveled frequently between the Land of Israel and Babylonia, performing the valuable service of sharing the teachings of one group of scholars with the other. Indeed, his sayings were usually preceded by the phrase, "When Dimi came." For example, when R. Abbaye asked, "What do people [most] carefully avoid in the West [i.e., Land of Israel]?" Dimi replied: "Putting others to shame [lit., 'making faces white']." He added R. Hanina's belief that after death everyone descended into Gehinnom but subsequently returned, except for those who had performed any of three unpardonable sins: "He who committed adultery with a married woman, publicly shamed his neighbor, or fastened an evil epithet [degrading nickname] upon him . . . even if he was accustomed to it" (BM 58b).

An honorable man, when Dimi once realized that he had incorrectly related a *halachic* ruling by a sage in the Land of Israel, he immediately sent word confessing his mistake: "The things I told you were in error" (Shab. 63b). Dimi eventually settled permanently in Babylonia to escape the persecutions of Emperor Constantine in the Land of Israel, becoming head of the academy at Pumbedita.

Dimi bar Hinena, Babylonian *amora* (fourth century).

The Talmud relates that their father left Dimi and his brother Rava "two bondwomen [servants], one of whom knew how to bake and cook and the other how to spin and weave. They came before Rava [to decide whether one could force the other to divide them, with the brother who received the more valuable servant giving compensation]." The sage replied: "No. A partner has no right to say, 'You name a price or let me name a price'" (BB 13b).

Dimi bar Joseph, Babylonian *amora* (third century).

When a divorced woman came to R. Samuel denying that a specific child was her son, he instructed his student Dimi bar Joseph to "test her case" (i.e., to determine whether the child knew its mother). So Dimi bar Joseph "placed her among a row of women and, taking hold of her child, carried him in front

41

of them. When he came up to her, [the child] looked at her face with joy, but she turned her eye away from him." Convinced of their relationship, Dimi bar Joseph ordered the woman to "lift up your eyes; come and take away your son" (Ket. 60a).

Dimi the brother of R. Safra, Babylonian *amora* (fourth century).

According to Dimi, "He who makes a vow, even though he fulfills it, is designated a sinner." When asked the biblical source for this conclusion, Dimi cited a verse in Deuteronomy (23:23)—"If you do not vow, you will not have sinned"—implying that the making of a vow must be a sin (Ned. 77b). Dimi also stated, "A man should never speak in praise [lit., 'good'] of his friend, because by praise of him he brings about his blame [lit., 'evil']." This meant that by pointing out a person's favorable qualities or actions, one also inadvertently draws attention to his negative attributes and misdeeds (BB 164b).

Dimi of Nehardea, Babylonian *amora* (fourth century).

Before becoming head of the academy at Pumbedita, Dimi of Nehardea earned his living as a fruit merchant. According to the Talmud, Dimi of Nehardea once brought a load of figs to sell at the market. At that time, Talmudic scholars were permitted to sell their produce earlier than other merchants, so that they could return to their studies as soon as possible. The exilarch asked the esteemed Rava to see whether Dimi was truly a scholar and deserving of the privilege. Rava assigned this task to R. Adda bar Abba, instructing him to test Dimi of Nehardea's scholarship (lit., "go and smell his jar"—to assess whether the wine [his knowledge] was good). When Dimi was unable to answer the difficult questions posed to him, they refused to "reserve the market for him" and thus "his figs were a dead loss" (BB 22a).

Dimi of Nehardea maintained that showing hospitality to a guest was more important than learning Torah in the study hall (Shab. 127a). In a discussion of whether it was better to teach a large amount of material superficially or delve into the depths of a smaller subject matter, Rava said: "If there are two teachers, one who goes through the lessons quickly but with mistakes and the other slowly but without mistakes, we appoint the one who goes quickly, because mistakes correct themselves in time." Dimi of Nehardea disagreed: "We appoint the one who goes slowly but makes no mistakes, for once a mistake is implanted [in a student's mind] it is difficult to unlearn" (BB 21a). On another educational issue, Rava said that if one has a teacher for his children and there is a second who could do a better job, one should "not replace the first by the second, for fear that the second [when appointed] will become lazy [i.e., have no competitor for the post]." Dimi of Nehardea disagreed, maintaining that the second "would exert himself still more if appointed, for the jealousy of scribes increases wisdom [i.e., the jealousy of the one who has been replaced will stimulate the second not to disgrace himself]" (BB 20a).

Dosa ben Harkinas, Palestinian *tanna* (first/second century).

In his famous statement in Pirkei Avot (3:14), Dosa ben Harkinas warned against wasting time that could be used profitably for study: "Late morning sleep [beyond the time prescribed for the saying of the *Shema*], midday wine [making one too sleepy to study or meditate], [listening too much to] children's chatter, and sitting in the assemblies of the ignorant [and following their worthless pursuits] remove a man from the world [i.e., prevent him from accomplishing his mission on earth—the study of Torah]."

Dosa ben Harkinas was highly respected by his colleagues. When fading eyesight and old age made it impossible for him to come to the academy, his fellow scholars often came to his home to discuss important issues (Yev. 16a). According to the Mishnah, Rabban Gamaliel II once accepted the testimony of two witnesses who claimed to have seen the new moon, despite the fact that Dosa ben Harkinas and R. Joshua ben Hananiah believed that they were false witnesses. Rabban Gamaliel II did not take any steps against Dosa ben Harkinas, presumably because of his age and honored status, but the *nasi* ordered R. Joshua ben Hananiah "to appear before me with your staff and your money on the day which, according to your reckoning, should be the Day of Atonement [since the month in question was Tishrei, in which Rosh Hashanah and Yom Kippur fall]." Dosa ben Harkinas advised R. Joshua ben Hananiah to obey the *nasi*, since "if we call in question the decisions of the *bet din* of Rabban Gamaliel II, we must call in question the decisions of every *bet din* that has existed since the days of Moses up to the present time" (RH 2:8–9).

Dostai ben Yannai, Palestinian *tanna* (second century).

Dostai ben Yannai observed in the name of his teacher, R. Meir: "Whoever forgets anything of his Torah learning [by failing to review it regularly], Scripture considers it as if he bears guilt for his soul [as having committed a capital offense]" (Avot 3:10). Responding to the question of why the thermal springs of Tiberias were not found in Jerusalem, Dostai ben Yannai answered that otherwise Jews would have come to the capital for the pleasure of the baths rather than for the sake of pilgrimage to the Temple (Pes. 8b).

The Talmud (Nid. 31b) relates the following set of questions and answers between the disciples of Dostai ben Yannai and their teacher: "Why [in matrimony] does a man go in search of a woman and no woman goes in search of a man? This is analogous to the case of a man who lost something. Who goes in search of what? He who lost the thing goes in search of what he lost [i.e., Adam's rib, from which God formed Eve]. Why does the man lie face downwards and the woman face upwards towards the man? He [faces the elements] from which he was created [the dust of the earth] and she [faces the man] from whom she was created [the rib]. Why is a man easily pacified and a woman not? He [derives his nature] from the place from which he was created [the earth, which yields], and she [derives hers] from the place from which she was created [the unyielding bone of a rib]. Why is a woman's voice sweet and a man's voice not? He [derives his] from the place from which he was created [tapping the earth produces no note], and she [derives hers] from the place from which she was created [a bone can be made to produce certain tones]. Thus it is said, 'For your voice is sweet, and your face is comely' [Song 2:14]."

Dostai ben Yannai taught: "Observe that the ways of God are not like those of flesh and blood. If a man brings a present to a king, it may be accepted or not; and even if it is accepted, it is still doubtful whether he will be admitted to the presence of the king. Not so with God. If a man gives but a penny to a beggar, he is deemed worthy to receive the Divine Presence, as it is written (Ps. 17:15): 'I shall behold your face in righteousness [*tzedakah*], I shall be satisfied when I awake with the vision of You'" (BB 10a).

E

Eleazar ben Arach, Palestinian *tanna* (first century C.E.).

A leading disciple of R. Yochanan ben Zakkai, Eleazar ben Arach was praised by his teacher as "like an overflowing spring" (Avot 2:11), from whom emanated seemingly endless novel insights into the Torah. It was said, "Were all the sages of Israel placed in one scale, and Eleazar ben Arach in the other, he would outweigh them all" (Avot 2:12). In response to a question about what acquisition should be the goal of man, other students suggested a "good eye," a "good friend," a "good neighbor," and "one who considers the outcome of a deed." Eleazar ben Arach answered, "a good heart." Yochanan ben Zakkai replied that he preferred Eleazar ben Arach's response, "for your words [those of all the other students] are included in his words" (Avot 2:13). To a question regarding the worst characteristic a person should avoid, the answers given included an "evil eye," a "wicked friend," a "wicked neighbor," and "one who borrows and does not repay." Again, Yochanan ben Zakkai preferred Eleazar ben Arach's response, "a wicked heart" (Avot 2:14). His motto was: "Be diligent in the study of Torah and know what to answer a heretic [lit., 'the Epicurean']; know before Whom you toil; and know that your Employer can be relied upon to pay you the wages of [reward you for] your labor" (Avot 2:19).

Surprisingly, there are few *halachot* and only a single *halachic midrash* associated with Eleazar ben Arach. An explanation is that after Yochanan ben Zakkai's death, when his disciples remained at Yavneh to study together, Eleazar ben Arach chose instead to move to his wife's home in Emmaus, a town located between Jerusalem and Jaffa that was famed for its pure water, pleasant climate, and warm baths. Isolated from other scholars, the keen mind of Eleazar ben Arach deteriorated, and it was said that he completely forgot all that he had learned (ARN 14).

The Talmud relates that when Eleazar ben Arach was traveling with his teacher, he asked Yochanan ben Zakkai to instruct him in some of the secrets of *Ma'aseh ha-Merkavah* (the mystical *Work of the Chariot*). The sage replied: "Have I not taught you that it is forbidden to teach such speculation to a single individual, unless he is a sage and 'understands of his own knowledge' [i.e., is able to think and speculate for himself]"? Eleazar ben

Arach then asked permission to expound some Chariot mysticism he had already learned. Immediately, Yochanan ben Zakkai dismounted from his donkey, wrapped himself in his *tallit*, and sat upon a stone beneath an olive tree. Responding to Eleazar ben Arach's surprise at these actions, Yochanan ben Zakkai explained: "Is it proper that while you are speaking of Chariot mysticism, with the Divine Presence and the ministering angels accompanying us, that I should ride on the donkey!" As Eleazar ben Arach began to expound on the subject, "Fire descended from heaven and enveloped all the trees in the field, which broke forth in [Divine] song." Then Yochanan ben Zakkai kissed his student on his head and said, "Blessed be the Lord, God of Israel, who has given a son to our father Abraham, a descendant who is capable of understanding, speculating, investigating, and expounding on the Divine Chariot." He added, "There are some who preach well but do not act well, others act well but do not preach well, but you preach well and act well. Happy are you, O Abraham our father, that Eleazar ben Arach has come forth from your loins" (Hag. 14b).

In several places, Eleazar ben Arach was said to be identical to "Nehorai," who was so named "because he enlightened [*manhir*] the eyes of the sages in *halachah*" (Shab. 147b; Er. 13b). To him they applied Nehorai's maxim (Avot 4:18): "Exile yourself to a place of Torah [move to a site where there are other Torah scholars]. Do not say that it will come after you [i.e., that scholars will follow you to a place devoid of them]. Only your colleagues will cause it [Torah knowledge] to remain with you, and 'do not rely on your own understanding' [Prov. 3:5] by studying alone." *See also* Yochanan ben Zakkai.

Eleazar ben Azariah, Palestinian *tanna* (first/second century).

Tracing his priestly ancestry for ten generations back to Ezra (JT Yev. 1:6), Eleazar ben Azariah was an extremely wealthy man (Shab. 54a). Indeed, it was said, "whoever sees Eleazar ben Azariah in a dream can expect riches" (Ber. 57b). When Rabban Gamaliel II was temporarily deposed from the presidency of the Sanhedrin for his autocratic behavior toward R. Joshua ben Hananiah, Eleazar ben Azariah was chosen to succeed him. In addition to his scholarly accomplishments and aristocratic lineage, his selection as *nasi* was also influenced by his great wealth, since the president of the Sanhedrin was responsible for shouldering a substantial portion of the expenses of the office (Ber. 27b). The Talmud notes that Eleazar ben Azariah, who was only about eighteen years old when appointed *nasi*, feared that he would not be respected because of his young age. However, "Eighteen rows of hair [on his beard] miraculously turned white" so that he could claim to be "like an old man" (Ber. 28a). Eleazar ben Azariah immediately reversed the practice of his predecessor and opened the academy to all who wished to study, adding hundreds of benches to the *bet midrash*. The scope of the discussions was broadened, so that "there was no doubtful *halachah* that was not fully elucidated." Although Rabban Gamaliel was soon reinstated, Eleazar ben Azariah was retained as *av bet din* (vice president) and allowed to lecture one Sabbath out of four (Ber. 28a).

Eleazar ben Azariah was so skilled at answering questions on all facets of Jewish learning—Bible, Mishnah, Midrash, *halachah*, and *aggadah*—that Judah ha-Nasi was reported as having praised him as being "a basket of spices [incense]" and "a dealer in perfumes." He believed that "the words of the Bible are to be construed literally" (Kid. 17b). Unlike R. Akiva, Eleazar ben Azariah did not attach any special significance to the repetition of verbs and other grammatical intricacies, instead arguing that "the Bible speaks in the language of human beings" (BM 31b). His homiletic technique often employed the rule of contiguity, in which one biblical passage was explained or supplemented by another that immediately preceded or followed it. Thus he maintained, "Whoever relates or accepts slander, or gives false testimony against his neighbor, deserves to be cast to dogs." He based this on the verse, "You shall throw it to the dogs" (Exod. 22:30), which is followed by, "You must not carry false rumors; you shall not join hands with the guilty to act as a malicious witness" (Exod. 23:1) (Pes. 118a; Mak. 23a). From the verse, "For on this day [Yom Kippur] expiation shall be made for you to purify you of all your sins; you shall be pure before the Lord" (Lev. 16:30), Eleazar ben Azariah derived the lesson that the efficacy of the Day of Atonement extends only to sins "between man and God"; sins between man and his fellow human, however, are not forgiven unless one has "pacified his fellow" (i.e., the offended party has first been reconciled) (Yoma 85b).

In Pirkei Avot (3:21), Eleazar ben Azariah states: "If there is no Torah, there is no *derech eretz* [worldly occupation; proper behavior]; if there is no *derech eretz*, there is no Torah. If there is no wisdom there is no fear of God [and vice versa] . . . ; if there is no knowledge, there is no understanding [and vice versa] . . . ; if there is no flour [*ein kemach*] there is no Torah [and vice versa]." Thus Torah knowledge is essential for fair business dealings, and the mere accumulation of knowledge is meaningless; proper nourishment of the body is essential to the study of Torah, but the acquisition of material possessions is not the end in life.

Comparing the relative values of study and performing *mitzvot*, Eleazar ben Azariah observed (Avot 3:22): "Anyone whose wisdom exceeds his good deeds, to what is he likened?—to a tree whose branches are numerous but whose roots are few; then the wind comes and uproots it and turns it upside down. . . . But one whose good deeds exceed his wisdom, to what is he likened?—to a tree whose branches are few but whose roots are numerous; even if all the winds in the world were to come and blow against it, they could not budge it from its place." He based this on the verse, "He shall be like a tree planted by the waters, sending forth its roots by a stream; it does not notice the coming of heat, its leaves are ever fresh; it has no care in a year of drought, it does not cease to yield fruit" (Jer. 17:8).

Regarding the Torah prohibition against eating the flesh of a pig, Eleazar ben Azariah stated: "One must not say, 'I do not like the flesh of swine and therefore I cannot eat it.' On the contrary, he should say, 'I would gladly eat it but must abstain because my Father in Heaven has forbidden it'" (Sifra 11:22). With respect to the statement that a Sanhedrin that ordered an execution once in seven years should be branded "bloody," Eleazar ben Azariah added that this designation should apply even if a death sentence is issued once in seventy years (Mak. 7a).

R. Joshua ben Hananiah exclaimed, "The generation in which Eleazar ben Azariah lives is not forsaken" (Tosef. Sot. 7:12). When he died, his colleagues sadly noted: "With the death of Eleazar ben Azariah, the crowns of wisdom have departed" (Sot. 49b).

Eleazar ben Harsom, Palestinian *tanna* (second century).

Eleazar ben Harsom was listed among the Ten Martyrs who were executed by the Romans for disobeying the prohibition against teaching Torah. When describing Eleazar ben Harsom's immense wealth, the Talmud related that "his father left him 1,000 cities on the continent [land] and 1,000 boats on the sea" (Yoma 35b). Nevertheless, Eleazar ben Harsom was a wandering scholar: "Every day he would take a sack of flour [to bake the bread he needed] on his shoulder and go from city to city and from province to province to study Torah."

When Eleazar ben Harsom returned home after a prolonged absence, "his servants [not knowing who he was] seized him for public service." (In another version of the tale, the servants believed he was a thief and beat him.) Eleazar ben Harsom served as high priest for eleven years (Yoma 9a). "His mother made him a tunic [priestly garment] worth 20,000 minas. His fellow priests would not allow him to wear it because he appeared naked [it was transparent]" (Yoma 35b; JT Yoma 3:5–6). To rectify this situation, Eleazar ben Harsom soaked the garment in water so that the loose weaving of the fine thread became thick and the whiteness of the garment lost its sheen. He then walked around the altar seven times so that the heat of the burning wood could dry the garment.

The Talmud cites Eleazar ben Harsom as the epitome of the wealthy man. If a man betrothed a woman under the assumption that he was wealthy, "it is not necessary that he be as wealthy as Eleazar ben Harsom" (Kid. 49b). In a discussion of various excuses offered for not engaging in Torah study, the Talmud relates that one rich man called before the heavenly tribunal offered the excuse that he was "worried about my possessions." This was discounted with the words, "Were you wealthier than Eleazar ben Harsom?" (Yoma 35b).

Eleazar ben Hisma, Palestinian *tanna* (second century).

Extremely poor, Eleazar ben Hisma was one of the subjects, with R. Yochanan ben Nuri, of a comment by R. Joshua ben Hananiah to Rabban Gamaliel II: "Marvel at two of your disciples, who are able to calculate how many drops there are in the ocean, but have neither bread to eat nor clothes to wear." Knowing that these students were very clever, Rabban Gamaliel decided to appoint them as supervisors at the academy at Yavneh so they could earn a living. He sent for them but they did not come, because they were too humble to accept a position of honor. When they finally responded to a second request, the sage said: "You thought I was going to offer you to rule [i.e., a position of authority]. [Instead,] I give you servitude!" (Hor. 10a–b).

Eleazar ben Hisma is best known for his *halachic* ruling that, although the Bible permitted a laborer while harvesting grapes to eat of the fruit (Deut. 23:25), an employee was not entitled to a proportion of his employer's produce greater than the amount of his wages (BM 7:5). He applied the biblical verse, "But you have not worshiped me, O Jacob" (Isa. 43:22), to one "who while reading the *Shema* blinks with his eyes, gesticulates with his lips, or points with his fingers." To Eleazar ben Hisma, these were indications that a person was not devout in his prayers, but instead communicating with his neighbors by sign language and not fulfilling his obligation (Yoma 19b).

Although well versed in the sciences, Eleazar ben Hisma noted: "The laws of bird-offerings and the beginnings of menstrual periods are the essential laws; astronomy and mathematics [i.e., the sciences] are only seasonings [condiments] of wisdom" (Avot 3:23). Thus one must pay attention to areas of study that at first blush seem uninteresting for the true scholar, reserving what may appear more appealing pursuits—including the mystical study of the numerical value of Hebrew letters—to a time when one has filled his stomach with the study of Torah and Talmud.

Eleazar ben Jose, Palestinian *tanna* (second century).

The second of the five scholarly sons of R. Jose ben Halafta (Shab. 118b), Eleazar is often cited in the Tosefta but never in the Mishnah. A maker of leather goods (Shab. 49b), Eleazar ben Jose once accompanied R. Shimon bar Yochai to Rome, where they succeeded in having the government repeal the harsh Hadrianic decrees. According to legend, in Rome they saw several items that Titus had carried there from Jerusalem: the curtain of the Holy of Holies stained with "many drops of blood from the bullock offered up for an error of the congregation and from the male goats offered up for idolatry" (Yoma 57a), and the golden headband of the high priest inscribed with the words, "Holy to the Lord" (Suk. 5a). In Alexandria, Eleazar ben Jose spoke to an old man who invited him to various places to see hair and bones allegedly of the Israelite slaves trapped in a building prior to the Exodus from Egypt: "See what [cruelties] my ancestors did to yours; some of them they drowned in the sea, some they slew by the sword, and some they crushed in the buildings" (Sanh. 111a). In other *aggadic* tales, Eleazar ben Jose was said to have viewed the insect that entered the nostrils of Titus and penetrated to his brain (Gen. R. 10:7), as well as fragments of the throne of Solomon that originally had been carried off by Nebuchadnezzar (Babylonian conqueror of Jerusalem) and eventually reached the treasure house of Rome (Esth. R. 1:12).

Explaining why "I have never given testimony [in a court case]," Eleazar ben Jose said: "Once I gave testimony [which was misunderstood] and they raised a slave to the priesthood through my evidence" (Ket. 28b). He stressed the value of philanthropic works: "All the charity and deeds of kindness which Israel performs in this world [help to promote] peace and good understanding between them and their Father in Heaven" (BB 10a). As he observed, "A person who sins and repents and thereafter leads an upright life is immediately forgiven; but one who says, 'I shall sin and then repent,' will be forgiven [only] three times but no more" (ARN 40).

Eleazar ben Judah of Bartota, Palestinian *tanna* (second century).

Known for his philanthropy, Eleazar ben Judah of Bartota urged his colleagues to be generous in giving charity to the poor: "Give God what is His [lit., 'give Him of His own'], for you and your possessions are His." He based this on the statement of King David (1 Chron. 29:14), "For everything is from You, and from Your own we have given You" (Avot 3:8). In his personal life, Eleazar ben Judah of Bartota was faithful to this creed. It was related that he was so extravagant in giving away all he possessed that collectors for the poor would hide themselves to avoid meeting him. Once while making purchases for his daughter's upcoming marriage, he saw the collectors hiding and ran after them to ask about their current mission. When they replied that they were seeking funds to assist a pair of orphans who wished to marry, Eleazar ben Judah exclaimed, "That couple takes precedence over my daughter," and he took all that he had and gave it to them. "He was left with one *zuz*, with which he bought wheat to deposit in the granary." When his wife soon afterward tried to open the room in order to see what her husband had bought, it was so full of wheat that the door would not open. His daughter rushed to the house of study with the good news: "Come and see what your Friend [God] has done for you!" However, Eleazar ben Judah of Bartota also consecrated that grain to charity, saying: "You have no more right to share in them [the benefits resulting from a miracle] than any poor person in Israel" (Taan. 24a).

Eleazar ben Mattai, Palestinian *tanna* (second century).

Also known as Matya, Eleazar ben Mattai was mentioned as one of the four scholars of the Sanhedrin at Yavneh who "understood seventy languages" (JT Shek. 5:1). According to legend (Tosef. Sot. 8:6), he was among the sages who examined and approximated the weight (forty *se'ah*) of the twelve stones that Joshua had ordered the Israelites to set up in the middle of the Jordan where the priests carrying the Ark of the Covenant had stood while the people crossed the river to the western shore, and which were later brought to Gilgal (Josh. 4).

In discussing the limits of what a child must do to honor his parents, Eleazar ben Mattai said: "If my father orders me to give him a drink of water while I have a mitzvah to perform, I disregard my father's honor and perform the mitzvah, since both my father and I are bound to fulfill the commandments" (Kid. 32a). However, the Talmud adds the view of R. Issi ben Judah, who maintained: "If the mitzvah can be performed by others, it should be performed by others, while he should attend to his father's honor" (and the *halachah* agrees with the latter). Eleazar ben Mattai also observed, "No man has the misfortune to hear [a curse] unless he has sinned. . . . He who sees transgressors deserved to see them, while one who sees pious persons has merited seeing them" (Tosef. Shev. 3:4).

Eleazar ben Parta, Palestinian *tanna* (second century).

Eleazar ben Parta was one of the sages arrested with R. Hananiah ben Teradion by the Romans for the capital offense of violating Hadrian's decree forbidding the public teaching of Torah and observance of the commandments. However, Eleazar ben Parta was saved from a martyr's death, probably because of his membership in the party advocating peace with Rome.

According to the Talmud, when Eleazar ben Parta was apprehended, he tried to comfort his fellow prisoner: "You should be happy because you have been arrested on one charge; woe is me, for I am arrested on five charges." R. Hananiah ben Teradion replied that the opposite was true, since Eleazar ben Parta would be rescued; whereas he was to be executed: "For you have occupied yourself with the study of Torah and with benevolent acts, whereas I was engaged in Torah study alone." At trial, the authorities asked Eleazar ben Parta why he was studying the Torah and stealing (as a member of the bands of robbers devastating the country at that time). He replied that if they suspected him of one of these activities, they could not accuse him of the other, since he could not be pursuing both at the same time. When the judge asked why the people called him "Rabbi," he answered that he was "the teacher of weavers." To test his knowledge of weaving, they brought two coils of cloth and asked which was for the warp and which for the woof. At that moment a miracle occurred, as a female bee flew down and settled on a thread of the warp and a male bee landed on the woof (Av. Zar. 17b).

The Mishnah states three statements of Eleazar ben Parta that were approved by the sages: "People in a besieged town or a ship storm-tossed at sea, and a man who has been brought to court to be tried [for his life], are presumed to be alive [as long as they are not known to be dead; thus the wife of a priest would be entitled to eat of the tithes offered a priest (*terumah*) because he might still escape alive]. However, people in a besieged town that has been captured or a ship that has been lost at sea, or a man who has been led out to execution, are presumed to be either alive or dead, according to whichever view has the greater stringency. Therefore, the daughter of an ordinary Israelite who has married a priest or the daughter of a priest who has married an ordinary Israelite may not eat of the *terumah* [if the husband has disappeared in this latter way, for in the former case the husband is presumed to be dead, but in the latter case, alive]" (Git. 28b).

Eleazar ben Parta offered proof that gossip was severely punished because of the power of an "evil tongue." If God so severely punished the spies, sent by Moses to scout out the Land of Israel, who slandered only "wood and stones" (trees and rocks), how much greater will be the punishment of one who "brings up an evil report against his neighbor!" (Ar. 15a).

Eleazar ben Pedat, Palestinian *amora* (third century).

Born in Babylonia of priestly descent and a student of R. Samuel and Rav, Eleazar ben Pedat moved to Tiberias to study with R. Yochanan and eventually became head of his academy. He is usually referred to in the Talmud without his patronymic, while references to Eleazar without patronymic in the Mishnah and Tosefta generally refer to the later Eleazar ben Shammua. Eleazar bed Pedat became so famous as a *halachist* that he received numerous questions from Babylonia, earning the title in his native land of "master [legal authority] of the Land of Israel" (Yoma 9b). Many of his sayings related to knowledge and scholarship (Sanh. 92a). "He who possesses knowledge is as great as if the Temple were rebuilt in his days"; "He who has knowledge will eventually be wealthy, as it is written, 'By knowledge are its rooms filled with all precious and pleasant things' (Prov. 24:4)"; and "Just as a child must be nursed by his mother every hour during the day, so every man should devote each hour of the day to Torah" (JT Ber. 9:5). Conversely, "The house in which the words of the Torah are not heard at night shall be consumed by fire"; and "Whoever does not benefit a scholar, his goods will never see a sign of blessing." Yet Eleazar ben Pedat did not favor the study of esoteric material: "Why attempt to find out what is hidden from you? Why search out what is deeper than Sheol [the netherworld]? Reflect [only] on what is permitted to you. Hidden things are of no concern to you" (JT Hag. 2:11).

Extremely poor and living in a room without windows (Ber. 5b), Eleazar ben Pedat stated: "He who executes charity and justice is regarded as though he had filled all the world with kindness"; and "The reward of charity depends entirely upon the extent of the kindness in it [i.e., the grace, tenderness, and compassion that accompany the act]." Moreover, "Charity atones for all sins and is more important than sacrifices. Just as armor is made up of small pieces, in charity one adds penny to penny until it grows into a considerable sum" (Suk. 49b). Ironically, Eleazar ben Pedat remarked that the community should be "thankful" to those who asked for charity though they did not need it. "Were it not for these swindlers, anyone who refused to give charity when asked would be punished at once. As it is, such a person can claim that he suspected the charity seeker of being a fraud!" (JT Pe'ah 8:9). In response to his rhetorical question, "Why did God create human fingers in their present shape?" Eleazar ben Pedat explained, "So that a person might plug his ears when he hears improper words" (Ket. 5b).

Eleazar ben Pedat offered a parable to explain why the righteous were often afflicted with suffering. "This can be compared to the owner of two cows, one strong and one weak. Upon which does he impose? Is it not upon the strong one? Similarly, God does not test the wicked, because they cannot bear it, as it is written, 'But the wicked are like the troubled sea.' Whom does God test? The righteous." As support, he cited three biblical verses: "The Lord tests a righteous man" (Ps. 11:5); "Some time afterward God put Abraham to the test" (Gen. 22:1); and "After a time, his master's wife cast her eyes upon Joseph" (Gen. 39.7) (Song R. 2:16).

Eleazar ben Pedat insisted that Babylonian Jews strictly observe the second day of festivals, as was practiced throughout the Diaspora (Betz. 4b). This custom of celebrating an extra day arose during periods when the Romans prevented messengers from the Sanhedrin in the Land of Israel to go to Babylonia to announce the beginning of the new month. Although the Babylonian Jews followed the lunar calendar and thus could have determined the new moons themselves, the exilarch added a day to the holidays lest his calculations inadvertently be different. When the Romans permitted the messengers to travel freely and announce the new month, the Babylonian Jews generally ignored the extra day. To provide uniformity of practice, Eleazar ben Pedat instructed all Jews living outside the Land of Israel to observe the second day of holidays.

Eleazar ben Pedat believed that "a man who has no wife" or "a man who owns no land" is "not a proper man" (Yev. 63a). As he stated, "Even when a sharp sword rests on his neck, a man should not stop from prayer [abandon hope of mercy], based on the verse from Job [13:15], 'Though He slay me, yet will I trust in Him'" (Ber. 10a). Stressing the sanctity of the Land of Israel, he observed: "Whoever resides in Israel lives without sin" and "Those who die outside Israel will not be resurrected" (Ket. 111a). Why did God exile Israel among the nations?—only so that proselytes might join them" (Pes. 87b). Eleazar ben Pedat declared, "Harmful speech is worse than monetary wrong because it affects his [the victim's] person, while the latter only [affects his] money" (BM 58b). "One should always set his table [properly] for the Sabbath evening meal, even if [he is not hungry and] needs only a meal the size of an olive" (Shab. 119b). According to Eleazar ben Pedat, "Who is destined for the World to Come? He who is modest and humble, who bows on entering and leaving, and learns Torah constantly without claiming merit for doing so" (Sanh. 88b). *See also* Hanina bar Hama; Mar Ukba; Ulla; Zerika.

Eleazar ben Shammua, Palestinian *tanna* and one of the Ten Martyrs (second century).

One of R. Akiva's last students, Eleazar ben Shammua was a renowned teacher of traditional law. Indeed, all statements in the Mishnah and Tosefta quoted in the name of Eleazar without further identification are considered to be the opinions of Eleazar ben Shammua. References to Eleazar without patronymic in the Gemara usually refer to the earlier Eleazar ben Pedat. According to one of his students, Judah ha-Nasi, Eleazar ben Shammua's academy was so crowded that there was not enough room for the scholars to sit comfortably ("six pupils used to sit there in the space of one cubit") (Er. 53a).

Eleazar ben Shammua's motto was: "Let the honor of your student be as dear to you as your own; the honor of your colleague as the reverence for your teacher; and the reverence for your teacher as that for Heaven" (Avot 4:15). When asked by his disciples to what he ascribed his long life, Eleazar ben Shammua replied: "I have never used the synagogue as a short cut [for the sake of my convenience], nor stepped over the heads of the holy people [come late to the academy and disrupted the concentration of attentive students by stepping between them], nor pronounced the priestly blessing without first offering a benediction" (Meg. 27b; Sot. 39a).

In response to the question, "What must a man do to be spared the pangs of the Messiah [the tribulations preceding the Messianic Era]?" he replied, "Let him engage in Torah study and benevolent deeds" (Sanh. 98b). For

Eleazar ben Shammua, "[The world rests] on one pillar, the name of which is 'Righteous,'" based on the verse from Proverbs (10:25): "The righteous is the foundation of the world [or 'an everlasting foundation']" (Hag. 12b). He compared three kinds of scholars to three types of stones. The first, like a stone pointed at one end, had studied only Midrash. The second was like a two-pointed stone, having learned both Midrash and Halachah. Both of them could reply only to questions in these fields. The third type of scholar was like a stone hewn on all sides, for he had studied Midrash, Aggadah, and Tosefta. "Whatever such a scholar is asked, he is able to answer" (ARN 28).

Among Eleazar ben Shammua's other statements are: "Living in the Land of Israel is equivalent to all the *mitzvot*" (Sifre Deut. 80); and "The Bible and the sword came down from heaven bound together. God said to the Jews, 'If you keep what is written in the book, you will be saved from the sword, but if not you will be killed by the sword'" (Sifre Deut. 40).

Eleazar ben Shimon, Palestinian *tanna* (second century).

Son of R. Shimon bar Yochai, Eleazar hid in a cave with his father for twelve years to avoid persecution by the Romans. After the death of Shimon bar Yochai, Eleazar ben Shimon entered the academy of Shimon ben Gamaliel II, where he became the colleague of the patriarch's son, Judah ha-Nasi, the compiler of the Mishnah.

The Talmud relates that Eleazar ben Shimon was appointed by the hated Roman authorities to track down and arrest thieves. R. Joshua ben Korcha severely chastised him: "Vinegar, son of wine [degenerate product of a righteous father]! How long will you deliver up the people of our God for slaughter [i.e., how can you send fellow Jews to be punished by the Romans]!" Eleazar ben Shimon replied, "I [only] weed out thorns from the vineyard." R. Joshua ben Korcha then retorted, "Let the owner of the vineyard himself [God] come and weed out the thorns" (BM 83b–85a).

In opposition to his colleagues, Eleazar ben Shimon ruled that *Kiddush* may be recited over beer (Pes. 107a). He taught, "Children die as a punishment for the [unfulfilled] vows of their parents" (Shab. 32b).

Eleazar ben Shimon once feared that he inadvertently may have been responsible for the execution of an innocent man. Consequently, he imposed upon himself the most painful penance. Convinced that the aid he had given to their persecutors would prevent his people from according him a decent burial, Eleazar ben Shimon made his wife promise to keep his body under her roof after his death. This gave rise to legends of the dead Rabbi pronouncing verdicts when litigants argued their cases in his house. After many years, Eleazar ben Shimon's former colleagues were determined to bury him with full honors, but the local citizens refused permission to remove the body since they believed that the sage's remains miraculously protected them from wild beasts. Eventually, people from a neighboring town spirited the body away, and Eleazar ben Shimon was buried beside his father in Meron. *See also* Joshua ben Korcha.

Eleazar Hakapar, Palestinian *tanna* (third century).

Eleazar Hakapar's most famous saying is from Pirkei Avot (4:28): "Jealousy, lust, and [the desire for] honor remove a man from this world [shorten his life]." A believer in Divine determinism, Eleazar Hakapar stressed, "Everything that happens is according to the plan" of God, who is "Fashioner, Creator, Discerner, Judge, Witness, and Plaintiff . . . in Whom there is no iniquity, no forgetfulness, no favoritism, and no acceptance of bribery." He warned, "Let not your evil inclination promise you that the grave will be an escape [place of refuge] for you—for against your will were you created, . . . born, . . . will live, . . . will die, and against your will you are destined to give an accounting [of your life] before the King of kings, the Holy One, Blessed be He" (Avot 4:29).

Warning against excessive pride, Eleazar Hakapar counseled: "Do not strive to be like the highest stair, but rather like a doorstep on which everyone treads. For when the house is being destroyed, the doorstep remains in place until the very end" (ARN 26). He also taught, "It is forbidden for a person to buy an animal or bird unless he can feed it properly" (JT Ket. 4:8).

According to the Jerusalem Talmud, "A person will be called to account on judgment day for every permissible thing that he might have enjoyed but did not" (JT Kid. 4:12). In the Babylonian Talmud, Eleazar Hakapar agreed: "A Nazirite is considered a sinner [and required to bring a sin offering after the completion of his vow] because he afflicted himself by abstaining from wine. How much more so if he ascetically refrains from all permitted types of enjoyment? Therefore, a person who fasts unnecessarily is called a sinner" (Ned. 10a).

Eleazar Harsena. *See* Eleazar ben Harsom.

Eleazar (Eliezer) of Modi'in, Palestinian *tanna* (first/second century).

Born in the home of the Hasmoneans, Eleazar of Modi'in was primarily known as an *aggadist*. According to tradition, he was the uncle of Bar Kochba and was with him in Betar during the siege. For three years, Hadrian, the Roman general, was unable to conquer Betar because Eleazar of Modi'in sat in sackcloth and daily prayed to God "not to sit in judgment" that day. When the Romans were about to abandon his siege, a Samaritan told Hadrian the secret of Betar's defense and received permission to slip into the city. With

Eleazar of Modi'in so engrossed in prayer that he was oblivious to what was occurring around him, the Samaritan went over to the sage and pretended to whisper in his ear. Bar Kochba's guards, who witnessed this incident, were suspicious and reported that Eleazar of Modi'in was plotting to surrender the city. When learning of this event, Bar Kochba immediately confronted Eleazar of Modi'in, but his uncle honestly denied any knowledge of having such a conversation. The enraged Bar Kochba kicked Eleazar of Modi'in, instantly killing him, and Betar soon was captured (JT Taan. 4:6; Lam. R. 2:2).

After hearing the opinions of all the scholars assembled in Yavneh, Rabban Gamaliel II often remarked, "We still need [the interpretation of] the Modi'ite" (Shab. 55b; BB 10b). However, some of the other Rabbis protested his often overblown *aggadic* interpretations: "How long will you rake words together and bring them up against us [try to impress us with unsubstantiated statements]?" (Yoma 76a).

In Pirkei Avot (3:15), Eleazar of Modi'in stated: "One who desecrates sacred things, who disgraces the festivals, who humiliates his fellow in public [causes his face to blanch], who nullifies the covenant of our forefather Abraham [by trying to disguise his circumcision in order to hide his Jewish origin], or who perverts the Torah contrary to *halachah*—even though he may have [knowledge of] Torah and good deeds [to his credit]—he has no share in the World to Come." Eleazar of Modi'in deemed observance of the Sabbath as the quintessential element of Judaism: "If the Jews were to observe the Sabbath as it should be observed, God would reward them with six gifts: the Land of Israel, the World to Come, a new world order, the reestablishment of the kingdom of David, the priesthood, and the Levites. (Mechilta de-Rabbi Ishmael, Vayassa)" (Bader, 219).

Eliezer ben Hyrcanus, Palestinian *tanna* (first/second century).

Also known as Eliezer ha-Gadol (the great), Eliezer ben Hyrcanus had a phenomenal memory, which his teacher, R. Yochanan ben Zakkai, compared to "a cemented cistern that loses not a drop [of learning]." "If all the sages of Israel were in one scale of the balance and Eliezer ben Hyrcanus in the other, he would outweigh them all" (Avot 2:11–12).

According to tradition, Eliezer ben Hyrcanus was born into a wealthy family of Levites. He worked on his father's estates until his early twenties, when he disobeyed his father's wishes and left for Jerusalem to study with R. Yochanan ben Zakkai. Although arriving with little education and living in poverty, Eliezer ben Hyrcanus became one of the outstanding students at the academy. Some time later, his father came to the capital determined to disinherit his son. However, when entering the *bet midrash*, he found his son sitting at the head, with all the great scholars of Jerusalem facing him. Seeing his son expounding the Torah, "transcending what was said to Moses at Sinai, his countenance as luminous as the light of the sun, and beams emanating from him as the rays from Moses," he changed his mind and instead decided to give Eliezer his entire fortune. The young scholar was elated by their reconciliation, but insisted that he would only accept a share equal to that of his brothers (ARN 6).

Eliezer ben Hyrcanus married Imma Shalom, the learned sister of the Rabban Gamaliel II (Shab. 116a). During the Roman siege of Jerusalem, he and a colleague, R. Joshua ben Hananiah, carried Yochanan ben Zakkai in a coffin outside the city walls for his meeting with Vespasian (Git. 56a). Accompanying his teacher to Yavneh, Eliezer ben Hyrcanus became a member of the Sanhedrin. Later, he moved to Lydda to establish his own academy (Sanh. 36b).

The Talmud states that Eliezer ben Hyrcanus adopted the exemplary qualities of his teacher, Yochanan ben Zakkai: "During his whole life he never used profane speech, nor walked four cubits without [studying the] Torah or [wearing] *tefillin*; nor did any man arrive earlier than he at the house of study, nor did he sleep or [even] doze while there; nor when finding himself in a filthy alleyway did he meditate [on his studies or other sacred subjects]; nor did anyone ever find him sitting in silence, but only engaged in study; no one but himself ever opened the door to his disciples; never in his life did he say anything [i.e., give a legal decision in public] that he had not heard from his teacher; he never said, 'It is time to leave the house of study,' except on the eve of Passover [when it was necessary to rush home for the seder before the children would fall asleep] and on the eve of the Day of Atonement [when the final meal of the day had to be eaten early before the fast began]" (Suk. 28a).

Although Eliezer ben Hyrcanus was the head of his own academy before the destruction of Jerusalem, he made a point of not answering any question unless he had received a definite tradition or interpretation from his teacher (Yoma 66b). He believed that one who debated the teaching of his master or offered an opinion that he had not heard from him "caused the Divine Presence to depart from Israel" (Ber. 27b). After a disciple had given a legal decision in his presence, Eliezer ben Hyrcanus remarked to his wife: "I wonder whether this man will live through the year," and the student soon died. "Are you a prophet [that you could foretell his death]?" "No, I am neither a prophet nor the son of a prophet, but I learned from my teacher that anyone who gives a legal decision in the presence of his Master incurs the penalty of death [at the hands of Heaven]" (Er. 63a).

Eliezer ben Hyrcanus was a conservative traditionalist and follower of the school of Shammai, unlike all of the other scholars and the *nasi*, who were adherents of the school of Hillel. Unwilling to teach anything that he had not heard from his masters, Eliezer ben Hyrcanus attempted to limit the use of hermeneutical rules as a basis for deriving new *halachot*. As an honored guest on the Festival of Sukkot, he once was asked whether it was permitted to spread a covering over the *sukkah* to provide shade. Having no precedent from his teachers on this issue, he repeatedly quoted his teachers on other subjects rather than offer his own opinion on the issue at hand (Suk. 27b).

Zealous in his views and remarkably unreceptive to other opinions, Eliezer ben Hyrcanus was incapable of reaching a compromise of any kind. He was known as the sage who argued relentlessly with his colleagues regarding the ritual purity of the "oven of Achnai" (BM 59b). He called for several miraculous events to prove his point ("If the law is according to my view, may . . . prove it"): a carob tree uprooting itself and moving one hundred cubits, the stream outside the academy changing course, and the walls of the school house falling inward, but these signs failed to persuade the Rabbis. Finally, Eliezer ben Hyrcanus summoned a voice from heaven to support his view. A *bat kol* cried out: "Why do you dispute with Eliezer ben Hyrcanus, seeing that in all matters the *halachah* agrees with him?" Referring to a verse in Deuteronomy (30:12), R. Joshua ben Hananiah calmly replied: "It [*halachic* decision] is not in heaven, and we pay no attention to a *bat kol*. For it is written in the Torah, 'One must follow the majority' [Exod. 23:2]," meaning that the *halachah* must be decided by human authorities following the guidelines given to Moses at Sinai. The Talmud then offers a denouement to this story. R. Nathan met Elijah the prophet and asked what God did when the sages rejected the words of the *bat kol*. Elijah answered, "He laughed [with joy], saying, 'My children have defeated Me, My children have defeated Me'" (BM 59b).

Although universally admired by his contemporaries, who even referred to him as "the great" during his lifetime, the unwillingness of Eliezer ben Hyrcanus to accept the majority view of his colleagues led to his being excommunicated by his brother-in-law Rabban Gamaliel II. "They [the other Rabbis] brought all the objects that Eliezer ben Hyrcanus had ruled were pure and burned them" in an effort to avenge his refusal to accept their authority. According to the *aggadah*, this ostracizing of an eminent sage incurred Divine wrath. The tears of Eliezer ben Hyrcanus caused the destruction of crops and food ("the world was smitten in one-third of the wheat, one-third of the olives, and one-half of the barley"). The destruction "was so great on that day that every place where Eliezer ben Hyrcanus cast his eyes immediately was burned. On that same day, Rabban Gamaliel was aboard a ship, when a storm caused huge waves that almost drowned him. The sage attempted to justify his actions toward Eliezer ben Hyrcanus by claiming that he had not acted for his honor or that of his father's house, but solely for the honor of God, "in order that disagreements do not multiply in Israel." Apparently this plea was accepted, for "the sea immediately rested from its anger" (BM 59b).

The excommunication did not prevent the Rabbis from having *halachic* discussions with Eliezer ben Hyrcanus, although he was not permitted to enter the academy and visitors were required to keep a distance of four cubits from him. As fewer students visited, he became increasingly isolated, frustrated with the realization that he had a wealth of knowledge that he was unable to transmit to the next generation. On his deathbed, Eliezer ben Hyrcanus placed his arms over his heart and exclaimed: "Woe to you, two arms of mine, which have been like two Scrolls of the Law that are wrapped up [i.e., wound so that they could never be read]. Much Torah have I studied, and much have I taught [before the ban of excommunication]. Much Torah have I learned, yet I have but skimmed from the knowledge of my teachers as much as a dog laps from the sea. Much Torah have I taught, yet my disciples have only drawn from me as much as a paint brush from its tube" (Sanh. 68a).

Though excommunicated, Eliezer ben Hyrcanus is quoted extensively in the Mishnah and Talmud. Whenever there is a reference to Rabbi Eliezer with no other title or patronymic, Eliezer ben Hyrcanus is meant. He offered his views on such widely disparate subjects as repentance (Sanh. 97b), writing on the Sabbath (BB 157a), levirate marriage (Yev. 26a), the beginning of the mourning period (Ket. 4b), and the education of women (Sot. 3:4). He also was considered the putative author of *Pirkei de-Rabbi Eliezer*, though internal evidence conclusively proved the later origin of the work.

Among his most famous statements are two maxims from Pirkei Avot (2:15): "Let the honor [reputation] of your friend be as dear to you as your own and do not anger easily"; and "Warm yourself by the fire of the sages, but beware of their glowing coal lest you be burnt—for their bite is the bite of a fox, their sting is the sting of a scorpion, their hiss is the hiss of a snake, and their words are like fiery coals [i.e., keep close to Torah scholars and learn from their ways, but never be so intimate that you become casual and disrespectful and merit a stinging warning]." He also noted, "Whoever has a piece of bread in his basket and says [in complaint], 'What shall I eat tomorrow?' is one of little faith" (Sot. 48b).

Is it possible for a human being to be without sin? Although the Mechilta (to Exod. 10:48a) said, "The first patriarchs were without traces of sin," Eliezer ben Hyrcanus retorted, "If God wished to apply strict justice to Abraham, Isaac, or Jacob, not [even] they could stand in the face of His rebuke!" (Ar.17a). Discussing the importance of a *minyan* for prayer, the Talmud observes: "Once Eliezer entered a synagogue [to pray] and did not find ten men there, so he freed his slave and used him to complete the requisite number" (Ber. 47b).

Education was always a topical issue in the Talmud. Some Rabbis stressed the educational value of mnemonics, while others emphasized the importance of reciting the lesson aloud: "Open your mouth and read the Scriptures, open your mouth and learn the Talmud, that your studies may be retained and that you may live long." The text continues, "Eliezer ben Hyrcanus had a disciple who studied his lessons in a low voice [without speaking them audibly]. The result was that after three years he forgot his learning" (Er. 54a). The Rabbis had divergent views on the need for educating Jewish girls. In the same *mishnah*, Ben Azzai said, "A man has an obligation to teach his daughter Torah," whereas Eliezer ben Hyrcanus declared, "Whoever teaches his daughter it is as though he taught her lewdness" (Sot. 3:4). In the view of Eliezer ben Hyrcanus, "Let the words of the Torah be destroyed by fire rather than be imparted to women" (JT Sot. 3:4).

During a drought, Eliezer ben Hyrcanus approached the Ark to pray for rain. Even though he recited the prescribed twenty-four blessings for fast days, his prayer was not answered. R. Akiva came to the Ark after him and simply said, "Our Father, our King, we have no King but You; our Father, our King, for Your own sake have mercy upon us," and rain immediately fell. A *bat kol* (heavenly voice) explained that the prayer of R. Akiva was not answered because he was greater, but because he practiced forgiveness (forbearance) while Eliezer ben Hyrcanus did not (Taan. 25b).

In discussing the duty to honor one's father, Eliezer ben Hyrcanus related the story of Dama ben Nethina, a gentile who owned a diamond that he wanted to sell at a 600,000 gold *dinarii* profit for the *ephod* of the high priest. However, when the priests came to buy it, Dama's father was asleep and the key to the box with the diamond was lying under his pillow. Dama refused to wake his father, even though it caused him a great financial loss. The following year God gave Dama his reward—"a red heifer was born in his herd. When the sages of Israel went to him to buy it, he said to them, 'I know that even if I asked you for all the money in the world you would pay me. But I ask of you only the money that I lost through my father's honor.'" As a colleague observed, "If one who is not commanded [to honor his parents] does so and is thus [rewarded], how much more so one who is commanded and does so!" (Kid. 31a).

Eliezer ben Hyrcanus was cited as having developed the rules of conjugal duty, a schedule of minimal sexual activity for men based on their occupations. "The times for conjugal duty prescribed in the Torah [Exod. 21:10] are as follows: for men of independent means [i.e., who have no need to pursue an occupation to earn their living], every day; for laborers [e.g., tailors, weavers, and builders, who according to Maimonides, lack the strength to cohabit more frequently because, although they are home every night, their work is so strenuous], twice a week; for donkey-drivers [who must travel during the week to bring grain to sell in the market and were typically away from home for six days at a time], once a week; for camel-drivers [merchants who travel longer distances from their homes], once every thirty days; for sailors [whose sea voyages take them away for many months at a time], once in six months" (Ket. 5:5).

In response to a disciple's question regarding how to be "worthy of life in the future world," Eliezer ben Hyrcanus replied: "Be careful of the honor of your colleagues, restrain your children from meditation [variously interpreted as foolish talk or philosophical speculation], and seat them before [lit., 'between the knees of'] the sages, and when you pray know before Whom you stand" (Ber. 28b). He also urged his students to "repent one day before your death." When asked how one can know on what day he will die, the sage replied, "All the more reason that one should repent every day, lest he die tomorrow; thus his whole life should be spent in repentance" (Shab. 153a).

Despite their quarrels, when his former colleagues heard of Eliezer ben Hyrcanus's approaching demise, the most prominent among them hastened to his bedside at Caesarea. They praised him with laudatory statements, calling him "more beneficial to Israel than rain and the sun" (Sanh. 101a). When Eliezer ben Hyrcanus succumbed, while they were asking him *halachic* questions, they rent their garments in mourning. R. Joshua ben Hananiah immediately revoked the sentence of excommunication. The *aggadah* (Song R. 1:3) relates that R. Joshua ben Hananiah even kissed the stone on which Eliezer ben Hyrcanus had been seated, saying: "This stone is like Mount Sinai, and he who sat upon it like the Ark of the Covenant." According to one tradition, in this world the *halachah* is according to R. Joshua ben Hananiah, because his pragmatic and humane views are better suited to current existence. However, with the coming of the Messiah, the *halachah* will follow the perfection and purity of the Torah as expressed by Eliezer ben Hyrcanus (Steinsaltz, 64). *See also* Ben Azzai; Imma Shalom; Onkelos; Yochanan ben Zakkai.

Eliezer ben Jacob, Palestinian *tanna* (second century).

In Pirkei Avot (4:13), Eliezer ben Jacob is quoted as saying: "He who fulfills even a single mitzvah gains for himself one advocate [to plead on his behalf on the day of judgment], and he who commits even a single transgression gains for himself one accuser. Repentance and good deeds are like a shield against punishment." This has been interpreted as meaning that if one's transgressions outweigh *mitzvot*, Divine punishment can be averted by repentance (if one is about to die) and by good deeds (if he live on).

Eliezer ben Jacob once gave up his seat of honor to a poor blind man who was visiting the town. This encouraged others to give so generously to this needy person that he effusively praised Eliezer ben Jacob for his good fortune. "You have shown kindness to one who is seen but cannot see; may He who sees but is unseen accept your prayers and deal kindly with you" (JT Shek. 5:4).

Among the numerous sayings cited in the name of Eliezer ben Jacob are: "If a man entertains a scholar in his house and lets him enjoy his possessions, Scripture accounts it to him as if he had sacrificed the daily burnt-offering"; "A man should not stand on a high place when he prays, but he should pray in a lowly place, as it is written, 'Out of the depths have I called you, O Lord' [Ps. 130:1]"; and "When one prays, he should place his feet in proper position [close together and level], as it says, 'And their feet were straight feet' [Ezek. 1:7; the prophetic vision of the creatures bearing the Divine Chariot]" (all in Ber. 10b); and "A man must not marry a woman if it is his intention to divorce her," based on the verse in Proverbs (3:29), "Do not devise harm against your fellow who lives trustingly with you" (Yev. 37b).

Eliezer ben Jose ha-Galili, Palestinian *tanna* (second century).

One of the last disciples of R. Akiva, Eliezer ben Jose ha-Galili (the Galilean) was an expert in the area of *aggadah*. Indeed, as his colleagues advised, "Wherever you find the words of Eliezer ben Jose the Galilean in an *aggadah*, make your ear like a funnel [to receive the teaching, just as the funnel at the top of the mill receives the grain]" (Hul. 89a). Eliezer ben Jose ha-Galili developed a set of thirty-two rules for interpreting the Bible, expanding on the traditional thirteen hermeneutical principles.

Torah scholars were highly honored in rabbinic society. Interpreting the verse, "And the Lord blessed Obed-Edom and all his house . . . because of the Ark of God" (2 Sam. 6:12), Eliezer ben Jose ha-Galili noted: "If such was the reward for keeping the ark, which did not eat or drink but only required cleaning and dusting, how much more deserving of blessing is one who hosts a Torah scholar in his home, gives him food and drink, and allows him to use his possessions!" (Ber. 63b).

Commenting on the dead whom Ezekiel brought back to life (Ezek. 37:11–14), Eliezer ben Jose ha-Galili said: "[They] went up to Palestine, married wives, and sired sons and daughters" (Sanh. 92b). In this way, he used this biblical passage as proof that, just as the dry bones were revived by the prophet, so the exiled Jews would someday return to the Land of Israel.

Urging persistence, Eliezer ben Jose ha-Galili observed, "If one begins to fulfill a commandment but does not complete it, and another person finishes the work, credit is given to the one who completed the task" (Gen. R. 5:3). Other maxims include: "A person in distress is forbidden to pray" (JT Ber. 5:1); and "Even if 999 argue against a man [in the Heavenly Court], while one [an angel advocate, based on his repentance and good deeds] argues in his favor, he is acquitted" (Shab. 32a).

Elisha ben Abuyah, Palestinian *tanna* known as *"Acher"* (the Other) (first/ second century).

A wealthy Jerusalemite and teacher of R. Meir, Elisha ben Abuyah joined three other colleagues (R. Akiva, Ben Azzai, and Ben Zoma) in mystical speculations. "Four [sages] entered paradise . . . Ben Azzai looked and died; Ben Zoma went mad; Acher cut down the plants [of the heavenly garden]; R. Akiva alone came out unhurt" (Hag. 14b). The meaning of "cut down the plants" (mutilated the shoots), usually translated as "apostasy," has been the subject of numerous interpretations. A common phrase in the *tannaitic* litera- ture meaning "wanton destruction" (BK 8:6), later sources extended it to the destructive consequences of sin (Gen. R. 19), specifically to one who learned Torah but did not fulfill its precepts. According to the Jerusalem Talmud, Elisha ben Abuyah stopped learning Torah and gave up observing the Sab- bath. Even worse, when seeing a budding scholar succeeding in Torah learn- ing, Elisha ben Abuyah would kill him. When entering the *bet midrash* and seeing pupils in front of their teacher studying Torah, he would ask why they were not instead learning a viable occupation. "What are you sitting here for? This one's trade is a builder, that one should be a carpenter; this one a hunter, that one a tailor." When they heard this, the children abandoned their studies and left the academy. In response to the repeated attempts by his disciple R. Meir to convince his master to repent, Elisha ben Abuyah stated: "Once I was passing by the Holy of Holies riding on my horse on the Day of Atonement, which fell on the Sabbath, and I heard a heavenly voice saying, 'Return, O children'—except for Elisha ben Abuyah" (JT Hag. 2:1).

The Rabbis offered various explanations for the source of Elisha ben Abuyah's heresy. Taking the Talmudic story at face value, it can be viewed as a polemic against the dangerous consequences of mystical speculation, which was strongly discouraged by the Rabbis. Some maintained that Elisha ben Abuyah greatly envied R. Akiva, feeling humiliated that a man of unknown origin, who only began his studies late in life, should be so exalted by the people. This may have been the basis for his famous maxim: "One who stud- ies Torah as a child, to what can he be compared?—to ink written on fresh paper [which retains its clarity and sharpness]. And one who studies Torah as an old man, to what can he be compared?—to ink written on smudged paper [which causes the ink to run and become illegible]" (Avot 4:25). This has generally been interpreted as meaning that one should learn Torah when he is young and his mind is fresh and receptive.

Another Talmudic legend suggests that Elisha ben Abuyah's religious doubts began when he saw a man climb a tree and remove a nest containing both fledglings and the mother bird. Although this violated an explicit Torah law (Deut. 22:6–7), nothing happened to the man. The next day, he saw another man follow the Divine commandment to first chase away the mother bird before taking her young. Although the Torah clearly stated that the reward for fulfilling this mitzvah is long life, when the man climbed down he was bitten by a snake and promptly died.

Other explanations for his apostasy were the impure nature of Elisha ben Abuyah's conception and birth and the trauma of experiencing the sufferings of the righteous—the tongue of Hutzpit the Interpreter dragged by a pig, which caused him to wail in grief, "The mouth that uttered pearls licks the dust" (Kid. 39b). Having experienced the destruction of the Temple, the failure of the Bar Kochba rebellion and the resulting political collapse of the Jewish community in the Land of Israel, and the Roman edicts forbidding the study of Torah and observance of the commandments, Elisha ben Abuyah may have wholeheartedly accepted the basic tenets of Gnosticism. This Greek philosophical system believed that there were two powers in the universe, a supreme good power and an evil power of lower authority. For Elisha ben Abuyah, the good force may be the more powerful, but it was remote from human events, whereas the evil power appeared to exert practical control over the real world.

Regardless of the motivation for his apostasy, it is clear that Elisha ben Abuyah eventually used his extensive knowledge of Jewish law to aid the Roman authorities in their relentless persecution of the people. The hatred of the Rabbis for their former comrade became so intense that they even refused to pronounce his name, instead referring to him in terms used to designate some vile object (*acher*, lit., "another thing"). Of all the *tannaim*, only R. Meir remained in contact with Elisha ben Abuyah.

After Elisha ben Abuyah's death, his impoverished daughter appeared before Judah ha-Nasi and begged, "Master, help me!" After learning the identity of her father, Judah asked in amazement: "Are any of his children left in the world? For it is written, 'He shall have no son, nor son's son, among his people, nor any survivor where he once lived' [Job 18:19]. She answered, 'Remember his [vast knowledge of] Torah and overlook his deeds!' Immediately, fire came down from heaven and burned the bench where Judah ha-Nasi was sitting. Then the sage wept and said, 'If this can happen on account of those who dishonor the Torah, how much reward is there for those who glory in it!'" (Hag. 15b). In the Jerusalem Talmud version, Judah ha-Nasi debated whether to receive Elisha's daughters, then wept and ruled that they could receive support from public funds, thus bringing them back into the Jewish community (JT Hag. 2:1).

According to rabbinic tradition, "One who sees Elisha ben Abuyah in a dream, let him fear calamity" (ARN 40).

G

Gamaliel I, Palestinian *tanna* (first century C.E.).

Grandson of Hillel and son of Shimon, Gamaliel I succeeded his father and grandfather as *nasi* (patriarch) and was the first to be given the honorific title *Rabban* (master). Like his grandfather, Hillel, he was known as *ha-Zaken* (the elder). The Christian Bible (Acts 22:3) mentions Gamaliel I as the teacher of Paul and describes him as a "Pharisee" and a "doctor of the law" much honored by his people.

The tradition does not depict Rabban Gamaliel I as either exceptionally learned or a gifted teacher, probably because the school of Hillel, which he headed, always appeared collectively in its controversies with the school of Shammai, so that the opinions of individual scholars were not cited. Thus, while R. Yochanan ben Zakkai was praised with the words, "When he died, the glory of wisdom [scholarship] ceased," the following line noted, "When Rabban Gamaliel the Elder died, the honor [outward respect] of the Torah ceased, and purity and piety perished" (Sot. 49a).

"From the days of Moses up to Rabban Gamaliel I, the Torah was studied only standing. When Rabban Gamaliel I died, feebleness descended on the world, and they studied Torah sitting" (Meg. 21a). The scholars and students may have been weaker because of the relentless Roman persecution and political instability that resulted in a scarcity of food. "When Turnus [or Tinneius] Rufus the wicked destroyed [lit., 'ploughed up'] the Temple, Gamaliel I was condemned to death" and a high officer was sent to arrest and execute him. Gamaliel I went into hiding, but the officer found him and spoke to him in secret: "If I save you will you bring me into the World to Come?" After an affirmative response, the officer made Gamaliel I swear that this was true and the sage took the oath. The officer then climbed to the roof and jumped to his death. According to Roman tradition, "If a sentence of death was not carried out because one of their leaders dies, the decree is annulled [i.e., they regard it as punishment for an evil decree]." Thereupon, a heavenly voice (*bat kol*) announced: "This high officer is destined to enter into the World to Come" (Taan. 29a).

As the Talmud observes, "Formerly, the cost of burial was harder for the family to bear than the death itself, so that sometimes they fled to escape the expense. This was so until Rabban Gamaliel I [a wealthy man] insisted that he be buried in a plain linen shroud instead of costly garments" (MK 27a–b), which remains the traditional practice. In Pirkei Avot (1:16), Gamaliel I is quoted as saying: "Secure for yourself a teacher and remove yourself from uncertainty [i.e., even a Rabbi should consult another scholar who is a greater authority]; and do not give excess tithes by estimating [instead of measuring]."

When serving as the *nasi*, Gamaliel I made numerous innovations in *halachah* designed to lighten the burden of the laws. He permitted a widow to remarry on the basis of the testimony of a single witness that her husband had died (Yev. 122a), an important problem during the Roman persecutions of the time. Gamaliel I eased restrictions on Sabbath travel, especially for midwives on their way to care for women in labor, "or one who comes to rescue someone from a fire, bandits, a river in flood, or a collapsed building" (RH 23b).

In a letter to the Jews of the Land of Israel and neighboring countries, Gamaliel I explained that the Sanhedrin ruled that some years contain thirteen months because "the time of Passover is drawing near, but there is no sign of spring and we have no lambs for the Passover offering. There are no lambs to be sacrificed by those women who have given birth, nor will there be new barley for the offering of the sheaf (*omer*)" (Bader, 126).

In one intriguing but cryptic observation, Gamaliel I compared his students to a classification of fish from various parts of the Land of Israel: (1) a son of poor parents, who has memorized everything by study but has no understanding, is like a ritually impure fish; (2) a son of rich parents who has learned and understood everything, is like a ritually pure fish; (3) a student who has learned everything but does not know how to respond is like a fish from the Jordan River; and (4) a student who has learned everything and knows how to respond is like a fish from the great ocean (Mediterranean Sea) (ARN 40).

Gamaliel II, Palestinian *tanna* (first/second century).

Gamaliel II was the grandson of Gamaliel I, son of Shimon ben Gamaliel, and the recognized head of the Jewish community in the Land of Israel for thirty years. He was too young to succeed his father as *nasi* when Shimon ben Gamaliel died soon before the destruction of the Second Temple. R. Yochanan ben Zakkai assumed this position, establishing the Sanhedrin at Yavneh after Jerusalem fell in 70 C.E. His successor was Gamaliel II, who returned the leadership of the Jews in the Land of Israel to the house of Hillel. With his descendants, the title of *nasi* (later patriarch) became hereditary, and the Roman authorities officially recognized Gamaliel II as the head of the Jewish community. In an attempt to end factionalism and unify the tradition, Gamaliel II finally succeeded in ending the opposition between the schools of Hillel and Shammai, which had survived even the destruction of the Temple. According to legend, a voice from heaven (*bat kol*) declared: "The words of both are the words of the living God, but the *halachah* is in agreement with the rulings of the house of Hillel" (Er. 13b; JT Ber. 3b).

Several Talmudic tales describe discussions between Rabban Gamaliel II and philosophers or heretics. Relating to the biblical verse "For the Lord your God is a consuming fire, a jealous God" (Deut. 4:24), a philosopher asked Gamaliel II, "Why does God express His jealousy against the worshipers rather than against the idol itself?" The sage replied with a parable: "This may be compared to a human king who had a son who reared a dog to which he gave his father's name. Whenever he swore an oath, the son exclaimed, 'By the life of this dog, my father!' When the king heard of it, with whom was he angry—his son or the dog? Surely he was angry with his son!" The philosopher said to him, "You compare the idol to a dog; but does it not have some powers?" When Rabban Gamaliel asked what powers it possessed, the philosopher replied, "Once a great fire broke out in our city, and the whole town was burnt with the exception of an idolatrous shrine." The sage said, "Let me give you another parable. This is like a human king against whom one of his provinces rebelled. If he goes to war against it, does he fight with the living or the dead? Surely he wages war with the living!" (i.e., because the idol is a dead thing, God does not wage war against it, and thus God destroyed the idolaters without destroying the idol) (Av. Zar. 54a).

A legendary story of the creation of woman effusively praised her. A heretic once said to Gamaliel II, "Your God is a thief!" for taking away one of Adam's ribs while he slept. "Let me answer him," said the heretic's daughter. Turning to her father, she asked for a judge who could prosecute the thief who broke into their home and stole a silver pitcher, leaving a golden one in its place. "Would that such a thief visited us every day!" he exclaimed. "So," she retorted, "was it not better for Adam that a rib was taken from him and instead he was given a wife [lit., 'a maid to serve him']?" (Sanh. 39a).

Drawing an incorrect inference from the different verbs used to denote "creation" of the mountains and winds (Amos 4:13), a heretic concluded that these indicated the presence of two creators. Gamaliel II replied, "If that is so, then the words 'And God created' (Gen. 1:27) followed by 'And the Lord God formed' (Gen. 2:7) should mean that He who formed man did not create him!" The sage continued, "There is in the human body an area of one handbreadth in which there are two openings [the eye and the ear]. Would you say that He who created one of them did not create the other? Indeed, Scripture declared [Ps. 94:9], 'Shall He who implants the ear not hear? He who forms the eye not see?' Does that mean that there are two different gods involved?" (Sanh. 39a).

A heretic (or a Roman emperor) challenged Gamaliel II: "You maintain that whenever ten Jews are assembled [i.e., the quorum required for public worship], the *Shechinah* [Divine Presence] is found. How many *Shechinahs* are there then?" In response, Gamaliel II summoned the heretic's servant and hit him on the neck, asking, "Why did you allow [the light of] the sun to intrude into your master's house?" The heretic exclaimed, "[But] the sun shines upon the whole world! [i.e., how can one prevent its light from entering a house?]." Gamaliel II calmly retorted: "If the sun, which is but one of the countless millions of God's servants, can shine on the entire world, how much more would this be true for the Divine Presence of the Lord [i.e., to be able to be in many places at once]!" (Sanh. 39a).

Gamaliel II antagonized the Rabbis by his harsh attacks on colleagues and his reckless use of the ban of *herem*, even against his own brother-in-law, R. Eliezer ben Hyrcanus (BM 59b). After publicly humiliating R. Joshua ben Hananiah, Gamaliel II was temporarily removed from his leadership position in favor of R. Eleazar ben Azariah, though he soon was reinstated into a joint presidency after apologizing for his actions (Ber. 27b–28a).

During his term in office, Gamaliel II organized the final text of the *Amidah* (*Shemoneh Esrei*, or Eighteen Benedictions) and mandated that its recitation was a religious duty to be performed three times a day by each Jew (Ber. 28a). To counter the dangerous threat of sectarians, he commissioned R. Samuel ha-Katan to compose a prayer against the *minim* (heretics) to be added to the *Amidah*. The canonization of the early synagogue prayers by Rabban Gamaliel II met with intense opposition because of the danger that this would severely limit spontaneity. Nevertheless, most Rabbis recognized that fixed forms of prayer and regularity of worship were essential to a person's religious life. While waiting for the rare flash of inspiration conducive to prayers of self-expression, a person could forget the art of prayer, be incapable of praying even when that rare spiritual instant arrived, and end up never praying at all! (Milgrom, *Jewish Worship*, 26–27).

Following the destruction of the Temple, Rabban Gamaliel II was primarily responsible for designing the Passover evening ceremony. The Hagaddah quotes him as saying, "Whoever has not explained these three things on Passover [during the seder] has not discharged his duty. These three things are the Passover offering [*pesach*]; unleavened bread [*matzah*], and bitter herbs [*maror*]" (Pes. 10:5).

When his beloved gentile slave Tabi died, Gamaliel II "accepted condolences for him" though he had taught that this was not appropriate. He replied, "My slave Tabi was not like other slaves. He was a good man" (Ber. 16b). Elsewhere, he described Tabi as a "scholar" (Suk. 20a) who was "worthy to be ordained" (Yoma 87a). The Talmud relates that Gamaliel II wanted to free Tabi, but could find no excuse for doing so. When he accidentally blinded Tabi in one eye, Gamaliel assumed that this would allow him to free his slave according to Torah law, but he was informed by another sage that this would not be permitted since there were no witnesses to the accident (BK 74b).

When Gamaliel II commanded his slave to purchase the best thing to eat from the market, he brought home a tongue. The next day the sage asked his slave to buy the worst thing in the market, and he again brought home a tongue. When asked for an explanation, the wise slave replied: "There is nothing better than a good tongue, and nothing worse than an evil tongue [*lashon ha-ra*]" (Lev. R. 33).

When Gamaliel II gave his daughter in marriage, she asked for his blessing. He said, "May I not see your return." When her son was born and she again asked for a blessing, her father said, "May it be God's will that the words 'woe is me' never leave your mouth." The shocked daughter asked why her father would "curse me on my two days of rejoicing." The sage replied, "These are indeed blessings and not curses. If your family life is at peace, you will never return to live in my home. And if your son is strong and hearty, you will continually say 'woe is me,' followed by complaints such as 'the child has not eaten; he did not drink; he has not gone to school'" (Gen. R. 26:4).

Despite the general rabbinic view against the teaching of secular knowledge, the Rabbis "permitted the household of Gamaliel II [the patriarch] to study Greek wisdom because they had close associations with the government [and represented the Jewish people before the Roman authorities]" (Sot. 49b). He was well versed in mathematics and astronomy and had numerous drawings of the phases of the moon in his house. When ignorant witnesses came to announce sighting of the new moon, Gamaliel II would ask them to point to the picture that most nearly resembled what they saw (RH 2:8). He also fashioned an instrument to measure distances (Er. 43b).

Gamaliel II understood that communal leadership entailed assuming serious responsibility. Knowing that two of his disciples were extremely clever, but very poor, he decided to appoint them as supervisors so they could earn a living. He sent for them, but they did not come, since they were too humble to accept a position of honor. When they finally responded to a second request, the sage said: "You thought I was going to offer you to rule [a position of authority]. [Instead,] I give you servitude!" (Hor. 10a–b).

Upon the death of Rabban Gamaliel II in 110, his close friend Onkelos paid for a lavish funeral. Although at times irascible, Gamaliel II was a respected leader who was mourned by the entire community. *See also* Eliezer ben Hyrcanus; Hanina ben Dosa; Imma Shalom; Onkelos; Samuel ha-Katan.

Gamaliel III (second/third century).

The eldest son of Judah ha-Nasi, Gamaliel III assisted his father in editing the Mishnah and was named by him to be his successor as *nasi* (Ket. 103a). Three of the sayings of Gamaliel III are preserved in Pirkei Avot (2:2–4). "It is good to combine Torah study with an occupation, for the exertion of them both makes sin forgotten. All Torah study that is not joined with work will cease in the end and lead to sin. Let all who work for the community do so in the name of Heaven [not for selfish motives such as financial benefit or to exercise authority over others]." The Rabbis interpreted this as meaning that if a scholar has no work by which he earns a steady livelihood, he will have to seek work at random, thus wasting time that he could otherwise have devoted to the Torah study. If unsuccessful in finding honest work, he might be tempted (or driven) to dishonest means of obtaining a livelihood. Consequently, one of the major duties of a father was to prepare his son to earn a living. "He who does not teach his son a craft/trade, teaches him to be a robber" (Kid. 29a).

Presumably on the basis of his own experience with the Roman authorities, Gamaliel III cautioned: "Beware of [dealing with] the ruling authorities, for they befriend someone only for their own benefit, they act friendly when it is to their own advantage, but they abandon him when he is in need." With respect to one's relationship with God, Gamaliel III declared: "Treat His will as your own, so that He may make your will like His own ['He will fulfill the desire of those that fear Him'; Ps. 145:19]; nullify your will before His will [when they conflict], so that He will set aside the will of others before yours."

Gamaliel IV (third century).

Son and successor of the patriarch Judah II, and father of the patriarch Judah III, Gamaliel IV headed the Sanhedrin from 250 to 265.

Gamaliel V (fourth century).

Son and successor of the patriarch Hillel II, Gamaliel V was head of the Sanhedrin from 365 to 380. He is best known for completing his father's work in developing a permanent Jewish calendar.

Gamaliel VI (fourth/fifth century).

The last patriarch of the Jews of the Land of Israel, Gamaliel VI succeeded his father, Judah IV, as *nasi* in 400. During his reign, the Roman Empire was divided in two: an eastern portion with its capital at Constantinople, and a western part with its old capital in Rome. A decree of the Roman emperors Honorius and Theodosius II in 415, which stripped Gamaliel VI of all power and removed him from office, charged that he had disregarded the special laws against the Jews, had built new synagogues, and had judged disputes between Jews and Christians. The death in 426 of Gamaliel VI, who left no heirs, marked the end of the 400-year dynasty of the house of Hillel.

Halafta, Palestinian *tanna* (first/second century).

A senior contemporary of Rabban Gamaliel II, Halafta was a leader of the Jewish community in Sepphoris and conducted a rabbinic school there during the Hadrianic persecutions. Although most *halachot* in his name were transmitted by his more renowned son, Jose, in two places Halafta's opinions were cited regarding the proper procedures for blowing the shofar (Taan. 16b; RH 27a).

Halafta ben Dosa, Palestinian *tanna* (second/third century).

A contemporary of R. Akiva, his best known teaching is in Pirkei Avot (3:7): "If ten people sit together and engage in Torah study, the Divine Presence rests among them, as it is said: 'God stands in the Divine assembly [a minimum of ten, as in a *minyan*]' [Ps. 82:1]. How do we know this even of five? For it is said, 'He has established his bundle [a quantity of sheaves held in the fingers of one hand] upon earth' [Amos 9:6]. How do we know this even of three? For it is said, '[God stands] in the midst of judges [minimum of three judges in a *bet din*], He shall judge' [Ps. 82:1]. How do we know this even of two? For it is said, 'Then those who fear God spoke to one another [i.e., therefore two], and God listened and heard' [Mal. 3:16]. How do we know this even of one? For it is said, 'In every place where I cause My Name to be mentioned, I will come to you and bless you' [Exod. 20:21]."

Hama, Babylonian *amora* (fourth century).

Known as the "*amora* of Nehardea" (Sanh. 17b), Hama served as head of the academy at Pumbedita for twenty years. When King Shapur of Persia wondered whether burial of the dead was simply a Jewish folk custom or a biblical commandment, he asked Hama, "From what passage in the Torah is the law of burial derived?" The sage "remained silent and made no answer." A colleague complained that he should have cited the verse, "You shall surely bury [Deut. 21:23]," but that "might merely have meant that he should be placed in a coffin [i.e., not necessarily placed in the ground]." Other suggested proofs were the emphatic doubling of the Hebrew words indicating burial in the verse "the fact that the righteous were buried" (i.e., the Bible stated that the patriarchs were buried, but this occurred prior to the giving of the Torah); and that God buried Moses (Deut. 34:6). However, the commentaries explained that Hama remained silent for fear of offending the sensibility of the king, since the ancient Persians regarded the earth as sacred ground and did not bury their dead lest they defile it with decomposing bodies (Sanh. 46b).

Hama made a living by selling goods whose price varied according to the locale. To avoid the prohibition against interest, he would give merchandise on credit and charge the higher cost prevailing in other markets, with the purchaser transporting the goods there at Hama's risk. He argued that the increased credit price was permitted since, by bearing the risk, the goods remained his until brought to the more expensive locale, so that they really sold his wares there and thus he was entitled to the price they would cost at that place. Why would this scheme work? "They are pleased that it [the merchandise effectively] remains in my possession, so that wherever they go they [receive the privilege of being] exempt from taxation and the market is held up for them" (BM 65a).

Hama bar Bissa, Palestinian *tanna* (second/third century).

The Talmud relates that Hama bar Bissa left his family and "spent twelve years at the house of study" (Ket. 6a–b). When he returned, rather than behave like a colleague who had entered his house unexpectedly and nearly scare his wife to death, Hama bar Bissa sent word of his arrival from the local study hall. There he engaged in a *halachic* discussion with a brilliant young man, who unbeknownst to Hama bar Bissa, was his son, R. Oshaia. Hama bar Bissa became depressed, realizing, "Had I been here [i.e., remained at home and attended to the education of my son], I also could have had such a child." Finally returning home, Hama was sitting with his wife when R. Oshaia entered the house. Assuming that the young man wished to continue their discussion, Hama bar Bissa rose to greet him. Surprised, his wife asked, "What father stands up before a son?!" (Ket. 62b). To Hama bar Bissa, his father, and his son—three generations of scholars all living at the same time—R. Rami ben Hama applied the verse from Ecclesiastes (4:12), "And a threefold cord is not readily broken" (BB 59a).

Hama ben Hanina, Palestinian *amora* (third century).

Like his father, Hama ben Hanina was head of the academy at Sepphoris (JT Shab. 6:2), where he used some of his wealth to build a synagogue (JT Pe'ah 8:9). Commenting on the biblical verse, "You shall walk after the Lord your God" (Deut. 13:5), Hama ben Hanina asked: "Is it possible for a human being to walk after the *Shechinah*? Has it not been said, 'For the Lord your God is a consuming fire' (Deut. 4:24)?" Hama ben Hanina explained that the meaning was "to walk after [emulate] the attributes" of God. "Just as He clothed the naked ['And the Lord God made garments of skin for Adam and his wife, and clothed them'; Gen. 3:21], so you shall clothe the naked. Just as God visited the sick ['And the Lord appeared to him (Abraham) by the oaks of Mamre'; Gen. 18:1], so you shall visit the sick. Just as God comforted mourners ['After the death of Abraham, God blessed Isaac his son'; Gen. 25:11], so you shall comfort mourners. And just as God buried the dead ['God buried him (Moses) in the valley'; Deut. 34:6], so you shall bury the dead" (Sot. 14a).

Hama ben Hanina made several comments relating to evil speech. "Just as the hand can kill, so can the tongue [slanderous words]" (Ar. 15b); and "What is the remedy for slanderers? If he be a scholar, let him engage in the Torah [based on a variant translation of Prov. 15:4, 'The healing for a tongue is the tree of life (Torah)']. . . . But if he is an ignorant person, let him become humble" (Ar. 15b). He interpreted the verse "As iron sharpens iron" (Prov. 27:17) as meaning that two scholars sharpen each other's mind by engaging in intense *halachic* discussions (Taan. 16a). He added, "One who regularly takes black cumin will not suffer from heartburn" (Ber. 40a).

Hama ben Hanina understood the critical need for water in the Land of Israel, declaring that the day when rain falls "is as great as the day when heaven and earth were created" (Ber. 32b). Among his other sayings are: "If a person sees that his prayers are not answered, he should pray again" (based on Ps. 27:14, "Look to the Lord, be strong and of good courage! O look to the Lord") (Ber. 5b); "As soon as a man takes a wife his sins are buried" (based on the verse from Prov. 18:22, "He who finds a wife has found happiness and has won the favor of the Lord") (Yev. 63b); and "Great is penitence, for it brings healing to the world" (Yoma 86a).

Hama ben Papa, Palestinian *amora* (fifth century).

Hama ben Papa was quoted as saying, "Every man who is endowed with grace [loving kindness] is without doubt a God-fearing man" (Suk. 49b).

Hamnuna I, Babylonian *amora* (third/fourth century).

Hamnuna I is often referred to in the Talmud as Hamnuna Zuta (the younger). When requested by the Rabbis to sing something at the wedding of R. Mar bar Ravina, Hamnuna I said, "Alas for us, that we must die!" When asked by his colleagues what they were to respond as a refrain, Hamnuna I replied: "Where is the Torah and where is the mitzvah that will shield us [from the punishment that is to come]?" (Ber. 31a).

On concluding his prayers, Rava added the following: "My God, before I was formed I was not worthy [to be formed], and now that I have been formed, I am as if I had not been formed. I am dust in my lifetime, all the more in my death. Behold I am before You like a vessel full of shame and confusion. May it be Your will, O Lord my God, that I sin no more, and that the sins I have committed before You be wiped out in Your great mercies, but not through evil chastisements and diseases!" Hamnuna I adopted these words as the formula for the confession that he used to recite on the Day of Atonement, which is still included in the Yom Kippur liturgy (Ber. 17a).

Hamnuna I asked: "How many important laws can be learned from these verses relating to Hannah (1 Sam. 1:10–16)? 'Now Hannah, she spoke in her heart'—from this we learn that one who prays must direct his heart. 'Only her lips moved'—from this we learn that he who prays must frame the words distinctly with his lips. 'But her voice could not be heard'—from this, it is forbidden to raise one's voice in the *Tefillah* [*Amidah*]. Therefore Eli thought she had been drinking—from this, a drunken person is forbidden to say the *Tefillah*" (Ber. 31a).

The Talmud relates a bizarre event when the coffins containing the bodies of Rabbah bar Huna and Hamnuna I were transported to the Land of Israel for burial. "As they came to a bridge, the camels carrying the coffins halted. A certain Arab said to those [who accompanied the cortege], 'What is that? [i.e., what does this strange behavior indicate?].'" When they replied that the deceased Rabbis were doing honor to each other, each saying that the other should proceed first, the Arab observed, "[In my judgment], it is right that Rabbah son of R. Huna [a notable who is the son of a notable] should take precedence." After the camel bearing Rabbah bar Huna passed along first, "The molars and teeth of that Arab fell out [a proverbial expression, meaning that the Arab received what he deserved for his irreverence]" (MK 25a–b).

Hamnuna II, Babylonian *amora* (third century).

Often referred to in the Talmud as Hamnuna Saba (the elder), Hamnuna II was a longtime disciple of Rav (BK 106a) and succeeded his master as head of the academy at Sura. Indeed, the Talmud suggests that all statements listed from "the school of Rav" come from Hamnuna II. He extensively cited his teacher as an authority and did his utmost to prevent others from deviating from customs instituted by his master. When one scholar decided a ritualistic point contrary to the opinion of Rav, Hamnuna II promptly put him under a ban, a form of excommunication that generally lasted for 30 days (Shab. 19b). A close friend of R. Hisda, Hamnuna II became recognized as one of the outstanding scholars of his generation and was frequently consulted by the exilarch on points of law (Shab. 119a).

As a strong proponent of education, Hamnuna II maintained: "Jerusalem was destroyed only because they [its inhabitants] neglected [the education of] school children" (Shab. 119b). He urged that as soon as a child learned to talk, his father must teach him to say the biblical verse (Deut. 33:4), "Moses commanded us a Law, an inheritance of the congregation of Jacob" (Suk. 42a). Consequently, after the Roman victory, the Rabbis worked tirelessly to keep the study of Torah alive in the Land of Israel.

Hamnuna II declared, "Just as learning precedes practice, so the judgment of human beings [in the World to Come] is based more on the study of Torah than performing *mitzvot*" (Kid. 40b). He used *gematria* (numerology) to support R. Simlai's declaration that the Israelites received 613 commandments at Mount Sinai. Hamnuna II observed that the numerical value of the Hebrew letters in the word "Torah," which Moses communicated to the people, equaled 611. When added to the first two of the Ten Commandments, which were communicated to them directly by God, the total is 613 (Mak. 23b–24a).

Among the several blessings ascribed to Hamnuna II is one that is said before engaging in Torah study: "[Blessed are You . . .] who has chosen us from all the nations and given us Your Torah. Blessed are You, O Lord, who gives the Torah," which is still recited at public readings of the Torah in the synagogue (Ber. 11b). This blessing contains a grammatical inconsistency that has been invested with great theological significance. The first portion of the blessing uses the past tense, while the second part is in the present tense. According to the Rabbis, this indicates that the Torah is not merely a static and lifeless text. Instead, Revelation is a continuing process, with subsequent interpretations of the Torah (Oral Law) also being Divine and thus binding.

In one Talmudic anecdote, after R. Hisda praised Hamnuna II to R. Huna, the latter asked to meet the young scholar. When he arrived, R. Huna saw that he wore no head covering. When asked why, Hamnuna II replied, "Because I am not married." R. Huna turned away from Hamnuna and said, "See to it that you do not appear before me [again] before you are married." This was in accord with R. Huna's belief, "He who is twenty years of age and is not married spends all his day in sinful thoughts" (Kid. 29b). *See also* Rabbah bar Huna.

Hana bar Bizna, Babylonian *amora* (third/fourth century).

A judge in Pumbedita, Hana bar Bizna was a renowned *halachist* who preserved the name and teachings of Shimon ha-Tzadik (Simeon the Just), who was rarely cited by any other sage. These include: "He who prays should regard himself [i.e., behave] as if the *Shechinah* were before him" (Sanh. 22a); "Better a man throw himself into a fiery furnace than shame his neighbor in public" (Ket. 67b); and "A fast in which none of the sinners of Israel participate is no fast" (Ker. 6b), meaning that those who have transgressed must not be excluded as being unworthy of joining their fellow Jews in prayer. He related Shimon ha-Tzadik's interpretation of the verse, "And I will take away My hand, and you shall see My back" (Exod. 33:23), as teaching that "God showed Moses the knot of the *tefillin*" (Men. 35b).

Hanan I, Palestinian *tanna* (second century).

Based on three verses from Isaiah, Hanan I concluded: "There are three [kinds of dreams which signify] peace, [ones about] a river, a bird, and a pot." As explanations, he added: "A river, for it is written, 'Behold I will extend peace to her like a river' [Isa. 66:12]; a bird, for it is written, 'Like birds that fly, so will the Lord of Hosts shield Jerusalem' [Isa. 31:5]; and a pot, for it is written, 'Lord, may you establish [the Hebrew also means placing a pot on a fire] peace for us' [Isa. 26:12]" (Ber. 56b). Hanan I also said, "Even if the Master of dreams says to a man [i.e., one dreams] that tomorrow he will die, he should not desist from prayer," based on the verse (Eccles. 5:6), "For much dreaming leads to futility and superfluous talk, but fear God" (Ber. 10b).

Hanan II, Palestinian *amora* (third century).

Born in Babylonia and a student of Rav in his later years (Yoma 41b), Hanan II taught: "He who invokes the judgment of Heaven [God's retribution] on his neighbor is himself punished first." As an example, he noted that just as Sarah called on God to judge between her and Abraham (Gen. 16:5), soon thereafter the Bible (Gen. 23:2) noted that "Sarah died . . . and Abraham proceeded to mourn for Sarah, and to weep for her" (BK 93a). Hanan II further maintained that the enslavement of the Israelites in Egypt was Divine retribution for the sons of Jacob selling Joseph. Just as Joseph was sold as a slave, so each year the descendants of Jacob repeat at the seder, "We were slaves of Pharaoh in Egypt" (Mid. Ps. 10:2).

Hanan bar Abba, Babylonian *amora* (third century).

A student of Rav, Hanan bar Abba maintained that one who responds "Amen" "should not raise his voice above the one who says the blessing [prayer leader]" (Ber. 45a). As a proof text, he cited the verse, "Exalt the Lord with me; let us extol His name together [i.e., not one louder than the other]" (Ps. 34:4).

Hanan ha-Nechba, Palestinian *tanna* (first century C.E.).

Like his grandfather, Honi the Circle-Drawer, "when the world was in need of rain the Rabbis would send school children to take hold of the hem of his garment" and beg Hanan ha-Nechba to beseech God to send rain. Then Hanan ha-Nechba would pray: "Master of the Universe, do it [send rain] for the sake of these [children] who are unable to distinguish between the Father who gives rain and the father who does not" (Taan. 23b). The text then explains that Hanan ha-Nechba received his appellation "because he used to lock [*michabeh*] himself in the privy [out of modesty]."

Hananel bar Papa, Babylonian *amora* (fourth century).

In his only mention in the Talmud, Hananel bar Papa asked: "Why are the words of the Torah compared to a prince?" He then answered: "To tell you that just as a prince has the power of life and death [over his subjects], so have the words of the Torah [the potentialities] of life and death" (Shab. 88b).

Hananiah, Palestinian *tanna* (second century).

To remove Hananiah from sectarian influences in Capernaum, his uncle R. Joshua ben Hananiah sent him to Babylonia. There he opened a school in Nehar-Pekod, west of Nehardea, which eventually achieved great fame (Sanh. 32b). Hananiah returned to the Land of Israel to share with his uncle *halachot* communicated to him by a Babylonian scholar. However, after the failure of the Bar Kochba rebellion, Hananiah again emigrated to Babylonia. Believing that Jewish institutions in the Land of Israel would collapse in the wake of the crushing Roman victory, Hananiah strove to establish an authoritative body in Babylonia that would be independent of the Sanhedrin in his native home. However, the unexpected death of Hadrian and the repeal of his harsh decrees led to a revitalization of Jewish learning in the Land of Israel. The surviving Rabbis, including students of R. Akiva, reorganized the Sanhedrin at Usha under Rabban Gamaliel II. Unwilling to permit any rival to the new central authority, they sent messengers to Hananiah asking him to acknowledge the authority of the Sanhedrin so as not to fragment the religious unity of Israel. Although Hananiah initially resisted this call, he eventually realized that he had no choice but to submit to the authority of the sages in the Land of Israel.

Hananiah ben Akashia, Palestinian *tanna* and one of the Ten Martyrs (first/second century).

Hananiah ben Akashia's only Talmudic citation is a *beraita* (Mak. 23b): "The Holy One, blessed be He, desired to make Israel a worthy people. Therefore, He gave them the Law [to study] and many commandments [to fulfill]." As a proof text, he used the verse from Isaiah (42:21), "The Lord desires His [servant's] vindication, so that he may magnify and glorify [His] Torah." The Soncino edition of the Talmud interprets this as a polemic against the Pauline conception that the Law was given because of Divine anger to increase both the sins of Israel and their need for Divine mercy. Instead, this passage indicates that the Law was a manifestation of Divine love, designed to instill moral holiness in Israel to make them more worthy in the eyes of God.

Hananiah (Haninah) ben Hakinai, Palestinian *tanna* (second century).

Hananiah ben Hakinai studied with R. Akiva for twelve years without returning home (Ket. 62b), leading his wife to be praised by the Rabbis as an example of a "helper" for him because of her forbearance (Gen. R. 17:3). Hananiah ben Hakinai was a superb scholar and linguist (JT Shek. 5:1), and R. Akiva considered him worthy of being taught the mysteries of the *merkava* (celestial chariot depicted in Ezekiel) (Hag. 14b).

Hananiah ben Hakinai was one of the Ten Martyrs executed by the Romans for teaching Torah. He is best known for his saying in Pirkei Avot (3:5): "He who keeps awake at night, or who walks alone at night and turns his mind to idle thoughts [lit., 'makes room in his heart for that which is futile'], is guilty of [responsible for] harming his own life."

Hananiah (Hanina) ben Teradion, Palestinian *tanna* (second century).

Hananiah ben Teradion's daughter, Beruriah, was married to R. Meir. A classic Talmudic text concerning the martyrdom of Hananiah ben Teradion encapsulates the rabbinic view of euthanasia (Av. Zar. 18a). During the Hadrianic persecutions, Hananiah ben Teradion disregarded the imperial edict against teaching Torah and was condemned to death. Unlike R. Eleazar ben Parta, who was arrested with him, Hananiah ben Teradion admitted that he had been teaching Torah, since it was a Divine command. When the renowned sage was to be burned at the stake, the Romans wrapped him in a Torah scroll and secured tufts of wet wool around his heart to prolong his suffering. His daughter exclaimed, "Father, that I should see you in this state!" He replied, "If it were I alone being burnt it would have been a thing hard to bear; but now that I am burning together with the Scroll of the Law, God who will have regard for the plight of the Torah will also have regard for my plight." His disciples called out, "Rabbi, what do you see?" He answered them, "The parchments are being burnt but the letters are soaring on high" (even if scrolls of the Torah are destroyed, its spirit is immortal and indestructible). As the fire raged, the Rabbi's disciples urged him to "open your mouth so you can end it quicker." However, he refused, saying that only God who gave him life could take it away. This is the primary argument against *active* euthanasia, any attempt to accelerate death by taking a step that would terminate life faster than it would naturally cease. However, Hananiah ben Teradion did permit removal of the wet wool around his heart, which was applied to sadistically prolong his suffering, and he soon died. This is interpreted as meaning that in some circumstances *passive* euthanasia is permitted, the removal of artificial life support keeping alive a person who will soon perish (i.e., not shortening life, but rather removing any impediment to the natural process of dying, especially if one is in severe pain). This

Talmudic section concludes by relating that the executioner was so moved by the sage's sufferings and death that he threw himself into the fire. A heavenly voice then exclaimed that both "are assigned to the World to Come." When Judah ha-Nasi heard this he wept and said, "One may acquire eternal life in a single hour, another only after many years."

Hananiah ben Teradion's most famous saying appears in Pirkei Avot (3:3): "If two people sit together and do not exchange words of Torah, this is a meeting of scorners [who do not avail themselves of an opportunity to study]; but if two sit together and there are words of Torah [spoken] between them, the *Shechinah* [Divine Presence] abides among them, as it is said, 'Then they who feared the Lord spoke with one another' [Mal. 3:16]." As the text continues, even a person who studies Torah alone will receive a Divine reward. *See also* Eleazar ben Parta.

Hanin, Palestinian *amora* (fourth century).

The Talmud recounts that Hanin was named for his father, who died on the very day his son was born (MK 25b). In the name of R. Hanina bar Hama, Hanin said, "If one prays long, his prayer does not go unanswered" (Ber. 32b). He observed: "Wine was created for the sole purpose of comforting mourners and rewarding the wicked [for the little good they may have done in the world]" (Er. 65a).

Hanina bar Hama, Palestinian *amora* (second/third century).

Most often referred to simply as Hanina, but also known as Hanina ha-Gadol (the Great), he was born in Babylonia and came to the Land of Israel, where he settled in Sepphoris and became a wealthy honey trader (JT Pe'ah 7:4). One of the prominent disciples of Judah ha-Nasi, Hanina bar Hama was said to have built the academy at Sepphoris, which he directed, from the money he earned from one especially profitable transaction (JT Pe'ah 7:3).

One of Hanina bar Hama's most famous sayings is, "Everything is in the hand of God [lit., 'Heaven'] except the fear of God" (Ber. 33b), meaning that although all of a person's qualities are fixed by nature, his moral character depends on his own choice. Although convinced that all was predestined—"no man bruises his finger here on earth unless it was so decreed against him by Heaven" (Hul. 7b)—Hanina bar Hama nevertheless declared that fevers and chills were exceptions (BM 107b), and that ninety-nine out of one hundred people died through their own fault in not avoiding colds (JT Shab. 14:3). Hanina bar Hama himself lived a long and healthy life—it was reported that at age eighty he was able to balance himself on one foot while taking off and putting on his shoes—which he attributed to the warm baths and oil treatments that he received as a child (Hul. 24b).

Comparing charity to a garment, Hanina bar Hama observed: "Just as a garment is woven out of single threads, so charity is composed of single coins that [eventually] add up to a large sum" (BB 9b). In distributing charity, the needs of scholars should be considered first, for a person who insulted a scholar was regarded as a heretic who had insulted the Torah and did not deserve a share in the World to Come (Sanh. 99b). At the same time, scholars had an obligation to teach all who wished to learn. Those who claimed that they "do not have the strength" to instruct others will soon reach that state (Lam. R. 1:38).

R. Yochanan maintained, "Israel is immune from planetary influence [i.e., Jews are not affected by astrology]." However, Hanina bar Hama disagreed: "The planetary influence gives wisdom, the planetary influence gives wealth, and Israel stands under planetary influence" (Shab. 144b).

Hanina bar Hama once rebuked his fellow citizens of Sepphoris for their immorality, saying that they had no right to complain if God punished them (JT Taan. 3:4). However, he noted that God was "indulgent of idolatry, but not of profanation of the Name" (Lev. R. 22:6). Consequently, "It is better to commit a sin in secret than to publicly profane the Name of God" (Kid. 40a). He argued, "A heathen who smites a Jew is worthy of death [at the hand of Heaven]. . . . One who raises a hand against his fellow, even without hitting him, is called 'a wicked man'" (Sanh. 58b). He warned that a judge should not listen to a litigant who came before him in the absence of his opponent in an effort to present his arguments and thus secure a verdict in his favor (Sanh. 7b).

Hanina bar Hama stressed the importance of the Sabbath, indicating that each person should have two sets of garments, one for weekdays and the other for the seventh day (JT Pe'ah 8:8). Each Sabbath eve, he wrapped himself in a special robe and called to his friends and disciples, "Come, let us go forth to welcome the Sabbath Queen" (Shab. 119a). In Hanina bar Hama's name, R. Eleazar ben Pedat said: "The disciples of the wise increase peace in the world, as it says, 'And all your children shall be taught of the Lord, and great shall be the peace of your children' [Isa. 54:13]. Read not 'your children' [banay-ich] but 'your builders' [bonayich, here meaning learned men]" (Ber. 64a). These words are said after *Ein Keloheinu* and before *Aleinu* during the *Musaf* (additional) service on Sabbaths and festivals in the Ashkenazic rite. When learning of Hanina bar Hama's death, his distinguished pupil, R. Yochanan, tore his clothes and the thirteen woolen garments (or lengths of precious silk) he had with them, lamenting: "Gone is the man before whom I was in awe [on account of his great learning]" (MK 24a).

Hanina bar Hama loved his adopted home in the Land of Israel. Using a Hebrew term that can be translated as either "glorious" or "deer," he said:

"Just as the skin of a deer cannot hold its flesh [because the skin shrinks after the death of the animal], so the Land of Israel when it is inhabited can find space [for everyone], but when not inhabited it contracts" (Git. 57a). Strongly opposed to anyone leaving the Land of Israel, Hanina bar Hama refused to write a letter of recommendation to the Babylonian scholars on behalf of one of his young students, R. Shimon bar Abba. "I cannot give this to you, for tomorrow I may see your parents [i.e., I may die] and they may complain to me that they had owned a beautiful flower in the Land of Israel and that I had allowed it to be transplanted to a foreign land" (JT MK 3:1). In the same section, he accused anyone wishing to leave the Land of Israel as having "abandoned the bosom of his mother and embraced the bosom of a stranger."

Hanina bar Hama once said, "There are those who sin against earth [i.e., their fellow men] but not against Heaven, and others who sin against Heaven but not earth. However, he who utters slander sins against both Heaven and earth" (Eccles. R. 9:13). *See also* Hanin.

Hanina ben Abbahu, Palestinian *amora* (fourth century).

Sent by his father from Caesarea to study at the academies of Tiberias, Hanina ben Abbahu spent all his time performing pious deeds, such as burying the dead. His exasperated father wrote to him: "Is it because there are no graves in Caesarea that I have sent you to Tiberias? Study must precede practical works" (JT Pes. 3:7).

In a parable, Hanina ben Abbahu related that a king had a child who would not stop crying. He took the child onto his lap and then raised it in his arms, but to no avail. Finally, he placed the child on his shoulders. But when the child soiled him, the king immediately put the child down on the floor. "How different was the child's ascent from its descent! The former was gradual, the latter sudden. Thus it was with Israel. At first God took him by the arms (Hos. 11:3), then He caused him to ride (Hos. 10:11); but when he sinned, 'He cast down from heaven unto the earth the beauty of Israel'" (Lam. R. 2:1).

In reconciling a *halachic* difference between two Rabbis, one who argued that the name of the Messiah will be "*Tzemach*" (sprout) and the other who maintained that it will be "*Menahem*" (comforter), Hanina ben Abbahu observed that "there is no difference of opinion between them," since the numerical value of the Hebrew letters in both words is the same (138) (JT Ber. 2:5). *See also* Abbahu of Caesarea.

Hanina ben Dosa, Palestinian *tanna* (first century C.E.).

A student of R. Yochanan ben Zakkai and famed for his piety and as a miracle worker, Hanina ben Dosa's prayers were said to have healed the children of both his teacher and Rabban Gamaliel II (Ber. 34b). There are two versions of the miraculous encounter between Hanina ben Dosa and a poisonous lizard. In the Jerusalem Talmud (Ber. 5:1), the sage was so focused on his prayers that he did not realize that he had been bitten by a poisonous lizard. When the lizard was found dead, his students exclaimed: "Woe to the man who is bitten by a poisonous lizard, and woe to the lizard that bites Hanina ben Dosa!" The text goes on to explain that the result of a lizard's bite depends on which reaches water first; if the man, the lizard dies (and vice versa), and in the case of Hanina ben Dosa, a spring miraculously opened under his feet. In the Babylonian Talmud (Ber. 33a), Hanina ben Dosa learned of a poisonous lizard that used to injure people. He asked to see its hole and put his heel over it; when the lizard came out and bit him, it died.

Hanina ben Dosa once was journeying on the road (in another version, carrying a sack on his head) when it began to rain. He exclaimed, "Master of the Universe, the whole world is happy but Hanina is suffering," and the rain stopped. When he reached home he cried out, "Master of the Universe, the whole world is in distress but Hanina feels content," and the rain fell again. Referring to his power to control the rain, the Rabbis said, "Beside Hanina ben Dosa's prayers, those of the high priest himself are of no avail" (Yoma 53b; Taan. 24b).

According to legend, after Hanina ben Dosa prayed for the sick he could predict which would live and which would die. "Are you a prophet?" the Rabbis inquired. "No," he replied, "I am neither a prophet nor the son of a prophet, but I learned this from experience. If my prayer comes fluently, I know that it is accepted; but if not, I know that it has been rejected" (Ber. 5:5). When the son of Rabban Gamaliel II became ill, the sage sent two disciples to request that Hanina ben Dosa pray for his recovery. After praying in the upper chamber of his home, Hanina ben Dosa came down to the messengers and told them that the boy's fever had passed and he would recover fully. The disciples carefully noted the exact moment of Hanina ben Dosa's pronouncement and reported it to Rabban Gamaliel, who informed them that "at that very time the fever left him and he asked for water to drink." On another occasion, when Hanina ben Dosa was studying Torah with Yochanan ben Zakkai, the sage's son became ill and Hanina ben Dosa was asked to pray for him. Hanina ben Dosa "put his head between his knees and prayed for him and he lived." Yochanan ben Zakkai observed that had he stuck his head between his knees for the whole day, it would have been to no avail. When his wife asked if that meant that Hanina ben Dosa was greater than he, Yochanan ben Zakkai replied: "No; but he is like a servant before the king [who has permission to go to him at any time] and I am like a nobleman before a king [who appears before him only at fixed times]" (Ber. 34b).

Hanina ben Dosa worked hard as a stone cutter in the Galilee but was extremely poor, surviving on the fruit of a carob tree "from one Sabbath eve to another" (Taan. 24b). The family of Hanina ben Dosa was the subject of several miracles related in the Talmud. Every Friday afternoon, the wife of Hanina ben Dosa would heat her oven and throw in a smoke-causing substance, embarrassed that she had nothing to bake to honor the Sabbath. An insensitive neighbor, knowing how poor Hanina ben Dosa was, decided to discover what was producing all the smoke. When she knocked on the door, Hanina ben Dosa's humiliated wife fled to the inner chamber. The neighbor entered the house and, miraculously, there was an oven full of bread and a kneading trough full of dough. When the neighbor called out, "Bring your shovel or your bread will burn!" Hanina ben Dosa's wife replied, "I just went to fetch it," because she "was accustomed to having miracles wrought for her" (Taan. 24b–25a).

One Friday evening, Hanina ben Dosa's daughter was distraught when she mistakenly filled the Sabbath lamp with vinegar instead of oil. Hanina ben Dosa consoled her, saying: "He who has endowed oil with the power of burning may give vinegar the same ability." The light continued to burn the entire day, and they took light from it to kindle the Havdalah candle the next evening.

The wife of Hanina ben Dosa once asked how long they would suffer for lack of food. When her husband asked what he could do, she advised, "Pray that something may be given to you." As he began to pray, an arm appeared, holding out a golden table leg. Later she dreamed that in the World to Come all the pious would eat at golden tables with three legs, but her husband's table would only have two legs. She said to her husband, "Are you content that the righteous [in the World to Come] will eat at a perfect table while we sit at an imperfect table? Pray that the leg be taken back." He prayed accordingly and the table leg was taken back. "It is taught that the miracle of taking away the gift was even greater than the miracle when it was presented, for it is customary for Heaven to bestow gifts but not to take them back" (Taan. 25a). As the Talmud relates, "When Hanina ben Dosa died, men capable of performing miracles ceased to exist" (Sot. 49a).

Two of his maxims appear in Pirkei Avot. The first teaches that fear of sin and the performance of good deeds are more important than wisdom (acquiring knowledge), which should not be made an end in itself (3:11–12). The second notes that God is pleased with a person "if [he behaves in such a way that] the spirit of one's fellows is pleased with him" (3:13).

Hanina ben Papa, Palestinian *amora* (third/fourth century).

A student of R. Samuel bar Nachmani, Hanina ben Papa's most famous saying is: "To enjoy this world without [reciting] a benediction is like robbing the Holy One, blessed be He, and the community of Israel" (Sanh. 102a).

Hanina of Sepphoris, Palestinian *amora* (fifth century).

After studies with R. Mani, Hanina moved to Sepphoris, where he became head of the religious community (JT Ned. 9:4). When R. Mani fled the Land of Israel in the wake of the Roman persecutions at Tiberias, Hanina resigned his leadership position in favor of his teacher, an act of self-denial and humility celebrated by the Rabbis as having few parallels (JT Pes. 6:3). However, Hanina was again forced to flee to Babylonia, where he became an associate of R. Ashi (BB 25a). His daughter married the son of Ravina (Nid. 66a), one of the editors of the Babylonian Talmud.

Hanina Segan ha-Kohanim, Palestinian *tanna* (first/second century).

As *segan ha-kohanim* (the deputy high priest), Hanina's role was to stand beside the high priest on the Day of Atonement, prepared to take over if some occurrence prevented him from carrying out his prescribed ritual duties. As an overseer and superintendent in the Temple, Hanina transmitted details about the Temple service from his knowledge of his father's customs (Shek. 6:1; Zev. 9:3) and those of the other priests (Pes. 1:6; Eduy. 2:1–2), as well as other widespread customs during Temple times (Eduy. 2:3; Men. 10:1). This was especially important to him since he believed that the Temple would soon be rebuilt, and thus he wanted to make certain that the customs in the new structure would be similar to those in the old one.

In Pirkei Avot (3:2), Hanina Segan ha-Kohanim taught: "Pray for the welfare of the government [i.e., Rome], because if people did not fear it, one man would swallow another alive." This related to Jeremiah's advice to those carried off to Babylonia (Jer. 29:7), "Seek the welfare of the city to which I have exiled you and pray to the Lord on its behalf; for in its prosperity you shall prosper [lit., 'in its peace you shall have peace']." He added, "Great is peace, which is equal to the whole act of Creation" (Sifre, Naso). Emphasizing the value of adhering to Torah principles, Hanina Segan ha-Kohanim said, "A person who takes the words of the Torah to heart . . . will have removed from him fear of the sword, of famine, of evil desires, and of the yoke [oppressive rule] of human beings" (ARN 20).

One of the preeminent scholars during the last years of the Second Temple, the peace-loving Hanina Segan ha-Kohanim was probably one of the Ten Martyrs executed by the Romans after the fall of Jerusalem.

Helbo, Palestinian *amora* (third/fourth century).

Born and educated in Babylonia, Helbo studied with R. Huna at the academy in Sura. In the name of his teacher, Helbo made several observations on prayer: "When a man leaves the synagogue, he should not take large steps [i.e., an action that might be misconstrued as indicating that he was glad to have finally fulfilled his obligation]"; "Whoever has a fixed place for his prayer has the God of Abraham as his helper"; and "A man should always take special care about the afternoon prayer [for this was the only time that Elijah was favorably heard]" (Ber. 6b). Also in R. Huna's name, Helbo said, "If one knows that his friend is used to greet him, let him greet him first," based on the verse, "Seek peace and pursue it" (Ps. 34:15). Similarly, "If his friend greets him and he does not return the greeting, he is called a robber" (Ber. 6b).

In the name of R. Ulla of Biri, Helbo maintained: "It is a man's duty to recite the *Megillah* [Book of Esther] at night and to repeat it the next day" (Meg. 4a), based on the rabbinic application to Mordechai and Esther of the verse from Psalms (30:13), "To the end that my glory may sing praise to you [by day] and not be silent [by night], O Lord, my God, I will give thanks to you for ever." He blamed wine as the cause for the dispersal of the Ten Lost Tribes of Israel, arguing that they were so preoccupied with this and other pleasures of the flesh that they neglected learning and lost faith, which ultimately led to their exile and disappearance (Er. 65a). Helbo's most famous maxim is: "One must always honor his wife, because blessings enter his home only on account of her, as it is written (Gen. 12:16), 'And he [Pharaoh] treated Abram well for her [Sarah's] sake'" (BM 59a).

Helbo had an extremely negative attitude toward converts. In at least four places he was quoted as saying, "Proselytes are as hard for Israel [to endure] as a [skin] sore" (Yev. 109b; Kid. 70b), believing that they were insincere and would lower the moral standards of Judaism. When R. Kahana announced that Helbo was sick, none of the sages visited him because his house was always messy. R. Kahana rebuked them, citing a similar tale in which the students of R. Akiva failed to visit one of their comrades who was ill. R. Akiva himself "entered [his house] to visit him, and because [finding the room a mess] he swept and sprinkled the ground before him, he [the student] recovered. 'My master,' said the student, 'you have revived me!' [Immediately,] R. Akiva went forth and lectured: 'He who does not visit the sick is like one who sheds blood'" (Ned. 40a).

Hezekiah, Palestinian *amora* (fourth century).

Hezekiah's most famous statement was: "A father is obligated to find a wife for his son and to teach him a craft [for a livelihood]" (Kid. 30b). As the text continued, some added that a father must also teach his son how to swim, for "his life may depend on it." Citing the verse from Isaiah (66:23) that "all flesh shall come to worship Me" on the New Moon and Sabbath," Hezekiah concluded: "A man's prayer is not heard unless he makes his heart [soft] like flesh" (Sot. 5a).

Hezekiah ben Hiyya, Palestinian *amora* (third century).

Born in Babylonia, Hezekiah moved to the Land of Israel with his twin brother (R. Judah ben Hiyya) and their father (R. Hiyya Rabbah bar Abba). According to legend, their mother suffered agonizing pangs of childbirth because, although twins, Hezekiah was born three months later than his brother (Yev. 65b). His most famous saying is: "Peace is more important than anything else. A person must observe all the commandments if they are at hand. . . . But where peace is concerned, he must go out of his way to pursue it. The value of peace is so great that the Bible refers to all the wanderings of the children of Israel in the desert in the plural because they traveled in discord and even rested in discord. But when they reached Mount Sinai the singular is used, for then they were at peace and united. It was then that God said, 'Now the time has come that I should give the Torah to my children'" (Lev. R. 9:9).

Hidka, Palestinian *tanna* (second century).

In a debate regarding how many meals one must eat on the Sabbath (Shab. 117b), the Rabbis said three, but Hidka maintained that the number was four. Their dispute stemmed from the verse concerning the manna, which was sent by God to nourish the Israelites in the desert (Exod. 16:25): Moses said, "Eat it today; for today is a Sabbath to the Lord; you shall not find it today in the field." Because the word *hayom* (lit., "the day") is mentioned three times, the Rabbis deduced that there must be a requirement to eat three meals during the whole of Shabbat. Hidka disagreed, arguing that the word *hayom* referred only to "the day" and did not include the fourth meal eaten on Friday night. However, Hidka's view was ultimately rejected, and the rule today is that three meals must be eaten on the Sabbath.

In a discussion of the seven Noahide laws that are incumbent on non-Jews and form the basis of any civilized society, Hidka thought the practice of castration should be added to the list of prohibitions (BM 90b; Sanh. 56b).

Hidka's most famous maxim is: "A man's own soul testifies against him," based on the verse, "Keep the doors of your mouth from her that lies in your bosom [i.e., the soul]" (Mic. 7:5).

Hillel, greatest sage of the Second Temple period (first century B.C.E./first century C.E.).

Hillel was known as *ha-Zaken* (the Elder), a title given to those who were leaders of the Jewish community or members of the supreme *bet din*. Born in Babylonia, Hillel moved to Jerusalem in his late thirties to study with Shemaiah and Avtalyon. Sleeping on the roof of the academy in the snow when he could not afford the admission fee, Hillel became a brilliant scholar and leader of the Pharisees and the liberal school of interpretation of Jewish law. From 30 B.C.E. to 10 C.E., Hillel served as *nasi*, the president of the Sanhedrin. Although the tyrant Herod was hated and viewed as merely the tax collector for Rome, Hillel was revered as a religious leader. Many hoped that Hillel's high status was a harbinger of the restoration of the House of David, from which he descended on his mother's side. This led to the introduction of the blessing for the return of the Davidic dynasty in the *Amidah*, and one of the blessings after the *haftarah* reading on the Sabbath: "Gladden us, Lord our God, with Elijah the prophet, your servant, and with the kingdom of the House of David, Your anointed, may he come speedily and cause our heart to exult. On his throne let no stranger sit, nor let others inherit his honor."

A paragon of modesty, Hillel said: "My humiliation is my exaltation; my exaltation is my humiliation" (Lev. R. 1:5), meaning that one who humbles himself will be raised up, while one who exalts himself will be brought low. The sages interpreted the verse, "You shall open your hand to him [i.e., your poor brother] and provide him all that he is lacking" (Deut. 15:8), as including the trappings of wealth that a formerly rich man had enjoyed. The Talmud relates that when a man from a wealthy family became poor, Hillel provided him with a horse and a servant to run before him. Once when no servant could be found, Hillel "himself ran before him for three miles" (Ket. 67b).

For Hillel, learning was of paramount importance. In a famous quote from Pirkei Avot (2:8), he says: "The more flesh, the more worms; the more possessions, the more worry; the more wives, the more witchcraft; the more maidservants, the more lewdness; the more manservants, the more theft; [However,] the more Torah, the more life; the more study, the more wisdom; the more counsel, the more understanding; the more charity, the more peace. One who has gained a good reputation has gained it for his own benefit; one who has gained Torah knowledge for himself has acquired life in the World to Come." He added, "An unlearned person cannot be scrupulously pious" (Avot 1:6), and "He who does not increase [his Torah learning] decreases it; he who refuses to teach [Torah] deserves death" (Avot 1:13). Hillel cautioned, "Do not say 'when I am free [i.e., have leisure time] I will study,' for perhaps you will never become free" (Avot 2:5).

R. Shimon ben Lakish declared Hillel to be as important as Ezra, for just as Ezra renewed the Torah after it was forgotten by the people, so Hillel came from Babylonia to teach the Torah, which had been neglected after the deaths of Shemaiah and Avtalyon. Hillel was the first of the *tannaim* to establish a rigorous system for Torah interpretation, developing seven rules of logic for uncovering the underlying meaning of the text. His chief intellectual adversary was Shammai, who espoused a stricter approach to Jewish law. They and their disciples were known as Bet Hillel (school [lit., "house of"] Hillel) and

Bet Shammai, respectively, with later Rabbis almost always siding with the more liberal and popular approach of the former.

Hillel taught that mere study was not sufficient: "Do not separate yourself from the community" (Avot 2:5). In his legal decisions, Hillel always was concerned primarily with the welfare of the people, and he established regulations aimed at reconciling the ancient law with new conditions. One of his innovations, the *prosbul*, made it possible for the poor to borrow money at the approach of the seventh (sabbatical) year, when people were reluctant to lend money since all debts would be cancelled at the end of that year (Git. 37a). Hillel warned that a person must be sympathetic to the plight of others: "Do not judge your fellow until you have been in his place" (Avot 2:5). His tolerance was illustrated by the famous story of the heathen who asked Hillel to teach him all of the principles of Judaism "while standing on one foot." In contrast to his major adversary, Shammai, who chased the man away, Hillel replied: "Do not do to your neighbor what you would not have him do unto you. This is the whole law; the rest is commentary. Now go and study it" (Shab. 31a).

Two other stories (Shab. 31a) illustrate the different approaches of Hillel and Shammai. A heathen once asked Shammai, "How many Torahs do you have?" Shammai answered, "Two, a Written Torah and an Oral Torah." When the heathen said, "I am willing to accept the Written Law but not the Oral Law—convert me to Judaism on the condition that you teach me the Written Torah [only]"—Shammai "scolded and repulsed him in anger." When the heathen came to Hillel, the sage agreed to convert him under the same condition. On the first day, Hillel taught him the first four letters of the Hebrew alphabet. On the following day, he reversed the sequence of the letters. When the prospective convert complained, "But yesterday you did not teach them to me in this order," Hillel replied, "Must you then not rely on me [as to what the letters are; i.e., the very names of the letters depend on an oral tradition]? Then also depend on me with respect to the Oral Torah." In the second tale, another heathen who had passed by a synagogue and heard of the special garments of the high priest asked Shammai to convert him to Judaism on the condition that *he* be appointed high priest. Shammai "pushed him out with the builder's cubit-measure that was in his hand." When the heathen came before Hillel, the sage asked him: "Can any man be made a king without knowing the arts of government [court procedure]? Go study them [in context, the laws pertaining to the functions of the high priest]." When the prospective convert learned that even King David could not become high priest because he was not of the family of Aaron, he realized why the condition he had set was impossible. Some time later, the converts met and observed: "The impatience of Shammai sought to drive us from the world, but Hillel's gentleness brought us under the wings of the *Shechinah* [Divine Presence]."

Once when asked by his disciples where he was headed, Hillel answered that he was going "to perform a religious duty . . . to bathe in the bath house." His surprised students questioned whether that was truly a "religious duty." Hillel replied: "If somebody is appointed to scrape and clean the statues of the king that are erected in the theaters and circuses, is paid to do the work, and even associates with the nobility, how much more should I, who am created in the Divine image and likeness, take care of my body!" (Lev. R. 34:3). Because the body is a vessel for the soul, the instrument through which one worships God and carries out the Divine will, taking proper care of it is a religious duty, for only a healthy body is capable of sustaining a holy soul: "Physical cleanliness leads to spiritual purity" (Av. Zar. 20b).

A fervent seeker of peace, Hillel's first statement in Pirkei Avot is: "Be among the disciples of Aaron, loving peace and pursuing peace, loving people, and bringing them closer to Torah" (Avot 1:12). When debating with fellow scholars, Hillel expressed his opinions calmly, stressing the truth of his statements rather than declaring them in a strident manner. Returning from a journey and hearing a great cry from the city, he assured his disciples, "I am confident that this does not come from my house" (Ber. 60a). His most famous sayings are: "If I am not for myself, then who will be for me? And if I am only for myself, then what am I? And if not now, when?" (Avot 1:14).

Hillel was the rabbinic ideal of emotional equanimity. As the Talmud relates, two men agreed that whoever could make Hillel lose his temper would receive 400 *zuzim*. One Friday afternoon toward dusk, one of the men knocked on Hillel's door as he was preparing for the Sabbath. When asked what he wanted, the man replied that he had a question to ask. "Why are the heads of the Babylonians so round [Hillel himself was a Babylonian]?" "My son, you have asked a good question," Hillel answered, "it is because they do not have skillful midwives [i.e., they improperly shape the head of the infant at birth]." The man departed, waited a while, and then returned with another question. "Why are the eyes of the Palmyreans round?" Hillel answered, "because they live in a very sandy place [i.e., they have smaller eye sockets so that during windstorms they are better protected from the blowing sand]." The next time, the man asked, "Why are the feet of Ethiopians [Africans] so wide?" and Hillel replied, "Because they live in swamplands [so that their feet do not sink into the marshy earth]." The man persisted: "I have many more questions to ask, but fear that you may become angry with me." Hillel reassured him, "Ask all the questions you want." Hoping to irritate Hillel by appearing as if he had been unaware of his stature, the man said, "Are you [the great] Hillel who they call the *nasi* [patriarch, the religious head of the people] of Israel?" When Hillel admitted that this was so, the man retorted, "May there not be many like you among the Jewish people!" The incredulous Hillel asked, "My son, why [do you say such a thing]?" The angry man exclaimed, "Because of you I have lost 400 *zuzim*!" After he revealed the wager, Hillel calmly replied: "It is far better that you have lost 400 *zuzim*, and even another 400 *zuzim*, because of Hillel than that Hillel become angry [and lose his patience]" (Shab. 31a).

According to Hillel, "A name made great is a name destroyed. This teaches that one's name should not come to the attention of the government. For once that happens, the end is that it [the government] casts its eye upon him, slays him, and takes away all his wealth" (ARN 11).

The *aggadah* (Sifre on Deut. 34:7) draws a parallel between the lives of Hillel and Moses, dividing their 120-year life spans into three periods of 40 years each. At the age of 40, Hillel moved from Babylonia to Israel; he devoted 40 years to intense study; and he spent the last third of his life as the spiritual head of the Jewish community in his adopted land. Hillel became viewed as the embodiment of the religious and moral teachings of Judaism, the sage who revived the art of Jewish scriptural exegesis. After his death, the Hillel dynasty persisted in the Land of Israel for 400 years. *See also* Avtalyon; Shammai.

Hillel II, son and successor of Judah III as patriarch and president of the Sanhedrin (*nasi*) (fourth century).

Hillel II is best known for developing a permanent calendar (in the year 360), based on astronomical calculations to adjust for discrepancies between the lengths of the solar and lunar years, adding an extra day or even intercalating an extra month when needed to make possible the universal celebration of the festivals on the days designated in the Bible (e.g., Passover must be observed in the spring [Deut. 16:1]). For many years previously, these changes had been decided at meetings of a special commission of the Sanhedrin. However, because these meetings were periodically prohibited as part of the relentless Roman persecution of the Jews, and because messengers often were prevented from disseminating the decisions throughout the Diaspora, Hillel II determined to provide an authorized calendar for all time to unite the Diaspora and the Land of Israel. However, this eliminated the only remaining important role of the *nasi*, effectively rendering it an empty title.

Hinena bar Idi, Babylonian *amora* (third century).

Hinena said, "Whoever fulfils a precept as it is commanded [i.e., with its proper spirit], no evil will befall him" (Shab. 63a). He based this on the scriptural verse, "He who keeps the commandments shall know no evil thing" (Eccles. 8:5).

Hisda, Babylonian *amora* (third century).

Born into a priestly family, Hisda's early years were spent in poverty. However, he became so wealthy as a brewer (Pes. 113a) that he was able to pay for the rebuilding of the academy at Sura, which he later headed for the last ten years of his life. A disciple of Rav and one of the most frequently quoted scholars in the Babylonian Talmud—more than 1,500 citations—Hisda also appears prominently in the Jerusalem Talmud because he spent considerable time in the Land of Israel studying the traditions and decisions of its sages. He and his colleague R. Huna were called "the pious ones of Babylon" (Taan. 23b).

Hisda stressed the importance of *halachah*, though numerous *aggadic* sayings were ascribed to him. He adopted an extreme attitude to modesty, stating that a man should not converse even with his own wife in the street (Ber. 43b). Hisda advised his daughters: "Act modestly in the presence of your husbands: do not eat bread before your husbands [you may eat too much]; do not eat herbs at night [because of their odor]; do not eat dates nor drink beer at night [because of their laxative properties; . . . and when someone calls at the door, do not say *mi hu* [who is he?] but *mi hi* [who is she?]." To demonstrate that what is hidden elicits great curiosity, Hisda took a precious jewel in one hand and a worthless seed in the other, showing his daughters only the stone. When they were "suffering" from their desire to know what he had hidden, Hisda opened his hand to prove the folly of curiosity (Shab. 140b).

A person should never pray in a dirty or elevated place. According to Hisda, if one is walking in a dirty alley, he should not recite the *Shema*; if he is reciting his prayers while walking and realizes that he is in a filthy area, he should stop (Ber. 24b). Clarifying the statement of R. Huna, "Whoever prays at the rear of a synagogue is called wicked" (Ber. 6a), Hisda observed that this statement applied only to one who remained at the rear entrance near the door, lest it appear that he was anxious to leave (Ber. 8a). He believed that, since the destruction of the Temple, "All gates [for prayer] are locked, except for those through which pass the cries of people who have been wronged" (BM 59a).

Hisda offered advice to his poor students: "When a scholar has but little bread, let him not eat vegetables, because it whets [the craving for food]. I did not eat vegetables when poor or when rich. When poor, because vegetables excite the appetite [which I could not satisfy]; when rich, because I would rather eat fish and meat [which are more nutritious]." However, when purchasing vegetables, Hisda urged that they "buy long ones, for one bunch is like another [in thickness], and so the length comes of itself [i.e., the additional length is extra value, since presumably the price was not increased]" (Shab. 140b). He noted, "A dish of beets is beneficial for the heart and good for the eyes and even more so for the bowels" (Ber. 39a). Hisda recommended that a scholar who has only a little bread should not divide it into small portions, but instead should eat it all at one time so that he would be satisfied at least once during the day. He accused one who can eat barley bread but instead consumes bread made from more expensive wheat as being wastefully extravagant and violating the commandment "You shall not destroy" (Deut. 20:19). He also suggested: "If a scholar buys raw meat he should buy the neck, because it contains three types of meat [fatty, lean, and tough sinews]"; "A scholar should not sit upon a new mat, because it ruins his clothing [since it is hard]"; and "A scholar should not send his garments to his hostess [the keeper of the boardinghouse where he stays] for washing, for this is not in good taste, lest she see something [a euphemism for semen] on it and he will become repulsive to her" (Shab. 140b).

Always friendly, Hisda went out of his way to be the first to greet everyone, including heathens, in the marketplace (Git. 62a). Believing in the value of introspection, Hisda remarked: "If a man finds himself plagued by great pain, let him examine his conduct" (Ber. 5a).

Hisda devised a series of ingenious analogies to derive the biblical sources for rabbinic statements. For example, the Talmud asks why the Mishnah permitted a person to go 2,000 cubits (3,000 feet) away from his place on the Sabbath, whereas the Torah explicitly states, "Let no man leave his place on the seventh day" (Exod. 21:13). Hisda observed that the word "place" (*makom*) was also found in the verse, "And I shall set up a place for you" (Exod. 21:13), which referred to the cities of refuge to which a person who committed an accidental murder could flee to escape the blood avenger. How far may one "flee"? Another verse explained, "Beyond the boundary of his city of refuge, to which he flees" (Num. 35:26), so that the word "boundary" can be seen as equivalent to the original phrase, "Let no man leave his place." Elsewhere it is stated, "And you shall measure for the east side 2,000 cubits outside the city" (Num. 35:5). Using a chain of comparisons with the words "outside, border, flee, and place," Hisda concluded that the maximum a person can go on the Sabbath is 2,000 cubits (Er. 51a).

Hisda utilized a similar comparison of words found in various biblical verses to conclude that the law of "searching out leaven" before Passover was to be performed with one candle. One biblical verse commands, "For seven days there shall be no leaven found in your house" (Exod. 12:9), while in the story of Joseph's cup found in the sack of his younger brother, it is written: "And he searched, beginning with the eldest and ending with the youngest, and the cup was found [in Benjamin's sack]" (Gen. 44:12), proving that "finding" and "searching" are linked together. Another verse dealing with searching says, "I will search Jerusalem with candles" (Zeph. 1:12), indicating that searching means using candles. Finally, to determine the number of candles to use, he cited a verse from Proverbs (20:27): "The spirit of man is the candle of the Lord, searching all the innermost parts of the belly." Combining all these observations, Hisda concluded that to properly document that there was no leaven in the house, one must search for it with a single candle (Pes. 7b).

Hisda also deduced: "One praying on behalf of another need not mention his name," based on the prayer of Moses for God to heal his sister—"Please God, heal her now" (Num. 12:13)—in which he never mentioned the name of Miriam (i.e., God knows for whom a prayer is meant without the need to mention the person's name) (Ber. 34a).

Although fearing that his words might prompt some of his students to leave him, Hisda advocated that students sample multiple teachers: "He who learns the Law from [only] one master will never achieve great success" (Av. Zar. 19a). Time devoted to sleep was not available for learning: "The daughters of R. Hisda once asked their father [who spent his nights in prayer and study], 'Would not the Master like to sleep a little?' He replied, 'Soon will come days that are long and short' [i.e., the days in the grave are long in quantity but short in quality, since there one cannot continue his studies or perform any other *mitzvot*]" (Er. 65a).

Many folk practices have evolved for preventing or counteracting the Evil Eye. Believing that the most frequent cause of the Evil Eye was jealousy, the Rabbis offered several practical measures to avoid engendering envy in others. They warned against excessive praise, especially of children, and ostentatious displays of riches. For example, Hisda noted: "If the firstborn child is a daughter, it is a good sign for sons that are born subsequently. Some explain that this is because she rears her brothers; but others say it is because the Evil Eye has no influence over them" (BB 141a). Because sons were so highly valued, the birth of a male child first might cause the envy of other women, who either were childless or only had daughters.

According to Hisda, "A bad dream is better than a good dream," because the anxiety it produces serves as a reprimand that spurs one to repentance. In the case of a good dream, "The pleasure of the dream is enough even if it is not fulfilled" (Ber. 55a).

When a father who refused to support his child was brought before him, Hisda would say: "Make a public pronouncement and proclaim, 'The raven cares for its young, but this man does not care for his children'" (Ket. 49b).

In a legend similar to that involving King David (Shab. 30b), the Talmud notes that Hisda was so devoted to his studies that the Angel of Death, who is powerless to take a person who is studying, "could not approach him." To create a diversion, the Angel of Death "perched on a cedar just outside the school house. As the tree cracked under him, Hisda paused [in his studies] and the Angel overpowered him" (Mak. 10a). *See also* Huna; Rabbah bar Shila; Rafram bar Papa; Rava; Zerika.

Hiyya, Palestinian *tanna* (second century).

Also called Rabbah (the Great), Hiyya was born in Babylonia but moved to the Land of Israel, settling in Tiberias, where he established a thriving silk business. The Talmud relates that Hiyya was "constantly tormented by his wife," who suffered such pains giving birth to twin sons (who later became famous sages) that she drank a sterilizing potion and became barren. Nevertheless, he regularly brought her gifts, believing that husbands should be grateful to their wives for raising the children and keeping them from sin (Yev. 63a, 65b). In contrast to several of his colleagues, who stated that a wife received her maintenance by being effectively a bondwoman of her husband, Hiyya taught that menial tasks would have an adverse effect on her womanly grace. "A wife [should be taken] mainly for the sake of her beauty and having children . . . [and] for the wearing of a woman's finery. He who wishes his wife to look graceful should clothe her in linen garments. He who wishes his daughter to have a bright complexion on the approach of her maturity should feed her with young fowls and give her milk to drink" (Ket. 59b).

When at dinner with the illustrious Judah ha-Nasi, Hiyya's two sons, though learned, were too shy to speak. His guest gave them "plenty of strong wine so that they may say something," but once their tongues were loosened, their words angered the sage. To apologize for their behavior, Hiyya resorted to *gematria*, observing that the numerical value of the letters of the Hebrew words *yayin* (wine) and *sod* (secrets) are identical (70), for "when *yayin* [wine] goes in, *sod* [secrets] comes out" (Sanh. 38a). He also developed a special method for interpretation based on the transposition of letters, known as the "*Atbach*" of Hiyya (Suk. 52b).

An outstanding pupil of Judah ha-Nasi and considered second in learning only to him, Hiyya developed a school that was primarily involved with *beraitot*, *halachic* material that his master did not include in the Mishnah. Some of these were based on rulings that Hiyya heard directly from Judah ha-Nasi (JT BM 5:7), while others were opposite to what his master had taught (Ket. 59b). He ended his prayers with the following: "May it be Your will that our Torah may be our occupation, and that our heart may not be sick nor our eyes darkened" (Ber. 16b).

A superb educator, Hiyya often traveled to remote towns to instruct Jewish children, thus keeping Torah learning alive. "To make certain that the Torah would not be forgotten, what did I do? I sowed flax, and from the flax cords I made nets. With the nets, I trapped deer, gave their meat to orphans to eat, and used their skins to prepare scrolls. On these I wrote the Five Books of

Moses. Then I went to a town that had no teachers and taught each of the five books to five different children, and each of the six orders [of the Mishnah] to six different children. I told them, 'Until I return, teach each other the Torah and the Mishnah.' In this way, I kept the Torah from being forgotten in Israel" (BM 85b).

Hiyya believed that the Babylonian Jewish community should be treated with more respect by the Rabbis in the Land of Israel. As he stated, "God knows that Israel is unable to endure the cruel decrees of Edom [i.e., Rome], and therefore He exiled them to Babylonia" (Pes. 87b). Consequently, against the wishes of Judah ha-Nasi, Hiyya attempted to permit the Babylonian sages to be more independent of the central authority of the Land of Israel (Sanh. 5a). Acknowledging the rabbinic dictum that the Jewish worshiper should direct his prayers to the "Holy of Holies," Hiyya considered that this referred to the "Holy of Holies above [i.e., Heaven]," rather than to the site of the former Temple in Jerusalem. Similarly, he interpreted the name "Mount Moriah" (the site of the *Akedah*, the binding of Isaac) as the place "from which fear goes forth," rather than the traditional "from which teaching goes forth to the world" (JT Ber. 4:5). His statement, "You should not make the fence higher than the essential object [i.e., the Torah], lest it fall and destroy the shoot" (Gen. R. 19:3), was a warning against the rabbinic imposition of increasingly severe restrictions on Jewish life. Hiyya metaphorically compared the first rays of dawn to the future redemption of the Jews: "at first it comes gradually, but the longer it continues, the greater it becomes" (JT Ber. 1:1).

Hiyya was sensitive to the rabbinic abhorrence of putting another to shame. According to a classic legend, once when Rabbi (Judah ha-Nasi) was delivering a lecture, he noticed a smell of garlic and immediately ordered the person who had eaten it to leave the room. Hiyya arose and left, and then all the other scholars went out. In the morning, Rabbi's son asked Hiyya, "Was it [really] you who caused that annoying odor yesterday?" Hiyya replied, "Heaven forbid," implying that he and his fellow scholars had acted solely to save the real offender from humiliation (Sanh. 11a). Similarly, Hiyya said to Rav, "When Rabbi is engaged with one tractate [of the Mishnah] you must not ask him about another, lest he not be conversant with it and answer you incorrectly, so that you would have put him to shame. In this instance he gave you the correct answer [but this does not alter the general principle]" (Shab. 3b).

Among Hiyya's many recorded statements are: "Such is the punishment of a liar, that even if he tells the truth he is not listened to" (Sanh. 89b); and the practical economic advice, "A person should not put all his money in one corner" (Gen. R. 76:3). According to a popular belief among the Rabbis, from the time that Hiyya and his sons moved from Babylonia to the Land of Israel, "there ceased to be shooting stars, earthquakes, storms and thunders; their wines never turned sour, and their flax was never blighted" (Hul. 86a).

Hiyya's most eminent student was his nephew Rav, who founded the prestigious Babylonian academy at Sura. When Hiyya lectured, Rav served as his interpreter, expounding in a popular style on what his master had spoken (Yoma 20b). According to the Talmudic rating of their intellectual stature, "Rabbi [Judah ha-Nasi] was the tallest man in his generation and Hiyya reached to his shoulder; and Hiyya was the tallest in his generation and Rav reached to his shoulder" (Nid. 24b). *See also* Ammi.

Hiyya bar Abba, Palestinian *amora* (third century).

Although born in Babylonia of priestly descent, Hiyya bar Abba moved to the Land of Israel as a child. A poor man, Hiyya bar Abba was forced to take time from his studies to travel from town to town, lecturing for a small fee. His financial straits eventually eased when he was awarded a commission from the patriarch Judah II to collect money from the public to help with the expenses of the decaying patriarchate.

Hiyya bar Abba's major teacher was R. Yochanan, whom he quoted on several hundred occasions in the Talmud. He cited three statements of his teacher concerning the righteous (Yoma 38b): "No righteous man dies out of this world before another, like himself, is created, as it is said: 'The sun rises, and the sun goes down' [Eccles. 1:5]"; "[God] saw that the righteous are but few, and therefore He planted them throughout all generations," citing the verse, "For the pillars of the earth are the Lord's; He has set the world upon them (1 Sam. 2:8)"; and "Even for the sake of a single righteous man does the world endure," for "the righteous is the foundation of the world [or 'an everlasting foundation' [Prov. 10:25]." On this same page of Talmud, Hiyya bar Abba also quoted his teacher as saying, "When the majority of a man's years have passed without sin [i.e., resisting some temptation], he will sin no more." Later he cited his teacher's comments on the historical development of the Havdalah ceremony that concludes the Sabbath. Initially, the Men of the Great Assembly inserted the Havdalah prayers into the *Amidah*. However, when the Israelites prospered and could afford wine, they instituted the practice that Havdalah be recited over a cup of wine. But when Israel again became poor, they replaced the prayer into the *Amidah*, but decreed that the person who says Havdalah "must [also] say it over the cup [of wine]" (Ber. 33a). Hiyya bar Abba also said in the name of his teacher, "All the prophets foretold only what will occur in the days of the Messiah [the ideal future state here on earth]. But as for the World to Come, no eye except Yours, O God, has seen" (Ber. 34b).

Hiyya bar Abba stated, "A father and son, or a master and disciple, even if they argue vigorously for their opinions while studying Torah [lit., 'become enemies of each other'], they do not part until they come to love each other" (Kid. 30b).

When R. Abbahu lectured on *aggadah* in the same city where Hiyya bar Abba was teaching *halachah*, virtually everyone went to hear the former. Afterward, R. Abbahu consoled his distraught colleague with a parable comparing two merchants, one who was selling precious jewels and the other inexpensive trinkets. "To whom would the people run [lit., 'the buyers descend']? Would it not be to the seller of cheaper goods?" (Sot. 40a).

Nevertheless, several *aggadic* statements are attributed to Hiyya bar Abba. For example, he interpreted the verse, "They have forsaken Me and not kept My law" (Jer. 16:11) as meaning, "Would they were to forsake Me, as long as they keep My law, for as a result of occupying themselves with it, its light will bring them back to the right path" (Lam. R., Proem 2). He also believed, "A meal without soup is no meal" (Ber. 44a).

The Talmud relates examples of Rabbis bringing about a cure by taking the hand of a sick person. When Hiyya bar Abba fell ill, R. Yochanan visited and asked the ailing sage, "Are your sufferings welcome to you?" From his sickbed, Hiyya bar Abba replied, "Neither they nor their reward [i.e., the implication that if one lovingly submits to his sufferings, he will receive a great reward in the World to Come]." Then R. Yochanan cured his colleague by the touch of his hand. When R. Yochanan later became ill, R. Hanina performed a similar service. The Talmud asks why, if he could cure Hiyya bar Abba, R. Yochanan could not heal himself. The answer: "The prisoner cannot free himself from jail [and similarly, the patient cannot cure himself]" (Ber. 5b).

Hiyya bar Abba stated, "The Sabbath was given for enjoyment," while R. Samuel bar Nachmani said, "The Sabbath was given for studying." How could these two comments be reconciled? Hiyya referred to scholars who spent the week studying Torah; when the Sabbath came, they enjoyed themselves. In contrast, Samuel bar Nachmani was speaking about laborers, who were so busy with their work all week that only on the Sabbath did they have time to study Torah (Pes. Rab. 117b). *See also* Ahhabu of Caesarea; Yochanan.

Hiyya bar Ammi, Babylonian *amora* (fourth century).

A student of R. Ulla, Hiyya bar Ammi quoted his teacher as saying, "A man who lives from the labor [of his hands] is [far] greater than one who fears Heaven [but relies for his living on the help of other people]." As justification for this claim, he noted: "With regard to the one who fears Heaven it is written, 'Happy is the man who fears the Lord' [Ps. 112:1]; whereas with regard to the man who lives from his own work it is written, "When you eat the labor of your hands, you shall be happy [in this world] and you shall prosper [in the World to Come]' [Ps. 128:2]" (Ber. 8a). He continued, "A man should always live in the same town as his teacher," explaining that out of respect for his teacher, Solomon did not marry the daughter of Pharaoh while his teacher was alive.

Hiyya bar Ashi, Palestinian *amora* (third century).

In virtually all his Talmudic citations, Hiyya bar Ashi quoted his teacher, Rav. As an example, "The disciples of the wise have no rest either in this world or in the World to Come [because they are always striving to progress spiritually]," based on the verse, "They go from strength to strength, every one of them appears before God in Zion" (Ber. 64a). He also noted, "In the time to come, all the wild trees of the Land of Israel will bear fruit," a statement based on the verse in Joel (2:22), "For the wild tree has borne its fruit, the fig tree and the vine have yielded their strength" (Ket. 112b); and "One who regularly eats small fish will not suffer with his bowels. Moreover, small fish stimulate propagation and strengthen a man's whole body" (Ber. 40a).

In the name of Rav, Hiyya bar Ashi observed: "Three things should follow immediately one on the other. The killing [of the sacrifice] should follow immediately on the laying on of hands [*semichah*]; *Tefillah* [the *Amidah*] should follow immediately after *ge'ulah* [the blessing concluding *ga'al Yisrael*; 'Who redeems Israel']; and grace [after meals] should follow immediately after the washing of hands" (Ber. 42a). He added, "Whoever washes his hands first at the end of the meal has the right to say grace" (Ber. 46b). Explaining the reason for washing the hands after a meal, Hiyya bar Ashi explained: "Because there exists a certain salt of Sodom [used during the meal] that causes blindness [and washing removes it from the fingers that may have touched it]" (Er. 17b).

Hiyya bar Rav, Babylonian *amora* (third century).

The Talmud relates several items of practical advice that Hiyya bar Rav was given by his illustrious father and teacher. "Do not take drugs [even as medicine, because they are habit forming], and do not jump straight into a pool of water [or 'do not jump over a brook,' because the strain affects the eyesight]. Do not have a tooth extracted [a toothache will eventually stop], and do not provoke serpents or quarrel with a heathen [lit., 'a Syrian woman']" (Pes. 113a). Rav also counseled his son: "If you are invited to eat porridge, [you may even go] a parasang [ancient Persian unit of distance, equal to about 3.5 miles] for it; to eat beef, even three parasangs. You must never expectorate before your teacher, except [after eating] a pumpkin or porridge, because they are like lead pellets [i.e., it is dangerous to swallow the saliva left in the mouth after consuming these]; expectorate this even in the presence of King Shapur [of Persia]" (Ket. 77a; Ned. 49b).

Honi the Circle-Drawer, renowned miracle worker in the Second Temple period (first century B.C.E.).

Honi's name relates to a Talmudic tale (Taan. 19a) describing how his prayers for rain were answered. When the people asked him to pray for rain, Honi prayed but no rain fell. He then drew a circle and stood within it, exclaiming to God that he would not move from it until God showed mercy to His children and let it rain. When a few drops fell, Honi protested that this was not enough, whereupon there was a torrential downpour. Once again Honi exclaimed that he had prayed for a rain of blessing and bounty, and rain then fell in the normal way. R. Shimon ben Shetach then sent a message to Honi: "Had it been anyone else but you I would have had him excommunicated for practicing witchcraft. But what can I do to you after you implored God and He acceded to your request? You are just like a child before an indulgent father who begs his father one moment to give him a warm bath, then asks for a cold shower. Then the child requests nuts, almonds, peaches, and pomegranates. Whatever he wants, his father gives him. Of you Scripture says, 'Your father and mother will rejoice; she who bore you will exult' [Prov. 23:25]" (Taan. 23a).

Another classic tale involving Honi begins with R. Yochanan relating, "All his life that righteous man [Honi] was troubled by the biblical verse, 'When the Lord restored those who returned to Zion we were like dreamers' [Ps. 126:1]. He thought, 'How can seventy years compare to a dream [that lasts] one night?'" Honi once chided an elderly man for planting a carob tree, since he surely would not live the seventy years necessary before it would bear fruit. The old man replied: "Just as I found [ready grown] carob trees when I came into the world, so I am now planting carob trees for my grandchildren to enjoy." After eating a meal, Honi went to sleep. "As he slept a rocky formation enclosed upon him, hiding him from sight, and Honi continued to sleep for seventy years. When he awoke he saw a man gathering the fruit of the carob tree and he asked him, 'Are you the man who planted the tree?' The man replied: 'I am his grandson.' Honi exclaimed: 'It is clear that I slept for seventy years.' Returning to his home, he asked, 'Is the son of Honi the Circle-Drawer still alive?' The people answered, 'His son is no more, but his grandson is still living.' When Honi identified himself as the Circle-Drawer, no one would believe him. Entering the study hall, Honi overheard the scholars saying, 'the law is as clear to us as in the days of Honi the Circle-Drawer, for whenever he came to the study hall he would settle for the scholars any difficulty that they had.' Honi again identified himself, but the scholars would not believe him nor give the honor due to him. Honi was deeply hurt and his prayer for death was granted" (Taan. 23a).

In one anachronistic version of this tale, Honi lived during the final days of the First Temple and slept throughout the years of the Babylonian Exile, awakening only when the Jews began to return to the Land of Israel and build the Second Temple (JT Taan. 9:1). This enabled Honi to understand the puzzling biblical verse, for just as he did not sense the passing of time, so the exiles who returned to Zion after seventy years felt as if they had awakened after a short dream.

According to Josephus (Antiquities 14:22), a courageous act led to Honi's murder. During the period of fratricidal warfare between the Hasmonean brothers, Hyrcanus besieged Jerusalem while Aristobulus was encamped on the Temple Mount. Soldiers of Hyrcanus captured Honi and ordered him to pray to God to curse Aristobulus and make them victorious. However, Honi prayed: "Master of the Universe, [have mercy on both sides]. These men are Your people, and those who are besieged are Your priests; I pray that You shall not do what they ask [i.e., heed the curses of one against the other]." Furious, the soldiers of Hyrcanus stoned Honi to death.

Honi's only surviving ethical teaching is: "If a man does not enjoy the society of his fellows, it is as if he were dead."

Huna, Babylonian *amora* (third century).

Succeeding his teacher Rav as head of the academy of Sura, Huna continued in this position for four decades until his death around 296. Renowned for both his wisdom and piety and always referred to without his patronymic, Huna was the undisputed leader during the period when scholars in the Babylonian academies became equal in authority to those in the Land of Israel (Git. 6a). "Huna's discourses were so popular that he routinely spoke to 800 students and was assisted by thirteen 'interpreters' (*meturgemen*), each of whom repeated his words loudly in the vernacular to a section of the crowded audience." So large was the number of devoted disciples who sat learning at his feet that it was said: "When the Rabbis stood up after Huna's discourses and shook out their garments, the dust rose [so high] that it obscured the [light of] day even in the West [Land of Israel]" (Ket. 106a). Huna and his colleague R. Hisda were called "the pious ones of Babylon" (Taan. 23b).

Although related to the family of the exilarch, Huna was so poor at the beginning of his career that he was forced to pawn his belt and use a rope instead, in order to have money to buy wine for consecrating the Sabbath. Hearing this story, Rav exclaimed, "May it be the will of heaven that you be [one day] smothered in robes of silk" (Meg. 27b). When his teacher Rav blessed him with riches, Huna demonstrated great generosity. Before sitting down to a meal, Huna would open the door wide and invite anyone who was hungry to join him (Taan. 20b). An expanded version of Huna's Aramaic invitation is found near the beginning of the Passover Haggadah: "Whoever is hungry, let him come and eat. Whoever is needy, let him come and celebrate Passover."

At that time, a judge who was not paid by the community for his services and was forced to take time off from his usual occupation to preside over a court was permitted to accept a fee, as long as it was paid equally by both parties in the litigation (i.e., considered as just compensation rather than a bribe). Thus, whenever Huna would hold court, he would say to the litigants: "Provide me with a man who will irrigate my fields in my place and I will take up your case" (Ket. 105a).

Huna is cited more than 2,500 times in the Talmud, offering numerous *halachot* in his name and that of Rav, of whom he observed: "We have an established rule that in ritual matters the law is in agreement with Rav, regardless of whether this leads to a relaxation or a restriction" (Nid. 24b). Almost all of the *amoraim* of the succeeding generation transmitted his teachings. Similarly, Huna was esteemed in the Land of Israel, where R. Ammi and R. Assi, the religious leaders of Tiberias, accepted his authority (Git. 59b).

Huna expounded on a broad range of topics, including the proper time to search for *hametz* (leaven) on the day before Passover (Pes. 2a, 3a), the correct height of an *eruv* (Er. 84a, 88a), proper behavior in synagogue (Ber. 24b), and who may or may not blow the shofar for others (RH 29a). Among his many sayings are: "He who occupies himself only with the study of the Torah [and does not act generously toward his fellows] is like a man who has no God" (Av. Zar. 17b); "When a man sins once and twice [without any consequences], it appears to him as if it is permitted [i.e., that his behavior is acceptable]" (Yoma 86b); and "He who is accustomed to honor the Sabbath with light will have children who are scholars; he who is observant of [the commandment of the] *mezuzah* will merit a beautiful dwelling; he who observes the rule of *tzitzit* [fringes] will have fine clothes; and he who consecrates the Sabbath and the holy days will be privileged to fill many barrels of wine [i.e., will be wealthy]" (Shab. 23b). According to Huna, if two witnesses gave evidence in the exact same words, he would thoroughly investigate their testimony since it was likely unreliable. However, if they told the identical story in different words, he was confident that they were telling the truth (JT Sanh. 3).

"Every Friday afternoon before the Sabbath, Huna would send a servant to the market to buy up any vegetables that had not been sold and throw them into the river. [This protected the growers against loss and made them willing to bring an abundant supply of produce to the market on Friday, which otherwise they could not have sold again until Sunday, by which time it would have begun to wilt and spoil (Rashi).] Should he not instead have distributed them among the poor? He feared that they would learn to rely on his gifts, rather than coming to the market to buy their own goods. Why did he not give the vegetables to the domestic animals? He believed that food meant [by God] for people should not be degraded by being given to animals. Then why did he buy them at all? Huna feared that if the food were not purchased, the farmers would lower their supply and raise their prices in the future, thus causing a hardship for the poor" (Taan. 20b).

Huna declared: "For four merits were the Israelites delivered from Egypt: Because they did not change their names, change their language, or inform against one another; and because there was no sexual immorality among them. They did not change their names—Reuben and Shimon they went down to Egypt, and as Reuben and Shimon they went up from it. They did not call Reuben 'Rufus,' nor did they call Shimon 'Luliani,' nor Joseph 'Listis,' nor Benjamin 'Alexander.' They did not change their language—in another context it is written, 'A fugitive brought the news to Abraham the Hebrew,' and later it is written, 'The God of the Hebrews has met with us' [implying that Hebrew remained the language of the people]" (Song R. 4:12).

To solve the frequent problem in small communities where one person was needed to complete a *minyan*, some authorities permitted a minor holding a Torah, or merely being present with the Torah in the ark, to be counted as the tenth person (JT Ber. 7:2). Huna was quoted as saying that if nine adults were present, the ark could be counted as the tenth person so that a full service could be held. However, he later qualified this to mean, "If nine look like ten, they may be joined together" (so the absence of one is not so noticeable) (Ber. 47b). However, these ingenious innovations never received widespread support.

Huna said, "Whoever has a fixed place for his prayer has the God of Abraham as his helper. And when he dies, people will say of him: 'Where is the pious man, where is the humble man, one of the disciples of our father Abraham?'" (Ber. 6b). He also noted, "Whoever prays at the rear of a synagogue is called wicked" (Ber. 6a), though R. Hisda clarified this statement to apply only to one who remained at the rear entrance, lest it appear that he was anxious to leave (Ber. 8a). Other sayings of Huna (all cited by R. Helbo) include: "When a man leaves the synagogue, he should not take large steps" (Ber. 6b); and "If one knows that his friend is used to greet him, let him greet him first [based on the verse, 'Seek peace and pursue it'; Ps. 34:15]; and if his friend greets him and he does not return the greeting, he is called a robber" (Ber. 6b).

The dictum that employees must be paid a fair wage was illustrated in the tale of Huna, who had 400 barrels of wine that turned into vinegar. Hearing of this, several sages urged Huna to "examine his actions," implying that he might have deserved his misfortune through some sin. When Huna asked whether they were accusing him of some wrongdoing, they calmly replied, "Shall we then suspect the Holy One of punishing unjustly?" After having heard rumors that "The Master did not give his tenant-farmer his lawful share of the vintage," Huna angrily retorted: "Did he leave me any? He stole it all [i.e., he took more than his rightful share]!" The other sages reminded him of the proverb, "Whoever steals from a thief is also a thief." Stung by this rebuke, Huna admitted that he underpaid his tenant-farmer and shamefully said, "From now on I promise to give him his proper share." There are two endings to this story. In one, the vinegar became wine again; in the other, the price of vinegar rose dramatically until it cost as much as wine (Ber. 5b).

God highly regards even the smallest meritorious acts, and the Talmud recounts incidents in which seemingly miraculous occurrences were attributed to the great merit of prominent Rabbis, but actually were related to less-esteemed persons. "Once a large fire that miraculously did not spread to the neighborhood where Huna lived was attributed to his great merit." However, it was really "due to the merit of a certain woman who [on the eve of Sabbaths] would heat her oven and permit her neighbors to use it [to bake bread, without accepting any compensation]" (Taan. 21b).

The Talmud relates that when Huna died, the Rabbis wanted to place a Torah scroll on his bier. However, they refrained from doing this when informed by R. Hisda that Huna did not approve of this practice. In his eulogy, R. Abba quoted Huna as saying that he "was worthy that the *Shechinah* [Divine Presence] should rest upon him, but [the fact of his being in] Babylonia prevented it" (MK 25a). *See also* Adda bar Ahava; Hamnuna II; Helbo; Rafram bar Papa; Sheshet; Ulla; Zerika.

Huna bar Hinena, Babylonian *amora* (fourth century).

The exilarch wanted to have a banquet at a dining hall in his orchard on the Sabbath. However, taking food from his house to the garden area would violate the Sabbath prohibition against carrying from the private to the public domain. Consequently, he asked Huna bar Hinena: "Will the Master make some provision whereby we might be able to dine there tomorrow?" Huna bar Hinena accordingly constructed a passage from the house to the banquet hall by putting up a reed fence on either side, with the reeds spaced closely enough that the passage assumed the status of a domain in which it was permitted to move objects on the Sabbath (Er. 25b).

Huna bar Joshua, Babylonian *amora* (fourth century).

When his close friend and business partner, R. Papa, became head of the academy at Naresh, Huna bar Joshua joined him as *rosh kallah* (head of the general assembly) (Ber. 57a). His most famous saying is: "May I be rewarded [by God] for never walking more than four cubits bareheaded" (Shab. 118b), one of the proof texts used for wearing a *kippah*. A notoriously slow eater, it was said that during the same time that Huna bar Joshua ate, Papa and Ravina consumed four and eight times as much, respectively (Pes. 89b). Among the *halachic* debates in which Huna bar Joshua participated were discussions of how mourning is to be observed on a festival (MK 19b) and whether it is permissible to light one lamp from another on the Sabbath (Shab. 22b). *See also* Sheshet.

Huna bar Nathan, Babylonian *amora* (fourth century).

In a discussion on the requirement that the "benediction of the bridegroom" must be said in the presence of ten persons (*minyan*), Huna bar Nathan derived the rule from the verse in Ruth (4:2), in which "he [Boaz] took ten elders of the town and said, 'Be seated here'" (Ket. 7a). Huna bar Nathan was the subject of a debate concerning the rabbinic concept of proper etiquette at mealtime. Invited to dine at the home of R. Nachman bar Isaac, he responded "Rav Huna" (mentioning his rabbinic title) when other guests asked his name. When beckoned to "sit down on the couch," he complied, even though at that time this was an honor reserved for distinguished persons. Asked why he did as requested rather than the common practice for ordinary guests to sit on stools, Huna bar Nathan replied, "Whatever your host tells you, do." In the sequence that followed, he accepted wine at its first offering from another distinguished guest rather than waiting for a second invitation ("because one must not refuse a great man") and "drank it in two drafts without turning his face away [while drinking]." As Huna bar Nathan later explained, he was taught that "One who drinks his cup in one draft is a guzzler; in two drafts, is following proper manners; in three drafts, is arrogant," and that "only a bride averts her face [but not others]" (Pes. 86b).

Hutzpit the Interpreter, Palestinian *tanna* (second century).

Hutzpit the Interpreter was one of the Ten Martyrs slain by the Romans for defying the prohibition against the teaching of Torah. As an interpreter, Hutzpit stood next to a sage teaching Torah and was responsible for translating the Hebrew words into the Aramaic vernacular and explaining their meaning to the audience. According to legend, before killing Hutzpit, the executioner cut out his tongue and threw it away. When the sages later saw dogs carrying the tongue, they wailed "The tongue that poured forth pearls lay in the dust" (Kid. 39b, Hul. 142a).

I

Ilai I, Palestinian *tanna* (second century).

He was sometimes referred to as Ilai the Elder, to distinguish him from an *amora* of the same name (Hag. 16a). The father of the well-known *tanna*, Judah ben Ilai, his major teacher was R. Eliezer ben Hyrcanus. Ilai I is best known for two sayings, the first of which is a Hebrew pun: "A person's character can be judged by three things: by his cup [*bekoso*; the effect of drink on his mind, or the amount he consumes]; by his purse [*bekiso*; the amount of money he spends on charitable causes, or how he deals in money matters]; and by his anger [*beka'aso*]" (Er. 65b). Referring to this last indication, Pirkei Avot (5:14) maintains: "There are four types of temperament: (a) one who is easily angered and easily appeased—his gain is offset by his loss; (b) one who is hard to anger and hard to appease—his loss is offset by his gain; (c) one who is hard to anger and easy to appease—the saint; and (d) one who is easily angered and hard to appease—the wicked."

The other saying of Ilai I is a sober view of the human condition: "If a man sees that his evil inclination (*yetzer ha-ra*) is conquering him [i.e., he cannot control his sexual urge], he should go to a place where he is unknown, dress in black clothes [either because somber garments may subdue his lust or this was the sign of a discredited Roman official], and do as his heart desires, rather than publicly profane the Name of God [by sinning where he was known]" (Kid. 40a; MK 17a).

Ilai I was the source for the *halachic* ruling that the laws governing the first fleece sheared from the sheep (Deut. 18:4) do not apply to countries outside the Land of Israel (Hul. 136a).

Ilai II, Palestinian *amora* (third/fourth century).

Ilai II said that it was permissible to "modify a statement [i.e., tell a lie] in the interests of peace" (Yev. 65b). As an illustration, he cited the statement of Joseph's brothers, who related that their father Jacob, before he died, had commanded them to tell Joseph to forgive their past sins (Gen. 50:16–17). Even though there is no indication in the text that Jacob had done so, the brothers were permitted to attribute the request to him for the sake of preserving peace between themselves and Joseph.

Ilai II believed in the importance of self-control: "The world exists only on account of [the merit of] those who restrain themselves in strife [challenging situations]" (Hul. 89a). The Jerusalem Talmud (JT Betz. 5:2) relates that on one Friday Ilai II was compelled to work at the academy until late in the evening. Returning home and finding the entrance barred and his family asleep, he spent the night on the steps of his house rather than knock on the gate and desecrate the Sabbath.

Ilfa (Ilfi), Palestinian *amora* (third century).

According to the Talmud, Ilfa and R. Yochanan studied the Torah together. "Finding themselves in financial distress, they said to each other: 'Let us go and engage in commerce [become business partners]' so that we may fulfill the verse, 'That there be no needy among you' (Deut. 15:4)." While sitting and eating under a crumbling wall, two ministering angels came by and R. Yochanan overheard one saying to the other, "Let us throw this wall upon these [people] and kill them, because they occupy themselves with temporal matters and forsake eternal life." The other angel disagreed: "Leave them alone because one of them has still much to achieve." R. Yochanan heard this conversation, but Ilfa did not. Consequently, R. Yochanan concluded that he must be the one who still had much to achieve. Citing the verse, "For there will never cease to be needy ones in your land" (Deut. 15:11), R. Yochanan left Ilfa and went back alone to the study hall. When Ilfa finally returned years later, R. Yochanan had become the head of the school. His disciples observed to Ilfa, "Had you remained here and studied Torah you might have been presiding [as head of the academy]." Ilfa then suspended himself from the mast of a ship and exclaimed, "If I am asked any *baraita* and cannot find an allusion to it in a mishnah, I will cast myself into the sea and drown," but his life was spared as he succeeded in finding all of them (Taan. 21a).

Once during a drought, Judah ha-Nasi ordered a fast, but no rain fell. Famed for his piety, Ilfa prayed before the ark, "He causes the wind to blow and the rain to fall," and immediately the wind blew and the rain began to fall. When Judah ha-Nasi asked, "What is your special merit?" Ilfa replied: "I live in a poverty-stricken remote place where wine for *Kiddush* and Havdalah is unobtainable, but I take the trouble to procure these items and thus help others to also fulfill their duty" (Taan. 24a).

The Talmud relates that Ilfa "contrasted two phrases [from the Divine Attributes of Mercy]—'abundant in goodness' and 'in truth'—At first, 'truth', and at the end 'abundant in goodness.'" (RH 17b). Although ideally God should rule the world according to absolute truth, human beings, given their inherent moral failings, could not survive. Therefore, God substituted the attribute of mercy in His relations with mortal men.

Imma Shalom, wife of R. Eliezer ben Hyrcanus and the sister of Rabban Gamaliel II (first/second century).

Receiving a superb education, Imma Shalom was described as one of the most brilliant women of Talmudic times. Despite his antagonism against educating women ("Whoever teaches his daughter it is as though he taught her lewdness"; Sot. 3:4), R. Eliezer ben Hyrcanus appreciated Imma Shalom's intellectual accomplishments and even discussed the tradition with her. In one variant of an *aggadic* tale, Imma Shalom overheard a skeptic taunting her brother: "Your God is not strictly honest, or He would not have stolen a rib from sleeping Adam" (Gen. 2:21). She urged the skeptic to immediately call a policeman, because on the previous evening she was robbed of a silver bowl by a thief who left a gold one in its place. When the skeptic replied that he wished "that thief would visit me every day!" she retorted: "You objected to the removal of the rib from sleeping Adam! Did he not receive in exchange a woman to wait on him?"

The marriage of Imma Shalom and R. Eliezer ben Hyrcanus was blessed with extraordinarily handsome children. Imma Shalom attributed this to the fact that "He [my husband] does not 'converse' [i.e., have sexual relations] either at the beginning or at the end of the night, but only at midnight [when no other woman would be on the street]" (Ned. 20a). As one Rabbi warned, "One may not drink out of one goblet and think of another [i.e., sleep with one woman and fantasize about another]" (Ned. 20a–b).

The Talmud relates that a certain "philosopher" (sectarian) in Imma Shalom's neighborhood was a judge who had the undeserved reputation of never accepting bribes. Attempting to expose him (lit., "make sport of him") by showing his true character, Imma Shalom and her brother contrived a lawsuit concerning the division of the estate inherited from their father, Rabban Shimon ben Gamaliel I. Before submitting the case, Imma Shalom brought a golden lamp (as a bribe) to the judge, who ruled that the estate should be divided equally. Rabban Gamaliel II protested that the Torah clearly stated that where there is a son, the daughter does not inherit. But the judge retorted, "Since the day that you were exiled from your land, the law of Moses has been superseded by a new law stating that a son and daughter inherit equally." The next day, Rabban Gamaliel II sent him a Libyan ass (as a more expensive bribe). When the siblings again came before the judge, he had "reconsidered" his view, arguing that he had looked further into the book, where it was written: "I did not come to subtract from the law of Moses but to add to it," so that the daughter does not inherit where there is a son." Imma Shalom declared, "Let your light shine forth like a lamp [an allusion to the lamp that she had presented to him on the preceding day]," while Rabban Gamaliel II remarked, "An ass came and kicked over the lamp!"

After her brother Rabban Gamaliel II excommunicated her husband R. Eliezer ben Hyrcanus, Imma Shalom feared that God would answer her husband's prayers against her brother. Therefore, she asked R. Eliezer ben Hyrcanus not to offer the Tachanun prayer calling for deliverance from enemies. Her husband complied with her request, and she reminded him of it at the proper time each day. Forgetting to do so one morning and finding R. Eliezer ben Hyrcanus in the midst of the prayer, Imma Shalom was disconsolate: "Cease, you have killed my brother!" Soon afterward, Rabban Gamaliel II died. When asked why Imma Shalom had expected such dire consequences, she replied that there was a tradition in her family that while all other gates of prayer are sometimes locked, "the gates of wounded feelings [cries of oppression] are never closed" (BM 59b).

Isaac bar Joseph, Palestinian *amora* (fourth century).

A student of R. Abbahu and R. Jeremiah, Isaac bar Joseph transmitted numerous statements of the R. Yochanan (Jeremiah's teacher) on a broad variety of issues. When Isaac bar Joseph emigrated to Babylonia, he brought with him many *halachic* decisions from the Land of Israel and became a close friend of R. Abbaye. Visiting the Babylonian sage on a festival, Isaac bar Joseph saw him reciting a blessing over each cup of wine during a meal, contrary to the ruling of R. Joshua ben Levi. When asked about this practice, R. Abbaye replied: "I have just changed my mind [i.e., he had not intended to take more wine after the meal]" (Ber. 42b).

Citing R. Yochanan, Isaac bar Joseph stated that a man who sends an agent to contract a marriage, without specifying the precise woman, becomes forbidden to marry any woman. The reason: "It is presumed that the messenger carries out his commission, and since he did not specify [the woman], he does not know which [woman] he betrothed for him" (Naz. 11b–12a).

Isaac bar Mesharsheya, Babylonian *amora* (fourth/fifth century).

Isaac bar Mesharsheya is best known for his actions when invited for a meal at the home of R. Ashi, where "he was served with cheese, which he ate, and then was served with meat, which he also ate without washing his hands [between the courses]." When a colleague cited the ruling that "a fowl and cheese may be eaten without restriction," but not meat and cheese, Isaac bar Mesharsheya replied: "That is the rule only at night. But by day I can see [that my hands are clean and thus there is no reason to wash them between courses]" (Hul. 104b).

Isaac Nappacha, Palestinian *amora* (third/fourth century).

Usually mentioned in the Talmud simply as R. Isaac, Isaac Nappacha (whose patronymic referred to his occupation as a blacksmith, *nappacha* in

Aramaic) lived in Tiberias with his master R. Yochanan, becoming recognized as both a *halachic* and *aggadic* authority. Once when R. Ammi and R. Assi were sitting before Isaac Nappacha, one asked for *halachic* instruction. When Isaac Nappacha complied and began a legal discourse as requested, he was prevented from continuing by the other, who was adamant that Isaac Nappacha instead lecture on *aggadah*. The sage then responded with the following parable: "A man had two wives, one young and one old. The younger wife pulled out his white hair [because she wanted her husband to look young], while the older wife pulled out his black hair [so that he would appear old]." Between the two of them, "the man became completely bald!" (BK 60b).

Isaac Nappacha stressed the value of *aggadah* as a way to encourage the people living through a particularly difficult time: "In the past, when money was plentiful, people used to yearn to study in Mishnah and Talmud. Now that money is in short supply, and we also suffer from the government, people want to be consoled by words of Scripture and *aggadah*" (PdRK 12:3).

During Talmudic times, certain local officials were appointed by the head of the Jewish community: the patriarch in the Land of Israel and the exilarch in Babylonia. The most important requirement was that their choices met with public approval. As Isaac Nappacha said, "We must not appoint a leader over a community without first consulting it." He offered a *midrash* based on the verse, "See, the Lord has called by name Bezalel, the son of Uri [to be the lead architect for the Tabernacle]" (Exod. 35:30). When God asked Moses if he considered Bezalel suitable, Moses replied, "Sovereign of the Universe, if he is acceptable to You, surely he must also be to me!" But God persisted, "All the same, go and consult the people" (Ber. 55a). Similarly, "No law may be imposed on the people unless a majority of the community can endure it [i.e., is able to comply with its terms]" (Hor. 3b).

Although esteeming charity, Isaac Nappacha considered kind words to the poor to be of even more value than money: "He who gives a small coin to a poor man obtains six blessings, but he who addresses him with words of comfort obtains eleven blessings" (BB 9b). Isaac Nappacha considered prayer essential. "Why were our ancestors [Abraham and Isaac] childless? Because God longs to hear the prayers of the righteous" (Yev. 64a). He also observed, "Whoever offends his neighbor, even if only with words, must pacify him; if he has a monetary claim against you, open the palm of your hand to him [give him what you owe]; and if not, send many friends to him [to intercede and obtain forgiveness]" (Yoma 87a).

Isaac Nappacha stressed the power of the prayers of the righteous, which he compared to a pitchfork: "As a pitchfork turns the sheaves of grain from one position to another, so the prayer of the righteous turns the attribute of God from wrath to mercy" (Yev. 64a). According to Isaac Nappacha, "Just as the olive tree bears fruit only after many years [lit., 'at the very end'], so Israel will flourish at the end of time." Based on a biblical verse (Eccles. 12:5), he observed: "Every righteous person is given an abode in heaven according to the honor he deserves. This may be compared to a king who enters a town together with his servants. They all enter through the same gate [i.e., all people die in the same way], but when they spend the night each is given accommodations according to his status" (Shab. 152a).

The Talmud offers divergent views regarding the relative value of agricultural work versus commerce and handicrafts. For the purposes of investment, Isaac Nappacha advised, "One should always divide his money into three parts: one-third [should be invested] in land, one-third in merchandise, and one-third ready at hand" (BM 42a). Each of these alternatives has an advantage over the others. Real estate is secure, but the investment in merchandise yields higher profits. The advantage of having money readily available is that one can benefit from business opportunities that may suddenly arise. The Rabbis understood that market prices fluctuate with the hour of the day (BB 90b), and that a fear of upcoming scarcity can drive up the prices of vital commodities (Taan. 2:9). In the debate over whether prices should be regulated, Isaac Nappacha argued that this was a good policy since it thwarted the activity of swindlers, who would wait for honest merchants to sell most of their goods at a competitive price and then substantially increase what they charged (BB 89a).

Isaac Nappacha observed, "If a man says to you, 'I have labored and not found,' do not believe him. If he says, 'I have not labored but still have found,' do not believe him. If he says, 'I have labored and found,' you may believe him. This is true with respect to words of Torah [i.e., the effort to gain enlightenment from it], but regarding business, everything depends on the assistance of Heaven. And even for words of Torah, this is true only of penetrating to the meaning [lit., 'sharpening' the understanding], whereas remembering what one has learned completely depends on the assistance of Heaven" (Meg. 6b). He also noted, "If you see a wicked man upon whom fortune is smiling, do not contend with him" (Ber. 7b). Isaac Nappacha took a cynical view about the allure of premarital (and extramarital) sex: "Since the destruction of the Temple, sexual pleasure has been taken [from those who practice it lawfully] and given to sinners, as it is written, 'Stolen waters are sweet, and bread eaten in secret is pleasant' [Prov. 9:17]" (Sanh. 75a).

In various Talmudic tractates, the Rabbis listed classes of people who would or would not have a share in the World to Come. R. Yochanan said: "There are three persons who have a share in the World to Come—he who dwells in the Land of Israel, he who raises his children to the study of Torah, and he who honors the Sabbath" (Pes. 113a). For Isaac Nappacha, "the wives of scholars, who chase the sleep from their eyes [sitting up all night waiting for the return of their husbands from the house of study] in this world achieve thereby the life of the World to Come [as a reward for the consideration they showed to their studious husbands]" (Ket. 62a).

According to the Jerusalem Talmud, "A person will be called to account on judgment day for every permissible thing that he might have enjoyed but did not" (JT Kid. 4:12). Opposed to those who vowed to abstain from world pleasures, Isaac Nappacha wryly noted: "Are not the things that the Torah has forbidden enough for you, that you wish to add more to them?!" (JT Ned. 9:1). *See also* Rabin bar Adda.

Ishmael ben Elisha, Palestinian *tanna* (first/second century).

Usually referred to in the Babylonian Talmud without patronymic, Ishmael ben Elisha came from a wealthy priestly family in Upper Galilee. His grandfather, R. Ishmael ben Elijah, served as high priest and was one of the Ten Martyrs executed by the Romans after they conquered Jerusalem. According to legend, when R. Joshua ben Hananiah was visiting Rome he was informed that among the Jewish captives was "a child with beautiful eyes and face and curly locks." After asking the boy several questions and realizing his brilliance, R. Joshua ben Hananiah exclaimed, "I am certain that this one will be a great teacher in Israel. I swear that I will not budge from here before I ransom him, whatever price may be demanded." He succeeded in raising the huge sum required, and soon the youngster, Ishmael ben Elisha, became a recognized sage and a leading member of the Sanhedrin at Yavneh (Git. 58a). Later he was forced to move to Usha, where he established his own academy (BB 28b).

Ishmael and his contemporary, R. Akiva, had different approaches to biblical interpretation. R. Akiva believed that the Torah was complete, with nothing lacking or superfluous. Therefore, any repetition of words or extra letters must have some special meaning, as did even simple connecting words and articles like if, but, also, the, and even the Hebrew word *et* before a direct object. Conversely, Ishmael ben Elisha maintained that the Torah was "conveyed in the language of man," so that extra or missing words and letters could not be the basis for new deductions (Sanh. 51b). For him, the plain sense of the biblical text was the only reliable guide to proper interpretation. Consequently, he developed a set of thirteen hermeneutical rules for *halachic* exegesis that were universally adopted by his successors and are still found in traditional prayer books. Ishmael ben Elisha also established the principle that the chapters of the Torah were not written in strict chronological order of the events. He and his school laid the foundation for the *Mechilta* and the

Sifrei, respectively the *halachic midrashim* on Exodus and Numbers. (The *Sifra* on Leviticus and the *Sifre* on Deuteronomy come from the school of R. Akiva.)

A kind and gentle person, Ishmael ben Elisha urged his students to "be yielding to a superior, pleasant to the young, and receive every person cheerfully" (Avot 3:16). Sensitive to the plight of poor young women with plain features, Ishmael ben Elisha would supply them with funds, arranging for them to be attractively clad so that they could obtain husbands (Ned. 9:10). His academy taught: "Four times a year judgment is passed on the world—on Passover with respect to produce, on Shavuot with respect to fruit, and on Sukkot with regard to rain. Man is judged on Rosh Hashanah and his fate is sealed on Yom Kippur" (RH 16a). It also described the six shofar blasts blown on the eve of the Sabbath. With the first, those working in the fields ceased their work. Those near to town waited until the more distant ones arrived, so that they could all enter together. However, the shops remained open until the second blast, when the shutters were removed and the shops locked up. Pots remained in the oven until the third blast, when what was needed for the evening meal was removed, what had been prepared for the next day was stored away, and the candles were lit. After that the people waited "for as long as it takes to bake a small fish or to place a loaf in the oven" before the final three blasts ("a *tekiah*, a *teruah*, and a *tekiah*") were sounded to formally usher in the Sabbath (Shab. 35). Interpreting the biblical verse, "My [God's] word is like fire, like a hammer that shatters rock" (Jer. 23:29), the school of Ishmael emphasized that "Just as a hammer splits a rock into many pieces, so one biblical verse may convey many teachings [i.e., is subject to many interpretations]" (Sanh. 34a).

Other sayings from the school of Ishmael include: "If the *yetzer ha-ra* [evil inclination] attacks, drag it into the *bet midrash* [school house; i.e., overcome it by devotion to study]. If it is of stone [hard as a rock], it will dissolve; if [it is as strong as] iron, it will be crushed into fragments" (Suk. 52b); and "Whoever shears off part of his possessions and dispenses it in charity is delivered from the punishment of Gehinnom. Picture two sheep crossing a river, one shorn and the other not shorn; the shorn one gets across [wades through the water], the unshorn one does not [remains behind]" (Git. 7a).

The majority of Rabbis believed that human beings and God were partners, not antagonists, in aiding the sick. The *aggadah* relates that once Ishmael ben Elisha and R. Akiva were walking on the streets of Jerusalem with another man. When they met a sick person who asked how he could be healed, the Rabbis recommended he take a certain medicine until he felt better. Their companion asked, "Who made this man sick?" to which the Rabbis replied, "the Holy One, Blessed be He." "Why then," asked the man, "do you presume to interfere in an area that is not yours [i.e., God afflicted him and you dare to heal]?" The Rabbis asked the man his occupation and, upon learning that he was a "tiller of the soil," they asked, "Who created the field and the vineyard?" When the man replied, "The Holy One, blessed be He," they challenged the farmer: "How do you dare move into an area that is not yours? He [God] created these and you eat their fruit!" The farmer was incensed: "Don't you see the sickle in my hand? If I did not go out and plow the field, cover it, fertilize it, and weed it, nothing would grow!" The Rabbis retorted, "You are a fool. Just as a tree does not grow if it is not fertilized and cared for—and even if it already grew but is not watered it dies—so the body is like a tree, medicine is the fertilizer, and the doctor is the farmer" (Mid. Sam. 4:1)

Euphemisms are neutral words that are substituted for ones that are coarse, unseemly, blasphemous, or taboo. The Rabbis taught, "Wherever an indelicate expression is written in the text, we substitute for it a more polite and delicate reading" (Meg. 25b). Examples cited in this section include "lie with" instead of "ravish" and "deposit . . . water of his feet" instead of "excrement . . . urine." As the school of Ishmael stressed, "One should always carry on a discussion using decent language" (Pes. 3a).

Is the requirement to study Torah all-consuming, or can a Jew take time out to earn a living? Two prominent sages had differing opinions on this issue, based on their interpretation of biblical verses (Ber. 35b). According to Ishmael ben Elisha, "This book of the law shall not depart out of your mouth" (Josh. 1:8) could be taken literally to imply that a Jew must devote all his time to Torah study. Therefore, the Bible also says, "And you will gather in your grain" (Deut. 11:14), indicating that a Jew must combine Torah study with a worldly occupation or be forced to beg for charity and abandon learning altogether.

According to legend, the son and daughter of Ishmael ben Elisha were taken captive and sold to two different masters. Some time later, these two men happened to meet, spoke glowingly of the beauty of their purchases, and agreed to have them marry and share their children. That night they put the slaves across from each other in a room so dark that the siblings did not recognize each other. After being informed about the proposed marriage, the son of Ishmael ben Elisha declared, "I am of a priestly family. Shall I marry a bondwoman?" His sister also protested against this arranged marriage, saying: "I also am of priestly descent. Shall I be married to a slave?" So they passed the night in tears. With the light of dawn, they finally recognized each other, embraced, and continued weeping until their souls departed from them. To this episode the Rabbis applied the lamentation of Jeremiah (Lam. 1:16), "For these things do I weep, my eyes flow with tears" (Git. 58a).

Asking why human beings have "fingers pointed like pegs," the Rabbis answered, "So that if we hear 'improper words' [i.e., *lashon ha-ra*] we can plug up our ears with them." The school of Ishmael taught that the outer ear is rigid, but the earlobe is soft, so that if one hears an unsavory word he can place the earlobe over the ear to cover it (Ket. 5a–b). It also deemed slander as serious a transgression as the three cardinal sins of "idolatry, incest and adultery, and the shedding of blood" (Ar. 15b).

Ishmael ben Elisha said that mourning over the destruction of the Second Temple would seem to demand abstinence from meat and wine, were it not for the principle that no restriction is imposed on the public unless the majority can endure it. Similarly, the prohibition against the study of the Torah and the observance of its precepts, instituted by the Roman authorities after the unsuccessful Bar Kochba revolt in 135, would seem to require that one should not marry or have children. However, all that this would accomplish would be that "the seed of Abraham our father would come to an end and might cease of itself. But let Israel go their way. It is better that they err in ignorance than presumptuously [and thus we do not tell them, since they would continue marrying and having children anyway]" (BB 60b).

For Ishmael ben Elisha, "All Israel are to be regarded as princes [i.e., there can be no distinctions among Jews]" (BM 113b). The Talmud notes that vows made in error can be overturned. "If one vows not to marry that ugly woman, whereas she is beautiful, that black woman whereas she is fair, that short woman who in fact is tall, he is permitted to marry her, not because she was ugly and became beautiful, or black and turned fair, or short and grew tall, but because the vow was made in error."

As an example, the story is told of a young man, living at a time of extreme hardship and poverty, who vowed not to marry the daughter of his sister. "So she was taken into the house of Ishmael ben Elisha and made beautiful." Incredulous, the Rabbi asked, "My son, did you really vow not to marry this one?" When he replied that he did not, the sage released him from his vow. "At the same time, Ishmael ben Elisha wept and said, 'The daughters of Israel are beautiful, but poverty makes them ugly [destroys their beauty].' And when Ishmael ben Elisha died, the daughters of Israel lamented his passing" (Ned. 9:10). *See also* Ben Dama; Shimon bar Yochai.

Ishmael ben Jose ben Halafta, Palestinian *tanna* (second century).

The eldest son of Jose ben Halafta (Shab. 118b), Ishmael succeeded his father as the leader of the community of Sepphoris (Er. 86b) and transmitted many of his father's teachings. Serving with R. Eleazar ben Shimon as a judge who assisted the Roman authorities in the arrest of Jewish criminals, Ishmael ben Jose ben Halafta was condemned by his fellow Jews. Challenged by Elijah the prophet, "How long will you deliver the people of our God to execution!" Ishmael ben Jose ben Halafta replied, "What can I do. It is the royal decree." However, the prophet had the last word: "Your father fled to Asia [after being ordained by R. Judah ben Bava in defiance of the Hadrianic edict]. You can flee to Laodecia!" (BM 83b–84a).

Ishmael ben Jose ben Halafta took care to maintain his impartiality and to ensure that there never was a hint of his taking a bribe, even one of mere words. His land tenant used to bring him a basket of fruit every Friday, as rent from the owner's orchard. When once he brought it on Thursday, the Rabbi asked, "Why the difference today?" The tenant answered, "I have a lawsuit [to be tried in your court] today, and thought that I would bring [the basket of fruit] on the way." Ishmael ben Jose ben Halafta refused to accept it from him, saying, "[Now] I am disqualified to judge your case" (Ket. 105b).

Several of the maxims of Ishmael ben Jose ben Halafta reflected his expertise in civil law: "One who withdraws from judgment [i.e., either a judge who refrains from passing a verdict and instead encourages the parties to come to an agreement, or a private person who avoids litigation and as an alternative seeks a friendly compromise] removes from himself hatred, robbery, and [the responsibility for] an unnecessary oath; but one who is too self-confident in handing down legal decisions is foolish, wicked, and an arrogant spirit. Do not judge alone, for none may judge alone except the One [i.e., God]; and do not say [to your judicial colleagues], 'Accept my view,' for they are permitted [to agree with you] but you are not [allowed to compel them to concur with your view]" (Avot 4:9–10).

Ishmael ben Jose ben Halafta was known for his huge girth. "When he and R. Eleazar ben Shimon met, [their waists were so large that] one could pass through with a yoke of oxen under them and not touch them" (BM 84a). At a dinner, "They offered him a goblet, which he accepted at the first invitation and drank in one draft." When asked, "Do you not agree that he who drinks his goblet in one gulp is greedy?" Ishmael retorted: "This was not said when your goblet is small, your wine sweet, and my stomach broad" (Pes. 86b). In response to an associate's strict ruling, Ishmael ben Jose ben Halafta cited a statement of his father: "Wherever you see an opportunity of relaxing the laws of *eruv*, seize it [i.e., make it easy]" (Er. 80a).

Based on two verses from Job, Ishmael ben Jose ben Halafta taught: "The older scholars grow, the more wisdom they acquire ['With aged men is wisdom, and in length of days understanding' (Job 12:12)], but as for the ignorant, the older they are, the more foolish they become ['He removes the speech of the trusty, and takes away the understanding of the elders' (Job 12:20)]" (Shab. 152a).

Ishmael ben Yochanan ben Beroka, Palestinian *tanna* (second century).

One of the four elders of his time (Er. 38b), Ishmael ben Yochanan ben Beroka often was quoted together with Rabban Shimon ben Gamaliel II, either presenting agreeing or opposing views. Most of his statements dealt with *halachic* issues, such as dietary laws, sacrifices, and levitical cleanness. He said, "I heard from the mouth of the sages in the vineyard of Yavneh that every woman must wait three months [to remarry after her husband's death or divorce to eliminate any question about the father of any offspring]" (Yev. 42b), a rule that persists to the present day. In Pirkei Avot (4:6), Ishmael ben Yochanan ben Beroka declared: "One who studies in order to teach is given the means to study and to teach; and one who studies in order to practice is given the means to study and to teach, to observe and to practice." This implied that although learning is an essential activity and using that knowledge to teach others is even more important, transforming the results of study into the performance of good deeds is its ultimate purpose.

J

Jacob ben Korshai, Palestinian *tanna* (second century).

Referred to in the Mishnah without patronymic, Jacob was the grandson of Elisha ben Abuyah and a teacher of Judah ha-Nasi. He observed, "There is not a single precept in the Torah whose reward is stated that is not dependent on the resurrection of the dead [i.e., on the World to Come]." After noting the verse relating to honoring one's father and mother (Deut. 5:16), Jacob ben Korshai cited the biblical verse, "Let the mother bird go and take only the young, in order that you may prosper and have a long life" (Deut. 22:7). He then related an incident that seemed to contradict this promise. A dutiful son, in obedience to his father's wish, climbed a tree after some birds. After shooing away the mother bird, he took the fledglings, but as he climbed down he fell and died. From this event, Jacob ben Korshai concluded that in this world there is no reward for good deeds; rather, the promised rewards will be granted in the World to Come, which is completely good and immeasurably long. Many decades later, the Babylonian R. Joseph ben Hananiah remarked, "Had Acher [Elisha ben Abuyah] interpreted this verse [i.e., the promise of reward and a long life] as Jacob ben Korshai, his daughter's son, he would not have sinned" (Kid. 39b).

Jacob ben Korshai's most famous saying is: "The world is like a vestibule before the World to Come. Prepare yourself in the vestibule so that you may enter the banquet hall. Better one hour of repentance and good deeds in this world [when one can elevate himself spiritually] than the entire life of the World to Come [when one receives the reward for accomplishments in this world]; and better one hour of spiritual bliss in the World to Come than the entire life [all the pleasures] of this world" (Avot 4:21–22). He also said, "One who walks on the road while reviewing [a Torah lesson] but interrupts his review and exclaims, 'How beautiful is this plowed field!'—Scripture considers it as if he bears guilt for his soul" (Avot 3:9). One interpretation of this maxim is that any journey exposes a person to harm, which is exacerbated by interrupting the study of Torah (which protects from danger). *See also* Zerika.

Jeremiah, Babylonian *amora* (fourth century).

Cited in the Talmud without patronymic, Jeremiah bar Abba was a lackluster student (Ket. 75a) before moving to the Land of Israel. There he studied under R. Hiyya bar Abba and R. Zeira, developing into a recognized scholar. However, his endless challenging on subtle points of esoteric law, which were of no practical value and perceived as verging on the disrespectful, led to Jeremiah's expulsion from the academy (BB 23b). Nevertheless, after the death of the great teachers, the scholars were so perplexed about a legal issue that they were forced to present it to Jeremiah. Prefacing his solution with the words, "Although I am not worthy [to be consulted by you], your pupil's opinion inclines this way," his colleagues were so impressed with his modesty and humility that they reinstated him (BB 165b).

Jeremiah became the undisputed head of the scholars at Tiberias, and his judgments were highly respected both in the Land of Israel and in Babylonia. Indeed, when a contemporary or later Babylonian scholar introduced a statement with the phrase, "It is said in the West," it was generally assumed that it reflected the view of Jeremiah (Sanh. 17b). When R. Abbaye remarked to Rava, "one scholar in the Land of Israel is worth two of ours," his colleague retorted, "yet when one of ours moves to the Land of Israel he is as good as two of them. As an example, take Jeremiah. While he was here he could not understand what the Rabbis were saying, but when he went up there [he achieved such status that] he refers to us as 'the stupid Babylonians'" (Ket. 75a). Jeremiah consistently deprecated the sages in his native land: "The Babylonians are fools. They dwell in a land of darkness and they engage in dark [obscure] discussions [without knowing the true meanings of the laws]" (Pes. 34b; Yoma 57a; Bek. 25b).

A strong believer in the ultimate redemption, Jeremiah requested that at the time of his death: "Clothe me in white shrouds, put stockings and sandals on my feet, place a staff in my hand, and bury me by the side of the road. Thus when the Messiah comes, I will be ready [to follow him]" (JT Kil. 9:3).

Jeremiah bar Abba, Babylonian *amora* (third century).

A disciple of Rav, Jeremiah bar Abba often cited the *halachic* decisions of his teacher. His most famous statement (Sanh. 103a) uses biblical proof texts to detail the four types of people who will never be admitted into the Divine Presence (*Shechinah*): (1) scoffers, based on the verse, "He withdrew his hand from scoffers" (Hos. 7:5); (2) liars, from the verse, "One who lies shall not be established before My eyes [i.e., live in my house]" (Ps. 101:7); (3) flatterers, from the verse, "No flatterer shall come before Him" (Job 13:16); and (4) slanderers (lit., "those who speak *lashon ha-ra*"), based on the verse, "You are not a God who desires wickedness; evil ['slander,' in context] cannot abide with You" (Ps. 5:5).

Jeremiah ben Eleazar, Palestinian *amora* (third century).

A master of *aggadah*, Jeremiah ben Eleazar inferred from a verse in Psalms (139:5), "You hedge me [hemmed me in] before and behind," that "God created two full faces in the first man [one of which became Eve]" (Ber. 61a; Er. 18a). Elsewhere, he said that Adam was formed as a hermaphrodite (Gen. R. 8:1). From the verse, "And He brought her to the man," Jeremiah ben Eleazar derived the teaching that "God acted as Adam's best man [attending to the wedding arrangements]. Here the Torah teaches a maxim of behavior, that a man of eminence should associate himself with a lesser man in acting as best man" (Ber. 61a). Focusing on the verse from the Flood story, "In its [the dove's] bill was a plucked-off olive leaf" (Gen. 8:11), Jeremiah ben Eleazar stated that the dove said to God, "May my food be as bitter as the olive but entrusted to Your hand, rather than sweet as honey and dependent on one of flesh and blood [Noah]" (Er. 18b).

Jeremiah ben Eleazar maintained that the builders of the Tower of Babel were divided into three groups with different motivations: to dwell there, to establish a cult of idolatry, and to wage war against God. The first group was dispersed; the second was punished by a confusion of language; and the third was "turned to apes, spirits, devils, and night-demons" (Sanh. 109a). Among his maxims are (Er. 18b): "Only a part of a man's praise may be said in his presence, but all of it in his absence"; and "Any house in which words of Torah are heard at night will never be destroyed."

Jonah, Palestinian *amora* (fourth century).

Lifelong friend as well as business partner of R. Jose, the two headed the Sanhedrin in Tiberias. A student of R. Ilai II and R. Ze'iri (disciples of R. Yochanan) and frequently mentioned with R. Jose in the Jerusalem Talmud, Jonah established principles for studying the Talmud and understanding the Mishnah. Jonah stated that numerous incidents in the Bible and the Mishnah were not related in order to establish the *halachah* for future generations, but rather to show how they were practiced in earlier generations (JT Shev. 1:7), and that the minimum quantities given by the Talmud, such as the volume of an olive or egg, were of rabbinic rather than biblical origin (JT Pe'ah 1:1).

In the Babylonian Talmud, Jonah is cited as one of "the great men of Palestine." It relates that "When the world was in need of rain, Jonah, the father of R. Mani, would go into his house and say to his [family]: 'Get my haversack and I shall go and buy grain for a *zuz*.' When he left his house he would go and stand in some hidden, low-lying spot [based on the verse, 'Out of the depths have I called You, O Lord'; Ps. 130:1] dressed in sackcloth and pray [fervently], and rain came." When Jonah returned home, his family asked whether he had brought the grain. He replied, "Now that rain has come, the world will feel relieved" (Taan. 23b).

Jonah said in the name of R. Ze'iri: "If a man does his own business before he says his prayers, it is as if he had built a [forbidden] high place [for idolatrous worship]"; and "Whoever goes seven days without a dream is called evil" (Ber. 14a).

Jonathan ben Eleazar, Palestinian *tanna* (third century).

Born in Babylonia but moving to the Land of Israel as a young man, Jonathan ben Eleazar is often referred to in rabbinic writings simply as Jonathan, without patronymic. A grain merchant who lived in Sepphoris, Jonathan ben Eleazar directed an academy where his most prominent disciple was R. Samuel bar Nachmani, who often repeated Jonathan's *aggadic* sayings.

Jonathan ben Eleazar stressed the importance of impartial judgments in Jewish courts. "A judge should always imagine himself as if [he had] a sword lying between his thighs [or 'over his head'] and Gehinnom [the pit of damnation] open beneath him" (Yev. 109b). "A judge who delivers a correct ruling causes the *Shechinah* to dwell in Israel . . . but he who gives an improper ruling causes the *Shechinah* to depart from the midst of Israel . . . and a judge who unjustly takes the possessions [lit., 'money'] of one and gives them to another will lose his life" (Sanh. 7a). Even the suspicion of impropriety must be avoided. When a woman brought him a basket of figs, Jonathan ben Eleazar refused the gift. He noted that if the basket had been uncovered when she arrived it must also be uncovered when she left, lest people suspect that the woman brought a basket of gold [for a bribe] but was taking back a basket of figs (JT BB 2:11).

Jonathan ben Eleazar taught: "He who teaches Torah to his neighbor's son will be privileged to sit in the Heavenly Academy . . . and he who teaches Torah to the son of an *am ha-aretz*, God will annul all decrees against him" (BM 85a). Among other sayings of Jonathan ben Eleazar transmitted by R. Samuel are: "Whoever performs a mitzvah in this world, it precedes him in the World to Come; but whoever commits a transgression in this world, it clings to him and precedes him for the Day of Judgment" (Sot. 3b); "He who loses his temper is exposed to all the torments of Gehinnom" (Ned. 22a); "Whoever reproves his neighbor for pious intent [a purely religious motive] is deemed worthy to the grace of God [i.e., to be in the portion of the Holy One]" (Tam. 28a); "Seven sins bring the punishment of leprosy—immorality, arrogance, robbery, bloodshed, false oath [perjury], slander, and envy" (Ar. 16a); and "A man is shown in a dream only what is suggested by his own thoughts [i.e., they derive from within, not from a prophetic source]" (Ber. 55b). He also said, "Great is repentance, because it brings about redemption [or in a second version, 'because it prolongs the years of man']" (Yoma 86b).

Jonathan ben Eleazar was a master of *aggadah*. Although the Bible explicitly referred to the sins of Reuben, the sons of Eli, the sons of Samuel, David, Solomon, and others, Jonathan ben Eleazar offered ingenious interpretations and cited other biblical references in their defense, prefacing each explanation with the phrase, "Whoever maintains that so-and-so sinned is in error!" (Shab. 55b–56a). Commenting on the verse, "Let us make man in our image" (Gen. 1:26), Jonathan ben Eleazar related that when Moses wrote down the daily acts of creation, he asked God the reason for the use of the plural form "we," which heretics could claim as evidence that there was not One Creator. God replied, "Whoever wishes to err, let him err. From this man that I have created, great and small men shall spring. If the great man should ask, 'Why do I need to request permission from one of less importance than I,' they will answer him: 'Learn from your Creator, who fashioned all that is above and below. Yet when He came to create man, He consulted with the ministering angels'" (Gen. R. 8:8).

Jonathan ben Joseph, Palestinian *tanna* (second century).

Usually cited without patronymic, Jonathan ben Joseph was a student at the academy of R. Ishmael ben Elisha with R. Josiah, with whom he is almost invariably quoted in *halachic* interpretations of biblical texts. Later a disciple of R. Akiva, Jonathan ben Joseph is cited only once in the Mishnah: "Whoever fulfills the Torah despite poverty, will ultimately fulfill it in wealth; but whoever neglects the Torah because of wealth, will ultimately neglect it in poverty" (Avot 4:11).

In a discussion defining the term "*am ha-aretz*," Jonathan ben Joseph applied it to one who "has sons and does not rear them to study Torah" (Sot. 22a). In the Mechilta (Bo 1), Jonathan ben Joseph was quoted as saying, "Eclipses may frighten gentiles, but they have no significance for Jews."

Contradicting the generally accepted rabbinic view that a "rebellious son" never was executed and that communal apostasy never occurred, Jonathan ben Joseph declared: "I saw him [a rebellious son who was executed at his parents' demand] and sat on his grave . . . [and] I saw it [a condemned city] and sat upon its ruins" (Sanh. 71a). Once R. Hanina and Jonathan ben Joseph were walking and came to a fork in the road, with one path leading past a place of idol worship and the other by a house of prostitution. One said, "Let us go past the place of idolatry, the inclination for which has been abolished." However, the other countered, "Let us go by the harlots' place and defy our inclination and have our reward." As they approached the house of prostitution, the "harlots withdrew" (abstained from solicitation), presumably observing that they were Rabbis (Av. Zar. 17a–b). *See also* Josiah; Rava.

Jonathan ben Uzziel, Palestinian *tanna* (first century B.C.E./first century C.E.).

According to legend, whenever Jonathan ben Uzziel studied Torah, every bird that flew over him was instantly burned up by the fire of the ministering angels who gathered to listen to his teachings. Termed Hillel's most distinguished pupil (Suk. 28a; BB 134a), Jonathan ben Uzziel was said to have composed an Aramaic translation of the Book of Prophets from the tradition handed down by the last three prophets—Haggai, Zechariah, and Malachi. When he was working on this project, the entire earth shook over an area of four hundred parasangs and a *bat kol* (heavenly voice) was heard asking, "Who is the one who has revealed My secrets to mankind?" Jonathan ben Uzziel immediately stood up and admitted that he had done so. "However, it is fully known to You that I have not done this for my own honor or for the prestige of my father's house. I have done it only for Your sake, so that controversies will not multiply in Israel [i.e., through different interpretations of various prophetic allusions]." When Jonathan ben Uzziel subsequently wanted to publish his translation (or inner meaning) of the later Writings, a heavenly voice called out, "You have done enough!" The reason was that he included calculations relating to the end of days and the coming of the Messiah (Meg. 3a).

A man once had sons who behaved so badly that he disinherited them, instead writing a will in which he bequeathed his entire estate to Jonathan ben Uzziel. What did the sage do? "He sold a third [retaining the proceeds for himself], consecrated a third [to the Sanctuary], and returned a third to the dead man's sons." Shammai vehemently objected to this course of action, arguing that Jonathan ben Uzziel had not honored the last wishes of the deceased. Jonathan ben Uzziel replied, "If you can take back what I sold and what I devoted to the Sanctuary, then you can also take back what I have returned [to the dead man's sons]." The thrust of his argument was that once he had assumed legal possession of the property, Jonathan could do whatever he wanted with it. Therefore, Jonathan was not violating the wishes of the deceased, for it no longer was the latter's property. Shammai went home, muttering: "The son of Uzziel has confounded me!" (BB 133b–134a).

Jose ben Halafta, Palestinian *tanna* (second century).

Often referred to in the Talmud as Jose, without patronymic, he was born in Sepphoris to a family of Babylonian origin (Yoma 66b). Tracing his heritage back to Jehonadav ben Rechev, who helped Jehu (king of Israel) destroy the house of Ahab and thus eliminate idolatry from the Northern Kingdom (JT Taan. 4:2), Jose ben Halafta was proud of his Babylonian roots. He stated, "All countries are as dough in comparison with the Land of Israel, but the Land of Israel is as dough relative to Babylonia" (Kid. 71a). One of the major disciples of R. Akiva, Jose ben Halafta fled to Babylonia after his master was murdered by the Romans (Yev. 63b) and was considered among those who "reestablished the Torah" (Yev. 62b). The Talmud states that the *halachah* was established in accordance with the view of Jose ben Halafta whenever his colleagues disagreed with him (Er. 46b).

According to legend, the mystical Jose ben Halafta often met with Elijah the prophet. Once while traveling along the road, Jose ben Halafta stopped and "entered into one of the ruins of Jerusalem to pray." Elijah appeared and, after waiting until Jose ben Halafta had finished the *Amidah*, asked why Jose had not prayed on the road. When Jose replied, "I feared that passersby might interrupt me," Elijah informed him that he should have offered an abbreviated prayer. The prophet asked Jose ben Halafta if he had heard anything while in the ruins. He answered, "I heard a Divine voice, cooing [crying] like a dove and saying: 'Woe to the children, on account of whose sins I destroyed My house and burned My temple and exiled them among the nations of the world!'" Elijah observed, "I swear that sound is heard not just once, but three times every day. However, whenever a Jew goes into the synagogue and responds, 'May His great Name be blessed!' [the principal congregational response in the *Kaddish*], the Holy One is comforted and says, 'Happy is the king whose subjects praise him in that way!'" (Ber. 3a).

Jose ben Halafta was reputed to be the author of *Seder Olam* (Order of the World), a book chronicling the events from Creation to the Bar Kochba revolt (Nid. 46b). Jose ben Halafta observed, "Whoever honors the Torah is himself honored by the people; and whoever disgraces the Torah [by using it for personal gain or living a debased life] is himself disgraced by the people" (Avot 4:8). On several occasions, Jose ben Halafta entered into discussions with non-Jews. When a gentile scholar asked why God did not select as sacrificial animals those that symbolized His greatness, Jose ben Halafta answered that God specifically chose those that were hunted rather than those who killed their prey to show His love for the weak. Thus Jews were ordered to sacrifice the ox that runs away from the lion; the goat that flees the tiger; and the sheep that runs from the wolf (Lev. R. 27:5).

R. Jose ben Halafta permitted the testimony in a capital case of a witness proven to have previously provided false testimony in a monetary case (Sanh. 27b). Attacking the "blindness" of usurers, he observed: "If a man calls another person wicked, [the insulted party] maintains a deep-seated animosity against him [and would be ready to kill him]." In contrast, "Usurers summon witnesses and a scribe, pen and ink, and record and attest [i.e., sign their own names to the document], thus denying the God of Israel [by brazenly defying the biblical law against lending to a fellow Jew at interest, which is tantamount to rejection of God, the highest degree of wickedness]" (BM 71a).

In a classic legend, a Roman matron asked Jose ben Halafta, "What has your God been doing since finishing the creation of the world?" He replied, "God has been busy making matches." When she retorted that she could marry off all her many male and female slaves in an hour, Jose ben Halafta cautioned, "That which seems easy in your eyes is as difficult for God as dividing the sea." Undeterred, the matron arranged her slaves in two lines, pairing them off at random. Only when they returned the next day, bearing an assortment of injuries and protesting that she had chosen the wrong mates for them, did the matron realize the wisdom of Jose ben Halafta's words (Gen. R. 68:4; PdRK 2:4).

Another Roman matron once told Jose ben Halafta that the verse "He gives wisdom to the wise, and knowledge to those that have understanding" (Dan. 2:21) made no sense, insisting wisdom should rather be given to fools. The Rabbi asked her, "Do you have any jewels?" When she replied in the affirmative, he said: "If someone comes and wants to borrow them, will you lend them to him?" "Of course I will, if he is a man of responsibility." The Rabbi said, "Since you will only lend your jewels to a worthy borrower, should God give His wisdom to fools?" (Tanh. Miketz 97a–b).

A very old person may seek death because of diminished strength and a dismal quality of life. When a woman fitting this description complained to Jose ben Halafta, he asked what great merit had permitted her to live so long. She replied, "I go to synagogue services every morning and allow nothing to interfere with this practice." Jose ben Halafta urged the woman to refrain from going to the synagogue for three consecutive days. She followed his advice and died (Yalkut Shimoni, Ekev 871).

Jose ben Halafta expressed the hope that his share in the World to Come be among those who eat three meals on the Sabbath; praise God daily; pray at sunset; die of intestinal trouble (the suffering effects atonement, according to Rashi) or on their way to fulfill a commandment; greet the Sabbath in Tiberias, in a valley, where it began earlier, and end it in Sepphoris, on a mountain, where it finished later; usher in their students to the academy rather than force them to rise and depart; and collect charity but not be involved in its distribution lest they be suspected of acting improperly (Shab. 118b). After his death, Jose ben Halafta was praised by his pupil, Judah ha-Nasi: "The difference between the generation of Jose ben Halafta and ours is like the difference between the Holy of Holies and the most profane" (JT Git. 6:9). *See also* Meir; Zerika.

Jose ben Hanina, Palestinian *amora* (third century).

A student of R. Eliezer ben Jacob, whose statements he often cited (Ber. 10b), Jose ben Hanina is best known for his opinion, based on three biblical verses, that the prayer services of *Shacharit* (morning), *Minchah* (afternoon), and *Ma'ariv* (evening) were instituted by the patriarchs (Ber. 26b). Abraham "rose up early in the morning and hurried to the place where he had stood [in the presence of the Lord]" (Gen. 19:27), and "standing" always means "praying"; Isaac went out "to meditate in the field toward evening" (Gen. 24:63); and Jacob prayed before he went to sleep on his stone pillow and dreamt of angels ascending and descending the ladder connecting the earth to heaven (Gen. 28:11).

In a discussion about the where Israel received the Torah, Jose ben Hanina said "it has five names: The Wilderness of Zin, [meaning] that Israel was given commandments there [from a connection with the Hebrew word, *zivah* (he commanded)]; the Wilderness of Kadesh, where the Israelites were sanctified [*kadosh*], the Wilderness of Kedemot, because a priority [*kedumah*] was conferred there [i.e., Israel was made pre-eminent by its acceptance of the Torah]; the Wilderness of Paran, because Israel was fruitful [*paru*] and multiplied there; and the Wilderness of Sinai, because on the mountain there descended hostility [*sin'ah*] toward idolaters. What was its [real] name? Its name was Horeb" (Shab. 89a–b).

Regarding seeking forgiveness on Yom Kippur, Jose ben Hanina said: "One who asks pardon of his neighbor need do so no more than three times." As a proof text, he noted that when his brothers begged Joseph to forgive them, they used the term *na* (please) three times (Gen. 50:17). If the person one has wronged has subsequently died, "he should bring ten persons and make them stand by his grave and say, 'I have sinned against the Lord, the God of Israel, and against this one, whom I have hurt'" (Yoma 87a).

Explaining why the righteous often suffer in this world, Jose ben Hanina observed that the flax maker does not beat the flax too much when it hardens, lest it break. However, when the flax is of good quality, the more he beats it, the more it is improved. Similarly, God does not test the wicked, for they cannot bear it. However, He does test the righteous, as it is written: "God tests the righteous man" (Ps. 11:5) (Song R. 2:16).

Jose ben Judah (bar Ilai), Palestinian *tanna* (second century).

Although cited in numerous *halachic* discussions, especially with Judah ha-Nasi, Jose ben Judah is best known for the *aggadic* tale that inspired the seventeenth-century hymn, *Shalom Aleichem* (Peace Be upon You). This is traditionally sung in Ashkenazic homes as the family gathers around the table on Friday night to welcome the "angels of peace." Jose ben Judah related that two ministering angels—one good, one evil—accompany every Jew from the synagogue to his home on the Sabbath eve. If they find the candles burning, the table set, and the bed covered with a spread, the good angel exclaims,

"May it be God's will that it also be so on the next Sabbath," and the evil angel is compelled to respond "Amen." But if everything is disorderly and gloomy, the evil angel exclaims, "May it be God's will that it also be so on the next Sabbath," and the good angel is forced to say "Amen" (Shab. 119b).

Jose ben Judah of Kefar Habavli, Palestinian *tanna* (second century).

He is principally known for a statement in Pirkei Avot (4:27): "One who learns [Torah] from the young, to what can he be likened? To one who eats unripe grapes or drinks [unfermented] wine from his vat. But one who learns from the old, to what can he be likened? To one who eats ripe grapes or drinks aged wine."

Jose ben Kisma, Palestinian *tanna* (first/second century).

Jose ben Kisma was the focus of a famous story concerning the importance of residing in a stimulating, Torah-centered community. Once when the sage was walking on the road, a man approached and asked where he was from. "I come from a great city of scholars and sages." The man then made him a proposition. "Rabbi, would you be willing to live with us in our place? I would give you thousands upon thousands of golden dinars, precious stones, and pearls." Jose ben Kisma replied, "Even if you were to give me all the silver and gold, precious stones, and pearls in the world, I would dwell nowhere but in a place of Torah" (Avot 6:9).

Two scholars need to sharpen each other's minds by engaging in intense *halachic* discussions (Taan. 16a). However, this should not be taken to an extreme. Jose ben Kisma described an altercation at the synagogue in Tiberias, when two sages argued so intensely about whether a door bolt had a knob at the end that they ripped apart a Torah scroll in their excitement. He exclaimed, "I would not be surprised if this synagogue [which permits scholars to argue so vehemently] will not one day be turned into a house of idolatry" (Yev. 96b).

Jose ben Kisma offered the following riddle: "Two are better than three [i.e., the use of two legs when young is better than two legs plus a cane in old age], and woe for the one thing that goes and does not return. What is that?" Answered R. Hisda, "One's youth" (Shab. 152a). Jose ben Kisma was a member of the party that supported peace with Rome. When he died, "all the great men of Rome [officials in Caesarea where he lived] went to his burial and made great lamentation for him" (Av. Zar. 18a). Ironically, on their return from the funeral they discovered R. Hananiah ben Teradion teaching Torah, which led to that sage's execution.

Jose ben Yochanan (second century B.C.E.).

Jose ben Yochanan joined with Jose ben Yo'ezer of Zeredah to form the first of the *zugot*—the Hebrew name given to the pairs of sages responsible for maintaining the chain of the Oral Law from Antigonus of Sokho to Yochanan ben Zakkai. According to the Jerusalem Talmud, although both were renowned scholars, they also had the highest moral values and were known as the *Ashkolot* (lit., "clusters"), indicating that they united many virtues within themselves. Upon their deaths, the people said that all virtue had departed (JT Sot. 9:4).

Jose ben Yochanan's most famous statement is: "Let your house be open wide; treat the poor as members of your household; and do not converse excessively with a woman [not even your own wife]" (Avot 1:5). *See also* Jose ben Yo'ezer.

Jose ben Yo'ezer (second century B.C.E.).

Jose ben Yo'ezer joined with Jose ben Yochanan of Jerusalem to form the first of the *zugot*—the Hebrew name given to the pairs of sages responsible for maintaining the chain of the Oral Law from Antigonus of Sokho to Yochanan ben Zakkai. Born in the town of Zeredah in Persia and termed "the most pious in the priesthood" (Hag. 20a), Jose ben Yo'ezer served as *nasi* (president of the Sanhedrin) while his colleague was the *av bet din* (head of the religious court) during the religious persecutions of Antiochus Epiphanes. The two disagreed in the controversial issue of *semichah* (the physical laying of hands on sacrifices) on the Sabbath and festivals, with Jose ben Yochanan ruling that the practice should be performed and Jose ben Yo'ezer saying it should not (Hag. 2:2).

Attempting to stem the dispersion of Jews to neighboring lands, Jose ben Yo'ezer and Jose ben Yochanan ruled that all the countries surrounding the Land of Israel were "impure" and not appropriate places for Jews to live. Anyone who disobeyed this order was required to perform various purification rites before being permitted to enter the Land of Israel. They also ruled that all glass vessels made by non-Jews were impure, just as were earthen dishes.

Jose ben Yo'ezer was called "Jose the Lenient" because he permitted three things that were prohibited by the other authorities (Eduy. 8:4). During years of famine, when the people were unable to precisely identify the four types of locusts that the Bible permitted as food, he allowed Jews to eat the Ayal locust, which had invaded the Land of Israel from Babylonia. He permitted the people to use the blood and water on the floor of the slaughtering place in the Temple for household purposes, arguing that they were not susceptible to ritual uncleanness. Finally, he maintained that only a person who actually touched a corpse became ritually impure, because the ritual impurity was not transferable to anyone with whom he came in contact. This was important in order to allay the feat of contamination by those who were reluctant to join the rebellion against the Greeks because they feared contamination through contact with people who touched dead bodies.

Jose ben Yo'ezer's most famous statement is: "Let your house be a meeting place for scholars; sit amid the dust of their feet; and drink in their words with thirst" (Avot 1:4). These words were a direct challenge to the government, which was attempting to separate the people from their teachers by decreeing that anyone who converted his home into a place for instruction was liable to the death penalty. The Talmud relates that Jose ben Yo'ezer disowned his son because he "did not conduct himself in a proper manner," instead donating all his extensive property to the Temple for communal use (BB 133b).

Jose ben Yo'ezer's antigovernment activities led him to be sentenced to death and crucified. Ironically, this was the direct result of a relative, the high priest Alkimos, who attempted to curry favor with the authorities by ordering the destruction of all pious Jews who refused to submit to the Greek religion. Alkimos tried to convince Jose ben Yo'ezer to submit to the government and save his life, arguing that by obeying the government dictates the high priest had gained wealth and power. According to legend, Jose ben Yo'ezer replied, "If those who anger God live as well as you do, how great will be the share of those who obey His will?" When Alkimos challenged his relative to show him "another person who obeyed God's will more than you did," Jose ben Yo'ezer answered, "If those who do God's will end as I do, what a terrible end must await those who anger Him with their evil deeds." According to two versions of this story, the high priest was so moved by this discussion that he either committed suicide (Gen. R. 65) or died of a stroke (Josephus, *Maccabees*). *See also* Jose ben Yochanan.

Jose ha-Kohen, Palestinian *tanna* (first/second century).

Also known as Jose the Pious (Jose he-Hasid) and one of the most distinguished disciples of R. Yochanan ben Zakkai, Jose ha-Kohen was described by his teacher as "a scrupulously pious person" (Avot 2:11). His most famous maxims are: "Let the property [money] of your friend be as dear to you as your own; apply yourself to study Torah, for it is not yours by inheritance [i.e., each person must acquire knowledge through his own efforts]; and let all your actions be for the sake of Heaven [pure purpose and good intentions to serve God]" (Avot 2:17).

It was related of Jose ha-Kohen that he never sent a letter through a gentile, lest he forward it on the Sabbath (Shab. 19a). In answer to the question as to "the proper way to which a man should cling [to live meritoriously and inherit the life of the World to Come]," Jose ha-Kohen answered that a man should be "a good neighbor" (Avot 2:13–14). *See also* Yochanan ben Zakkai.

Jose the Galilean, Palestinian *tanna* (first/second century).

Coming from an area of uneducated inhabitants, Jose the Galilean shocked the scholars at Yavneh by showing that R. Tarfon and R. Akiva, the leaders of the academy, were mistaken regarding the rules on eating the flesh of a first-born animal (Zev. 57a). Since that day, Jose the Galilean was numbered among the most respected scholars. Although his views often differed from those of Akiva—he once said, "Were you to argue all day, I would not accept your opinion" (Zev. 82a)—their styles of *halachic* interpretation were similar. Jose established the principle that a person engaged in the observance of one commandment was absolved from fulfilling another at the same time (Suk. 26a).

However, several of his most famous rulings were not accepted. These included his teaching that fowl could be eaten with milk (since it could not be "cooked in its mother's milk"), as was done in his native town (Hul. 113a, 116a); and that during Passover it was permitted to enjoy any leavened product, as long as it was not consumed as food (Pes. 28b). Regarding the "rebellious [disobedient] son," Jose the Galilean disagreed with the general view that there were so many requirements that the biblical sentence of death would never be enforced. As he argued, "The Torah foresaw his ultimate destiny. After dissipating his father's wealth, he would turn to stealing to satisfy his [gluttonous] desires. . . . Therefore the Torah said, 'Let him die while yet innocent, rather than let him die guilty'" (Sanh. 72a).

Jose the Galilean suffered through a difficult marriage with an evil wife who frequently insulted him in front of his students. Finally divorcing her after years of claiming that he did not have enough money to pay her large *ketubah*, Jose had such a generous heart that he helped her and her blind second husband when they were in desperate straits (Gen. R. 17:3; Lev. R. 34:14). Known for his piety, it was said: "When because of their sins there is a drought in Israel and such a one as Jose the Galilean prays for rain, the rain comes immediately" (JT Ber. 9b). *See also* Beruriah.

Joseph, Babylonian *amora* (third/fourth century).

Always called Rav Joseph without the patronymic bar Hiyya, he was a close friend and colleague of Rabbah bar Nachmani. However, whereas Rabbah bar Nachmani was adept at intricate logical reasoning, Joseph's sayings were simple declarations that did not require complex analysis. This was possible because Joseph had an encyclopedic knowledge of Jewish tradition and practice. Indeed, he was called "Sinai," since all the laws of the Torah, along with the Mishnah and Tosefta, were systematically arranged in his mind as if they had been revealed to him directly from the mouth of God. When it was necessary to appoint a new head of the academy at Sura after the death of Huna bar Hiyya, Joseph was offered the post. However, he would not accept it, "because the astrologers had told him that he would be head for only two years." So Rabbah bar Nachmani became head and continued in this position for twenty-two years. Joseph succeeded him, but served for only two and a half years until his death in 333 (Ber. 64a).

As Joseph noted, "There are three kinds of people whose life is not worth living: the overly compassionate, the hot-tempered, and the [too] fastidious [sensitive] . . . and these [qualities] are all found in me" (Pes. 113b). When he became blind, Joseph was distraught because he could no longer fulfill all the commandments that required vision (BK 87a). Eventually, he suffered the loss of his memory and learning, not even recognizing his own interpretations when they were given in the study hall, "but Abbaye restored it to him" (Ned. 41a). Nevertheless, at a party marking his sixtieth birthday, Joseph wryly observed: "No matter how much I misbehave now, I can no longer die young" (MK 28a).

In response to the question, "Why is it uncommon for scholars to have sons who are Torah scholars?" Joseph answered: "So that no one may think that the Torah can be inherited" (i.e., lest others complain that it is useless for them to study, or the sons of scholars think that study is unnecessary). Other Rabbis asserted, "That they not be arrogant and consider themselves superior to the rest of the community" (Ned. 81a).

Joseph said, "A person should always be humble and learn from the behavior of his Creator. In giving the Ten Commandments to the people of Israel, God disregarded all the lofty mountains and instead caused the Divine Presence to rest on Mount Sinai [a relatively low mountain]. He also ignored all the stately trees and causes the Divine Presence to rest on the lowly thornbush [Burning Bush]" (Sot. 5a).

The Talmud condemns not only the thief, but also someone who knowingly received stolen property. R. Abbaye asked, "Why do we penalize the purchaser rather than the seller?" Joseph replied, "It is not the mouse that is the thief, but the hole that encourages him [i.e., a thief who cannot find a ready market will have less inclination to steal]." Abbaye protested, "If there were no mouse, how should the hole come by it?" However, Joseph was not convinced: "It is only reasonable that where the forbidden stuff is found [i.e., in the hands of the purchaser of stolen goods], there we should impose the penalty" (Git. 45a).

Numerous miraculous events are related in the Talmud. "There once was a man whose wife died, leaving behind a son to nurse. He could not afford to pay a wet-nurse, so a miracle was performed for him. His breasts grew to be like those of a woman, and he nursed his son himself. Joseph observed, 'Come and see how great was this man, that such a miracle was performed on his behalf!' But Abbaye disagreed. 'On the contrary, how inferior was this man, for the natural order [of Creation] had to be changed on his behalf!'" (Shab. 53b).

Among the many sayings of Joseph are: "Poverty suits Israel like a red trapping on a white horse" (Hag. 9b); "An artisan who makes a spoon will still burn his tongue if there is hot soup in it" (Pes. 28a); and "Even if you utter curses on a dog's tail, it will continue to wag [lit., 'do its work']" (MK 17a). *See also* Aviya.

Joshua ben Gamla, high priest (first century C.E.).

Joshua ben Gamla was appointed to the position after the payment of a large bribe to Herod Agrippa II from Joshua's wealthy wife, Martha, who came from the high priestly family of Boethus (Yev. 6:4). Despite the fact that he had bought the office of High Priest, the Rabbis praised Joshua ben Gamla for totally reorganizing the educational system and requiring universal instruction. Until his time, fathers taught their children at home. Joshua ben Gamla set up elementary schools, ordaining "that teachers of young children should be appointed in each district and each town [previously they were only found in Jerusalem], and that children should enter school at the age of six or seven." This accomplishment led the Talmud to exclaim: "Truly, the name of that man is blessed . . . since but for him the Torah would have been forgotten in Israel" (BB 21a).

During his brief one-year tenure in office, Joshua ben Gamla devoted funds to beautify the Temple. He had a golden vessel made to replace the boxwood container holding the two lots used on Yom Kippur to determine which of the two goats was sacrificed and which was sent off to Azazel (Yoma 3:9).

Joshua ben Hananiah, Palestinian *tanna* (first/second century).

Almost always known as Joshua without patronymic, he is quoted frequently throughout the Talmud. A Levite who served as one of the singers in the Temple, Joshua ben Hananiah was one of the major disciples of R. Yochanan ben Zakkai, who exclaimed of his student: "Praised is she who gave him birth" (Avot 2:11). Based on the verse from Ecclesiastes (4:12), "a threefold cord is not readily broken," Yochanan ben Zakkai referred to Joshua ben Hananiah as "the triple thread" (ARN 14), either because he had mastered the three branches of traditional Jewish learning (*midrash, halachah, aggadah*) or because he combined within himself the virtues of Torah, wisdom, and fear of God. During the Roman siege of Jerusalem, Joshua ben Hananiah and his colleague R. Eliezer ben Hyrcanus carried Yochanan ben Zakkai, hidden in a coffin, outside the city walls for his meeting with Vespasian, the Roman general (Git. 56a).

Accompanying his teacher to Yavneh, Joshua ben Hananiah became a member of the Sanhedrin and later headed his own academy at Peki'in. Joshua ben Hananiah objected to the exaggerated asceticism practiced by some Jews mourning for the destruction of Jerusalem. When some abstained from meat and wine on the grounds that they no longer could be brought as sacrifices or poured as a libation on the altar, Joshua ben Hananiah chided them: "But then we should no longer eat bread made of flour, because meal offerings can no longer be brought on the Altar." By extension, he added that they should no longer eat fruit (once brought to the Temple) or drink water (because of the water-drawing ceremony at the Temple on the second night of Sukkot). Joshua ben Hananiah concluded, "Not to mourn [the loss of the Temple] at all is impossible . . . [but] to mourn too much is also impossible, because we do not impose on the community a hardship that the majority cannot endure" (BB 60b).

Joshua ben Hananiah was the central figure in the rabbinic opposition to the efforts of Rabban Gamaliel II to impose dictatorial rule over the Sanhedrin. Ironically, although he was publicly humiliated by the *nasi*, Joshua ben Hananiah served as the mediator between his colleagues and Rabban Gamaliel II, which led to the latter being reinstated.

As an advocate of peaceful compromise, Joshua ben Hananiah warned: "An evil eye, the evil inclination, and hatred of other people remove a person from the world [destroy one's life]" (Avot 2:16). Furthermore, he declared that the world is spoiled by four types who are pious to a fault: "a pious fool [e.g., one who sees a woman drowning and does not save her for fear of touching her body, or one who does not save a drowning child because he has not yet taken off his *tefillin*]; sly sinners; an abstaining woman [who renounces her husband and worldly pleasures]; and the plague of the Pharisees [hypocrites who pretend to be saints]" (Sot. 21b).

Following the death of Rabban Gamaliel II, Joshua ben Hananiah became the spiritual leader of the Jewish people. When Hadrian reneged on his permission to rebuild the Temple, Joshua ben Hananiah quelled an imminent rebellion by relating an Aesop fable about the lion and the crane (Gen. R. 64). The Talmud relates numerous legendary debates between Joshua ben Hananiah, the Roman emperor, and the philosophers. In response to the question, "Where is the middle of the world," Joshua ben Hananiah pointed to the spot where he stood. When the incredulous philosophers asked how he knew this, Joshua ben Hananiah told them to take a line and measure the distance to convince themselves. Asked how the soul leaves the body of a bird when it dies, Joshua ben Hananiah answered that it leaves through the same place it entered at birth. Hadrian asked Joshua ben Hananiah to explain why the name of God is mentioned in the first five of the Ten Commandments but not in the others. Joshua ben Hananiah retorted, "Why is it that wherever a person looks he sees your statue, but in those places where a person goes to relieve himself he does not find your statue?" The emperor answered, "It is not fitting to place my image in unclean places." Joshua ben Hananiah replied, "Neither is it fitting to mention God's name together with murderers, adulterers, thieves, false witnesses, and other sinners who are the refuse of humanity." At another time, Hadrian asked why Sabbath foods have such a pleasant aroma. Joshua ben Hananiah answered, "We [Jews] have a certain seasoning called 'Sabbath' that we mix with food and improves its fragrance." When the emperor asked for some, Joshua ben Hananiah said: "Whoever does not observe the Sabbath will get no benefit from it" (Shab. 119a). On another occasion, Hadrian asked Joshua ben Hananiah to "see your God." Joshua ben Hananiah took the emperor outside "facing the sun during the summer solstice" and told him to look at it, but the latter said he could not do so. "If you cannot look at one of the ministers who attend the Holy One, blessed be He, how then can you presume to look upon the Divine Presence!" (Hul. 60a).

Joshua ben Hananiah was said to be quite homely in appearance. On one occasion, Hadrian's daughter addressed the sage as, "O glorious Wisdom in an ugly vessel." The sage replied to her [facetiously], "Does your father put his wine in [ugly] earthenware vessels?" When she answered that everyone did so, Joshua ben Hananiah retorted, "You nobles should put your wine in vessels of gold and silver!" She dutifully reported this suggestion to her father, who had the wine transferred to gold and silver vessels. When the wine turned sour, the irate emperor demanded to know who had given his daughter such bad advice. Learning that it was Joshua ben Hananiah, he ordered the sage brought to the palace for an explanation. After Joshua ben Hananiah had recounted the incident, the emperor asked, "But are there not beautiful people [in Israel] who are also learned?" "Yes," he retorted, "But if these very people were ugly, they would be even more learned [i.e., they would be humble and devote themselves more intensely to their studies]" (Ned. 50b; Taan. 7a).

In addition to Rabban Gamaliel II, Joshua ben Hananiah and Eliezer ben Hyrcanus were the two leaders of the Jewish community in the Land of Israel. Although close friends for years, they represented two different views on *halachic* issues. Joshua ben Hananiah followed the more liberal and pragmatic approach of Bet Hillel, while Eliezer ben Hyrcanus took the more conservative stances of Bet Shammai. Consequently, with few exceptions, the *halachah* was decided according to the opinions of Joshua ben Hananiah. Joshua ben Hananiah opposed Eliezer ben Hyrcanus in the famous dispute regarding the "oven of Achnai" by championing the fundamental principle of majority rule in deciding *halachic* issues. He also differed with Eliezer ben Hyrcanus in maintaining that righteous gentiles would also have a share in the World to Come.

"When the soul of Joshua ben Hananiah was about to go to its rest, the Rabbis said to him, "What will become of us at the hands of the unbelievers [i.e., who will represent us in our disputes with them]?" He replied, "Counsel is perished from the children, their wisdom is vanished" (Jer. 49:7), meaning that whenever the Jewish people lack leaders of stature, the same is true of other nations (Hag. 5b). With Joshua ben Hananiah's death and the loss of his moderating influence, radical forces gained control and precipitated the disastrous Bar Kochba revolt. *See also* Ben Zoma; Dosa ben Harkinas; Eleazar ben Hisma; Eliezer ben Hyrcanus; Ishmael ben Elisha; Onkelos; Rabbah bar Rav Hanan; Yochanan ben Zakkai.

Joshua ben Korcha, Palestinian *tanna* (second century).

Several major Talmudic commentators asserted that he was the son of R. Akiva, who was nicknamed "*Kereach*" (the bald) based on the statement of Ben Azzai that all Jewish scholars are worth no more than the skin of garlic except for the bald one (referring to R. Akiva). Therefore, he became known as ben Korcha or Karchah.

The Rabbis often differed in their opinions over legal matters. The Talmud states that the *halachah* follows the rule of Joshua ben Korcha: "In laws of the Torah [explicitly stated in scripture], follow the stricter view; in those of *Soferim* [rabbinic injunctions from the time of Ezra onward], follow the more lenient view" (Av. Zar. 7a; Tosef. Eduy. 1:5).

Opposed to any collaboration with the Romans, even in the arrest of criminals, Joshua ben Korcha bitterly castigated his student, R. Eleazar ben Shimon, for serving as a police officer under the Roman government. "Vinegar, son of wine [i.e., degenerate son of a righteous father]! How long will you hand over the people of our God for slaughter?!" Eleazar ben Shimon replied, "I weed out thorns from the vineyard [ridding the Jewish people of its evildoers]." Joshua ben Korcha retorted, "Let the Master of the vineyard [God] come and weed out His thorns Himself [God can deal with the wicked without your assistance]" (BM 83b). Joshua ben Korcha was also said to have verbally attacked sectarians (Judeo-Christians), as well as non-Jews, with whom he engaged in vigorous disputations (Lev. R. 4:6).

In the dire situation of the Land of Israel following the Bar Kochba revolt, Joshua ben Korcha observed that several Rabbis once were sitting among the trees when the wind blew and knocked the leaves against each other. Immediately they arose and fled, fearing that the Roman cavalry would chase and catch them. Soon looking and realizing that no one was there, they sat and wept: "Woe to us for whom the verse, 'And the sound of a driven leaf shall chase them' [Lev. 26:46], has been fulfilled" (Sifra Behukotai 7:4).

A non-Jew once asked Joshua ben Korcha, "Do you not claim that God sees into the future?" When the sage agreed, the man said: "But it is written in your Torah [Gen. 6:6], 'And the Lord regretted that He had made people on earth, and His heart was saddened' [i.e., if God knew that He would eventually regret creating human beings, why did He do it?]." Joshua ben Korcha asked the man if he had ever had a son. When he said yes, the sage asked the man what he did when his son was born. "I rejoiced and made everyone celebrate with me." Joshua ben Korcha said, "But did you not know that eventually the child would die?" The non-Jew replied, "At the time when one should be joyous, be joyous. And when it is time to mourn, mourn." Joshua ben Korcha said, "So, too, with God" (Gen. R. 27:4).

Among Joshua ben Korcha's best-known sayings are: "Whoever studies the Torah but does not review it is like a man who sows a field but does not harvest the crop" (Sanh. 99a); "Settling conflicts by arbitration is a meritorious act" (Sanh. 6b); "A man should always be prepared to perform a mitzvah" (Naz. 23b); and "He who shuts his eyes from [one who appeals for] charity is like one who worships idols" (Ket. 68a).

When Judah ha-Nasi asked the aged Joshua ben Korcha the secret of his long life, the latter was deeply offended and retorted, "Do you begrudge me my life?" Judah ha-Nasi reassured his colleague that he was simply asking "as a point of Torah that is important for me to learn." Then Joshua ben Korcha replied: "Never in my life have I gazed at the countenance [lit., 'likeness'] of a wicked man" (Meg. 28a). *See also* Eleazar ben Shimon.

Joshua ben Levi, Palestinian *amora* (third century).

A student of R. Bar Kappara and R. Judah ben Pedayah, Joshua ben Levi became head of the academy at Lydda. He stressed the importance of coming early to the synagogue to have the merit of being among the first ten to constitute a *minyan*, adding that "even if one hundred come after him he receives the reward of all of them" (Ber. 47b). However, he also stressed that one should "leave it [the synagogue] late that you may live long" (Ber. 8a). Among his many other maxims concerning the synagogue and prayers are the following: "Though a man has recited the *Shema* in the synagogue, it is a [meritorious] religious act to recite it again on his bed" (Ber 8a); "It is not permitted to pass behind a synagogue when the congregation is praying" (Ber. 8b); "The [thrice-daily recitation of the] *Amidah* was instituted [by the Men of the Great Assembly] to replace the daily sacrifices" (Ber. 26b); "One who prays [the *Amidah*] should go three steps backwards and then recite 'peace' [*Oseh Shalom*]" (Yoma 53b); "He who answers 'amen' during *Kaddish* is certain to have all decrees against him annulled" (Shab. 119a); "The [commandment to light the] Hanukkah lamp is obligatory upon women, for they also were concerned in that miracle"; "All oils are fit for the Hanukkah lamp, but olive oil is the best" (Shab. 23a); and "He who reads the section from the prophets must first read [a passage] in the Torah . . . [and] is not permitted to begin his recital until the Torah scroll is rolled up [so those who are rolling it can listen to it]" (Sot. 39b). Many of the rules he instituted regarding the synagogue service and the Torah reading are still in force today.

Joshua ben Levi cited the Men of the Great Assembly as having "observed twenty-four fasts so that those who write [Torah] scrolls, *tefillin*, and *mezuzot* should not become wealthy [lest they would not be willing to perform the tedious task of writing these religious articles]" (Pes. 50b). He observed, "Whoever compels his wife to the [marital] obligation will have unworthy children" (Er. 100b), and "He who teaches his grandson Torah [is regarded] as though he had received it [direct] from Mount Sinai" (Kid. 30a). Stressing the intimate relationship between the Jewish people and God, Joshua ben Levi declared: "Not even a wall of iron could separate Israel from their Father in Heaven" (Pes. 85b; Sot. 38b). When his son Joseph recovered from a serious illness and prolonged coma, Joshua ben Levi asked, "What vision did you have?" His son replied, "I saw an upside down world. Those who are at the top of things in this world are at the bottom in the next world . . . [and vice versa]." Joshua ben Levi observed, "My son, you have seen the real [lit., 'well-regulated'] world" (BB 10b).

According to legend, Joshua ben Levi risked his life by carefully tending to a man suffering from a deadly infectious disease known as *raatan*. Despite being warned of the danger, Joshua ben Levi sat studying Torah with him, arguing that it would protect him. This was in stark contrast to his close friend, R. Hanina ben Papa, who was renowned as a Torah scholar but never demonstrated love for his fellow man. When Hanina ben Papa was about to die, he asked the Angel of Death to hand over his sword lest he frighten the sage on the way to Paradise. Remembering the similar trick that Joshua ben Levi previously had played on him to avoid death, the Angel of Death was cautious. Hanina ben Papa protested, saying that he had been so dedicated to the tradition that the Angel of Death should bring him the Torah scroll to see that there was nothing in it that the sage had failed to observe. The Angel of Death retorted, "But have you attached yourself to the sufferers of *raatan* and thus engaged in the study of the Torah?" (Ket. 77b).

Agreeing with the rabbinic view of Torah study as the best medicine, Joshua ben Levi used various biblical verses to prove that this activity is the perfect cure for headache, sore throat, abdominal pain, bone pain, and even generalized pain throughout the body (Er. 54a). He noted that the Israelites made the golden calf to demonstrate both the opportunity and the power of repentance (Av. Zar. 4b). He compared Israel to an olive tree, explaining: "Just as the olive tree does not lose its leaves either in summer or in winter, so Israel will never be lost either in this world or the World to Come" (Men. 53b).

Although known as a *halachist* whose rulings were generally accepted, Joshua ben Levi also was an accomplished master of *aggadah*. However, he opposed committing it to writing, saying that those who did so would have no share in the World to Come. Joshua ben Levi once asked Elijah when the Messiah would come. The prophet replied, "Go and ask him." When the sage asked how he would recognize the Messiah, Elijah answered: "He is disguised as a filthy beggar, sitting among the lepers, untying and retying his bandages." He then asked Elijah, "When will you come and proclaim the Messiah?" Elijah replied, "Today, if you will only hear His voice [and obey the will of God]" (Sanh. 98a), implying that the good deeds of the Jewish people will determine when the Messiah comes.

Similar to the message of the biblical Book of Job, the Rabbis stressed that human beings can have only an extremely limited comprehension of God's ways. In a famous story, Joshua ben Levi asked to accompany Elijah on his wanderings and gain wisdom by observing his deeds. The prophet warned that Joshua would be shocked by what he saw and want to barrage him with questions, but if the sage asked even one question about the miracles Elijah would perform, he would have to return to his home. The two soon arrived at the hut of a poor couple, who invited them in, gave them food and drink, and asked them to stay the night. In the morning, Elijah prayed to God that the poor man's cow die, and this promptly occurred. When the heartbroken Joshua ben Levi began to ask why this was the reward to the poor couple's gracious hospitality, Elijah warned his companion of his agreement to ask no questions. The next night they stayed at the home of a wealthy man, who refused to feed them or treat them in a respectful manner. When they departed in the morning, Elijah prayed that a crumbling wall of the house be rebuilt immediately, and it was so. Joshua ben Levi was angry at this injustice, but held his peace. The next evening they lodged in the synagogue of a wealthy town, whose most important members sat on silver benches. However, when one asked the other who would provide for the poor visitors that night, the latter contemptuously retorted that Joshua ben Levi and Elijah should be content with their bread, water, and salt. Yet the next morning Elijah blessed the rich members of the synagogue that they all become leaders. That night, they were cordially welcomed in a different community, given the best food, and treated with the utmost respect. The next morning Elijah blessed them, praying that God set only one leader over them.

Joshua ben Levi could no longer keep quiet and demanded an explanation for Elijah's seemingly senseless actions. The prophet explained that, learning that Heaven had decreed that the wife of the poor man would die that same day, he had prayed that God would accept the cow as redemption for the wife's life. Had he not prayed that the miser's wall be rebuilt before it collapsed, the miser would have dug down to the foundation and discovered there a treasure of gold and silver. Elijah prayed that the hard-hearted wealthy members of the first synagogue all become leaders, since this would inevitably result in dissension and strife. Conversely, his prayer that the other community have only one head was for their benefit, since all would follow him and prosper. Elijah concluded that human beings should never wonder about Divine justice when a wicked man appears to thrive or a righteous one to suffer, for God alone is omniscient and supervises all the deeds of men.

Joshua ben Levi praised humility as the greatest virtue (Av. Zar. 20b), asserting that one "whose mind is lowly" is regarded by God as if he had offered the sacrifices (Sot. 5b), based on the biblical verse, "The sacrifices of God are a broken spirit" (Ps. 51:19). He stressed the need for pure speech, citing the biblical circumlocution, "Every clean beast . . . and of the beasts that are not clean" instead of "every *unclean* beast" (Pes. 3a). Joshua ben Levi attacked slander as one of two things (with bloodshed) for which there was "no atonement through sacrifices" (Av. Zar. 88b), and he cautioned against unnecessary speech: "A word is worth one *sela*, but silence is worth two" (Lev. R. 16:5).

According to legend, a rainbow, the Divine sign that God would never again destroy the world with a flood, was never seen during Joshua ben Levi's lifetime (Ket. 77b), because his merit was sufficient to save the world from destruction.

Joshua ben Perachyah (second century B.C.E.).

Joshua ben Perachyah served as *nasi* (president of the Sanhedrin) as one of the *zugot* (pairs of leading sages, with Nittai of Arbela). When King Alexander Yannai persecuted the Pharisees, Joshua ben Perachyah fled to Alexandria. From there, Joshua ben Perachyah wrote to the Jews in the Land of Israel that Egyptian wheat should not be eaten, since he believed that it was contaminated by a combination of unclean hands and the methods of fertilization employed. According to some, Joshua ben Perachyah's reasoning was based on irrigation and other artificial methods used to encourage plant growth in Egypt, which constituted unacceptable human interference with the natural course of development ordained by God. In any event, the prohibition against Egyptian wheat was ignored by the rabbinic leaders in Jerusalem (Tosef., Machshirin 3).

As with their predecessors, Joshua ben Perachyah and Nittai of Arbela disagreed regarding the controversial issue of *semichah*, the physical laying of hands on sacrifices on Sabbaths and festivals. Joshua ben Perachyah ruled that the practice was prohibited as constituting forbidden work, while Nittai of Arbela maintained that it could be performed (Hag. 2:2).

Joshua ben Perachyah observed: "At first, if anyone had suggested that I seek [a position of] power, I would have bound him and put him in front of a lion; but now that I have power [having assumed the office of *nasi*], if anyone were to suggest that I let it go, I would pour a kettle of boiling water over him.

So it was with King Saul. At first he shunned the throne [fled from power], but after he had reigned as king, he sought to kill David [who was a threat to his power]" (Men. 109b).

In Pirkei Avot (1:6), Joshua ben Perachyah is quoted as saying: "Provide yourself with a teacher (*rav*), find yourself [lit., 'acquire'] a friend, and judge everyone favorably." This probably reflected his belief that, given the political and religious upheaval in the Land of Israel, it was important to have an authoritative figure as a guide to emulate and a friend to correct one's errors. Joshua ben Perachyah personified the recommendation to judge everyone favorably. Forced to flee Jerusalem and seek refuge in Alexandria, he never made disparaging remarks about Yochanan, the high priest responsible for his exile.

According to early noncensored manuscripts of the Talmud (Sot. 47a; Sanh. 107b), Joshua ben Perachyah had a disciple named Jeshu, who "practiced magic and led Israel astray." When Joshua ben Perachyah lived in Egypt, he praised the kindness of an innkeeper to his students. Jeshu remarked, "She is not beautiful, for her eyes are almond-shaped." Rebuking his student, "Wicked man, are you concerned with such trifles," the sage then drove him away. Some have suggested that Jeshu was really Jesus, although this is chronologically impossible since the two lived about a century apart. *See also* Nittai of Arbela.

Joshua Hagarsi, Palestinian *tanna* (first/second century).

His name may have referred to his profession as a grinder of grits (*gerisim* in Hebrew), although some commentators have suggested that it related to his locality, either Garsis in Galilee or Gerasa in Transjordan. When the Romans cast R. Akiva into prison under close guard, the sage was forbidden to continue to teach his disciples. However, Joshua Hagarsi was permitted to stay with R. Akiva and attend to his needs, including providing water for his daily use. The warden once thought that Joshua Hagarsi was bringing in too much water for the use of a single prisoner. Accusing him of planning an escape, the warden poured out half the water from the pitcher. When Joshua Hagarsi came to R. Akiva's cell, the latter said: "'Joshua, do you not know that I am an old man and my life depends on yours?' [i.e., no one else was allowed to bring him food or drink]." Realizing that there was not enough water to both drink and wash his hands, R. Akiva said: "What can I do when for [neglecting] the words of the Rabbis one deserves death? It is better that I myself should die than that I should transgress against the opinion of my colleagues [who ordained the washing of the hands before meals]." Hearing of this incident, the sages concluded that if R. Akiva was so meticulous when a feeble old man in prison, how much stricter must have been his observance when a young man free in his own home (Er. 21b).

In one other Talmudic reference, a sectarian asked Joshua Hagarsi: "How do we know that *tefillin* may not be written upon the skin of an unclean animal?" The sage cited the biblical verse (Exod. 13:9), "And it [*tefillin*] shall be a sign on your hand, and a reminder between your eyes, that the Torah of the Lord may be in your mouth," implying that *tefillin* can only be written on something "that is permitted in your mouth" (Shab. 108a).

Josiah, Palestinian *tanna* (second century).

Born in Babylonia, Josiah moved to the Land of Israel, where he studied with R. Ishmael ben Elisha (Men. 57b). He is almost invariably quoted with his fellow-student and colleague R. Jonathan in *halachic* interpretations of biblical texts, although they often disagreed on how to apply their teacher's hermeneutical principles. As an example, Josiah taught that the land of Canaan was divided among those over age twenty who "came out of Egypt," based on the verse, "According to the names of the tribes of their fathers [who came out of Egypt] they shall inherit" (Num. 26:55). Jonathan disagreed, arguing that it was divided according to those "who entered the land," based on the verse, "Among these [who entered the land] shall the land be apportioned as an inheritance" (Num. 26:53). Therefore, if one man who left Egypt had one son (under age twenty) and another had four sons (under that age), how should the land be apportioned when they entered Canaan? According to Josiah, the son of the first man would receive a full share, but each son of the second would be allotted only a quarter share. According to Jonathan, all the sons would receive equal shares (BB 117a).

A maxim of Josiah was: "Whoever is faint [negligent] in the study of the Torah will have no strength to stand in the day of trouble," based on the verse (Prov. 24:10), "If you showed yourself slack in time of trouble, your strength will be small" (Ber. 63a). He also declared, "The deeds of the righteous yield fruit . . . the deeds of the wicked do not produce fruit, for if they produced fruit they would destroy the world" (Gen. R. 33:1). Josiah is not mentioned in the Mishnah, perhaps because he lived in the south (Sanh. 88b) and thus his teachings were unknown to the compiler of the Mishnah, Judah ha-Nasi, who lived in the north in Tiberias and Beit She'arim.

Judah II, Palestinian *amora* (third century).

Son of Gamaliel III, grandson of Judah ha-Nasi, and also known as Judah Nesi'ah and Yudan the patriarch, Judah II was the last of the descendants of Hillel to both head the Sanhedrin and lead the secular administration of the Jewish community (c. 230–270). Following his death, these two positions were separated and held by different persons. An advocate of the spread of elementary education throughout the small towns and villages of the Land of Israel, Judah II was quoted by R. Shimon ben Lakish (a former student) as having said: "The world endures only for the sake of the breath of school children"; and "School children may not be made to neglect [their studies] even for the building of the Temple" (Shab. 119b). Judah II apparently felt unworthy of his acclaimed forebears. Once during a drought, after ordering a fast and vainly praying for rain, he exclaimed: "What a difference between Samuel of Ramah [referring to the biblical verse, 1 Sam. 12:18] and Judah, the son of Gamaliel! Woe to the generation that finds itself in such a plight! Woe to him in whose days this has happened." In consequence of this self-abasement, "rain fell" (Taan. 24a).

Judah II made no administrative distinction between scholars and ordinary Jews, taxing them both equally. This policy, which was in opposition to the accepted principle that one who assumed the burden of the Torah should be exempt from that of the government, caused substantial resistance from the scholarly ranks. Unlike his forebears, Judah II permitted the use of oil bought from pagans (Av. Zar. 35b), but refused to cancel the prohibition against their bread (possibly untithed), lest he and his advisers be labeled "the permitting Court" (Av. Zar. 37a). The relative laxity of religious observance was criticized by the public, who favored a more rigorous interpretation of the law. Once when Judah II and his brother Hillel were bathing together in Cabul (a practice that was prohibited in the city), "The whole region criticized them, saying, 'We have never seen such [a thing] in [all] our days.'" When the murmurings of discontent reached them, Hillel felt compelled to immediately leave the bathhouse (Pes. 51a). The public at large also challenged some customs of Judah II's household because they differed from those followed by the general population. These included speaking Greek, growing their hair long, and decorating the walls with paintings and mirrors. However, as the scholars informed them, since Judah II and his retinue were "close to the government," such deviations from common practice were permitted (JT Shab. 6:5).

Judah III, Palestinian *amora* (third/fourth century).

Judah III was the son of Gamaliel IV and grandson of Judah II. Because the sources do not distinguish between Judah II and Judah III, and since the title *"Nesi'ah"* was borne by both in any Talmudic citation, it is necessary to look at the names of the scholars mentioned in the context to determine the correct person. Although the Roman government recognized Judah III as the head of the Sanhedrin, the Jewish community deemed R. Ammi and R. Yochanan their religious authorities. R. Ammi complained about the excessive number of fast days that Judah III had established in times of drought, saying that the community should not be overburdened. He successfully argued that if thirteen days did not produce rain, additional fasts would probably be of no avail (Taan. 14a–b).

As political unrest and the weakness of the Roman empire almost led to anarchy, scholarship suffered in the Land of Israel. Academies survived only in the Galilee, and Babylonia developed into the major center of Jewish learning. The most important event of Judah III's patriarchate was the visit to the Land of Israel by the Roman emperor Diocletian, who stayed in Tiberias while waging war against the Persians (JT Ter. 8:10; Gen. R. 63:8).

Judah bar Ezekiel, Babylonian *amora* (third century).

Judah bar Ezekiel was born in 220, on the same date that Judah ha-Nasi died in the Land of Israel (Kid. 72b). The most prominent disciple of Rav, in whose house he often stayed, Judah bar Ezekiel later studied with R. Samuel and founded a school of his own at Pumbedita. After the destruction of the town of Nehardea and the disbanding of its prominent center of Jewish learning, Pumbedita became one of the two prestigious Babylonian academies. Ironically, after the death of R. Huna in 297, Judah bar Ezekiel was chosen as his successor to head the academy at Sura, so that for the two years until his death, both of these major centers of learning were under the same leadership.

Judah bar Ezekiel devoted such time and energy to his studies that he even omitted daily prayer, praying only once every thirty days (RH 35a). This diligence, when combined with a prodigious memory, allowed Judah bar Ezekiel to collect and transmit hundreds of the *halachic* and *agaddic* sayings of his illustrious teachers. Judah bar Ezekiel himself was so widely known and respected that in the Talmud he is usually referred to as simply Judah, or Rav Judah, without patronymic.

In the name of Rav, Judah bar Ezekiel said: "There are four [classes of people] who have to offer thanksgiving: those who have crossed the sea, those who have traversed the wilderness, one who has recovered from an illness, and a prisoner who has been set free" (Ber. 54b). This is the source of the *gomel* blessing, which today is ideally said in the presence of a *minyan* and within three days of the event, to publicly acknowledge God's saving deed. Judah bar Ezekiel echoed his mentor's view that everything that happens has been preordained and does not occur by mere chance: "Forty days before the creation of a child, a *bat kol* (heavenly voice) issues forth and proclaims, 'The daughter of A is for B; the house of C is for D; the field of E is for F!'" (Sot. 2a). Judah bar Ezekiel also noted in the name of Rav, "Hospitality to wayfarers is greater than welcoming the presence of the *Shechinah*," based on Abraham's leaving God to attend to the needs of the three strangers (Gen. 18:3) (Shab. 127a); and "Wherever the sages have forbidden [an action] because of appearances [i.e., how it might be perceived in public, it also] is forbidden even in the innermost chambers [i.e., in strictest privacy]" (Betz. 9a).

Judah was opposed to Jewish scholars returning from Babylonia to the Land of Israel before the coming of the Messianic age, believing that, "Whoever lives in Babylonia is accounted as though he lived in the Land of Israel." Consequently, he would not give permission to his students to do so, considering it a transgression of a positive commandment. When R. Ze'ira and R. Abba decided to go to the Land of Israel, they were compelled to leave in secrecy, without his knowledge (Ket. 110b–111a). However, Judah bar Ezekiel believed that prayers should only be recited in Hebrew: "One should never petition for his needs in Aramaic [the vernacular among the Jews in Babylonia]" (Shab. 12b).

The Talmud describes two different opinions regarding whether the Torah scroll should be rolled closed while the Torah blessings are being recited (Meg. 32a). According to R. Meir, a person called up for an *aliyah* should open the scroll, look at the place where the reading is to begin, roll the scroll closed, recite the first Torah blessing, and then unroll the scroll for reading. His rationale was that if the scroll were left open, an uninformed person might mistakenly think that the blessings are being read from the scroll itself. Judah bar Ezekiel disagreed, arguing that there was no need to close the scroll because no one would be foolish enough to imagine that the blessings were written in it.

According to Judah bar Ezekiel, "He who delights in the Sabbath is granted his heart's desire" (Shab. 118b). With respect to the *Amidah*, Judah bar Ezekiel maintained, "A man should never petition for his requirements either in the first three benedictions or in the last three, but [only] in the middle ones" (Ber. 34a), a practice that continues today. Although considering it as "one-sixtieth part of death" (Ber. 57b), the Rabbis appreciated the healthful benefits of sufficient sleep. Judah bar Ezekiel observed, "Night was created for nothing but sleep" (Er. 62b).

Judah bar Ezekiel agreed with his teacher Rav that "God did not create a single thing without purpose. [Thus] He created the snail [as a cure] for a sore; the [application of a crushed] fly [to the wound as a cure] for the sting of a hornet; a [crushed] mosquito for [the bite of] a serpent; a serpent [as a remedy] for skin eruption; and a [crushed] spider for [a remedy for the bite of] a scorpion" (Shab. 77b). A lover of nature and a close observer of animal and plant life around him, Judah bar Ezekiel said: "When in springtime you see Nature in her glory, you shall thank God for forming such beautiful creatures and plants for the good of mankind" (RH 11a).

The Talmud relates that in times of drought, Judah bar Ezekiel, who was known as a wonderworker, needed to only remove one shoe as an indication of preparation for fasting, and rain would immediately begin to fall (Ber. 20a). For Judah bar Ezekiel, the day when rain fell was as great as the day when the Torah was given, based on the verse (Deut. 32:2), "My teaching

[Torah] shall drop like rain" (Taan. 7a). The underlying meaning was that rain is just as critical to the physical well-being of a Jew as the Torah is to his spiritual existence. Judah bar Ezekiel once ordered a fast when informed about an infestation of locusts. Subsequently told that these voracious eaters were not damaging the crops, he exclaimed: "Have they brought provisions with them?!" (Taan. 21b). He included "sitting long at the table [lit., 'drawing out one's meals']" as one of the three things that "prolongs a man's days and years," because it afforded an opportunity for a poor man to come in late and still receive something to eat (Ber. 55a).

The Bible unequivocally condemns male homosexual practice (Lev. 18:22). Judah bar Ezekiel forbade two bachelors from sleeping together under the same blanket (lit., "cloak"), for fear that this would lead to temptation. However, the other sages permitted it, deeming homosexuality so rare among Jews that such preventative legislation was unnecessary (Kid. 4:14).

The Talmud indicates that certain people were especially susceptible to being attacked by demons. According to Judah bar Ezekiel: "Three [types of people] require guarding [i.e., protection from evil spirits]: a sick person [invalid], a bridegroom, and a bride." Other Rabbis added "a woman who has [recently] given birth . . . a mourner . . . and disciples of the sages at night" (Ber. 54b). "Judah bar Ezekiel once saw two men throwing bread at one another and exclaimed, 'It seems that there is plenty in the world!' He gave an angry look [Evil Eye] and there was a famine" (Taan. 24b).

The pursuit of learning was the highest rabbinic goal. However, if a father had both himself and his son to teach, but the means for only one of them to study, who took precedence? The rabbinic majority ruled, "He [the father] takes precedence over his son." However, Judah bar Ezekiel disagreed: "If his son is industrious, bright [filled with a desire to learn] and has a retentive memory [lit., 'his learning endures in his hand'], his son takes precedence over him [since he will outlive the father]" (Kid. 29b).

In a discussion of the relative worth of various occupations, when one Rabbi urged that a father should not teach his son to be (among others) a camel driver or sailor, Judah bar Ezekiel disagreed: "Most camel-drivers are worthy men [their travels through the desert give them a sense of awe that leads to humility and a God-fearing spirit], and most sailors are pious [the dangers of the sea turn their thoughts to God]." He added, "The best of doctors are destined for Gehinnom," which may refer to the physician who arrogantly believes that the recovery of a patient was due to his own skill, with God playing no role in the process (Rashi), or who is convinced he knows everything and never seeks the advice of his colleagues; and "The worthiest of butchers is the partner of Amalek [i.e., they prevent a loss by selling ill animals as fit to eat]" (Kid. 4:14).

Judah bar Ezekiel stated that a shopkeeper may not cut prices (i.e., sell below the market price), but the other Rabbis disagreed, arguing that such a merchant "is to be remembered for good" because "he eases the market" (BM 4:12). Competition is healthy and, as a result of his initiative, other sellers would lower their prices as well, thus preventing the practice of holding back goods to raise prices.

The Rabbis stated that repentance required sincere remorse for having committed the sin. Judah bar Ezekiel defined a true penitent as one who encountered the object that caused his original sin on two subsequent occasions and yet was able to keep away from it. As he specified, "With the same woman, at the same time, in the same place" (Yoma 86b). *See also* Akabiah ben Mahalalel.

Judah bar Samuel bar Shilath, Babylonian *amora* (third century).

A student of Rav, Judah bar Samuel bar Shilath quoted his teacher on several occasions. For example: "How does one show his delight [in the Sabbath]? With a dish of beets, a large fish, and cloves of garlic" (Shab. 118b); and "Just as with the beginning of [the month of] Av rejoicings are curtailed, so with the beginning of Adar rejoicings are increased" (Taan. 29a). Judah bar Samuel bar Shilath also cited Rav's opinion that the sages wished to hide the Book of Ecclesiastes (eliminate it from the biblical canon) "because its words are self-contradictory," but they did not do so because its beginning and end "is religious teaching [lit., 'words of Torah']" (Shab. 30b).

Judah bar Shila, Palestinian *amora* (third/fourth century).

Judah bar Shila said, in the name of R. Assi and R. Yochanan: "There are six things, the fruit of which man eats in this world, while the principal remains for him for the World to Come: hospitality to wayfarers, visiting the sick, meditation in prayer, early attendance at the study hall, rearing one's sons to the study of the Torah, and judging one's neighbor in the scale of merit [i.e., seeking a favorable interpretation of his actions, even when they appear suspicious]" (Shab. 127a).

Judah ben Bathyra (Beteira), name of two Palestinian *tannaim* (first and second centuries, respectively).

Some scholars believe that they represent a single second-century sage. They argue that the tale of a rabbinic figure of this name preventing a pagan in Jerusalem from partaking in the offering of the Paschal lamb before the destruction of the Temple (Pes. 3b) may be merely an anachronistic story relating to a later person.

Judah ben Bathyra left Jerusalem to become head of the academy in Nisibis in Babylonia (Sanh. 32b). In a discussion of the proper ritual, Judah ben Bathyra said that when any close relative died, a person was required to make a single tear in his garment, whereas "for his father or mother [he makes] another rent" (MK 26). This statement was variously interpreted as meaning a tear for each, separate from any next of kin, or possibly an extension of the tear.

In a dispute concerning the teaching of R. Akiva that Zelophehad (the father of the five daughters who fought for their inheritance rights; Num. 27) was the person who violated the Sabbath by gathering sticks and was stoned to death for his crime (Num. 15:32–36). Judah ben Bathyra challenged his fellow sage: "Akiva! In either case you will have to give an account [for your statement]: if you are right, the Torah shielded him, while you reveal him; and if not, you cast a stigma upon a righteous man" (Shab. 96b). Judah ben Bathyra said, "Like fire, words of Torah are not susceptible to uncleanness" (Ber. 22a).

Judah ben Hiyya, Palestinian *amora* (third century).

Born in Babylonia, Judah ben Hiyya moved to the Land of Israel with his twin brother, R. Hezekiah ben Hiyya, and their father, R. Hiyya Rabbah bar Abba. According to legend, their mother suffered agonizing pangs of childbirth and, although twins, Judah ben Hiyya was born three months earlier than his brother (Yev. 65b). Judah ben Hiyya married the daughter of R. Yannai Rabbah. Devoted to his studies, Judah ben Hiyya spent his days in the academy and only returned home just before nightfall on the Sabbath eve. When Judah ben Hiyya once was so engrossed in his studies that he failed to come home at the appointed time, R. Yannai Rabbah ordered his bed to be covered, assuming his son-in-law to be dead, "for had Judah ben Hiyya been alive he would not have neglected the performance of his marital duties" (Ket. 62b). The Jerusalem Talmud (Bik. 3:3) related that it became a custom for Judah to visit his father-in-law every Friday afternoon. R. Yannai Rabbah would sit atop a high hill and, upon seeing the approaching Judah ben Hiyya in the distance, would rise out of respect. When asked by his students the reason for his actions, R. Yannai Rabbah explained that his son-in-law "equaled Mount Sinai in sanctity [i.e., as a profound scholar]," and no one was permitted to sit down in front of Mount Sinai.

Living at a time of severe Roman persecutions, which the Jews believed to be punishment for their sins, they complained that despite their repentance, their afflictions did not cease. Judah ben Hiyya observed, "Repentance avails against half of the punishment, while prayer may undo all of it" (Lev. R. 10:8). He added, "The suffering of exile atones for [the second] half of man's sins" (Sanh. 37b), so that they should not suffer in the World to Come. Comparing the Torah to a healing potion, Judah ben Hiyya remarked that Divine medication is far different from that dispensed by mortals: "When a human being administers a medicine to his friend, it may be beneficial to one limb [organ] but harmful to another. Not so God, who gave the Torah to Israel as a life-giving remedy for the entire body" (Er. 54a).

Judah ben Ilai, Palestinian *tanna* (second century).

Often cited without patronymic, Judah ben Ilai was so pious that, "When the phrase 'it once happened to a certain pious man' occurs, it refers either to Judah ben Bava or to Judah ben Ilai" (BK 103b).

Born in Usha and a pupil of his father and R. Tarfon, Judah was one of the last five students of R. Akiva who fled to Babylonia after their master was murdered by the Romans, returning to the Land of Israel at the end of the Hadrianic persecutions. After the Bar Kochba revolt, Judah ben Ilai was the leading scholar who reestablished the Sanhedrin in Usha and also at Yavneh. The *halachic* authority for the *nasi*, Judah ben Ilai was the teacher of Shimon ben Gamaliel's son, Judah ha-Nasi.

The Talmud relates a tale explaining why Judah ben Ilai was known as "first speaker on every occasion." Although they had executed his teacher, Judah ben Ilai admired Roman technical achievements. In a discussion among his colleagues, Judah ben Ilai praised the Romans for paving the streets and building bridges and baths. Jose ben Halafta "was silent" (disagreeing with Judah ben Ilai, but afraid to contradict him). However, R. Shimon bar Yochai was more outspoken: "Everything they did was for their own benefit. They built marketplaces to place harlots in them; baths to rejuvenate themselves; and bridges to collect tolls for them." When the Roman authorities learned of this conversation through an informant, their reaction was swift: "Judah ben Ilai, who exalted [us], shall be exalted [with the privilege of being the first to speak on all occasions]; Jose ben Halafta, who was silent, shall be exiled to Sepphoris [his native city in upper Galilee]; and Shimon bar Yochai, who censured [the Romans], let him be executed [he was condemned to death and forced to flee]" (Shab. 33b).

Despite his erudition and prominence, Judah ben Ilai lived in severe poverty. The Talmud relates that conditions were so dire that six of his disciples had to cover themselves with one garment between them, yet they studied the Torah (Sanh. 20a). His wife handmade a heavy coat that the couple shared; she wore it when going to market, he when on the way to the academy. Judah ben Ilai's appearance was so disheveled and his face was so red and shining that a noble Roman woman once accused him of being "a teacher and a drunkard." He replied that he drank no wine except for *Kiddush* and Havdalah and (the prescribed) four cups on Passover (from which he suffered from headaches until Shavuot), adding that "a man's wisdom makes his face shine" (Eccles. 8:1). When a Sadducee accused him of looking like a usurer or pig breeder, Judah ben Ilai simply responded, "Both of these are forbidden to Jews." Nevertheless, Judah ben Ilai refused all assistance, stating that he had become used to a simple existence and "do not wish to benefit from this world" (Ned. 49b–50a). His face never betrayed his poverty. Once when Judah ben Ilai was sitting before R. Tarfon, his teacher remarked, "Your face shines today." Judah ben Ilai replied, "Your servants went out to the fields yesterday and brought us beets, which we ate unsalted. Had we had some salt to eat with them, imagine how much more my face would have shone!" (Ned. 49b).

Judah ben Ilai said, "Eat an onion [*batzeil*] and dwell in the shade [*bitzeil*] of your house [i.e., do not spend too much on food, so you will be able to afford your house], and do not eat geese and fowl lest your heart palpitate [i.e., do not cultivate a greedy appetite so that you are always wanting to eat]" (Pes. 114a). Yet he had such pious reverence for the Sabbath that, "On the eve of the Sabbath a basin filled with hot water was brought to him, and he washed his face, hands, and feet, and he wrapped himself in fringed linen robes, producing the appearance of an angel of the Lord" (Shab. 25b).

Among his more than 3,000 statements in the Talmud, Judah ben Ilai's most famous maxim is: "Be meticulous [cautious] in learning, for a careless misinterpretation is considered tantamount to an intentional sin" (Avot 4:16). Judah ben Ilai was committed to study as the major pursuit in life: "See what a difference there is between the earlier and the later generations. The earlier generations made the study of the Torah their main concern and their ordinary work subsidiary to it, and both prospered in their hands. The later generations made their ordinary work their main concern and their study of the Torah subsidiary, and neither prospered in their hands" (Ber. 35b). Nevertheless, Judah ben Ilai also had high regard for the value of labor, which "honors the toiler" (Ned. 49b). He stressed the duty of a father to teach his son a trade, comparing one who does not to a person "who teaches his son to be a robber" (Kid. 29a). In the debate regarding whether it was more important to study the commandments or practice them, Judah ben Ilai favored the latter, and he would interrupt his studies to fulfill the mitzvah of joining a funeral process or leading a bride to the wedding canopy (Ket. 17a).

When a fast had been declared to pray for rain in order to avert a drought, Judah ben Ilai declared that the man who selected to speak to God on behalf of the community should "have a large family and no means of support, and draw his subsistence from [the produce of] the field [i.e., thus depending for his livelihood on rain, so he will pray with more devotion that his prayers be accepted], whose youth was unblemished, who is meek and is acceptable to the people; who is skilled in chanting, who has a pleasant voice, and possesses a thorough knowledge of the entire Tanach [Torah, Prophets, Writings] as well as the *midrash, halachot, aggadot*, and all the blessings" (Taan. 16a).

In answer to the question, "Why does this affliction [croup] begin in the bowels and end in the throat?" Judah ben Ilai related it to the development of the sin of slander: "The kidneys counsel, the heart gives understanding, the tongue speaks [gives form to the words], and yet the mouth completes it" (Shab. 33b).

Judah ben Ilai exclaimed, "One who has not seen the double colonnade [of the great synagogue] in Alexandria in Egypt has never seen the glory of Israel." This edifice was described as being so vast that the prayer leader signaled with a flag from the central reading platform to indicate the time for the congregation to respond "amen" (Suk. 51b). After declaring the value of charity, which "brings the redemption nearer," Judah ben Ilai noted: "Ten strong things have been created in the world [each one stronger than, and acting as a remedy for, the one preceding it]. A rock is hard, but iron cleaves it. Iron is hard, but fire softens [melts] it. Fire is strong, but water quenches it. Water is strong, but clouds carry it away. Clouds are heavy, but the wind scatters them. Wind is strong, but the human body withstands it. The human body is strong, but fear crushes it. Fear is strong, but wine banishes it. Wine is strong, but sleep overcomes its effects. Death is stronger than all, but charity saves one from death" (BB 10a).

Judah ben Ilai favored interpretations based on the plain meaning of the biblical text, but warned against giving a literal Aramaic translation of the Bible: "He who translates a verse literally is a liar, while he who adds to it is a libeler" (Tosef. Meg. 4:41). As support for the dictum that even the justified taking of the life of another is to be avoided whenever possible, Judah ben Ilai cited the biblical statement that when Jacob awaited the arrival of his estranged brother Esau and his host of 400 men, the patriarch "was greatly frightened and distressed" (Gen. 32:8). "Are not fear and distress the same thing?" He explained that Jacob was *afraid* that he might be killed, but was *distressed* that he might kill. Jacob thought, "If he defeats me, will he not kill me? But if I am victorious, will I not kill him?" (Gen. R. 76:2).

Judah ben Shimon, Palestinian *amora* (fourth century).

Known as Judah ben Pazi in the Jerusalem Talmud, he was famed for his *aggadic* teachings. Speaking of Adam, Judah ben Shimon noted that the first man was destined to live forever, but was eventually condemned to die "to inspire people with the fear of God" (Eccles. R. 3:17). Adam also was to have received the Torah, but once he failed to obey the single commandment not to eat of the fruit of the Tree of Knowledge, God realized that he could not be entrusted with the Torah and its 613 commandments (Gen. R. 24:5; Eccles. R. 3:14).

Extolling the great Divine love for Israel, Judah ben Shimon related a parable: "A king once had an orchard which grew figs, vines, pomegranates, and apples. The king turned the orchard over to a caretaker and went away. Sometime later, the king returned to see how his orchard was thriving and found it full of thorns and weeds. In great anger he ordered that the trees be cut down, but when he looked closely between the thorns, he noticed a beautiful rose. Bending over and inhaling its fragrance, he said: 'Because of this rose I will save the whole orchard.' So twenty-six generations after the Creation of the world, God saw its wickedness and decided to annihilate it. But among the thorns He saw a rose, the Jews who accepted the Ten Commandments, and for their sake He spared the entire world" (Lev. R. 23:3).

Judah ben Shimon discussed the sufferings of the Jews and their ultimate redemption. In the verse dealing with the binding of Isaac—"And Abraham lifted up his eyes and looked, and behold, *behind* (*achar*) him a ram was caught in a thicket by his horns; and Abraham went and took the ram, and offered him up for a burnt offering in place of his son" (Gen. 22:13)—Judah ben Shimon interpreted the Hebrew word "*achar*" as meaning "after" rather than "behind." As he observed, "After the passage of all the generations, your children will be caught by their sins and entangled in troubles but will finally be redeemed through the horns of this ram," based on the biblical verse (Zech. 9:14), "The Lord God will blow the horn and will go with the whirlwinds of the south" (JT Taan. 2:4). Similarly, he interpreted the verse "Arise O Lord, O God, lift up Your hand" (Ps. 10:12) as meaning, "Israel said to God, 'Lord of the Universe! Troubles are about to destroy us like a man drowning in the sea; stretch out Your hand and save us'" (Mid. Ps. 10:6).

Judah ben Tabbai (first century B.C.E.).

Judah ben Tabbai was paired with Shimon ben Shetach as the third of the *zugot*. The two disagreed over the degree of punishment to be meted out to witnesses who testified falsely in capital cases, with Judah ben Tabbai arguing that it was permitted to execute a false witness whose testimony, had it been accepted, would have caused the defendant to be put to death. During the persecutions of the Pharisees under Alexander Yannai, who favored the Sadducees, Judah ben Tabbai was forced to flee to Egypt and only returned after Alexander's death. After Judah ben Tabbai once had sentenced a single perjured witness to death, Shimon ben Shetach accused him of not following the tradition and thus shedding innocent blood. Recognizing his error and mortified by this rebuke, Judah ben Tabbai never again rendered a decision except in Shimon ben Shetach's presence. For the rest of his life, Judah ben

Tabbai "prostrated himself on the grave of the executed man." Those who heard his weeping voice in the distance were convinced it was that of the man who had been killed. However, Judah ben Tabbai assured them that it was his own: "It is my voice. You shall know this, for when I die the voice will be heard no more" (Hag. 16b; Mak. 5b).

Judah ben Tabbai's most famous maxim is: "[When serving as a judge] do not act as an attorney [for either side]; when the two parties in a case stand before you, consider them both as guilty; but when they depart, having submitted to your judgment, regard them both as innocent [since they have accepted the ruling]" (Avot 1:8).

Known for his modesty, Judah ben Tabbai warned of the harm that success could bring: "If someone had told me before I achieved greatness that I would succeed, I would have become his enemy for life. Now that I have attained greatness, if someone were to tell me that I might lose it, I would be prepared to pour boiling water on him" (ARN 10).

Once in Egypt, Judah ben Tabbai praised the generosity of an innkeeper to his disciples. One of the students said, "Rabbi, she had diseased eyes." The sage castigated him: "With one statement you have committed two wrongs. First, you suspected me of considering the beauty of that woman. Second, I see that you carefully looked at her face while I only noted her good deeds!" (JT Hag. 2:2). *See also* Shimon ben Shetach.

Judah ben Tema, Palestinian *tanna* (second century).

Termed a "master of the Mishnah" (Hag. 14a), Judah ben Tema related: "Adam reclined in the Garden of Eden, while the ministering angels roasted flesh and strained wine for him. The snake looked in, saw his glory, and became envious of him" (Sanh. 59b). Judah ben Tema observed, "The brazen go to Gehinnom, but the shamefaced goes to the Garden of Eden. May it be Your will, our God and God of our forefathers, that the Holy Temple be rebuilt speedily in our days, and grant us our share in Your Torah" (Avot 5:24).

Describing the stages of life, Judah ben Tema said: "At five, a child begins [the study of] Torah; at ten, Mishnah; at thirteen [he is responsible for performance of] the *mitzvot*; at fifteen, he begins [the study of] Talmud; at eighteen, [he is ready for] marriage; at twenty, he begins the pursuit [of a livelihood]; at thirty, [a person is at the fullness of] strength; at forty, [he reaches the time of] understanding; at fifty, [he can offer] counsel [no longer fit for heavy work]; at sixty, he enters his senior years [either appearance or intellectual maturity]; at seventy, he attains a ripe old age; at eighty, [his survival indicates] strength; at ninety, he becomes stooped over [in anticipation of the grave]; at one hundred, it is as if he were dead, passed away, and withdrawn from the world" (Avot 5:25).

Judah ben Tema's most popular maxim is: "Be bold as a leopard, light as an eagle, swift as a gazelle, and strong as a lion to carry out the will of your Father in Heaven" (Avot 5:23; Pes. 112a). The Rabbis urged that petty quarrels be healed promptly before they could flare into overt hostility. Later tradition ascribed to Judah ben Tema the saying: "If you have done your fellow a slight wrong, let it be a serious matter in your eyes; if you have done him much good, let it be a trifle in your eyes; if he has done you a slight favor, let it be a great thing in your eyes; if he has done you a great wrong, let it be a little thing in your eyes" (ARN 41).

Judah ha-Nasi, Palestinian *tanna* (second/third century).

The son of Rabban Shimon ben Gamaliel II, he is known as Judah the Prince in English and referred to simply as "Rabbi" in the Talmud. Judah ha-Nasi was even called *Rabbenu ha-Kodesh* (Our Holy Teacher) by his contemporaries as an indication of his unsurpassed piety and scholarship. Both the spiritual and political leader of his generation, the Talmud exults: "Between Moses and Rabbi we do not find one who was supreme both in Torah and in worldly affairs [lit., 'Torah and greatness in one place']" (Git. 59a). Nevertheless, Judah ha-Nasi was a humble man and devoted to his students: "I learned much [Torah] from my teachers, much more from my fellow students, but from my disciples most of all!" (Mak. 10a).

The crowning achievement of Judah ha-Nasi was his redaction of the Mishnah, the earliest major rabbinic book, completed in about 220. Fearing that centuries of traditions might be forgotten by later generations, especially in view of the increasing growth of far-flung Diaspora communities in the absence of an independent Jewish state, Judah ha-Nasi gathered, sifted through, evaluated, and edited the vast number of laws and customs of Jewish life as they were then accepted orally by the people as interpretations and supplements to the commandments of the Torah. He included the legal decisions that had been expressed over the centuries in the academies of learning, primarily by scholars in the Land of Israel. All the material in the Mishnah had originally been taught orally because of the prohibition against writing down the Oral Law (Git. 60b), lest it no longer be constantly developed by rabbinic decisions. The authorities whose opinions were assembled in the collection were known as the *tannaim*, from an Aramaic word meaning "repeater," since they acted as "living books" in imparting the Mishnah to their disciples.

The subject of numerous legends, Judah ha-Nasi was said to have been born on the same day that R. Akiva was executed by the Romans (Kid. 72b). A brilliant student trained by the best tutors, Judah ha-Nasi devoted time to the study of astronomy (to be able to determine the dates of the new months and the holidays) and the nature of various plants and animals (regarding the dietary laws). His knowledge of Greek enabled him to interact with the Roman authorities, although in his own household everyone spoke Hebrew, rather than Aramaic. Indeed, to revitalize Jewish settlement, Judah ha-Nasi said, "What has the Syrian tongue [Aramaic] to do with the Land of Israel? Speak either the Holy Tongue [Hebrew] or Greek" (BK 82b–83a). Contradicting the *halachah* that the *Shema* may be recited in any language, he was cited as having said that this quintessential Jewish prayer may be recited only in Hebrew (Tosef. Sot. 7:7). Judah ha-Nasi's academy and seat of the patriarchate was initially in Tiberias and then in Beit She'arim. He spent the last seventeen years of his life in Sepphoris, which he selected because the high altitude and pure air provided relief for his multiple illnesses (Ket. 103b).

Although extremely wealthy, Judah ha-Nasi used little of his resources for personal use. Instead, he gave generously to support needy students and feed the poor. During a famine, he opened his storehouses and distributed grain to the needy (BB 8a). He believed that "One who chooses the delights of this world will be deprived of the joys of the World to Come; one who renounces the former will receive the latter" (ARN 28). Judah concluded his daily prayers with one of his own that has been incorporated into the service: "Do not bring us into the power of error, nor into the power of transgression and sin, nor into the power of challenge, nor into the power of scorn. Let not the Evil Inclination dominate us. Distance us from an evil person and an evil companion" (Ber. 16b).

Judah ha-Nasi believed in the value of making shocking statements to keep his students awake. Once he "was lecturing and noticed that his audience was falling asleep. Suddenly he called out, 'A woman in Egypt gave birth to 6,000 children!' One student, Ishmael ben Jose, roused from his stupor and asked, 'Who could that be?' Judah ha-Nasi loudly replied, 'It was Jochebed, when she gave birth to Moses, because he is equal to 6,000 people'" (Song R. 1:15).

One day, Judah ha-Nasi returned home from the bathhouse to attend to community tasks. His servant placed a cup of wine before him, but he was too busy to drink it. Soon he observed that the servant had fallen asleep. The sage remarked, "The servant sleeps sweetly, but the public servant who is busy attending to the needs of the people is not allowed to sleep!" (Eccles. R. 5:10).

According to Judah ha-Nasi, the Day of Atonement brings pardon for transgressions against God even without repentance, except in cases of very serious sin (Yoma 85b). However, the forgiving quality of Yom Kippur is ineffective if one thinks, "I will sin and the Day of Atonement will procure atonement." Similarly, the person who says, "I will sin and repent, and sin again and repent," will not be given any opportunity to repent (Yoma 87a).

The Talmud relates numerous friendly encounters between Judah ha-Nasi and a Roman emperor named Antoninus, reflecting the cordial relationships between some Rabbis and Roman rulers during this time. Judah ha-Nasi is often depicted as a teacher, instructing his emperor-student on various theological and philosophical topics based on his religious experience and Torah knowledge. Antoninus once asked Judah ha-Nasi, "If a person has sinned, can the body and the soul both free themselves from judgment by pleading that the other was responsible?" The sage answered with this parable: "A human king owned a beautiful orchard that contained splendid figs. He appointed two watchmen, one lame and the other blind. One day, the lame man said to the blind, 'I see beautiful figs in the orchard. Put me on your shoulders so that we may pluck and eat them.' Some time later, the owner of the orchard returned and asked what had happened to his beautiful figs. The lame man replied, 'Have I feet to walk with?' The blind man answered, 'Have I eyes to see with?' What did the king do? He placed the lame upon the blind and judged them together. So will God bring the soul, [re]place it in the body, and judge them together" (Sanh. 91a–b).

According to legend, once when Judah ha-Nasi was studying Torah, a calf being taken to the slaughterhouse begged the sage to save him. "What can I do for you? For this you were created." As punishment for his insensitivity, Judah ha-Nasi suffered from a toothache for sixteen years. One day, a weasel ran past the sage's daughter, who was about to kill it. Judah ha-Nasi admonished her to let the animal live, citing the verse from Psalms (145:9), "The Lord is good to all; and His mercy is upon all His works." Because Judah ha-Nasi's compassion prevented the suffering and death of the harmless animal, his toothache ceased (BM 85a).

Judah ha-Nasi's most famous maxim, divided into three parts, is recorded in Pirkei Avot (2:1): "What is the proper path that a man should choose for himself? Whatever brings honor to himself and earns him the esteem of his fellow men; be as scrupulous in performing a 'minor' mitzvah as a 'major' one, for you do not know the reward given for the respective *mitzvot*. Calculate the cost of a mitzvah against its reward, and the reward of a sin against its cost; keep in mind three things and you will not be tempted to sin. Know what is above you—a watchful eye [Who sees all] and an attentive ear [Who hears and remembers everything], and [above all that] your deeds are recorded in a Book."

According to legend, as Judah ha-Nasi lay on his deathbed the impassioned prayers of the entire community to spare his life prevented the Angel of Death from accomplishing his task. Rabbi's handmaid, known for her wisdom and learning, "ascended the roof and prayed: 'Those above [the angels] desire Rabbi [to join them], but those below [mortals] desire Rabbi [to remain with them]. May it be God's will that those below overpower those above.' However, when she saw how often Rabbi went to the latrine because he was suffering from severe diarrhea, painfully taking off his *tefillin* to go to the bathroom and then putting them on again, she prayed anew: 'May it be God's will that those above overcome those below.' Hearing the Rabbis continually praying for heavenly mercy, she took a small earthenware jar and threw it from the roof to the ground. When the Rabbis heard the sound of the breaking vessel, they ceased praying [lit., 'remained silent'] for a moment, and the soul of Rabbi departed to its eternal rest" (Ket. 104a). Thus it is permissible in Jewish law to pray that someone in great pain from an incurable disease be mercifully released from his suffering by death. The Talmud added, "On the day that Rabbi [Judah ha-Nasi] died, a *bat kol* [heavenly voice] went forth and announced, 'Whoever was present at the death of Rabbi is destined to enjoy the life of the World to Come'" (Ket. 103b). With respect to the qualities that characterize the righteous man—"beauty, strength, wealth, honor, wisdom, old age, a manly beard, and successful children"—R. Shimon ben Menasia declared that they "were all realized in Rabbi and his sons" (Avot 6:8). *See also* Hananiah (Hanina) ben Teradion; Hiyya; Ilfa (Ilfi); Levi ben Sisi; Zerika.

Judah the Baker (ha-Nachtom), Palestinian *tanna* (first/second century).

A close friend of R. Akiva, Judah the Baker was one of the Ten Martyrs who were slain by the Romans for defying the ban on teaching Torah. According to the Jerusalem Talmud (JT RH 1:5), the legend of the tongue of Hutzpit the Interpreter, which the Roman executioner was said to have cut out and thrown to the dogs, was said to refer to Judah the Baker.

K

Kahana, Babylonian *amora* (third/fourth century).

A student of Rav, Kahana said: "By the time I was eighteen years old, I had studied the whole *Shas* [an abbreviation for *shishah sedarim*, the six orders of the Mishnah, which serve as the basis for the Talmud]." However, years later he admitted, "Yet I did not know that a verse cannot depart from its plain meaning," implying that a person should study intensely and subsequently understand (Shab. 63a). Describing Kahana's preparation for prayer, R. Ashi reported: "When there was trouble in the world, [I saw him] remove his cloak, clasp his hands, and pray, saying: '[I pray] like a slave before his master.' When there was peace, he would put it [his cloak] on, cover and enfold himself, and pray: 'Prepare to meet your God, O Israel'" (Shab. 10a).

Once Kahana "hid under Rav's bed. He heard him chatting [with his wife] and joking and doing what he required. [Thereupon] he said, 'The mouth of Rav is like one who has not tasted any food [i.e., he was as ravenous in his desires as a newlywed].' Rav said: 'Get out, because it is rude [lit., "it is not the way of the world"].' Kahana retorted, 'It is a matter of Torah, and I need to learn'" (Ber. 62a; Hag. 5b).

Rav advised Kahana: "It is better to deal in the bodies of dead animals than engage in idle talk [gossiping or quibbling]. Flay carcasses in the market place and earn wages and never say, 'I am a priest and a great man and it [such an occupation] is beneath my dignity [i.e., the most important person is not degraded by honest work]" (Pes. 113a). *See also* Helbo.

L

Levi, Palestinian *amora* (third century).

Focusing primarily on *aggadah*, Levi divided the Rabbis dealing in this area into two classes: those who can string pearls (i.e., cite appropriate biblical texts) but cannot perforate them (i.e., penetrate the depths of Scripture), and those who can perforate but not string them. Immodestly, he claimed skill in both arts (Song R. 1:10). A common technique he employed was to cite popular proverbs and compose fables and parables relating to them. For example, in commenting on the verse in Psalms (7:15), "He . . . has conceived mischief and brought forth falsehood," Levi said that when God ordered Noah to include two of every kind in the ark, Falsehood tried to enter, but Noah refused to admit him unless he brought his mate. Falsehood then searched for a mate and met Avarice. Falsehood asked whether Avarice would accompany him into the ark. Avarice would not agree to this unless being assured of material gain, so Falsehood promised all his earnings. When they left the ark, Avarice took everything that Falsehood had gained. When the latter demanded some share of his own, Avarice reminded Falsehood of their pact. Thereupon, Falsehood replied, "How could you ever believe that I meant to do as I promised?" Thus the lesson, "Falsehood begets falsehood" (Mid. Ps. to 7:15).

Levi described the human being as having six limbs, three of which were under his control and three of which were not. The eye, ear, and nose were outside his control. Conversely, the mouth can be controlled, employed either for the study of Torah or for gossip. Similarly, the hand can be used to fulfill commandments or to steal, and the foot leads a person wherever he chooses, into the synagogue and the academy or to see forbidden games (Gen. R. 66:3). As a guide to proper conduct, Levi recommended that one should eat according to his income, dress poorer than his income permits, and furnish his home better than his income allows (Gen. R. 20:30). In his lectures, Levi often put forward two different interpretations of the same text, one directed to the scholars in attendance and the other to the masses (Gen. R. 44:4; Eccl. R. 2:2).

According to the Talmud, in ancient times the *kohanim* recited the Ten Commandments daily as part of the Temple service as a reminder of the

Revelation (Tam. 5:1). Israelites outside the Temple were forbidden to recite them, so as to disprove claims by heretical sects (*minim*) that only the Ten Commandments and not the entire Torah were Divinely revealed at Mount Sinai (Ber. 12a). Therefore, the Ten Commandments were excluded from the liturgy, although in the Jerusalem Talmud, Levi insisted that they are alluded to in the three paragraphs of the *Shema* (Ber. 1:8).

Levi compared the giving of charity to three types of nuts: "soft-shelled, middling, and stony ones." Those who give charity unasked are like soft-shelled nuts, which "can be opened of themselves." Those who give immediately when asked are like middling nuts, which "break if you knock them." Those who refuse to give even if you press them repeatedly are like stony nuts, which are "very hard to break." Citing the proverb, "The door that is not open to charity is open to the doctor," Levi observed: "Those who do not give charity when healthy will either fall ill or promise to give charity when they are sick" (Pes. Rab. 42b).

Levi compared the defiant acts of rebellious children to "a man who lights a candle to use its light, but it falls down and burns his coat. He said, 'I lit this candle to enjoy its light, not to be burned by it'" (Mid. Sam. 7:1). Among his many sayings are: "Living without a wife is not living" (Gen. R. 17); "The punishment for [false] measures is more severe than for incest [lit., 'marrying forbidden relatives']" (BB 88b); and "Stealing from a fellow man is worse than robbing holy things [i.e., from God]" (BB 88b).

Levi yearned passionately for the arrival of the Messianic era. "If the Jews would keep but one Sabbath properly, the son of David [Messiah] would immediately come" (JT Taan. 1:1).

Levi ben Lahma, Palestinian *amora* (third century).

Levi ben Lahma addressed the issue of whether the shofar should be blown if Rosh Hashanah fell on the Sabbath. Traditionally, when this occurred the shofar was blown in the Temple but not in the countryside. After the Temple was destroyed, there was a difference of opinion among the major Rabbis. Fearing that an inexperienced blower might go for help to a more experienced person, thus violating the law of carrying on the Sabbath, they eventual concluded that the shofar should not be blown on the Sabbath, which remains the current practice. Levi ben Lahma maintained that this decision was based on the two descriptions of Rosh Hashanah in the Bible: *Yom Teruah* (Num. 29:1) and *Yom Zichron Teruah* (Lev. 23:24), respectively, "the day of the blowing" and "the day of remembering the blowing." The former was deemed to mean any day but the Sabbath, when the shofar would actually be *blown*, while the latter was considered as referring to the Sabbath, when all we do is *remember* the sound of the shofar and not blow it (RH 29b).

Also known as Levi bar Hama, he cited several sayings of his teacher, R. Shimon ben Lakish. "A man should always incite the good impulse [in his soul] to fight against the evil impulse, for it is written, 'Tremble, and sin no more; ponder it [lit., "commune with your own heart"] on your bed, and be still' [Ps. 4:5]." If one is successful in subduing the evil impulse, "well and good." If not, Levi bar Hama interpreted this verse as offering several suggestions: "'Commune with your own heart,' [meaning] let him study Torah; 'on your bed,' [meaning] let him recite the *Shema*; 'and be still,' [meaning] let him remind himself of the day of death" (Ber. 5a).

On the same page, Levi bar Hama rhetorically asked the meaning of the verse, "And I will give you the tablets of stone, and the law, and the commandment, which I have written that you may teach them" (Exod. 24:12). He answered that the tablets of stone are the Ten Commandments, the law is the Five Books of Moses, and the commandment is the Mishnah; "which I have written" refers to the Prophets and the Writings, while "that you may teach them" is the Gemara. "It teaches [us] that all these things were given to Moses on Sinai."

Levi ben Sisi, Palestinian *amora* (third century).

The most prominent of the last disciples of Judah ha-Nasi, Levi ben Sisi assisted his teacher in compiling and editing the Mishnah. He also collected numerous *beraitot* that were not included in that work. In the Babylonian Talmud, he is mentioned without a patronymic, whereas in the Jerusalem Talmud his father's name was used.

A merrymaker on festive occasions in the household of Judah ha-Nasi, Levi ben Sisi was an accomplished juggler who delighted visitors with his acrobatic feats. However, at one performance when he attempted to imitate how the priests used to prostrate themselves in the Temple, he dislocated his hip and was left with a permanent limp (Suk. 53a).

When the congregation at Simonias asked Judah ha-Nasi to send them someone to lecture, decide issues of law, and supervise general communal affairs, he sent Levi ben Sisi. However, when questions of law and exegesis were addressed to him, Levi ben Sisi left them unanswered. The Simonias congregation charged the patriarch with having sent an unfit man, but he assured them that he had selected a man as able as himself. When Judah ha-Nasi summoned Levi ben Sisi and asked him the questions originally submitted by the congregation, the latter answered every one correctly. When asked why he did not do so when the congregation asked those same questions, Levi ben Sisi replied that his courage had failed him (or that he became confused and did not know what to say) (JT Yev. 12:6).

After the death of Judah ha-Nasi, Levi ben Sisi moved to Babylonia, where he assisted in founding an academy at Nehardea (JT Suk. 4:3). Mourned by his colleagues at his death, Levi ben Sisi was eulogized as a superb scholar and God-fearing man, whose worth was "equal to that of all humanity" (JT Ber. 2).

Levitas of Yavneh, Palestinian *tanna* (second century).

In Pirkei Avot (4:4), Levitas of Yavneh is quoted as saying: "Be exceedingly humble in spirit, for the anticipated end of mortal man is [that he will turn to] worms."

Mani, Palestinian *amora* (fourth century).

Mani was head of the academy in Sepphoris (JT Pes. 6:1). From the *mishnah*, "He who says the *Shema* later loses nothing, being like one who reads from the Torah," Mani deduced: "He who recites the *Shema* in its proper time is greater than he who studies the Torah [i.e., if one who says it later is as good, the person who says it at the proper time must be better!]" (Ber. 10b).

In one tale, Mani was depicted as an inveterate complainer. While attending the lectures of R. Isaac ben Eliashab, he grumbled, "The rich members of the family of my father-in-law are annoying me." Isaac ben Eliashab then exclaimed, "May they become poor!" and so they did. Later Mani complained, "They press me [for support]." This time Isaac ben Eliashab said, "Let them become rich!" and so they did. On another occasion, Mani complained, "My wife is no longer acceptable to me." After ascertaining her name, Isaac ben Eliashab exclaimed, "May Hannah become beautiful!" and so she did. But this did not satisfy Mani, who grumbled again, "She is too domineering over me." In response, Isaac ben Eliashab said, "If that is so, let Hannah revert to her [former] ugliness!" and so she did (Taan. 23b).

On *halachic* issues, Mani debated the proper Torah readings when Rosh Hodesh Tevet (during Hanukkah) falls on a weekday (Meg. 29b), and how the rules of *shivah* and *keri'ah* differ when one learns on the Sabbath that a close relative has died, either less or more than thirty days before (MK 20b).

Mani bar Pattish, Palestinian *amora* (third century).

Mani bar Pattish considered the inability to control one's temper as a recipe for disaster. "Whoever becomes angry, even if greatness has been decreed for him by Heaven, will be cast down" (Pes. 66b). Mani bar Pattish derived this conclusion from the story of Eliab, the eldest son of Jesse. When David, Eliab's younger brother, saw the mighty Goliath, he asked: "What shall be done for the man who kills that Philistine and removes the disgrace from Israel? Who is that uncircumcised Philistine that he dares to defy the armies of the living God?" (1 Sam. 17:26). Then "Eliab became angry with David and said: 'Why did you come down here, and with whom did you leave those few sheep in the wilderness? I know your impudence and your impertinence; you came down to watch the fighting!'" (1 Sam. 17:28). When Samuel went to anoint a king from the House of Jesse, he saw Eliab and was certain that this was the chosen one. However, "the Lord said to Samuel, 'Pay no attention to his appearance or his stature, for I have rejected him'" (1 Sam. 16:6–7), implying that God had previously favored Eliab but then dismissed him because of his angry outburst.

Mar bar Rav Ashi, Babylonian *amora* (fifth century).

Although his real name was Tavyomi (BB 12b), he was always referred to as "Mar [Master], the son of Rav Ashi." Although a student of his father and a recognized scholar in his own right who continued the process of editing the Talmud, Mar bar Rav Ashi did not become head of the prestigious academy of Sura until 455, twenty-eight years after his father's death. *See also* Ravina II.

Mar bar Ravina, Babylonian *amora* (fourth century).

Mar bar Ravina was best known for the words he added after concluding his formal prayers (Ber. 17a), which today have been inserted, in a slightly modified form, at the end of every silent *Amidah*: "My God, guard my tongue from evil and my lips from speaking guile. To those that curse me, let my soul be silent, and may my soul be like dust to all. Open my heart to Your Torah, let my soul pursue Your commandments, and save me from evil occurrences, from the evil inclination, from an evil woman, and from all evils that threaten to come upon the world. As for those who plot evil against me, speedily annul their counsel and frustrate their designs! 'May the words of my mouth and the meditation of my heart be acceptable before You, O Lord, my Rock and my Redeemer!' (Ps. 19:15)."

Mar bar Ravina considered profanation of the Name of God the most horrible sin (Kid. 40a), and he believed that even those gentiles who observed the seven Noahide laws did not earn any heavenly reward (Av. Zar. 2b–3a). The Talmud (Ber. 57b) relates, "When Mar bar Ravina came to [the city of] Babylon, he used to put some dust in his kerchief and throw it out to fulfill the prophetic text: 'I will sweep it with the broom of extermination' (Isa. 14:23)." At the wedding feast for his son, when he observed "the Rabbis growing overly merry," Mar bar Ravina smashed a precious [crystal] glass worth 400 *zuzim* . . . and they [the Rabbis] became serious" (Ber. 30b). Some believe that this may be the origin of the custom of breaking a glass at a Jewish wedding ceremony.

Several Talmudic legends describe how Mar bar Ravina miraculously escaped from danger. When once he suffered from severe thirst while walking through the valley of Arabot, a well of water was miraculously created for him to drink. On another occasion, when a wild camel attacked him in Machoza, the wall of a nearby house fell and he escaped inside. Whenever Mar bar Ravina subsequently came to these places, he always said: "Blessed be He who produced miracles for me in . . ." (Ber. 54a).

Mar Ukba, Babylonian *amora* (third century).

A disciple of R. Samuel, Mar Ukba was a scholar in addition to serving as exilarch (political leader of the community). Thus he played a major role in the development of Jewish life in Babylonia. His major student was R. Hisda, who transmitted many of his sayings.

A wealthy man, Mar Ukba was renowned for his generosity, especially for giving charity to the poor while keeping his identity a secret (Ket. 67b). According to one story, each day Mar Ukba placed four silver coins on the doorstep of a poor man. Hoping to learn the identity of his benefactor, the recipient waited in his house until he heard someone at the door. To avoid being recognized as the door was flung open, Mar Ukba fled and "hid in a furnace from which the fire had just been swept," but it still was very hot and burned his feet. In another tale, every year Mar Ukba sent 400 silver coins to a poor neighbor on the eve of Yom Kippur. On one occasion he entrusted this task to his son, who returned with the money because he had seen the neighbor drinking expensive wine. Mar Ukba was furious, stating that if the neighbor had become used to a luxurious life, the money would help him maintain it (Bader, 682).

When about to die, Mar Ukba checked his accounts and saw that he had already donated the large amount of 7,000 golden dinars. Saying, "The provisions are scanty and the road [i.e., death] is long," he immediately gave half of his remaining wealth to charity, to be distributed to the poor after his death. When the Talmud asks how he was permitted to do this, since elsewhere it was ruled that a man who wished to spend liberally could not give more than a fifth of his wealth to charity, the Rabbis noted that this applied only during one's lifetime (since he might otherwise become impoverished, whereas it would not matter after his death).

On the *halachic* issue of how long one was required to wait after eating meat before consuming cheese, Mar Ukba said: "In this matter I am as vinegar is to wine [i.e., am inferior] compared with my father. For if my father were to eat flesh now he would not eat cheese until this same hour tomorrow [i.e., he would wait twenty-four hours], whereas I do not eat [cheese] in the same meal but I do eat it in my next meal" (Hul. 105a).

Mar Ukba once asked for advice from R. Eleazar ben Pedat, who was living in the Land of Israel: "There are certain people who are causing me problems. I can get them into trouble by reporting them to the government, but shall I do so?" Eleazar ben Pedat replied with a verse from Psalms (39:2): "I will take heed to my ways, so that I not sin with my tongue; I will curb my mouth while the wicked one is confronting me." When Mar Ukba wrote back complaining, "They are worrying me very much, and I cannot stand them," R. Eleazar ben Pedat answered with another biblical quotation: "Be patient and wait for the Lord" (Ps. 37:7), which he interpreted as meaning, "Wait for the Lord, and He will cast them down prostrate before you; go to the study hall early morning and evening and there will soon be an end of them." The text concluded, "R. Eleazar ben Pedat had hardly spoken these words when his major antagonist was placed in chains [for execution]" (Git. 7a).

Mar Zutra, Babylonian *amora* (fourth/fifth century).

The subject of numerous legends, it was said that when Mar Zutra's father was exilarch, he punished R. Hanina (head of the academy) for refusing to obey official orders. The shamed and resentful R. Hanina entered the synagogue at night, where he wept bitterly before falling asleep. He dreamed that he was cutting cedars in a forest, but when about to fell the last tree he was stopped by King David. When he awoke the next morning, R. Hanina learned that the entire house of the exilarch had perished, except for his pregnant daughter, who soon gave birth to a son (Mar Zutra).

While the lad was growing up under the tutelage of his grandfather, the exilarchate was administered by Mar Zutra's uncle. When Mar Zutra reached age fifteen, his grandfather presented him to the king as the legitimate ruler of the Jewish community. His uncle contested this action, but was killed by a fly that entered his nostril—the source of having a fly appear on the seal of all subsequent exilarchs. Mar Zutra later led an uprising against the Persian authorities and, according to legend, a pillar of fire always preceded his victorious army. He founded an independent Jewish state and established his residence at Machoza, where he imposed heavy taxes on all non-Jews. However, despite Mar Zutra's effective administration, immorality became rampant among the Jews and the pillar of fire disappeared. In a subsequent battle, Mar Zutra was taken prisoner and decapitated, with his body suspended from a cross on the bridge at Machoza.

The Talmud relates how Mar Zutra once deduced the identity of a thief. While the sage was staying at an inn, "a silver cup was stolen from his host. When Mar Zutra saw a young student wash his hands and dry them on his friend's garment, he said: 'This is the person [who stole the cup], for he has no consideration for the property of his neighbor'" (BM 24a). The Rabbis stated, "Who is forgiven his iniquity? A person who overlooks offenses committed against him" (RH 17a). An example of such meritorious conduct was Mar Zutra, who went to bed saying, "I forgive all who have aggravated me" (Meg. 28a).

In the case of a *met mitzvah* (lit., "an obligatory corpse"), an unidentified dead body whom the inhabitants of the nearest community are responsible to bury at their own expense, Mar Zutra declared that worn out coverings of Torah scrolls may be used for making the shrouds" (Meg. 26b). Among Mar Zutra's sayings are: "The merit of a fast day lies in the charity dispensed" (Ber. 6b); and "Even a poor man who himself subsists on charity should give charity" (Git. 7b). *See also* Amemar; Safra.

Mari bar Rachel, Babylonian *amora* (fourth century).

Perhaps uniquely, Mari bar Rachel was identified by the name of his mother rather than that of his father. The Talmud explains that Rachel, a daughter of Mar Samuel, had been taken captive. While in captivity, she married an idolater and gave birth to Mari. While Rachel was still pregnant, the father (Issur) embraced Judaism and became a convert (Yev. 45b). Against some opposition, Rava appointed Mari bar Rachel as a "purser" (a person with some supervisory authority over Jews in his jurisdiction, and a position that was open only to men of Jewish parentage), arguing that it was sufficient that his mother was a Jewess. On several occasions, Mari was described as "son of the daughter of Samuel" (Ber. 16a; Taan. 24b; BB 61b).

Mathia ben Heresh, Palestinian *tanna* (second century).

After studies in the Land of Israel, Mathia ben Heresh was described as among the scholars who, as they fled the Land of Israel (presumably after the fall of Betar to the Romans), tore their clothes in overwhelming grief, tearfully exclaiming that a person who lives in the Land of Israel was considered as if he had fulfilled all the commandments in the Torah (Sifre Deut. 80).

Mathia ben Heresh moved to the small Jewish community in Rome and founded a *yeshivah* (Sanh. 32b). In Pirkei Avot (4: 20) he is quoted as saying, "Be first in greeting [inquiring after the peace of] all men; and be a tail to lions rather than a head to foxes." This is traditionally interpreted as meaning that it is better to be a follower of the righteous (from whom one can learn) than the leader of the common people (ArtScroll Siddur, 569). This maxim may have reflected Mathia ben Heresh's preference for the small, but friendly and hospitable Jewish community in the capital of the powerful Roman empire, rather than the Jewish community in the Land of Israel, in which there were many erudite scholars.

Meir, Palestinian *tanna* (second century).

Although little is known of his origin, according to legend, Meir was a descendant of converts to Judaism. He was even described as descending from Nero, the Roman emperor (Git. 56a). Nevertheless, Meir married Beruriah, the brilliant daughter of R. Hananiah ben Teradion. Greatest of the students of R. Akiva, after the martyrdom of his teacher, Meir became leader of the post–Bar Kochba generation in the Land of Israel. He also was a student of R. Elisha ben Abuyah, the apostate known as Acher, and the only scholar who remained in contact with him. When asked how he could learn Torah from such a heretic, Meir replied that when he found a juicy pomegranate he ate the seeds and threw away the peel (Hag. 15b), meaning that he took the best of Elisha ben Abuyah's teachings and rejected all that was bad. According to tradition, he was called Meir (the illuminator) because he "enlightened the eyes of the sages in the *halachah*" (Er. 13b). In addition to the more than 300 laws in the Mishnah that bear his name, it is generally accepted that all laws whose authorship is not specified are attributed to him.

Meir was a champion of the three fundamental tenets of study, work, and prayer. He stressed the importance of labor ("A blessing rests only upon labor"; Tosef. Ber. 7:8), urging that a father "should always teach his son a clean and easy profession and earnestly pray to the One to whom all wealth and property belong [that he be financially successful]" (Kid. 4:14). With these words, the sage stressed that every profession has the potential to make one rich or poor, but this was all in the hand of God. Meir was an expert scribe, and he divided his earnings between living expenses and support for needy students. When his disciples asked why he was not setting aside any money for his own children, Meir replied: "If they are righteous they will be provided for, as it is written, 'I have not seen the righteous forsaken' (Ps. 37:25); and if they are not worthy, then why should I leave them anything?" (Pearl, 104).

Meir attached great importance to knowledge, even declaring that a gentile who occupied himself with the Torah was the equal of a high priest (BK 38a). "Whoever engages in Torah study for its own sake merits many things; furthermore, [the creation of] the entire world is worthwhile for his sake alone." Such a person is beloved of God and man, and study keeps him away from sin and causes others to seek out his advice. "[The Torah] gives him kingship and dominion and analytical judgment; the secrets of the Torah are revealed to him; he becomes like a steadily strengthening fountain and an unceasing river. He becomes modest, patient, and forgiving of insult to himself. [The Torah] makes him great and exalts him above all things" (Avot 6:1). Meir had nothing but contempt for the ignoramus—"Whoever marries his daughter to an *am ha-aretz* is as though he bound her and laid her in front of a lion" (Pes. 49b)—and he stressed the essential nature of Torah study: "Whoever forgets one word of the Torah is accounted by Scripture as if he had forfeited his life" (Avot 3:10). He also said, "Reduce your business studies and engage in Torah study. Be of humble spirit before every person. If you should neglect the [study of] Torah, you will come upon many excuses to neglect it; but if you labor in the Torah, God has ample reward to give you" (Avot 4:12). Unlike R. Jose bar Judah, who stressed the importance of learning from an older, experienced teacher, Meir cautioned: "Do not look at the vessel, but what is in it; there is a new vessel filled with old wine and an old vessel that does not even contain new wine!" (Avot 4:27).

Meir disagreed with those Rabbis who advocated studying with multiple teachers. Having studied with three masters—R. Akiva, R. Ishmael ben Elisha, and R. Elisha ben Abuyah—Meir likened one who studied with a single teacher to a person "who had a single field, part of which he sowed with wheat and part with barley, and planted part with olives and part with oak trees. Now that man is full of good and blessing. But when one studies with two or three teachers, he is like one who has many fields: one he sows with wheat and one he sows with barley, and plants one with olives and one with oak trees. Now [the attention of] this man is divided among many pieces of land, without good or blessing" (ARN 8). In the debate regarding whether it is permitted to visit the sick on the Sabbath, the day of joy on which sadness should not intrude, Meir believed that one should say, 'It [the Sabbath] may have compassion' [i.e., proper observance of the Sabbath will bring recovery in its wake]" (Shab. 12a).

The rabbinic maxim "More than the calf wishes to suck, does the cow desire to suckle" (Pes. 112a) implied that the desire of the teacher to teach was greater than the wish of the pupil to learn. According to Meir, a person should not be satisfied with acquiring knowledge of the Torah, but should also teach it to others (Sanh. 99a), lest he be considered one "who has spurned the word of the Lord" (Num. 15:31).

Meir also emphasized the importance of prayer. He interpreted the biblical verse relating to Hannah, "And it came to pass as she prayed long" (1 Sam. 1:12), as indicating that "whoever prays long is answered" (JT Ber. 4). In view of the myriad examples of the workings of God, the pious Jew recites numerous blessings. Indeed, Meir declared that it was the duty of every Jew to recite 100 blessings daily (Men. 43b). Consequently, the Rabbis formulated blessings for practically every aspect of human existence—from the common experiences of daily life such as rising from sleep, dressing, eating, and drinking, to unusual occurrences such as escaping from danger, recovering from illness, and seeing some marvelous natural event such as lightning or a comet. During the discussion of when the morning *Shema* may be read, Meir said, "From the time that one can distinguish between a wolf and a dog" (Ber. 9b).

The Talmud describes two different opinions regarding whether the Torah scroll should be rolled closed while the Torah blessings are being recited (Meg. 32a). According to Meir, a person called up for an *aliyah* should open the scroll, look at the place where the reading is to begin, roll the scroll closed, recite the first Torah blessing, and then unroll the scroll for reading. His rationale was that if the scroll were left open, an uninformed person might mistakenly think that the blessings are being read from the scroll itself. R. Judah bar Ezekiel disagreed, arguing that there was no need to close the scroll because no one would be foolish enough to imagine that the blessings were written in it. Ashkenazic Jews generally follow the ruling of Meir and close the scroll while the Torah blessings are recited (or cover it with the mantle or a special cloth). Sephardic Jews usually neither roll the Torah scroll closed nor cover it when reciting the blessings. As among most ancient peoples, Jews thought eclipses to be evil portents, particularly "because they are in-ured to blows." Indeed, Meir compared this "to a school teacher who comes to school with a strap in his hand. Who becomes apprehensive? He who is accustomed to be daily punished" (Suk. 29a). Whereas some of the Rabbis rejected the veracity of dreams outright, Meir remarked, "Dreams neither help, nor harm [i.e., they have no significance]" (Hor. 13b).

Meir had a deep love for the Land of Israel and the Hebrew language: "One who lives in the Land of Israel and speaks the holy tongue is assured of his share in the World to Come" (JT Shek. 3:4). Regarding prayer, Meir said, "A man's words should always be few in addressing God" (Ber. 61a), and that it was just as necessary to praise God for the evil as for the good (Ber. 48b). He believed in the power of repentance, for "on account of an individual who repents, the sins of the whole world are forgiven" (Yoma 86b).

Neighborhood highwaymen once vexed Meir, who prayed that they should die. When his wife Beruriah asked how such a prayer could be justified, he cited the statement, "Let the wicked be no more." However, she explained that the underlying meaning was not, "Sins will cease when there are no more wicked men; rather you should pray that they should repent and [in the ab-sence of any urge to sin] the wicked will be no more." Meir took her advice, prayed for them, and they repented (Ber. 10a).

Meir spoke out against subtle variants of lying: "A man should not urge his friend to eat with him if he knows that his friend will not do so. Nor should he offer him any gifts if he knows he will not accept them [i.e., he is merely gaining the gratitude of his friend through something which he had no inten-tion of doing]" (Hul. 94a).

Responding to a question of why a *tallit* must have a blue thread in its fringes, Meir said: "Because blue resembles [the color of] the sea, and the sea resembles [the color of] heaven, and heaven resembles [the color of] the Throne of Glory [based on Exod. 24:10 and Ezek. 1:26]" (Sot. 17a). His rul-ing that a person visiting a strange city should follow the local customs was derived from *midrashic* tales relating that when Moses ascended to heaven he neither ate nor drank, but when the angels descended to earth they consumed food (Gen. R. 48:16). Meir was renowned for using fables, especially of foxes, in his public discourses to illustrate his legal opinions (Sanh. 38b). Consequently, upon his death it was said: "The composer of fables has departed" (Sot. 49a).

Meir considered the period of separation during a woman's menstrual period to be of great benefit to the conjugal relations between husband and wife. "Being in constant contact with his wife, [a husband might] develop a loathing towards her. Therefore, the Torah ordained that she be unclean for seven days in order that she shall be as beloved by her husband as when she first entered the bridal chamber" (Nid. 31b). Meir used to criticize those who were weak enough to succumb to sexual temptation, maintaining that they could easily subdue their evil desires if they wished. "One day, Satan [the personification of the evil inclination] appeared to him in the guise of a woman on the opposite bank of the river. As there was no ferry [or bridge], Meir seized a rope tied to two trees on either side and proceeded across. When he had reached half way along the rope, he [Satan] let him go [by resuming his normal shape and thus freeing Meir from temptation], saying: 'Had they not proclaimed in heaven, take heed of Meir and his learning, your life would be worth to me no more than two small coins [i.e., I would have destroyed you as a worthless thing]'" (Kid. 81a), indicating that prominent Rabbis should not scoff at those who succumb to the wiles of the *yetzer ha-ra*.

In a famous story, a woman who enjoyed Meir's lectures once remained late at the academy to listen to him. When she returned home, her irate husband threw her out of the house and threatened to divorce her unless she would spit in the sage's face. When hearing of this demand, Meir summoned the woman and told her that he had an eye problem that his doctor said would be healed if a woman would spit in it seven times. Although the woman initially refused to comply with this unusual therapy, Meir finally persuaded her and she did as requested. Meir then said: "Go and tell your husband that not once, but seven times, did you spit in R. Meir's eye!" (JT Sot. 1:4).

When Meir died, his colleague, Jose ben Halafta, called him: "A great man, a holy man, a modest man" (JT Ber. 2:7). Some connect the tomb of Meir Ba'al ha-Nes in Tiberias on the shores of Lake Kinneret with Meir, who had established his school in that town. *See also* Beruriah; Dostai ben Yannai; Elisha ben Abuyah; Nathan; Nehorai; Shimon ben Gamaliel II.

Menasia bar Tachlifa, Babylonian *amora* (fourth century).

In his sole citation in the Talmud, Menasia bar Tachlifa quoted a famous observation of his teacher Rav: "This proves that there is no chronological order [lit., 'earlier and later'] in the Torah" (Pes. 6b).

Mesharsheya, Babylonian *amora* (fourth/fifth century).

In a well-known *halachic* ruling concerning rental property, Mesharsheya stated that it was the responsibility of the tenant, not the landlord, to provide the *mezuzah* (Pes. 4a; BM 101b; Av. Zar 21a). He applied the biblical verse "I gave them laws that were not good and rules by which they should not live" (Ezek. 20:25) to "two scholars who live in the same town and do not treat each other's halachic pronouncements respectfully" (Sanh. 77a).

Addressing the issue of why the Rabbis considered the scrolls of the Torah to be ritually unclean, Mesharsheya noted: "Originally the *terumah* [sacred food] was stored near the scrolls of the Law [since both were holy and it seemed fitting that they be placed together]"; but the food attracted mice, which injured the sacred books. To stop this practice, the Rabbis ruled that the scrolls were unclean, so that the *terumah* could no longer be stored near them (Shab. 14a). In another controversy involving *terumah*, which only members of a priestly family could eat, Mesharsheya postulated a case in which the child of a priest had "become interchanged with the child of her female slave [so that it was unclear which child was which]." His ruling was that "both may eat *terumah*"—one as a priest and the other as the slave of a priest (Git. 42b; Ter. 8a).

N

Nachman bar Hisda, Babylonian *amora* (fourth century).

Son of an illustrious scholar, Nachman pointed out the unusual spelling of the word *va-yetzer* (and He formed) in the verse, "And God formed man from the dust of the earth" (Gen. 2:7). He explained that the word is written with two *yuds* (only one is grammatically necessary) to indicate that God created human beings with two inclinations: a good inclination (*yetzer ha-tov*) and an evil inclination (*yetzer ha-ra*) (Ber. 61a). Nachman bar Hisda asserted that even though it may appear unjust that the righteous suffer in this world, unlike the wicked they will receive their reward in the World to Come (Hor. 10b).

Nachman bar Isaac, Babylonian *amora* (fourth century).

A student of R. Nachman bar Jacob and R. Hisda, Nachman bar Isaac succeeded Rava as head of the academy at Pumbedita. In his teachings, Nachman bar Isaac frequently used mnemonic formulas as memory aids (Shab. 60b; Taan. 10a; Kid. 20b; BB 147a; Sanh. 7a; Nid. 45b). His major contribution to the *halachah* was to collect, arrange, and transmit the teachings and decisions of his predecessors, which otherwise might have been lost. As he astutely observed of his own talents, "I am neither a sage nor a visionary [seer], nor even a scholar as contrasted with the majority, but I am a teacher and codifier of traditions, and the *bet midrash* follows me in its decisions" (Pes. 105b). Nevertheless, Nachman bar Isaac produced numerous maxims of his own, such as: "Why are the words of the Torah [wisdom] likened to a tree [in the verse, 'It [the Torah] is a tree of life to those who grasp it' [Prov. 3:18]? This teaches that just as a small piece of wood can kindle a larger one, so a younger scholar can sharpen the minds of older ones" (Taan. 7a). He added that he concurred with a famous comment of Judah ha-Nasi: "I learned much from my teachers, much more from my fellow students, but from my disciples most of all" (Mak. 10a). After demonstrating his great learning and being asked to take a more prominent place ("Please take a seat nearer us"), Nachman bar Isaac modestly refused, saying: "It is not the place that honors the man, but the man who honors the place" (Taan. 21b).

When astrologers told the mother of Nachman bar Isaac that her son was destined to become a thief, she never allowed him to leave the house with a bare head: "'Cover your head so that the fear of Heaven may be upon you, and pray [for Divine mercy that the Evil Inclination not overcome you].' Her son did not understand why she spoke these words to him. One day as he was sitting and studying under a palm tree, temptation [i.e., the Evil Inclination] overcame him. He climbed and bit off a cluster [of dates from a tree that did not belong to him] with his teeth" (Shab. 156b). This and other stories illustrate that the belief in planetary influence on Jews was not entirely rejected, but there was the concept that it might be counteracted by good deeds. *See also* Huna bar Nathan.

Nachman bar Jacob, Babylonian *amora* (third/fourth century).

Usually referred to without his patronymic, Nachman bar Jacob married Yalta, the daughter of the wealthy exilarch Rabbah bar Avuha, and established his academy in Nehardea. He lived in luxury and entertained esteemed scholars and strangers who stayed at his house and enjoyed his hospitality. After R. Isaac from the Land of Israel had dined at his home, Nachman bar Jacob asked his guest to bless him. R. Isaac offered a parable to indicate to what his experience could be compared. "Once a man journeying in the desert, who was hungry, weary, and thirsty, came upon a tree with sweet fruit, pleasant shade, and a stream of water flowing beneath it. He ate its fruit, drank the water, and rested under its shade. When about to continue his journey, he said: 'Tree, O Tree, with what can I bless you? Shall I say to you, may your fruit be sweet? They are sweet already; that your shade may be pleasant? It is already pleasant; that a stream of water may flow beneath you? A stream of water already flows beneath you. Therefore, I [merely] say, May it be [God's] will that all the plants that emerge from you be just like you. It is the same with you [Nachman bar Jacob]. With what shall I bless you? With learning [knowledge of the Torah]? You already possess it. With riches? You have riches already. With children? You have children already. Therefore [I say], May it be [God's] will that your descendants be like you'" (Taan. 5b–6a).

Nachman bar Jacob is one of the most cited sages in the Babylonian Talmud. Highly respected for his rulings in civil law, his opinions generally took precedence over those of his colleagues (Ket. 13a; Kid. 59b). However, Nachman bar Jacob was often harsh to his slaves and an arrogant judge, constantly hearing civil suits alone and thus rejecting the long-accepted rule that a court of three judges was required (Sanh. 5a). His haughtiness even led Nachman bar Jacob to remark, "If he [the Messiah] is among those living [today], it might be one like myself." He based this on the verse, "And their nobles shall be of themselves, and their governors shall proceed from the midst of them" (Jer. 33:21), since as the son-in-law of the exilarch he enjoyed great power and prestige (Sanh. 98b). Nachman bar Jacob made biting *aggadic* remarks about biblical personalities. "Haughtiness [conceit] does not befit women. The two prophetesses Deborah and Huldah had hateful names, namely 'bee' and 'weasel'" (Meg. 14b); and "Impudence avails even against Heaven; for God allowed Balaam to make the journey to Balak after He had first forbidden it [Num. 22:12, 20]" (Sanh. 105a). Hearing of a deadly plague in the Land of Israel, Nachman bar Jacob declared a fast, explaining: "If the mistress [Land of Israel] is stricken, then certainly the maidservant [Babylonia] is in danger!" (Taan. 21b), meaning that if a plague strikes the land that is under God's special providence, there is reason to fear that it will strike lesser lands as well.

Several Talmudic tales feature Nachman bar Jacob's outspoken wife, Yalta, who was the daughter of the exilarch. Nachman bar Jacob once was entertaining R. Ulla, who after saying the Grace after Meals, refused to send her the cup over which he had recited the blessing. Violently enraged, Yalta went to the wine store and broke 400 jars of wine. Commenting on R. Ulla's refusal, Yalta tartly remarked, "Gossip comes from peddlers and vermin from rags [i.e., what can one expect from a man like R. Ulla!]" (Ber. 51b).

Nachman bar Jacob had two daughters, who were captured by pagans. The Talmud describes them as "stirring a cauldron with their bare hands when they were boiling hot [i.e., without scalding their hands, presumably on account of their piety]." R. Ilish, who was captured with them, wanted to take them with him when he was about to escape, but did not do so when he discovered they were actually practicing witchcraft (Git. 45a). Nachman bar Jacob observed, "When a woman is talking she spins [i.e., a web to capture the male]" (Meg. 14b).

On his deathbed, Nachman bar Jacob requested that Rava pray to the Angel of Death to spare him from a painful death. Later, the deceased sage appeared to Rava in a dream. Rava asked whether Nachman bar Jacob had suffered much pain as he died. "It was as easy as taking a hair from a pitcher of milk. But were God to say to me, 'Go back to the world as you were before,' I would not want to go. For the fear of death is so great there" (MK 28a). *See also* Ahai ben Josiah; Anan; Bebai.

Nahum of Gimzo, Palestinian *tanna* (first/second century).

A teacher of R. Akiva (Ber. 22a; Shev. 26a), in folklore he is popularly known as Nahum of Gamzu, because of a pun between the place name (Gimzo, a town in southwestern Judea; 2 Chron. 28:18) and his famous motto. "Why was he called Nahum of Gamzu?—because whatever befell him he would declare, '*gam zu le-tovah*' [this also is for the best]" (Taan. 21a).

To appease the anger of the Roman emperor, who was threatening to impose new harsh decrees against them, "the Jews desired to send a gift to the Emperor." After intense discussion, and with no volunteers for this dangerous mission, they decided that Nahum of Gimzo should go "because he is accustomed to have miracles [performed on his behalf]." Carrying a bag full of precious stones and pearls for the emperor, Nahum of Gimzo stopped overnight at an inn. There thieves emptied the bag and filled it up with earth. Awaking in the morning and discovering what had happened, he exclaimed, "This also is for the best," and proceeded on his way. When he arrived at his destination, the emperor was enraged when he saw that the bag was full of earth. Screaming, "The Jews are mocking me," he ordered Nahum of Gimzo's execution. (In a second version, he determined to kill all the Jews.) As always, Nahum of Gimzo calmly replied, "This also is for the best." That night, Elijah the prophet appeared to the emperor in a dream and suggested, "Perhaps this is the earth of Abraham, the patriarch, who threw [at his enemies] earth that turned to swords, and straw that turned into arrows." Testing it against a neighboring province that they had not been able to conquer, the Romans threw some of the special earth against their enemy and the opposing forces were routed. Realizing the value of the earth that the Jews had sent him, the emperor ordered his servants to take Nahum to the royal treasury, fill his bag with precious stones and pearls, and send him back with great honor. On his return trip, when Nahum of Gimzo arrived to spend the night at the same inn, everyone was amazed. When asked what he had taken to the emperor to deserve such great honor, he replied, "What I took away from here I carried there." Therefore, they razed the inn to the ground, filled large boxes with earth, and took them to the emperor, boasting that the magical earth belonged to them. However, when the Romans tested it in battle and saw that it did not possess any miraculous properties, those who had brought the boxes of earth were immediately put to death for fraud (Taan. 21a, Sanh. 108–109a).

In later years, Nahum of Gimzo suffered from many bodily afflictions. According to one account, his hands and feet became paralyzed; in another, he was blind in both eyes and his arms and legs were amputated. Nevertheless, he bore his troubles patiently and even seemed to rejoice over them. His pupils were distraught when they saw how such a just man had to endure so many ills. "Master, since you are wholly righteous, why has all this befallen you?" In reply, Nahum of Gimzo related a story indicating that he had brought all his troubles upon himself. When traveling to the home of his father-in-law with three donkeys laden with food, drink, and "all kinds of dainties," he was stopped on the road by a poor man requesting something to eat. Asking the man to wait a moment until he unloaded something from his donkey, the man suddenly died from hunger. Grief stricken that his delay may have caused the man's death, Nahum of Gimzo cursed himself. "May my eyes which had no pity upon your eyes become blind, may my hands which had no pity upon your hands be cut off, may my legs which had no pity upon your legs be amputated . . . and may my whole body be covered with boils." When his stunned pupils repeated their misery at seeing him in such a devastated state, Nahum of Gimzo exclaimed: "Woe would it be to me had you not seen me in such a sore plight"—once again reaffirming his motto, "This also is for the best" (Taan. 21a).

Nahum of Gimzo lay in that condition in a dilapidated house on a bed with its legs immersed in water to keep away the ants, tended by his faithful disciples (JT Pe'ah 8:8; Shek. 5:4). When his students wanted to remove his bed from the house, Nahum of Gimzo asked them to take out the furniture first, certain that as long as he remained in the house it would not fall down. They complied with his request and, as soon they had carried him out on his bed, the decrepit structure collapsed.

Nathan, Palestinian *tanna* (second century).

Son of the exilarch, Nathan left Babylonia for some unknown reason and moved to the Land of Israel, where he was appointed head of the school at Usha (Hor. 13b). Nathan's chief opponent in *halachic* decisions was Judah ha-Nasi, though they highly respected each other, and Nathan is said to have assisted the patriarch in compiling the Mishnah (BM 86a). As a major Talmudic authority, numerous *halachic* rulings and *aggadic* sayings are recorded in his name. Noting that the commandment regarding *tefillin* is immediately followed in the Torah by the one to "write them on the doorposts of your house [*mezuzah*]," Nathan concluded that the *tefillin* should be bound on the weaker forearm, because the hand that writes must be the same hand that wraps—the stronger hand. (Nevertheless, left-handed people wear the *tefillin* on their "weaker" right arm) (Men. 37a).

Nathan was considered the author of the treatise titled *Avot de-Rabbi Natan*, a type of *tosefta* to the Mishnaic tractate Pirkei Avot, which contains a variety of social, ethical, and religious maxims. Discussing the characteristics of the many lands through which he traveled, Nathan observed: "There is no greater love than the love of Torah; there is no greater wisdom than the wisdom of the Land of Israel; there is no greater beauty than the beauty of Jerusalem; there is no greater wealth than the wealth of Rome; there is no greater valor than the valor of the Persians; there is no greater immorality than the immorality of the Arabs; there is no greater rudeness than the rudeness of the land of Elam; there is no greater flattery than the flattery of Babylonia; there is no greater witchcraft than the witchcraft of Egypt" (ARN 25).

R. Akiva declared the commandment "You shall love your neighbor as yourself" (Lev. 19:18) to be "a fundamental principle of the Torah." The Talmud presents the negative form of this commandment in the well-known story of the heathen scoffer who asked Hillel to condense the entire Law in the shortest form possible ("while standing on one foot"). Hillel replied, "What is hateful to you do not do to your fellow man," followed by, "This is the whole Torah, the rest is commentary; now go and learn!" (Shab. 31a). Nathan said, "Do not reproach your neighbor with a fault that you also have" (BM 59b), while R. Meir taught, "The same measure with which one measures others will be used to measure him" (Sanh. 100a).

Nathan ruled that when there was money left over from that collected for a person's burial, the extra should be used "for a monument on his grave" (Sanh. 48a).

Wine loosens the lips, so that "when wine enters [the body], the secrets come out" (Sanh. 38a). In response to a declaration that a judge who "drank a quarter of a log [about 2.5 ounces] of wine must not give a legal decision," Nathan believed this was too lenient, admitting that "before I drink a quarter of a log of wine my mind is not clear" (Er. 64a). *See also* Eliezer ben Hyrcanus; Shimon ben Gamaliel II.

Nathan bar Asia, Babylonian *amora* (third century).

As the Talmud relates, "Nathan bar Asia traveled from Rav's academy [in Sura] to Pumbedita on the second day of Shavuot, [whereupon] Joseph put him under the ban" (Pes. 52a). In the Diaspora, an extra day was added to each of the biblical festivals, except for Yom Kippur. This practice originated because of uncertainty in the Diaspora as to the day on which the Sanhedrin in Jerusalem announced the New Moon. After two reliable witnesses had actually sighted the crescent moon, the Sanhedrin dispatched messengers to disseminate the information, but they often were unable to reach distant communities in time to inform the people of the correct day. Therefore, a second day was added to each festival to prevent any chance of the people mistakenly failing to celebrate it on the biblically mandated date. Unfortunately for Nathan bar Asia, he was used to the tradition in Sura, where only a single festival day was observed, forgetting that this was not the practice elsewhere in Babylonia.

Nechunia (or Yochanan) ben Gudgada, Palestinian *tanna* (first/second century).

A Levite in charge of closing the gates of the Temple (Tosef. Shek. 2:14), Nechunia ben Gudgada was a colleague of R. Yochanan ben Zakkai. Even after the Temple was destroyed, Nechunia ben Gudgada continued to scrupulously observe all the laws relating to purity. Thus, throughout his life it was his custom to eat food "in the ritual purity required for sacred food" (Hag. 2:7).

Nechunia ben Gudgada offered several rulings detailing the implementation of biblical precepts. The traditionally accepted rule had been that a man who stole wood and used it in the construction of a building was required to destroy the building and return that specific wood to its rightful owner. However, Nechunia ben Gudgada decreed that it was only necessary to pay the value of the material that was stolen. Using similar reasoning, Nechunia ben Gudgada ruled that a person who sacrificed a stolen animal as a sin offering had fulfilled his obligation as long as he was unaware that the animal was stolen (Eduy. 7:9).

The Tosefta (Ter. 1:1) relates that the children of Nechunia ben Gudgada were deaf-mutes. According to the Talmud, his daughter's sons were dumb but not deaf and studied in the academy of Judah ha-Nasi. After they were healed in response to Judah ha-Nasi's prayers, it was discovered that they had complete knowledge of the whole Torah (Hag. 3a). One of Nechunia ben Gudgada's rulings was that a deaf-mute girl, given in marriage in a binding contract by her father, might be divorced by her husband, even though as a deaf-mute she would not be capable of giving consent (Git. 5:5).

Nechunia ben Hakanah, Palestinian *tanna* (first/second century).

Nechunia ben Hakanah taught: "Whoever takes upon himself the yoke of the Torah [the multitude of commandments] will be relieved of the yoke of the government [Roman taxation and oppression] and the yoke of the search for sustenance [anxieties and hardships related to earning a living] (interpretation of Maimonides in brackets). But whoever casts off the yoke of the Torah will have placed on him the yoke of the government and the yoke of worldly responsibilities" (Avot 3:6).

The short prayers Nechunia ben Hakanah used to recite as he entered and left the synagogue are recorded in the Talmud (Ber. 28b). On entering, he would pray: "May it be Your will, O Lord my God, that no mishap come about through me, that I may not err in a matter of *halachah*, that my colleagues may rejoice over me, and that I may not say something unclean is clean or that something clean is unclean. May my colleagues not err in a matter of *halachah* and may I rejoice in them." On leaving, he would say: "I thank You, O Lord my God, that You have set my portion with those who sit in the house of study rather than with those who sit [idly] in [street] corners [shopkeepers and ignorant people, according to Rashi]. For though we both rise early, I do so for words of Torah while they do so for frivolous talk; we both labor, but I receive a reward while they do not; we both run, but my way leads to the World to Come [eternal life] while they race to the pit of destruction [hell]."

When asked by his disciples, "By what virtue have you reached such a good old age?" Nechunia ben Hakanah replied: "Never in my life have I sought respect through the degradation of my fellow, nor has the curse of my fellow gone up with me upon my bed [i.e., he forgave all who troubled him before going to sleep], and I have been generous with my money" (Meg. 28a). On the same page of the Talmud, Nechunia ben Hakanah answered R. Akiva's identical question in a different way: "Never in my life have I accepted presents, nor have I insisted on retribution [when wronged], and I have been generous with my money."

Nehemiah, Palestinian *tanna* (second century).

An outstanding student of R. Akiva, Nehemiah was one of the five Rabbis ordained by R. Judah ben Bava, which led to the sage being executed for violating the Roman edict forbidding it. Nehemiah was among the scholars who gathered at Usha to revive the religious life of the people after the Bar Kochba rebellion (Song R. 2:5).

Nehemiah said: "As a punishment for causeless hate, strife multiplies in a man's house, his wife miscarries, and his sons and daughters die young" (Shab. 32b). He observed, "In the generation when the Messiah will come, people will not respect one another, honor will dwindle [or 'the most honored people will be corrupt' (Rashi) or 'those who should be honored will be scorned instead'], the vine will yield its fruit yet wine will be dear [i.e., all will be drunkards, so despite the abundant yield, wine will be scarce], and the government will be converted to heresy [godlessness] with none to rebuke them" (Sanh. 97a). According to tradition, it was Nehemiah who developed the rule of Hebrew grammar that the addition of the suffix *hei* at the end of a place name is equivalent to using the letter *lamed* as a prefix, with both meaning "to" (Yev. 13b). Other sayings attributed to Nehemiah include: "Beloved is suffering. For just as sacrifices bring atonement, so does suffering" (Sifre Deut. 32); and "A single person is as important as the whole of Creation" (ARN 31).

According to the Jerusalem Talmud, Nehemiah descended from the biblical Nehemiah and earned a meager living as a potter (JT Taan. 4:2). A man once came to Nehemiah asking for support. When asked about his usual diet, the man replied that it consisted of "fat meat and old wine." Nehemiah asked, "Would you consent [lit., 'put up with the inconvenience'] to live with me [only] on lentils?" The man agreed to do so, lived with him and ate only lentils, and died! Several Rabbis debated whether they should be sorry "for this man whom Nehemiah has killed" or "for Nehemiah who killed this man?"

They concluded that the man himself was to blame, for "he should not have cultivated his luxurious habits to such an extent" (Ket. 67b).

Nehorai, Palestinian *tanna* (second century).

Nehorai is most famous for the comment: "I abandon all my earthly work to teach my son nothing but Torah, for which a man enjoys the reward in this world while the principal remains for him in the World to Come. This is not the case with all worldly occupations. When a man falls ill, grows old, or is suffering and unable to do his work, he dies of starvation [i.e., he cannot earn a living]. But the Torah is not so, for it guards him from all evil in his youth and gives him a hopeful fate in his old age" (Kid. 4:14).

In Pirkei Avot (4:18), Nehorai said: "Exile yourself to a place of Torah [i.e., uproot yourself and move to a place where there are scholars from whom you can learn]. Do not assume that it will come after you [i.e., that Torah scholars will move to a place where currently there is no Torah learning]. For it is your colleagues who will cause it to remain with you [i.e., in an environment where Torah can be properly studied], 'and do not rely on your own understanding' [Prov. 3:5]."

When will the Messiah come? Many Rabbis believed that the political and social conditions would have to deteriorate to an appalling condition before the Messiah would arrive. Nehorai taught: "The Messiah will appear when the young will shame the old in public, when the old will stand in respect before the young, when daughters will rise up against their mothers, and daughters-in-law against their mothers-in-law. The leaders of that people shall be like dogs, and a son will feel no shame when rebuked by his father" (Sanh. 97a).

There is a tradition that Nehorai was another name for R. Meir (based on one Hebrew version of the explanation that the latter was so named because he "enlightened the eyes of the sages in the *halachah*") (Er. 13b). Using the same reasoning, elsewhere Nehorai was identified with R. Nehemiah and R. Eleazar ben Arach (Shab. 147b). *See also* Eleazar ben Arach.

Nittai of Arbela (second century B.C.E.).

Nittai of Arbela served as *av bet din* (head of the rabbinic court) as one of the *zugot* (with Joshua ben Perachyah). A native of Arbel in Lower Galilee, Nittai was a student of Jose ben Yoetzer and Jose ben Yochanan, the first pair of *zugot*. As with their predecessors, Joshua ben Perachyah and Nittai of Arbela disagreed regarding the controversial issue of *semichah* (the physical laying of hands on sacrifices) on Sabbaths and festivals. Nittai of Arbela said that it could be performed, while Joshua ben Perachyah ruled that it was prohibited as constituting forbidden work (Hag. 2:2).

In Pirkei Avot (1:7), Nittai of Arbela is quoted as saying: "Keep at a distance from an evil neighbor; do not make yourself an associate of a wicked man; do not abandon faith in [Divine] retribution." These harsh words, contrasting sharply with the gentle maxims of his colleague in the preceding line, were apparently intended to comfort the Pharisees with the thought that just punishment would befall John Hyrcanus, who had persecuted their party after deserting the Pharisees and joining the Sadducees. *See also* Joshua ben Perachyah.

O

Onkelos, translator of the Bible into Aramaic (second century).

His translation, Targum Onkelos, is printed alongside the Hebrew text of the Bible in many editions and is a valuable guide for explaining obscure passages. One Talmudic statement attributed to him was that the faces of the cherubim were turned sideways "as a pupil taking leave of his master" (BB 99a). Onkelos apparently developed a close relationship with Rabban Gamaliel II and arranged for a lavish funeral for the *nasi* (Av. Zar. 11a).

A convert to Judaism and student of R. Akiva, Onkelos was described by the Babylonian Talmud as "the son of Klonikos [Kalonymus], the son of the sister of [Roman emperor] Titus." According to the *aggadah*, when contemplating conversion, Onkelos succeeded through a necromancer in raising his uncle Titus from the dead and asked him, "Who is held in the highest regard in the Other World?" When Titus replied, "Israel," Onkelos asked what he would think about him joining them. Titus answered: "Their observances are so burdensome [numerous] you will not be able to endure them [carry them out]. Go and attack them in your world and you will become master over them, as it is written, 'Her enemies are now the masters' [Lam. 1:5]; whoever harasses Israel becomes a master of men." Onkelos next consulted Balaam by incantations and received the same initial reply. When he asked Balaam about joining Israel, the seer replied: "You shall never concern yourself with their welfare or benefit as long as you live [Deut. 23:7]." Finally, Onkelos raised by incantations the sinners of Israel (in one manuscript, Jesus). This time the response to his question was quite different: "Seek their welfare, seek not their harm. Whoever touches them touches the apple of God's eye. . . . Observe the difference between the sinners of Israel and the prophets among the nations of the world who worship idols" (Git. 56b–57a).

According to legend, while studying the biblical verse "[For the Lord your God] befriends the *ger* [convert], providing him with food and clothing" (Deut. 10:18), the *ger* Onkelos asked the stern R. Eliezer ben Hyrcanus: "Is food and clothing the reward for the *ger?*" "Is that a small thing in your eyes?" the sage replied. "When our ancestors asked for bread and clothing, they would make a vow (Gen. 28:20), while now God offers it to the *ger* on a platter!" Then Onkelos visited R. Joshua ben Hananiah, who began to comfort him with the words: "'Bread' refers to the Torah, as it says, 'Come, eat my food' [Prov. 9:5], while 'clothing' means the [scholar's] cloak. When a man is privileged to [study the] Torah, he is privileged to perform God's precepts. Moreover, they [the proselytes] marry their daughters into the priesthood, so that their descendants may offer burnt offerings on the altar" (Gen. R. 70:5).

In another version of the conversion of Onkelos (Av. Zar. 11a), the Talmud relates that when he became a proselyte, the Roman emperor sent a contingent of soldiers to arrest him. However, after Onkelos explained some scriptural verse to them, the soldiers converted to Judaism. The emperor then sent another contingent of soldiers and ordered them not to engage in any conversations with him. As they prepared to lead Onkelos away, he said to them: "Let me tell you just an ordinary thing. [In a procession,] one of lesser rank lights the way for those of higher rank, yet my God [who is the greatest] carries the light before Israel ['And the Lord went before them . . . in a pillar of fire by night to give them light' (Exod. 13:21)]." Hearing this, these soldiers also converted. The emperor then sent another cohort to apprehend Onkelos, ordering them to not even listen to him. As they were walking out of his house, Onkelos placed his hand on the *mezuzah* and said, "According to universal custom, the mortal king dwells within, and his servants keep guard on him without; but [in the case of] God, it is His servants who dwell within while He keeps guard on them from without ['The Lord shall guard your going out and your coming in, from this time forth and for evermore'; Ps. 121:8]." These soldiers also converted to Judaism, and the Roman emperor sent no more.

In the Jerusalem Talmud and other sources from the Land of Israel, similar stories are told regarding "Aquila," a name that closely resembles Onkelos in the Palestinian pronunciation. The Babylonian Talmud relates Onkelos to Titus and Rabban Gamaliel I, which would indicate that he lived at the time of the destruction of the Temple. It states that Onkelos translated the Torah into Aramaic under the guidance of R. Eliezer ben Hyrcanus and R. Joshua ben Hananiah. The Jerusalem Talmud connects Aquila with Hadrian and Rabban Gamaliel II of Yavneh, suggesting that he lived after the destruction of the Temple. It maintains that he translated the Torah into Greek. Scholars still debate whether Onkelos and Aquila were the same person. *See also* Aquila.

Oshaia, Babylonian *tanna* (third century).

A student of Rav, Oshaia quoted his teacher's statement about God's creation of the first man: "Adam's trunk came from Babylonia, his head from the Land of Israel [i.e., the most exalted part of his body from the loftiest country], his limbs from other lands, and his private parts [according to R. Aha] from Akra di Agma [a town near Pumbedita whose inhabitants were known for their moral depravity]" (Sanh. 38a–b).

Oshaia asked, "Why are the words of the Torah likened to three liquids—water, wine, and milk?" He explained that the verse "All who are thirsty, come for water, even if you have no money; come, buy food, and eat. Buy food without money, wine and milk without cost" (Isa. 55:1) teaches: "Just as these three liquids can only be preserved in the most inferior of vessels, so too the words of the Torah endure only with one who is meek minded." As an illustrative parable, Oshaia related the story of Emperor Hadrian's daughter, who addressed the learned but homely scholar, R. Joshua ben Hananiah. As another explanation: "Just as these three liquids can become unfit for consumption only through inattention [i.e., by negligently forgetting to cover them so that they become contaminated], so words of Torah are forgotten only through inattention [i.e., by neglecting constant review]" (Taan. 7a–b).

A *midrash* relates that a pagan philosopher once asked Oshaia: "If God wanted man to be circumcised, why was Adam not created already circumcised?" (By extension, how do we have the nerve to change what God has created?) The sage replied, "According to your reasoning, why should a man like you shave the hair with which you were born?" The pagan responded, "Because the hair grows in the days of foolish childhood." Oshaia then argued: "If so, a person should blind his eyes, cut off his hands, and break his legs because they grew in his foolish childhood." Unable to offer a meaningful answer, the philosopher exclaimed: "Have we come down to such garbage [a stupid argument]?" Oshaia calmly observed: "I cannot let you go without a proper answer. Observe that everything that was created during the six days of Creation needs finishing: mustard needs sweetening, wheat needs grinding, and even man needs finishing" (Gen. R. 11:6). Thus human beings were empowered by God to perfect Creation. *See also* Hama bar Bissa; Joshua ben Hananiah.

Oshaia Rabbah, Palestinian *amora* (third century).

The son of R. Hama bar Bissa and a student of R. Bar Kappara and R. Hiyya, Oshaia Rabbah established a school in Caesarea that rivaled the celebrated academy in Tiberias. Oshaia Rabbah was renowned for his collection of *baraitot* (*Mishnayot Gedolot*), which were studied in the academies, as well as his explanations of them, earning him the title *Av ha-Mishnah* ("Father of the Mishnah"; JT BK 4:6). As R. Zeira noted, "Any *baraita* that was not taught in the school of R. Hiyya and Oshaia Rabbah is not authentic and has no authority [lit., 'you should not put it forward as a refutation in the house of study']" (Hul. 141a–b). According to one version, Oshaia Rabbah ruled that any man wanting to convert to Judaism must undergo circumcision and immersion in a *mikveh* in the presence of three authoritative witnesses (Yev. 46b), which became the accepted law.

Oshaia Rabbah and R. Hanina earned their livings as cobblers. Dwelling on a street of harlots, they made shoes for these women and delivered them to their rooms. As Rava noted, "They [the harlots] looked at them, but they [these scholars] would not lift their eyes to look at them, and their [the harlots'] oath was 'by the life of the holy Rabbis of the Land of Israel.'" This demonstration of the chastity of Oshaia Rabbah and R. Hanina, in the face of great temptation, served to sanctify the Divine Name (Pes. 113b).

Oshaia Rabbah said: "God was gracious [lit., 'showed righteousness'] to the Jews by scattering them among the nations" (Pes. 87b). This meant that when the Jews suffer in one country and are faced with annihilation, they are treated kindly in another land. The Talmud states, "R. Hanina and Oshaia [Rabbah] spent every Sabbath eve studying *Sefer Yetzirah* [Book of Creation; a mystical text], by means of which they created a small calf and ate it" (Sanh. 65b). This was the only way they could properly celebrate the Sabbath, because they were too poor to buy sufficient food.

In response to a challenge from a philosopher who asked why men were not created circumcised, Oshaia Rabbah replied that circumcision enabled human beings to become partners with God in completing the Divine work of creation (Gen. R. 11:6). Among the Talmudic maxims of Oshaia Rabbah are: "He who is haughty falls into Gehinnom" (Av. Zar. 18a); and "Custom overrides law" (JT BM 7:1).

P

Papa, Babylonian *amora* (fourth century).

A student of Rava and R. Abbaye, after the death of his teachers, Papa founded a school at Naresh, a city near Sura. Papa was extremely wealthy, both as the result of "marrying a priest's daughter" (Pes. 49a) and by brewing beer (Pes. 113a). His teacher Rava once said of Papa, "Happy is the righteous man who is as prosperous on earth as only the wicked usually are!" (Hor. 10b). However, Papa sold his beer at a higher price than ordinary because he gave the buyer credit, even though the practice was considered a type of prohibited usury. He justified this act by saying, "My beer will not deteriorate and I am in no need of money, so I merely confer a benefit upon the purchaser [by letting him have it earlier]" (BM 65a).

In view of his great wealth, it is surprising that Papa frequently refused to aid the poor (BB 9a, 10a). "Once when Papa was climbing a ladder, his foot slipped and he narrowly escaped falling. 'Had that happened, I would have been punished like a Sabbath breaker and idolater [without having deserved it].'" But another Rabbi said to him, "Perhaps a beggar appealed to you and you did not assist him" (BB 10a).

Even those who believed that marriages were predestined must take enough time to make a prudent choice. Because of a nonharmonious relationship with his second wife, the daughter of R. Abba of Sura (Ket. 39b), Papa warned: "Be quick in buying land; but be slow and deliberate in choosing a wife. Come down a step [on the social ladder] in selecting a wife [lest a woman from a higher rank in society not be content with her husband's social or financial position], but go up a step in selecting your best man [to have a good example to emulate]" (Yev. 63a). On another occasion, when Papa heard an especially wise decision from R. Huna bar Nathan, he immediately "arose, kissed his student on his head, and offered him his daughter's hand in marriage" (Hor. 12b).

In what areas should a husband follow his wife's advice? According to Rav, whoever does so "will descend into Gehinnom [hell]." Yet Papa said, "if your wife is short, bend down and hear her whisper [i.e., follow her advice regardless of how 'lowly' she may appear to be]." Rather than viewing these as contradictory opinions, the Rabbis concluded that on general matters a man should not follow his wife's advice, but he should do so "on matters of the household," where she is the expert. Another interpretation is that the husband should follow the advice of his wife on secular matters but not on religious issues (BM 59a).

A less than erudite scholar, Papa's opinion was often the last one cited in a Talmudic discussion, often attempting to reconcile conflicting views. When two Rabbis offered different ways of saying a prayer, Papa typically said, "We should say both" (Ber. 59b; Meg. 21b). One student, R. Shimi bar Ashi, used to constantly humiliate him with questions that he was unable to answer. One day he observed, "Papa fell on his face [i.e., recited the prayer known as the *Tahanun*] and he heard him say, 'May God preserve me from the insolence of Shimi.' The latter immediately vowed silence and annoyed him no more [with questions]" (Taan. 9b).

Hugely obese, Papa was said to consume four times as much as an ordinary man (Pes. 89b). He disliked fasting since it did not agree with him (Taan. 24b). Papa stated, "At the door of a food shop there are many brothers and friends, but at hunger's door there are no brothers and no friends" (Shab. 32a); and "When the barley is gone from the pitcher, strife comes knocking at the door" (BM 59a).

Papa seemed to have a fascination with the occult. "One should not remove his shoes when entering a house in which there is a cat, because the cat may kill a snake and eat it, leaving little bones [on the floor] that can stick into his foot and not come out, thus endangering him" (Pes. 112b). He also observed, "A certain man made derogatory remarks about Mar Samuel, and a log fell from the roof and broke his skull" (Ber. 19a); and "A white horse is a favorable omen in a dream [since it signifies appeasement]" (Sanh. 93a). Eschewing violence, Papa said: "He who takes vengeance destroys his own house" (Sanh. 102b).

Papa urged his colleagues, "Plant [crops for the needs of your home] and do not purchase [it from the market], for even if the total cost is the same, those [crops that are] home grown are [natural and more] abundant. Sell [your possessions] and do not become poor [to avoid the disgrace of starvation or begging]." This latter rule applied to all household goods, "but not to a garment [since he may never find another one that was as good]." "If a small hole develops in a weak wall, plug it up immediately [so you will have no need for a major repair, as in the maxim, 'a stitch in time saves nine']. But do not [enlarge it in order to rebrick and] plaster [it for the sake of appearance]" (Yev. 63a).

R. Judah said in the name of his teacher Rav, "A person is forbidden to keep in his house a measure that is either smaller or larger than the normal capacity." As a later sage, Papa argued that this rule did not apply in those places where the Persian authorities controlled the weights and measures, since the utensils for weighing and measuring required official seals and marks. However, the other Rabbis disagreed on the grounds that customers may come at twilight, when people are in a hurry and accidentally accept the faulty measure (BM 89b).

Several prominent Rabbis taught, "Whoever has the power to prevent someone in his household from sinning but does not do so will be punished." Similarly, if one has the power to stop his fellow citizens, or even the entire world, from sinning but fails to speak out or act, he is responsible for their actions. Papa added, "The exilarchs (leaders of the Jewish community in Babylonia) are held accountable for the sins of the entire house of Israel" (Shab. 54b).

Papa was willing to go beyond the letter of the law on behalf of others. "A certain man once sold a plot of land to Papa because he was in need of money to buy some oxen. Eventually he no longer needed [the money and regretted making the sale]. Papa actually returned the land to him [though legally he did not have to do so]!" (Ket. 97a).

The Rabbis listed the appropriate breakfast time for those engaged in specific occupations. Dividing the day into twelve hours (6 a.m. to 6 p.m.), the Rabbis said: "The first hour [of the day] is the mealtime for gladiators, the second for robbers [thieves remain awake all night and sleep during the first hour of the day]; the third for heirs [property owners who do not have to work for a living and thus could eat earlier than others]; the fourth for laborers [in the field], the fifth for all [other] people." According to Papa, "the fourth [hour] is the mealtime for people generally, the fifth for [agricultural] laborers, and the sixth for Torah scholars." Having breakfast after that time "is like throwing a stone into a barrel [i.e., of no benefit]" (Shab. 10a).

According to a *midrash*, following the Exodus from Egypt, "Moses and Aaron walked in front with Nadab and Abihu [two of Aaron's sons] behind them, and all Israel followed in the rear. Then Nadab said to Abihu, 'When will these old men die, so that you and I can become the leaders of our generation?' But God said to them: 'We shall see who will bury whom.' [Nadab and Abihu died within weeks, after offering 'strange fire' to the Lord; Lev. 10:1–3]." Papa deemed this an illustration of the popular saying, "Many an old camel is laden with the hides of younger ones" (i.e., many older men surprise the young by outlasting or outperforming them) (Sanh. 52a).

Among Papa's many sayings are: "In a house of mourning it is well to keep silent" (Ber. 6b); "If you let a quarrel stand overnight, it disappears by itself" (Sanh. 95a); "The weasel and cat [when at peace with each other] had a feast on the fat of the luckless [i.e., they rid themselves of a common enemy]" (Sanh. 105a); "If you hear that your neighbor has died, believe it: if you hear that he has become rich, do not believe it" (Git. 30b); and "As you happen to pass by [your enemy], make your voice heard by your foe [interpreted as either 'appear before him to disorient him' (Rashi) or 'take revenge when the opportunity is offered']" (Sanh 95b).

Pappus ben Judah, Palestinian *tanna* (first/second century).

Even when civil authorities prohibited the study (and teaching) of Torah, Jews resolutely risked martyrdom to carry out this sacred task. In defiance of a Roman government decree forbidding Jews from studying the Torah, R. Akiva continued to publicly teach Torah to large gatherings of students. When Pappus ben Judah asked his master, "Are you not afraid of the government?" R. Akiva replied with a parable: "A fox walking on the riverbank saw swarms of fish swimming to and fro. 'From what are you fleeing?' the fox asked. They answered, 'From the nets cast for us by men.' The fox said, 'Come up on to the dry land, so that we can live together [in peace] just as our ancestors once did.' They replied: 'Are you the one they call the wisest of animals? You are not clever but foolish. If we are afraid in our natural environment, how much more fearful would we be in the element in which we would die!'" R. Akiva concluded, "So it is with us. If we are in danger in our [ideal] condition, when we sit and study the Torah, regarding which it is written, 'For that is your life and the length of your days' [Deut. 30:20], how much worse would be our peril if we neglect it [the study of Torah]!" Soon afterward, both R. Akiva and Pappus ben Judah were arrested and imprisoned next to each other. When Pappus ben Judah was asked by his teacher "For what sin were you brought here?" he replied: "Happy are you, Akiva, that you were arrested for busying yourself with words of Torah! Woe to Pappus, who was seized for occupying himself with meaningless things!" (Ber. 61b).

The Talmud observes that just as men differ in how they treat their food, so too they differ in how they treat their wives. If a fly falls into their cup, some men will put it aside and not drink it. This corresponds to the way of Pappus ben Judah who, when leaving his house, would lock his wife indoors. In the same situation, other men will throw away the fly and then drink the cup. This corresponds to the way of most men, who do not mind their wives talking with their brothers and relatives. A third response would be to squash the fly and then eat it. This corresponds to the way of a bad man who sees his wife go out with her hair unfastened and spin cloth in the street (Git. 90a).

Pinchas ben Yair, Palestinian *tanna* (second century).

The son-in-law of R. Shimon bar Yochai and a fellow disciple of Judah ha-Nasi, Pinchas ben Yair was renowned more for piety than for learning. Two men once visited the city where the scrupulously honest Pinchas ben Yair was living. They left two measures of barley with him and forgot about them when they departed. "He sowed the barley and each year stored the harvest. When after seven years the men returned to that town, he [Pinchas ben Yair] recognized them and told them to take what belonged to them [i.e., the accumulated grain]" (Deut. R. 3:3).

The Talmud relates that Pinchas ben Yair "never in his life said the [*hamotzi*] blessing over a piece of bread that was not his own [i.e., never accepted an invitation to a meal]; moreover, from the day he matured intellectually [became an adult] he derived no benefit [refused to eat even] from his father's table" (Hul. 7b). As an explanation for this unusual behavior, Pinchas ben Yair said that there are two kinds of people: those who are willing to be hospitable, but cannot afford it; and those who have the means, but are not willing to extend hospitality to others.

The *aggadah* records many miracles performed by Pinchas ben Yair. Once upon reaching the River Ginai on a mission to redeem captives, Pinchas saw that he could not cross to the other side because there was no boat or bridge. "Divide the waters for me," he ordered, but the river refused. "You are about to do the will of the Creator and so am I [i.e., by Divine command all rivers flow to the sea]. You may or may not accomplish your purpose [of redeeming captives], but I am certain of accomplishing mine!" But Pinchas ben Yair would not be dissuaded. "If you will not divide for me, I will decree that no waters ever pass through you [i.e., your sources will dry up]." Appreciating that Pinchas ben Yair could make good on his threat, the river immediately made a path for him. On subsequent occasions, Pinchas ben Yair succeeded in having rivers divide themselves for a "man who was carrying wheat for the Passover [i.e., 'engaged in a religious duty']" and an Arab "who had joined them on the journey." When hearing of these miraculous feats, R. Joseph bar Hiyya exclaimed: "How great is this man! Greater than Moses . . . for him [the sea divided itself] only on one occasion, while for him [Pinchas ben Yair it did so] three times!" (Hul. 7a). In another version of the tale, Pinchas ben Yair performed this miracle while en route to delivering a lecture. When the pupils following him asked if they also might safely cross the river in the same manner, he cautioned: "Only those who have never shamed another person may do so."

Pinchas ben Yair once stopped at an inn to feed his donkey. "They placed barley before his donkey, but it would not eat." Even carefully sifting it to remove any impurities had no effect. Pinchas suggested: "Perhaps it [the barley] has not been tithed?" Once it was tithed, the donkey ate its fill. Pinchas ben Yair concluded: "This poor creature is about to do the will of the Creator, and you would feed it with untithed produce!" (Hul. 7a–b). Pinchas ben Yair apparently believed that Divine punishment for failure to offer tithes was the cause of numerous communal problems, such as city wells not delivering enough water and a plague of mice, which were relieved as soon as the inhabitants paid scrupulous attention to fulfilling this commandment.

Pinchas ben Yair painted a depressing picture of his time: "Since the destruction of the [Second] Temple, scholars and noblemen are ashamed and cover their heads [i.e., the custom was for the masses to go bareheaded], men of deed are disregarded, and men of arms and men of tongue [demagogues] grow powerful. No one asks [about the plight of Israel] and no one prays [on their behalf], and no one inquires [about the welfare of his neighbor]. Upon whom can we rely? [Only] upon our Father who is in Heaven" (Sot. 49a).

In several different versions (Sot. 9:15; Av. Zar. 20b; Shek. 4:6), Pinchas ben Yair offered a famous teaching that became known as either the "ladder of righteousness" or the "saint's progress": "Study leads to precision," which successively "leads to diligence, [moral] cleanliness, restraint [abstinence], purity, piety, humility, fear of sin, saintliness, [possession of] Divine Inspiration, and [eventually] leads to life eternal [or 'resurrection of the dead that comes through Elijah of blessed memory']." In the eighteenth century, this sequence became the basis of the major ethical treatise *Mesilat Yesharim* (The Path of the Upright) by Moses Hayim Luzzatto.

R

Rabbah bar Abbuha, Babylonian *amora* (third century).

Related to the house of the exilarchs, Rabbah bar Abbuha lived at Nehardea until the city was destroyed in 259. He then moved with his student and son-in-law R. Nachman bar Jacob to Machoza, where he was appointed a judge (Yev. 115b) and head of the academy (Shab. 59b). Admittedly not a superb scholar (BM 114b), Rabbah bar Abbuha frequently relied on the view of his teacher, Rav, transmitting many sayings in his name. Commenting on the famous verse, "You shall love your neighbor as yourself" (Lev. 19:18), Rabbah bar Abbuha said that this must be observed even in the case of a criminal, who should be granted as easy a death as possible (Ket. 37b).

Rabbah bar Abbuha met Elijah the prophet, who was believed to have appeared to saintly men, and complained that his poverty forced him to work hard to eke out a living, thus depriving him of time to concentrate properly on his studies. "Elijah took him into the Garden of Eden and ordered him to fill the pocket of his cloak with leaves. As he was leaving, the sage heard a voice say: 'Who is consuming [his reward in the World to Come] like Rabbah bar Abbuha has done [i.e., miraculous assistance in this world is deducted from the reward in the future world]?' Immediately, he shook the leaves out of his pocket and threw them away. However, since he had carried the leaves in his cloak, the garment had absorbed their fragrance from the Garden of Eden. So he sold the cloak for 12,000 dinars and distributed [the money] among his sons-in-law" (BM 114b). He did not give the money to his own sons, because that still would be considered of benefit to him since they were his heirs.

Rabbah bar Bar Hana, Babylonian *amora* (third century).

Rabbah bar Bar Hana moved to the Land of Israel to study with R. Yochanan, whose sayings he often transmitted. However, upset by the lack of respect accorded him in the Land of Israel (e.g., R. Shimon ben Lakish refused to do him the honor of addressing him in public [Yoma 9b]), Rabbah bar Bar Hana returned to Babylonia and resided at both Pumbedita and Sura. He wanted to introduce the Palestinian habit of reciting the Ten Commandments during the daily prayer, but was dissuaded by R. Hisda because it was felt to be associated with Christian practice (Ber. 12a).

Rabbah bar Bar Hana became known for his marvelous travels. In some of these tales, he recorded personal observations, such as the identity of the most fertile part of the Land of Israel ("the land flowing with milk and honey"; Ket. 111b–112a); the distance between Jericho and Jerusalem (Yoma 39b); and the gourd of Jonah (Shab. 21a). Most popular were his fantastic adventures during sea voyages and journeys through the desert, replete with bizarre creatures of huge size. "Once we were traveling on board a ship and saw a [gigantic] fish [at rest] whose back was covered with sand out of which grew grass. Thinking it was dry land [an island in the sea], we landed, made a fire, and cooked our meal [on its back]. But when the fish felt the heat it rolled over, and had the ship not been so near we would have drowned" (BB 73b). Rabbah bar Bar Hana also described a journey through the desert led by an Arab guide who knew the route so well that he could tell from the odor of the sand when a spring was near. The Arab took him to see Mount Sinai, where he heard the voice of God speaking from the mountain and regretting sending Israel into exile. On one occasion, an Arab led Rabbah bar Bar Hana to the place where Korach and his followers had been swallowed by the earth (Num. 16:32). "I saw two cracks that emitted smoke, took a piece of clipped wool, dipped it in water, attached it to the point of a spear, and stuck it in there. When I took it out, it was singed. He [the Arab] said to me, 'Listen carefully. What do you hear?' I heard them [Korach and his followers] crying out, 'Moses and his Torah are true, and we are liars!'" However, some of his contemporaries were cynical about Rabbah bar Bar Hana's alleged exploits: "Every Abba [Rabbah equals Rab Abba] is an ass, and every bar Bar Hana is a fool!" (BB 73b–74a).

Rabbah bar Hana, Babylonian *amora* (third century).

Rabbah bar Hana accompanied his uncle, R. Hiyya, to the Land of Israel, where he studied with R. Yochanan and Judah ha-Nasi. When Rabbah bar Hana was about to return to his native land, R. Hiyya asked Judah ha-Nasi to give his nephew permission to decide matters of ritual law, monetary cases, and defects in a firstborn animal that could allow it to be slaughtered for food. Although this permission was rarely granted, Judah ha-Nasi agreed to do so in the case of Rabbah bar Hana (Sanh. 5a).

In answer to his question, "Why are the words of the Torah likened to fire" (Jer. 23:29), Rabbah bar Hana answered: "This is to teach you that, just as fire does not ignite itself, so too the words of the Torah do not endure with a person who studies alone" (Taan. 7a).

Rabbah bar Hana is often confused with Rabbah bar Bar Hana, who some believe was his son.

Rabbah bar Huna, Babylonian *amora* (third/fourth century).

After studying with his father, the head of the academy at Sura, and his successor R. Hisda, Rabbah bar Huna eventually achieved that prestigious position. However, Rabbah bar Huna was not always pleased with R. Hisda's lectures, complaining: "When I go to him he treats me to secular [not Torah] discourses! [Thus] he tells me, 'When one enters a privy, he must not sit down abruptly, nor strain too much, because the rectum rests on three teeth-like glands that might become dislocated and endanger [one's health].'" R. Huna disagreed with his son's assessment: "He treats matters of health and you call them secular discourses! All the more reason for going to him!" (Shab. 82a). Years later, Rabbah bar Huna and R. Hisda served together as judges (Shab. 10a). Rabbah bar Huna demonstrated respect for his teacher by accepting his advice not to include the Ten Commandments in the daily prayers at Sura "on account of the insinuations of the *minim* [sectarians]" (Ber. 12a).

When Rabbah bar Huna was appointed head of the academy of Sura, he became friendly with the exilarch, who often asked him *halachic* questions. Nevertheless, when Rabbah bar Huna "quarreled with members of the household of the exilarch," he stressed his independence from secular control, noting to the exilarch that he was not bound by his view: "I did not receive authority [to act as judge] from you, but from my father, who had it from Rav, and he from R. Hiyya, who received it from Judah ha-Nasi [in the Land of Israel]" (Sanh. 5a).

Described as a man of both true piety (Shab. 31a–b) and genuine modesty (MK 28a), Rabbah bar Huna said: "He who possesses learning without the fear of God is like a steward who is entrusted with the inner keys [of the storehouse] but not with the outer keys, and thus cannot gain access to the treasure" (Shab. 31a–b). Among his other maxims are: "An insolent person must be considered a sinner" (Taan. 7b); and "He who loses his temper, even the Divine Presence is unimportant in his eyes and God is not in his thoughts" (Ned. 22b).

The story is told that Rabbah bar Huna and R. Hamnuna I died at the same time, and camels walking side by side carried their coffins to be buried in the Land of Israel. Reaching a narrow bridge, the camels halted. When a passing Arab asked the men accompanying the procession why they had suddenly stopped, he was informed that the two scholars they were taking to be buried each modestly wanted his colleague to precede him. The Arab stated that in his opinion the famous son of an illustrious father should go first, and thus the camel bearing Rabbah bar Huna passed ahead. This course of action appeared to have upset the soul of Rabbah bar Huna, for "the molars and teeth of that Arab fell out [when Rabbah bar Huna's camel reared up and kicked him]" (MK 25b). *See also* Hamnuna I; Yannai.

Rabbah bar Mari, Babylonian *amora* (third/fourth century).

Rabbah bar Mari was a close friend and colleague of Rava, to whom he gave the biblical references for a series of thirteen popular proverbs (BK 92a–b). In explaining why Jacob used lentils in preparing the stew to comfort his father Isaac when Abraham died, and for which Esau sold his birthright, it was said in the name of Rabbah bar Mari: "Just as the lentil has no mouth [i.e., is not cleft, like other kinds of beans], so the mourner has no mouth [i.e., neither the ability nor desire to speak at the meal of consolation following the funeral]" (BB 16b).

Rabbah bar Nachmani, Babylonian *amora* (third/fourth century).

Whenever the Talmud mentions Rabbah without a patronymic, it means Rabbah bar Nachmani. A descendant of a priestly family of Judea that traced its lineage to Eli the priest (RH 18a), Rabbah bar Nachmani moved to Babylonia to study with R. Huna at Sura and R. Judah bar Ezekiel at Pumbedita. It appears that R. Huna infrequently decided a question of importance without consulting his distinguished student.

Although his brothers urged him to return to the Land of Israel and study with R. Yochanan (Ket. 111a), Rabbah bar Nachmani decided to remain in Babylonia. He focused on the *halachah*, especially an understanding of the fundamental reasons for the biblical and rabbinic laws and explanations of any apparent contradictions contained within them. Thus he often asked, "Why did the Torah command this?" and "Why did the sages forbid this?" A master of intricate logical reasoning who never hesitated to argue even if his was a minority opinion, Rabbah bar Nachmani was known as an "Uprooter of Mountains" because of his exceptional skill in dialectics (Ber. 64a).

Rabbah bar Nachmani eventually became the head of the academy in Pumbedita, where he served for twenty-two years. Before beginning his scholarly discourse, he would tell his students a humorous story to bring smiles to their faces and get them in a cheerful mood; then he would assume a more solemn air and proceed to discuss the difficult intricacies of *halachah* (Shab. 30b). Although widely respected by his fellow scholars, Rabbah bar Nachmani was hated by the general community in Pumbedita because of his outspokenness in criticizing their behavior (Shab. 153a).

Recognizing the importance for a growing child to be given things he can break as an outlet for surplus emotional energy, Rabbah bar Nachmani bought damaged earthenware vessels for his children to break if they so desired (Yoma 78b).

Rabbah bar Nachmani's popularity as a lecturer led to a tremendous increase in the number of students, but this ironically led to his tragic death. Local tax collectors complained that they were unable to get money from the many students who flocked to the academy at Pumbedita in Nisan and Tishrei, the months of popular Torah lectures before Passover and Rosh Hashanah. "There is an Israelite [teacher] who keeps back 12,000 Israelites [students] from the payment of the royal poll-tax one month in summer and one in winter." Blaming Rabbah bar Nachmani for their lost revenue, they determined to arrest him, but he escaped. After fleeing from town to town, Rabbah bar Nachmani died near Pumbedita. His body, which according to legend had been concealed by birds, was found in a thicket where he had hidden from his pursuers. It was said that at the moment of his death, a heavenly voice proclaimed: "Happy are you, O Rabbah bar Nachmani, whose body is pure and whose soul departed in purity!" (BM 86a). *See also* Abbaye.

Rabbah bar Rav Hanan, Babylonian *amora* (third/fourth century).

Rabbah bar Rav Hanan was said to have asked the question, "What is the law?" to which came the famous reply: "Go out and see how the people are accustomed to act" (Ber. 45a). The Talmud relates a dispute involving Rabbah bar Rav Hanan, who "had some date trees adjoining a vineyard of R. Joseph ben Hananiah. . . . Birds used to roost on the date palms and fly down and damage the vines." R. Joseph bar Hananiah asked Rabbah bar Rav Hanan to remove the date palms, but the latter refused based on a ruling by Rav that it was forbidden to cut down fruit-bearing trees. As further justification, he noted that R. Hanina had said that his son died young only "because he cut down a date palm before it was dead [lit., 'not its time']." Rabbah bar Rav Hanan concluded that if the master wanted the trees cut down, he was welcome to do it himself (BB 26a).

Rabbah bar Shila, Babylonian *amora* (fourth century).

After being appointed as a judge, Rabbah bar Shila warned his fellow jurists that a judge must not borrow anything from those under his jurisdiction unless he was in a position to lend them something in return, lest the transaction be considered as bribery or the impartiality of his judgment be influenced by the kindness of the litigant who had made the loan in question (Ket. 105b).

In the name of his teacher, R. Hisda, Rabbah bar Shila said (Shab. 33a): "He who puts his mouth to folly [speaks lewdly], Gehinnom [Hell] is made deep for him," based on the verse, "The mouth of a forbidden woman is a deep pit" (Prov. 22:14). He also remarked, "The day when rain falls is as hard [to bear due to the inconvenience and discomfort that it causes to people] as a day of judgment [according to Rashi, Mondays and Thursdays, when the *bet din* met and people could have their cases tried]" (Taan. 8b).

According to legend, Rabbah bar Shila once met Elijah and asked what God was doing. The prophet replied, "He utters traditions [*halachot*] in the name of all the Rabbis" except R. Meir, who studied under Acher (R. Elisha ben Abuyah, who became an apostate). Rabbah bar Shila complained, "Why is this? R. Meir [merely] found a [beautiful] pomegranate and ate [the juicy fruit] within it and discarded the peel!" (Hag. 15b), meaning that the sage extracted only that which was good from R. Elisha ben Abuyah's teaching. Convinced by this argument, Elijah asserted that from then on God would mention R. Meir's name.

Rabbah Tosfa'ah, Babylonian *amora* (fifth century).

Head of the academy at Sura, Rabbah Tosfa'ah was one of the last of the *amoraim* and assisted R. Ashi in completing the editing of the Babylonian Talmud. In concert with rabbinic efforts to avoid labeling a newborn a *mamzer*, Rabbah Tosfa'ah once ruled that a child born when his father "had gone to a country beyond the sea and remained there for a full year of 12 months" was legitimate, based on the assumption that the birth was delayed and the fetus remained in utero three months after the normal nine months of pregnancy (Yev. 80b). He also addressed the issue of the effectiveness of *zimmun* (the call to a public recitation of the *Birkat ha-Mazon*) when one of three eating together had already said the Grace after Meals for himself (Ber. 50a).

Rabin bar Adda, Babylonian *amora* (fourth century).

A disciple of R. Judah bar Ezekiel at Pumbedita, Rabin bar Adda transmitted several traditions of his teacher, R. Isaac. "How do you know that the Holy One, blessed be He, is to be found in the synagogue? For it is written, 'God stands in the Divine assembly' [Ps. 82:1]." The same verse explained why "if ten people pray together, the Divine Presence is with them" (for a congregation consists of not less than ten). "And how do you know that if three are sitting as a court of judges, the Divine Presence is with them? For it is said [in the same verse]: 'In the midst of the judges He judges' [and a *bet din* consists of three]." Finally, Rabin bar Adda asked: "And how do you know that if two are sitting and studying the Torah together, the Divine Presence is with them? For it is said: 'Then they that feared the Lord spoke one with another [a phrase denoting two], and the Lord paid heed and listened. A record was written before Him of those who feared the Lord and kept His name in mind' [Mal. 3:16]" (Ber. 6a). In the name of his teacher, R. Isaac, Rabin bar Adda said: "If a man is accustomed to attend synagogue [daily], but on one day he does not go, the Holy One, blessed be He, inquires about him" (Ber. 6b).

Rafram bar Papa, Babylonian *amora* (fourth century).

Rafram bar Papa once "was called up [in synagogue] to read the [Torah] Scroll. He recited 'Bless the Lord' and stopped, without adding 'who is to be blessed.' The whole congregation cried out, 'Bless the Lord who is to be blessed.' His teacher Rava rebuked him: 'You black pot [probably reflecting his swarthy complexion]! Why do you want to enter into controversy [i.e., follow a minority view]?'" (Ber. 50a). Later, Rava asked Rafram bar Papa, "Tell me some of the good deeds that R. Huna had done." Rafram bar Papa replied, "Of his childhood I do not recollect anything, but of his old age I do. On cloudy [stormy] days they used to drive him about in a golden carriage. He surveyed every part of the city and he ordered the demolition of any wall that was unsafe. If the owner was in a position to do so he had to rebuild it himself, but if not, then [R. Huna] would have it rebuilt at his own expense. Whenever R. Huna discovered some [new] medicine, he would fill a water jug with it and suspend it above the doorstep and proclaim: 'Whosoever desires it, let him come and take some.'. . . When he had a meal, he would open the door wide and declare: 'Whoever is in need, let him come and eat.'" Rava observed, "All these things I could carry out myself except the last one, because there are so many [poor people where he lived]" (Taan. 20b–21a).

In the name of R. Hisda, Rafram bar Papa quoted: "Since the day the Temple was destroyed, there has never been a perfectly clear sky, since it says, 'I clothe the heavens with blackness and make a sackcloth their covering' [Isa. 50:3]" (Ber. 59a). Rafram bar Papa eventually became head of the academy at Pumbedita.

Rami bar Ezekiel, Babylonian *amora* (third/fourth century).

Disregarding the advice of his younger brother, R. Judah bar Ezekiel, the founder of the academy at Pumbedita, Rami bar Ezekiel went to the Land of Israel to see the site where R. Akiva's academy once stood in Bnai Brak. He described it as truly "a land flowing with milk and honey [Exod. 3:8; Num. 13:27]" (Ket. 111b). Subsequently returning to Babylonia, Rami bar Ezekiel edited many of the sayings that his brother R. Judah bar Ezekiel had cited in the names of Rav and Samuel (Ket. 21a, 60a, 76b; Hul. 44a).

Rami bar Hama, Babylonian *amora* (fourth century).

A pupil of R. Hisda, Rami bar Hama married his teacher's daughter. When he died at an early age, Rava married his widow and declared that Rami bar Hama's premature death resulted from his having insulted R. Menashiah ben Tahalifa (a student of the law) by treating him as an ignoramus (Ber. 47b). Rami bar Hama was also criticized by Rava for attempting to decide questions of law independently, without taking the time to search for a *mishnah* or *baraita* to support his opinion. Described as a "man of pious deeds," his daughter married R. Ashi (Betz. 29b). *See also* Sheshet.

Rav, Babylonian *amora* (second/third century).

The founder of the academy at Sura, Rav was known as Abba Aricha (long Abba) because "he was the tallest man in his generation" (Nid. 24b). However, in the Talmud he is almost always referred to simply as "Rav" (master), just as his teacher Judah ha-Nasi was called "Rabbi." (The title *Rav* was subsequently awarded by the exilarch to all of the sage's successors who headed their own academies in Babylonia.) Rav bridged the eras before and after the Mishnah and was one of the very few *amoraim* who were permitted to dispute the opinions of a *tanna*. Born in Kafri, Rav came from a prominent Babylonian family that traced its lineage back to Shimea, a brother of King David (Ket. 62b). He spent many years in the Land of Israel, some with his uncle R. Hiyya, and even had the opportunity to participate in legal discussions with Judah ha-Nasi.

In 219, at the age of sixty-four, Rav eventually returned to Babylonia, an event generally considered as the beginning of the Talmudic age in that country. After several years as a lecturer at Nehardea under R. Shila, Rav established his own academy in Sura. This soon became the intellectual center of Babylonian Jewry, attracting thousands of students from throughout the Jewish world. Rav's close friend and intellectual adversary in *halachic* discussions was R. Samuel, who succeeded Shila as head of the academy at Nehardea. Their disputes on civil and ritual issues, as well as the massive number of opinions recorded in Rav's name, constitute the basis for the development of the Babylonian Talmud, which was then expanded by his numerous and influential disciples. As a general rule, it is said that the *halachah* follows the rulings of Rav on ritual law and of R. Samuel on civil issues.

Rav's basic method was to first understand the spirit of the rules laid down in the Mishnah and then derive from its teachings a variety of theoretical explanations and practical applications of the law. Over the years, Rav often changed his mind about specific issues. Consequently, various students cited many of his opinions in different ways. Departing from the tradition that precluded a student from expressing his opinion in the presence of his teacher, Rav permitted his students to decide legal cases. "In capital cases, one may instruct his disciple [giving the reasons for and against conviction] and pronounce judgment with him [the master and disciple each having separate votes]" (Sanh. 36a).

Rather than have his students depend on the charity of those who gave money to scholars to share in the reward of their learning, Rav established the institution of the *yarchei kallah* (months of study). Requiring his pupils to work for a living, Rav set aside only two months of the year, Adar and Elul, as times for study, when scholars and laymen gathered together to teach and learn a tractate of Talmud. Rav did not accept pupils until age six, believing that only then "can you stuff them with Torah like an ox," and he limited punishment of a pupil to "hitting with nothing harder than a shoelace" (BB 21a). Appointed by the exilarch as supervisor of the municipal market in charge of checking weights and measures, Rav also became involved in the manufacture of beer (from dates), a popular beverage in Babylonia that often was considered a substitute for wine. In addressing the issue of whether *Kiddush* could be said over beer, Rav ruled that this was not permitted, but that beer could be used for Havdalah (Pes. 107a).

Rav devoted much of his activities to developing the service in the synagogue, which he decreed must be the tallest structure in the city (Shab. 11a). He composed numerous prayers extemporaneously, either as the formal leader of the congregation or before opening his classes. According to Rav, on each of the four occasions when one bows during the *Amidah*, "one should bow at [the word] 'Blessed' and return to the upright position at [the mention of] the Divine Name" (Ber. 12b). On concluding the *Amidah*, Rav added the following: "May it be Your will, O Lord our God, and God of our fathers, to grant us long life, a life of peace, a life of good, a life of blessing, a life of sustenance, a life of bodily vigor, a life in which there is fear of sin, a life free from shame and confusion, a life of riches and honor, a life in which we may be filled with the love of Torah and the fear of Heaven, a life in which You will fulfill all the desires of our heart for good" (Ber. 16b). Today, this forms the central part of *Birkat ha-Hodesh*, the prayer that is recited on the Sabbath on which the upcoming New Moon is announced.

Tradition maintains that Rav composed the *Aleinu* prayer, organized the verses of the *Malchuyot, Zichronot,* and *Shofarot* sections recited during the *Musaf Amidah* on Rosh Hashanah, and arranged the *haftarot* (readings from the prophets recited after the Torah reading on Sabbaths and festivals). He maintained that "four [classes of people] have to offer thanksgiving [for God's mercy]: those who have crossed the sea [completed an ocean voyage], those who have traversed the wilderness [desert], one who has recovered from an illness, and a prisoner who has been set free" (Ber. 54b). Among the additions Rav made to prayers calling for an end to the dispersion of the Jewish people were: "Let the Almighty bring us with joy into our land and plant us within our own boundaries" for the Sabbath; "Gather up our scattered remnants from among the heathens and our dispersed ones from all lands of the earth" for holidays; and "Break off the yoke of the heathens from our necks and lead us proudly into our own land" in the daily service and the Grace after Meals. Rav described how the World to Come would be different from this world: "There will be no eating and drinking, no propagating or business activity; no envy or hatred or intrigue. The righteous will sit with crowns on their heads, feasting on the brilliant glow of the Divine Presence" (Ber. 17a).

A huge number of sayings are attributed to Rav. Among them are: "One should be careful not to wrong his wife, for being quick to weep, she is easily hurt [at the smallest trifle]" (BM 59a); "Whatever may not properly be done in public is forbidden even in the most secret chamber" (Shab. 64b); "A person will be called to account in the hereafter for each pleasure he denied himself [in this world] without sufficient cause" (JT Kid. 4:12); "A meal without salt is no meal" (Ber. 44a); "Whoever has no pity for his fellow man is no child of Abraham" (Betz. 32b); "God gave the commandments to refine the Jews, as the goldsmith takes gold in his crucible and refines the dross from it" (Mid. Sam. 4); "A man must always accustom himself to think that whatever God does is for the best" (Ber. 60b); "The study of Torah is more important than the rebuilding of the Temple" (Meg. 16b); and "A Jew, even though he has sinned, is still a Jew" (Sanh. 44b).

When Rav died at an advanced age, thousands of scholars from all over Babylonia came to his funeral. Every Jewish community in the country mourned Rav's death for twelve months. When hearing of Rav's death, R. Samuel tore thirteen garments (as a sign of mourning) and declared, "Gone is the man before whom I trembled [in awe of his great learning]" (MK 24a). *See also* Abba bar Zavda; Adda bar Ahava; Hiyya; Hiyya bar Ashi; Hiyya bar Rav; Huna; Judah bar Ezekiel; Judah bar Samuel bar Shilath; Kahana; Rava bar Hinena the Elder; Samuel; Samuel bar Shilath; Sheshet; Zutra bar Tobiah.

Rava, Babylonian *amora* (third/fourth century).

According to tradition, when Judah ha-Nasi died, Rava (an abbreviation for Rav Abba) was born (Kid. 72b). The son of R. Joseph bar Hama of Machoza, a wealthy and distinguished scholar, Rava was a student of R. Nachman bar Jacob and the closest friend and study partner of R. Abbaye, with whom he developed the dialectic methodic of *halachic* interpretation. Their discussions represent a considerable part of the Babylonian Talmud. Rava expanded the existing hermeneutical principles of interpretation and was known for his brilliant deductive reasoning. When he and R. Abbaye disagreed, in all but six cases Rava's decision became the accepted law (Kid. 52a). Later, Rava studied with R. Hisda at the academy in Sura.

Indicating that prophecy may be given to children, the Talmud relates that as R. Hisda's young daughter was sitting on her father's lap while he was teaching, in the front row of students were Rava and R. Rami bar Hama. When R. Hisda asked the child which of the two students she wished to have for her husband, she answered, "I want both." Immediately, Rava said, "Let me be the second" (BB 12b). This eventually occurred, with R. Hisda's daughter marrying R. Rami bar Hama; ten years after his death, the widow married Rava (Yev. 34b).

Returning to his birthplace, Rava founded a school at Machoza, which became one of the preeminent academic institutions in Babylonia and attracted thousands of students. As one student wryly noted to another, "Instead of gnawing bones in the school of R. Abbaye, why do you not eat fat meat in the school of Rava [where the teaching is so much superior]?" (BB 22a). Realizing that it was impossible for every Jew to totally devote his life to study, and that it was necessary to work to earn a living, Rava instructed his students to abandon the study hall during the months of Nisan (the spring harvest) and Tishrei (the fall pressing of the grapes and olives) so that they would have an income for the rest of the year. His students followed this advice, engaging in farming during these two months, except for celebrating the autumn holidays, and studying in Rava's *yeshivah* the rest of the year (Ber. 35b).

Rava opened his lectures to the general public to spread knowledge of the *halachah* among the masses. Believing that Torah study was essential, he considered it an antidote for the evil inclination (BB 16a) and declared that one who occupied himself with the study of Torah had no need for sacrifices (Men. 110a). "If done with the right intent, Torah study is a life-giving medicine; but it is a deadly poison if not done properly" (Yoma 72). He was critical of those who abandoned Torah study for any other pursuit, even attacking R. Hamnuna for "prolonging his prayers" and thus "forsaking eternal life and occupying himself with temporal life [praying for transient needs]" (Shab. 10a). Rava scorned as "dull-witted" those uncultured individuals who rose in deference to the Torah scroll but did not stand up to show respect to a learned man (Mak. 22b). He supported tax reductions and economic benefits for genuine scholars, though this raised the question of whether a scholar could inform others of his identity and describe his own accomplishments. Rava declared that this was permitted, but only in a place where the scholar was unknown. However, it was improper to boast of his attainments where he was known, based on the verse from Proverbs (27:2): "Let another man praise you, and not your own mouth" (Ned. 62a–b).

Based on the biblical description of the Ark, "Overlay it with pure gold, inside and out" (Exod. 25:11), Rava observed: "Any scholar whose inside is not like his outside is no scholar [i.e., both should be of the same upright character]" (Yoma 72b). He interpreted the verses, "[The Torah] is not in heaven . . . nor is it beyond the sea" (Deut. 30:12–13) as meaning that the Torah "cannot be found in a person whose pride is as high as the heavens . . . or whose smugness in his self-esteem is as wide as the sea" (Taan. 21b). Rava once observed, "I made three requests of Heaven, of which two were granted and one was not. [The prayers for] the scholarship of R. Huna and the wealth of R. Hisda were granted me; but the modest disposition [and humility] of Rabbah ben Huna was not" (MK 28a). Rava urged his disciples, "Set a fixed [regular] time for the study of Torah" (Er. 54b). He believed that if a student has problems learning, "It is because his teacher does not show him a cheerful countenance" (Taan. 7b–8a). Overcrowded classes were not considered conducive to learning. According to Rava, "The [maximum] number of [elementary] pupils assigned to one teacher is 25. If there are 50, we appoint two teachers. If there are 40, we appoint an assistant [senior student] at the expense of the town" (BB 21a).

Despite his stress on the great importance of Torah study, Rava did not consider it an end in itself. "The goal of wisdom is repentance and good deeds, so that a man should not study the Torah and Mishnah and then despise his father and mother, his teacher, and his superior in wisdom and rank" (Ber. 17a). According to Rava, "When a man is brought in for judgment [in the World to Come] he is asked: 'Did you deal faithfully [were you honest in your business dealings]; did you set aside fixed times to study Torah; did you have children; did you hope for redemption; and did you search for wisdom?'" (Shab. 31a). Why was Jerusalem destroyed?—"Only because men of faith [completely truthful and trustworthy] no longer resided there" (Shab. 119b).

The Talmud notes, "If someone is able to pray for his friend and does not, he is called a sinner." Rava added that if his friend is a Torah scholar, he must pray for him to the point of making himself sick" (Ber. 12b). On concluding his prayer, Rava added the following: "My God, before I was formed I was not worthy [to be formed], and now that I have been formed I am as if I had not been formed. I am dust in my lifetime, all the more in my death. Behold, I am before You like a vessel full of shame and confusion. May it be Your will, O Lord my God, that I sin no more, and the sins I have committed before You be erased in Your great mercies, but not through evil chastisements and diseases!" (Ber. 17a).

One day, a frantic man came to Rava asking for his advice. "The governor of my town has ordered me to kill a certain person, and if I refuse he will kill me." Rava replied, "Let him kill you rather than you should commit murder; do you think that your blood is redder [than his]? Perhaps his blood is redder [i.e., you have no right to murder him to save yourself, since his life is no less valuable than your own]" (Pes. 25b). A man who was given a purse of money for the ransoming of captives was attacked by thieves and handed over the money to them. He was summoned before Rava, who nevertheless declared him exempt from any wrongdoing. When R. Abbaye suggested that the man was guilty of "rescuing himself by means of money meant for another," Rava replied, "There could hardly be a case of redeeming captives more urgent than his own!" (BK 117b).

Rava observed, "If a man sees that painful sufferings afflict him, let him examine his conduct. If he finds nothing objectionable, let him attribute his difficulties to neglect of the study of Torah. If he finds that this is not the cause, it is certain that his sufferings are chastenings of love, for it is said: 'For whom the Lord loves, He rebukes [Prov. 3:12].' . . . If God loves a man, He crushes him with painful sufferings" (Ber. 5a).

Rava declared a "bad wife" to be "as troublesome as a stormy day" (Yev. 63b), offering an ingenious way to handle a bad wife whose *ketubah* specified such a high amount that he could not afford to divorce her. He recommended marrying another wife, so that the competition would cause his first wife to improve. This idea was based on the popular saying, "by her partner rather than by a thorn," meaning that a bad wife was more easily corrected by subjecting her to the unpleasantness of a rival than by any punishment (Yev. 63b). As in the Bible, the Talmud sanctioned polygamy but discouraged it. Rava said a man could marry as many wives as he could support (Yev. 65a), but the maximum number permitted was four (Yev. 44a), so that each could have marital intercourse on the Sabbath once a month. Nevertheless, there is no indication that any of the Talmudic Rabbis had more than one wife at a time. Rava once overheard a man praying that a certain girl might become his mate and chastised him: "If she is the right one for you, you will not lose her; if not, your unanswered prayer might lead you to lose faith in God" (MK 18b).

According to Rava, "One hundred *zuz* [invested] in business will provide meat and wine every day; one hundred *zuz* [invested] in land only lets one survive on salt and vegetables. Moreover, it [owning a farm] causes him to sleep on the ground [since he must remain in his field at night to guard his crops] and embroils him in strife [with the owners of adjoining fields]" (Yev. 63a). Rava continued, "Though a famine last seven years, it does not pass the artisan's gate [i.e., hunger need not be feared by those who have learned a trade]" (Sanh. 29a).

Rava supported R. Jonathan's view that dreams derive from within rather than from a prophetic source. As supporting proof for this concept, he noted: "A man is never shown in a dream a golden date palm or an elephant going through the eye of a needle [because he never thinks of such things]" (Ber. 55b). He also believed that internal temperament affects the content of dreams, suggesting that a good dream is caused by happiness, particularly that which follows the fulfillment of a commandment (Shab. 30b). The Rabbis maintained that dreams could be used by the dead to convey a message to the living: "Rava once prayed to God to send rain. His father appeared to him in a dream, saying: 'Is there anyone who troubles Heaven so much? Change your place [of sleeping, because you are in danger].' Rava obeyed and next morning he discovered that his bed had been slashed with knives" (Taan. 24b).

Rava advised his children: "When you are cutting meat, do not cut it upon your hand [either because of the danger or the possibility of spoiling the meat]; do not sit upon a gentile's bed [lit., 'the bed of an Aramean woman']); and do not pass behind a synagogue when the congregation is praying" (Ber. 8b). He claimed, "Wine and spices have helped to make me wise" (Hor. 13b), and observed, "At first the evil inclination is like a passerby, then he is called a guest, and finally he becomes master of the house" (Suk. 52b). As Rava maintained, "Length of life, children, and sustenance depend not on merit but [rather on] *mazal* [luck or destiny]" (MK 28a).

In a famous passage serving as a forerunner of the *golem* legend, Rava declared: "If the righteous desired it, they could [by living a life of absolute purity] be creators. . . . Rava created a man and sent him to R. Zei'ra, who spoke to him but received no answer [since the creature lacked the ability to speak]." Ze'ira then addressed the man: "You are a creature of the magicians [sages who mastered the secrets of creation]. Return to your dust" (Sanh. 65b). *See also* Abbaye; Aha ben Adda; Bar Hedya; Dimi bar Hinena; Dimi of Nehardea; Hamnuna II; Jeremiah; Nachman bar Jacob; Rafram bar Papa; Rami bar Hama; Safra; Ulla; Ze'iri.

Rava bar Hinena. *See* Dimi bar Hinena.

Rava bar Hinena the Elder, Babylonian *amora* (third century).

A disciple of Rav, Rava bar Hinena the Elder quoted several statements of his teacher concerning the recitation of the *Amidah* [*Tefillah*]: "In saying the *Tefillah*, when one bows [four times] one should bow at [the word] 'Blessed,' and when returning to the upright position one should return at [the mention of] the Divine Name. R. Samuel asked: What is Rav's reason for this? Because it is written: 'The Lord raises up those that are bowed down' [Ps. 146:8]" (Ber. 12a). "Throughout the year, one says in the *Tefillah*, 'the holy God' and the 'the King who loves righteousness and judgment' [in the third and twelfth benedictions, respectively], except during the ten days between New Year and the Day of Atonement, when he says, 'the holy King' and 'the King of judgment'" (Ber. 12b). Other sayings of Rav cited by Rava bar Hinena the Elder include: "If one is in a position to pray on behalf of his fellow and does not do so, he is called a sinner"; and "If one commits a sin and is ashamed of it [conscience stricken], all his sins are forgiven" (Ber. 12b).

Ravina I, Babylonian *amora* (fourth/fifth century).

Blessed with an extraordinary memory, Ravina I assisted R. Ashi in undertaking the editing of the Babylonian Talmud. Ravina I was the uncle of Ravina II, the final editor of the work. Often engaging in disputes with R.

Ashi on legal questions, the interpretations of Ravina I were more liberal and almost always prevailed.

Ravina II, Babylonian *amora* (fifth century).

Although his father R. Huna died when Ravina II was very young, his learned mother communicated to her son his father's opinions (Ber. 39b; Men. 68b). After his father's death, his maternal uncle (Ravina I) became his guardian (Ket. 100b). Ravina II served as a judge in Sura (Ket. 69a) and assisted R. Ashi in editing and finalizing the text of the Babylonian Talmud. After the deaths of R. Ashi and Rabbah Tosfa'ah, Ravina II was head of the academy at Sura for one year. The death of Ravina II in about 500 marked the end of the *amoraic* period, as well as the completion of the editing of the Talmud (BM 86a).

Ravina II believed that the dignity of a human being was more important than obeying the commandments. He once was walking behind Mar bar Rav Ashi on one of the Sabbaths preceding Passover, when it was usual to preach on the laws pertaining to the festival. "Suddenly, a corner of [Mar bar Rav Ashi's] garment with its fringe was torn away." Ravina II did not mention anything until they returned home. Mar bar Rav Ashi said, "Had you told me of what had happened, I should have immediately cast it off [since the garment no longer had the proper fringes, it would have been regarded as an unnecessary burden carried on the Sabbath]." Ravina II replied, "But has not a Master said, 'Great is the dignity of man since it overrides a negative precept of the Torah?' [i.e., since it would be undignified for a man of his eminence to remove his garment in the street, he was permitted to carry it on the Sabbath]" (Men. 37b).

As the Talmud relates, "When the soul of Ravina II went into repose, a certain orator opened [his eulogy] as follows:

You Palms, sway your heads [and deplore]
A Saint, a noble Palm that is no more.
Who days and nights in meditation spent;
For him, day and night, let us lament. (MK 25b)

Resh Lakish. *See* Shimon ben Lakish.

Reuben ben Estrobile (**Strobilius/Istroboli**), Palestinian *tanna* (second century).

Reuben ben Estrobile was a teacher of Rav, who cited two statements in his name (MK 18b). "From the Torah [Pentateuch], Prophets, and Writings it may be shown that a woman is destined to a man by God—from the Torah: 'Then Laban and Bethuel answered [referring to Rebecca's marrying Isaac], the matter was decreed by the Lord' [Gen. 24:50]; from the Prophets, 'but his [Samson's] father and mother did not realize that this was the Lord's doing' [Judg. 14:4]; and from the Writings, 'property and riches are bequeathed by the father, but an efficient wife comes from the Lord' [Prov. 19:14]." Rav also said in the name of Reuben ben Estrobile: "A person does not arouse suspicion unless he has done the [suspected] thing; and if he has not done it wholly, he has done it partly; and if he has not done it partly, he had the intention to do it; and if he had no such intention, he has seen others doing it and enjoyed [the sight of it]" (MK 18b).

Cultivating good relations with the authorities could be valuable to the community. The Roman government once issued a decree that prohibited Jews from observing the Sabbath or circumcising their children and required them to have intercourse with menstruating women. To disguise himself, Reuben ben Estrobile cut his hair in the Roman fashion and was able to mingle with important officers without being recognized. He asked them, "If one has an enemy, does he want him to be poor or rich?" When they opted for the former, he said: "Then let the Jews do no work on the Sabbath so that they become poor [i.e., by working only six days a week instead of seven]." The officers agreed with this logic and the decree was annulled. Reuben ben Estrobile continued, "If one has an enemy, does he want him to be weak or strong?" When they again chose the former, he said: "Then let their children be circumcised on the eighth day and they will become weak." Again they saw the wisdom of his words, and the decree was annulled. Finally, Reuben ben Estrobile asked them, "If one has an enemy, does he want them to multiply or to decrease?" When they replied that they wished their enemy to decrease, Reuben ben Estrobile said, "Then you should forbid the Jews from having intercourse with menstruating women," and the authorities agreed. However, once they discovered that Reuben ben Estrobile was a Jew, they reinstated the decrees (Me'il. 17a).

S

Safra, Babylonian *amora* (fourth century).

When Safra heard the dictum of R. Yochanan that among the three classes of people earning God's special approval was "a bachelor living in a large city without sinning," his "face lit up" for he had never fallen victim to the temptation of prostitutes (Pes. 113a).

The collectors in Caesarea debated whether Safra had the right to be exempt from paying taxes, a privilege accorded to scholars, because he could not answer a biblical question they posed to him. R. Abbahu noted that Safra was "a scholar of the Talmud" (lit., "Tannaitic teaching"), but not learned in scripture (Av. Zar. 4a). After completing his prayers, Safra would add: "May it be Your will, O Lord our God, to establish peace among the celestial family [the guardian angels of the different nations] and among the earthly family [the nations of the world], and among the disciples who occupy themselves with Your Torah, whether for its own sake or for other motives; and may it please You that all who do so for other motives may come to study it for its own sake!" (Ber. 16b–17a).

Known for his scrupulous honesty in business (Mak. 24a), Safra, according to several parallel stories, once refused to allow a prospective buyer for his donkey/wine to interrupt his prayers. Interpreting Safra's lack of response as a rejection of his offer, the buyer repeatedly raised his bids. However, when Safra had completed his prayers, the sage would not accept more than the price initially offered.

Once Safra and Rava were walking along the road when they chanced to meet Mar Zutra, the son of Nachman. Believing that they had come to meet him, Mar Zutra expressed his appreciation that two esteemed scholars would "take this trouble to come so far [to meet me]." Safra replied, "We did not know that you were coming; but had we known of it, we should have come even a longer distance to meet you." When asked by Rava why he had given an explanation that upset Mar Zutra, Safra answered, "But we would be deceiving him otherwise." Rava disagreed: "No, he would be deceiving himself [thinking that they had specially come to meet him]!" (Hul. 94b).

"When the soul of Safra went into repose, the Rabbis did not rend [their clothes] on account of him [at the news of his demise]," even though this was the general practice to mark the death of a scholar. Although they explained, "We have not learned from him [directly as his disciples]," R. Abbaye instructed his pupils to accord Safra the highest honors because "when a scholar dies, all are next of kin" (MK 25a).

Samuel, Babylonian *amora* (second/third century).

Born Samuel ben Abba ha-Kohen in Nehardea, his ability to independently determine the beginning of the months resulted in his being given the appellation *Yarchina'ah* (from the Hebrew word *yare'ach* meaning "moon") (BM 85b). Considered an expert in astronomy, Samuel stated: "I am as familiar with the paths of heaven [courses of the stars] as with the streets of Nehardea, with the exception of [the movements of] the comet, about which I am ignorant" (Ber. 58b). However, even though Samuel was able to calculate the order of the leap years and the precise time of the holidays, Babylonian Jews still had to celebrate an additional day for each festival because of the time-honored custom that they must wait to be informed of the sighting of the new moon by messengers sent from the Land of Israel. After moving with his father to the Land of Israel, Samuel studied with R. Hama ben Hanina. Having also studied medicine, Samuel became the physician of Judah ha-Nasi, whom he cured of an eye disease. His medical training led Samuel to permit kindling a fire on the Sabbath for a woman in childbirth and anyone who had been bled and felt chilly, even during the hottest period of the year (Er. 79b; Shab.129a).

Returning to Babylonia, Samuel was appointed judge of the court at Nehardea. When R. Shila died, Samuel became director of the Nehardea academy. Samuel and Rav, the head of the academy at Sura, were close friends and intellectual adversaries in *halachic* discussions. Their disputes on civil and ritual issues constitute the core of the Babylonian Talmud. As teachers of the highest rank in the Jewish world, Rav at Sura and Samuel at Nehardea (who later relocated to Pumbedita) established the intellectual independence of Babylonia, enabling aspiring young scholars to remain at home to study rather than being required to go to the Land of Israel. Indeed, R. Judah stated in the name of Samuel, "Just as it is forbidden to leave the Land of Israel for Babylonia, so it is forbidden to leave Babylonia [now a center of religion and learning] for other countries" (Ket. 111a).

As a general rule, it is said that the *halachah* follows the rulings of Rav in ritual law and of Samuel in civil issues (Bek. 49b). Samuel tended toward more lenient interpretations. He strenuously opposed unscrupulous merchants who demanded high prices for seasonal scarcities related to the holidays. Rather than requiring that dishes used for leavened food be destroyed before Passover, he permitted them to be stored during the holiday and then used again. Similarly, he ruled that dishes that had been used only for cold leavened food could be used on Passover (Pes. 30a). When sellers excessively raised the cost of myrtle branches (one of the four species used on Sukkot), Samuel threatened to declare that myrtle branches with broken tips be permissible unless the merchants lowered their prices to reasonable levels (Suk. 34b). In a rabbinic discussion of what constituted a price so exorbitant that it would render a transaction invalid, Samuel set the margin of profit at one sixth of the sale price (BM 40b).

Samuel introduced the concept that the plaintiff in a civil case had the burden of proof (BK 43b). Consequently, the defendant was not required to challenge the accusation until a creditor had produced some reasonable evidence that a debt had not been paid (Ket. 76b). Samuel wrote a short prayer that travelers could use if they did not have time to recite the entire *Amidah* (Ber. 29a), and he believed that customs generally accepted by the Jewish community might outweigh a law (BM 115b).

Samuel developed the overriding principle of *dina malchuta dina*—the law of the state is the law (Git. 10b; BK 113b)—meaning that even though Jews had their own civil courts, it was a religious duty for them to obey the laws of the country in which they lived. He taught, "A man should never exclude himself from the community" (Ber. 49b), implying that everyone was responsible for seeking to improve the lot of all in society. This may have been influenced by Samuel's friendly relationship with the Persian king, which led to the granting of special privileges to the Jews. However, Samuel had a cynical view of those in power. He sarcastically noted, "As soon as a man is appointed leader of a community, he becomes rich." Moreover, in concert with the prevailing view that every leader had to have a family skeleton, Samuel said: "Why did the kingdom of Saul not endure? Because his family was untainted!" (Yoma 22b).

Samuel demanded that judges always be above suspicion. Once when Samuel was crossing a river on a ferry, a man offered to assist him. When Samuel asked what business he had there, the man replied that he had a lawsuit to try. Knowing that he would be the judge in the matter, Samuel disqualified himself from the case, lest it appear that he rule in favor of one who had been kind to him (Ket. 105b). At times, Samuel could interpret laws harshly. Based on Jonah's prophetic warning to the people of Nineveh (Jon. 3:8), "Let everyone turn from his evil way and from the violence that is in his hands," Samuel understood the phrase to mean that "one who had stolen a beam and built it into his home must raze the entire structure to the ground and return the beam to its owner" (Taan. 16a). Samuel believed that it was important to show respect to all people. "It is forbidden to deceive anyone, even gentiles" (Hul. 94a). He also ruled that a person who put a slave to shame must compensate him accordingly (Nid. 47a).

The Rabbis strongly preferred early marriages as long as one made proper preparations: "First build a house, then plant a vineyard, and after that marry" (Sot. 44a). According to Samuel, "If a person wants to study Torah and to marry a wife, he should first study and then marry. But if he cannot [live] without a wife, he should first marry and then study" (Kid. 29b). The Talmud records a critical disagreement between Samuel and Rav concerning divorce (Ket. 77a). Samuel argued that a man should first be compelled to fulfill his duty to maintain his wife before divorcing her. He consistently attempted to use the powers of the court to preserve the marriage as long as possible rather than dissolve it, hoping that there might be reconciliation. Rav disagreed, stating that the husband's refusal to support his wife was merely one sign of his hostile attitude toward her. Convinced that by the time the situation had deteriorated to such a point the marriage should be ended immediately; Rav added that forcing her to remain with him would be like living "with a serpent in a basket."

Although Samuel often ruled in support of wives and widows, his statement "A woman's voice stimulates sexual desire" (Ber. 24a) became the basis for the development of the separation of men and women in the synagogue, either by a partition (*mechitza*) or in a separate room. In keeping with the goal of keeping men and women apart, Samuel stated that a man should not employ a female servant, either young or old, nor greet a woman in the street lest he be forced to hear her response (Kid. 70a). Similarly, he even prohibited a man from being alone with any of the female relatives that the Torah forbids him from marrying (Kid. 81b).

The way in which God is addressed and described in *berachot* (blessings) was the subject of a rabbinic controversy that resulted in a grammatical inconsistency. Rav maintained that a blessing should begin with the words *Baruch ata*, speaking of God in the second person as "You." Samuel thought this too familiar for the relationship between mere mortals and the Divine. The Rabbis ruled in favor of Rav, but decided to combine both opinions into what became the approved formula. The opening of every blessing stresses the nearness of God to each worshiper by addressing God as "You." However, as soon as we refer to God as the more distant and unapproachable *Melech ha-olam* (King of the universe), we become more formal and respectful. The remainder of every blessing switches into the third person, as in "Who sanctifies us by His commandments" and "Who creates the fruit of the vine" (Milgrom, *Sabbath*, 46).

Samuel favored enjoyment of worldly pleasures: "Hurry on and drink, since the world from which we must depart is like a wedding feast [which all too soon will come to an abrupt end]" (Er. 54b). Nevertheless, he cautioned that anything consumed must be preceded by the appropriate blessing, lest it be like making personal use of things consecrated to Heaven (Ber. 35a).

Despite his opposition to those who frequently fasted and denied themselves pleasure (Taan. 11a), Samuel once decreed a fast when he heard that an epidemic was ravaging a distant city. The people asked why this was necessary since the affected place was so far away. He replied, "Would a crossing prevent it from spreading [i.e., does a plague require a ferry or bridge to cross the river]?" (Taan. 21b).

As a physician, many of Samuel's opinions on health and diet are found in the Talmud. He opposed the belief that most diseases were due to the Evil Eye, declaring instead that they were caused by something noxious in the air (BM 107b). He attributed many disorders to a lack of personal cleanliness and wearing unclean garments (Shab. 133b) and others to a change in diet (i.e., a poor man used to eating only dry bread during the week may suffer from indigestion after eating meat and other expensive foods on Sabbaths and festivals) (BB 146a). Although he developed a well-known salve for the eye ailments that were widespread in his area, Samuel declared: "A drop of cold water in the morning, and washing the hands and feet in hot water in the evening, is better than all the eye-salves in the world" (Shab. 108b). He cautioned, "He who washes his face and does not dry it well, will have boils break out [on his face]. What is his remedy? Let him wash well in water [in which beets have been cooked]" (Shab. 133b).

In contrast to various Rabbis who contemplated how conditions would vary in the Messianic era, Samuel expressed a minority view. "There is no difference between this world and the days of the Messiah except freedom from bondage to foreign powers [i.e., heathen rulers], as it says: 'For the poor shall never cease out of the land' [Deut. 15:11], not even in the Messianic Era" (Ber. 34b).

When Samuel died, the sages lamented: "Alas! We have lost a pious man, a humble man, a true disciple of Hillel!" (Sanh. 11a). *See also* Abba bar Abba; Adda bar Ahava; Rav.

Samuel bar Ika, Babylonian *amora* (third/fourth century).

Samuel bar Ika maintained that if some forbidden food fell into a vat of beer, the beer could be consumed as long as the prohibited material constituted less than one-sixtieth of the total volume. This remains the rule for mixtures of forbidden and permissible food today, with the exception of *hametz* on Passover, which in any amount renders the food in which it is mixed forbidden.

Samuel bar Isaac, Babylonian *amora* (second/third century).

Quoting his teacher Rav, Samuel bar Isaac observed: "Whatever can be eaten in its natural state [raw] is not subject to [the rule against] the cooking of gentiles [i.e., it may be eaten even if cooked by a non-Jew]" (Shab. 51a; Yev 46a). In a discussion of rabbinic antics at weddings, Samuel bar Isaac was said to have "danced with three [twigs]," which Rashi says meant throwing one up after the other and catching them in turn (Ket. 17a). The Talmud relates that at the death of Samuel bar Isaac, "all trees were uprooted" (MK 25b), implying that his passing caused not only his colleagues but even the plants (botanical world) to be distraught.

Samuel bar Nachmani, Palestinian *amora* (third century).

A student of R. Yochanan, Samuel bar Nachmani was a spiritual leader of the people. He quoted his teacher frequently: "Why were the Egyptians compared to *maror* [Exod. 1:14]? To teach you that just as *maror* is soft when it begins to grow and hard at the end [the top is soft while the stalk hardens like wood], so were the Egyptians, who were soft at the beginning [during the time of Joseph when they treated the Israelites well] but hard at the end [when there arose a Pharaoh 'who knew not Joseph,' they treated them with severe cruelty]" (Pes. 39a). In other examples, Samuel bar Nachmani said in the name of R. Yochanan: "He who loses his temper is exposed to all the torments of Gehinnom [Hell]" (Ned. 22a); and "One whose wife requests him to perform his marital duty will father children such as were not to be found even in the generation of Moses" (Ned. 20b). He wryly noted, "Everything in the world was created by God, except for falsehood, which is the product of human imagination" (Pes. Rab. 24). He maintained that God's assessment that everything He had made during Creation was "very good" referred to man's evil desires (*yetzer ha-ra*), without which no man would build a house, marry a wife, sire children, or engage in business (Gen. R. 5:9; Eccles. R. 3:16).

Samuel bar Nachmani disagreed with the statement of R. Hiyya bar Abba that "the Sabbath was given for enjoyment," instead arguing, "The Sabbath was given for studying." How can these two comments be reconciled? The Talmud explains that R. Hiyya referred to scholars who spend the week studying Torah; when the Sabbath comes, they enjoy themselves. In contrast, Samuel bar Nachmani described laborers who are so busy with their work all week that only on the Sabbath do they have time to study Torah (Pes. Rab. 23:9). In a Talmudic discussion on whether harmful speech was worse than a monetary wrong, Samuel bar Nachmani declared that the former was more serious, "because money can be returned, but words once uttered cannot easily be recalled" (BM 58b).

Samuel bar Nachmani believed that the requirement to pray three times daily corresponded to three changes that occur every day. In the morning, one should thank God "for bringing me out of darkness into light." In the afternoon, a person should pray that it be God's will "to permit me to see the sun in the West even as You allowed me to see it in the East." Finally, at night one should pray that God "lead me out of the darkness into the light" as He had done previously (JT Ber. 4:1).

Samuel ben Nachmani was considered an authority on the *aggadah* (Pes. 15b). In response to the statement of R. Huna bar Berechia in the name of R. Eleazar ha-Kappar, "Anyone who makes the Name of Heaven a partner in his distress, God shall be his treasure and provide him with precious silver." Samuel ben Nachmani said: "His livelihood will fly to him like a bird [i.e., it will be provided him without difficulty]" (Ber. 63a). *See also* Hiyya bar Abba.

Samuel bar Shilath, Babylonian *amora* (second/third century).

Samuel bar Shilath was renowned as an educator who was completely devoted to teaching children. His teacher Rav offered him advice concerning the education of children. "Before the age of six do not accept pupils; from then on you can accept them and stuff them with Torah like an ox." Moreover, "When you punish a pupil, only hit him with a shoelace [i.e., do not hurt him too much]. The attentive one will read [for himself]; and if one is inattentive put him next to a diligent one [so that he will listen and gradually become studious]" (Ket. 50a; BB 21a). Once Rav found Samuel bar Shilath in his garden during school hours and asked, "Have you deserted your post [lit., 'your faith or trustworthiness']?" Samuel ben Shilath replied, "I have not seen my garden for thirteen years, and even now my thoughts are with the children" (BB 8b).

Samuel bar Shilath was cautioned by Rav: "Be fervent in [delivering] my funeral eulogy, for I will be standing there!" (Shab. 153a).

Samuel ha-Katan, Palestinian *tanna* (first/second century).

This famous student of Hillel was given his epithet meaning "small" either because of his extreme modesty or as an allusion to his being only slightly inferior to the prophet Samuel (JT Sot. 9:13). Like other Rabbis, Samuel ha-Katan went out of his way to spare his colleagues from shame. Rabban Gamaliel II once asked for seven scholars to convene in the upper chamber, where the Rabbis met to intercalate the year (i.e., add an extra month for a leap year). However, when he arrived in the morning and found eight, the sage announced that whoever came without permission must leave. Samuel ha-Katan arose and said, "I am the one who came without permission, not to participate in the intercalation, but merely to learn the practical application of the law." The Talmud observes that it was actually another scholar who had not been invited, but Samuel ha-Katan had taken the blame upon himself to save the uninvited one from embarrassment (Sanh. 11a).

So highly esteemed was Samuel ha-Katan among his colleagues that when a *bat kol* (heavenly voice) was heard declaring "There is one of you present who is worthy that the *Shechinah* should rest on him, but his generation does not merit it," the sages looked toward Samuel ha-Katan, assuming that he was the one intended (Sanh. 11a). Renowned as extremely pious, Samuel ha-Katan once ordered a fast during a period of drought, and rain fell before sunrise on the day he had designated. When the people believed that the rain "was due to the merit of the community," he offered a parable: "This can be compared to a servant who asked his master for a gratuity and the master exclaimed, 'Give it to him, and let me not hear his voice.'" Another time, "Samuel ha-Katan ordained a fast and rain fell after sunset." When the people again thought that it was due to the merit of the community, Samuel related another parable: "This can be compared to a servant who asked his master for a gratuity and the master exclaimed, 'Keep him waiting until he is made submissive and is distressed, and then give it to him.' What would be an instance of rain falling on account of the merit of the community? If they recited [the prayer], 'He causes the wind to blow,' and the wind blew; and if they recited, 'He causes the rain to fall,' and rain fell" (Taan. 25b).

Some have suggested that Samuel ha-Katan originated the invocation "*Ribbono shel Olam*" (Sovereign of the Universe) to avoid pronouncing the Name of God (Shab. 33a). Despising Judeo-Christians and informers, Samuel ha-Katan, at the request of Rabban Gamaliel II, was said to have composed the *Birkat ha-Minim*, the prayer condemning apostates that was incorporated into the daily *Amidah* (Ber. 28b–29a). Nevertheless, in Pirkei Avot (4:24), Samuel ha-Katan quoted verses from Proverbs (24:17–18): "If your enemy falls, do not exult; if he stumbles, let your heart not rejoice, lest the Lord see it and be displeased, and avert His wrath from him." Knowing that God always supported those who had been wronged, Samuel ha-Katan feared that this unworthy behavior on the part of Jews might result in Divine favor toward their adversaries—not because of their merits, but rather due to the failings of Israel—thus delaying the complete salvation of the Jewish people from their enemies.

Samuel ha-Katan was also known for the prophecy of the killing of the Ten Martyrs, which he uttered on his death bed: "R. Shimon and R. Ishmael [probably ben Gamaliel and ben Elisha, respectively, who were executed after the fall of Jerusalem] are doomed to destruction; their companions to death; the people to pillage; and bitter persecutions shall come upon the nation" (Sot. 48b). When Samuel ha-Katan died, his colleagues exclaimed in grief: "Alas the pious man! Alas the humble man! The disciple of Hillel [is no more]!" (Sanh. 11a).

Samuel ha-Katan was childless, and at his funeral Rabban Gamaliel II and R. Eleazar ben Azariah eulogized him: "For Samuel ha-Katan it is proper to cry and mourn. When kings die, they leave their crowns to their sons; when wealthy men die, they bequeath their riches to their children; but Samuel ha-Katan has departed and taken away with him all the desirable things in the world" (Sem. 8).

Samuel of Difti, Babylonian *amora* (fourth/fifth century).

Samuel of Difti disagreed with R. Aha bar Rava concerning the proper placement of the *hanukiah*. At that time, the Hanukah menorah was placed outside near the door, since houses opened into a courtyard rather than the street. R. Aha bar Rava maintained that it should be placed on the right side, as one entered the house, while Samuel of Difti said it should be on the left. "And the law is [in accordance with Samuel's view] on the left, so that the Hanukah lamp shall be on the left and the *mezuzah* on the right" (Shab. 22a).

Shammai, contemporary and rival of Hillel (first century B.C.E./first century C.E.).

Born in the Land of Israel, Shammai served as *av bet din* (vice president) of the Sanhedrin, joining Hillel as the last of the *zugot* (pairs) of scholars whose teachings formed the basis of the Mishnah. The Rabbis considered the disputes between Hillel and Shammai, and later controversies between their two schools, as arguments "for the sake of Heaven" (Avot 5:20), whose sole purpose was to determine the truth. This was in contrast to Korach's argument with Moses (Num. 16), which he initiated for reasons of personal honor. In general, the Talmudic sages decided the *halachah* in accordance with the opinions of Hillel and his school (Bet Hillel), which were more lenient and easier for the people to understand. In Messianic times, however, the *halachah* will revert to the stricter opinions of the school of Shammai (Bet Shammai), since people then will be able to understand and appreciate his great insights in matters of Torah.

Shammai took an extremely strict approach to religious issues. Although it was accepted practice that children did not fast on Yom Kippur, Shammai insisted that his young son abstain from eating on that day, although he relented at the insistence of his friends (Yoma 77b). When his daughter-in-law gave birth to a boy on Sukkot, Shammai broke open the plaster ceiling over the baby's bed and covered it with branches, so that his newborn grandson could fulfill the mitzvah of dwelling in a *sukkah* (Suk. 2:8). Shammai insisted that divorce was only permissible on the grounds of the wife's infidelity. He required direct testimony that her husband was dead before he would permit a woman to remarry, while Hillel (and most of the other Rabbis) ruled that she could remarry even on the basis of indirect evidence of her husband's death, thus easing the *agunah* problem. In a classic tale, the school of Shammai asked, "What words must we use when dancing before the bride?," to which the school of Hillel answered, "Beautiful and graceful bride." Bet Shammai then asked, "What shall we do if she is lame or blind . . . for does not the Torah direct to 'keep away from any lie?'" Bet Hillel replied: "If a person has purchased some bad merchandise in the marketplace, should one praise it [to make it look good to him] or disparage it [so that it looks bad to him]? Surely, one should praise it in his eyes" (Ket. 17a).

The school of Shammai maintained, "There will be three groups of people at the Day of Judgment—the completely righteous, the completely wicked, and those in between [intermediate]. The completely righteous will be immediately inscribed and sealed for life in the World to Come; the completely wicked are doomed to Gehinnom, as it is said: 'Many of those that sleep in the dust of the earth will awake, some to eternal life, others to reproaches, to everlasting abhorrence' [Dan. 12:2]. The intermediate will go down to Gehinnom and struggle and rise again, as it is said, 'The third part I will put into the fire, and I will smelt them as one smelts silver and test them as one tests gold. They will invoke Me by name and I will respond to them' [Zech. 13:9]. But the school of Hillel says that He who abounds in mercy inclines the scales of judgment to the side of mercy [and does not doom them to Gehinnom]" (RH 16b–17a).

The Torah unequivocally states that God created the entire universe, but the Rabbis disagreed as to whether heaven or earth was created first. Bet Shammai argued that heaven was created first, citing the initial verse in Genesis—"In the beginning, God created the heaven and the earth"—likening the situation to a king who made a throne for himself and afterward added a footstool. Conversely, Bet Hillel compared the situation to a king who erected a palace, first building the lower stories and then the upper (Gen. R. 1:15). R. Shimon bar Yochai observed, "I am amazed that the sages engage in controversy over this matter, for surely both were created simultaneously like a pot and its lid."

The two schools disagreed regarding whether Torah knowledge should be taught to the masses or only to the intellectual elite. According to a *midrash*, "The school of Shammai says one ought to teach only those who are talented and humble and of distinguished ancestry and rich. But the school of Hillel says one should teach every man, for there were many sinners in Israel who were drawn to the study of Torah, and from them descended righteous, pious, and worthy folk" (ARN 3).

The Talmud relates a debate concerning how the *Shema* should be read (Ber. 1:3). Taking the words, "when you lie down and when you rise up," literally, Bet Shammai ruled that the evening *Shema* should be recited while reclining, whereas in the morning it should be said standing upright. Bet Hillel argued persuasively that the verse merely referred to the times of the readings, with no special posture required.

Is it permitted to visit the sick on the Sabbath, the day of joy on which sadness should not intrude? Bet Shammai prohibited the practice, but the *halachah* agrees with Bet Hillel, which permitted such visits. One visiting a sick person on the Sabbath should say, "'It is the Sabbath, when one must not cry out, but [I wish you that] recovery will come soon.'" According to R. Meir, one should say, "'It [the Sabbath] may have compassion' [i.e., proper observance of the Sabbath will bring recovery in its wake]" (Shab. 12a).

Bet Shammai ruled that a man must have two sons to fulfill the biblical commandment, "Be fruitful and multiply" (Gen. 1:2). Bet Hillel disagreed, ruling that the requirement was a son and a daughter, based on the biblical verse (Gen. 5:2), "Male and female He created them" (Yev. 6:6).

Lighting an eight-branched menorah (*hanukiah*) on Hanukah is a rabbinically ordained commandment. "One light must be kindled in each house; the zealous require one light for each person; the extremely zealous add a light for each person each night." The schools of Hillel and Shammai disagreed on the number of candles that should be lit. Bet Shammai declared that eight candles should be lit on the first night, with the number reduced by one on each successive day. The *halachah*, as usual, follows Bet Hillel, which argued for lighting one candle on the first night, two on the second night, and so forth. This view was based on the principle that, in matters of holiness, one should increase rather than diminish (Shab. 21b).

The Talmud observes that the schools of Shammai and Hillel disagreed on so many issues that at times it seemed as if there were two Torahs instead of one (Shab. 88b). Nevertheless, this did not stop them from marrying women from families in the opposing camp (Yev. 14b). According to tradition, the disputes between the two groups continued until after the destruction of the Temple, when a conference of scholars was called at Yavneh to determine which school's rulings should be enforced. The contentious debate continued for three years until a *bat kol* (heavenly voice) announced that the opinions of both "are the words of the living God, but the *halachah* is in agreement with the rulings of Bet Hillel" (Er. 13b). The Rabbis then discussed why the views of the school of Hillel were preferred, maintaining that it was because the disciples of Hillel were considerate and respectful, studying not only their opinion but also the teachings of Bet Shammai. Moreover, they even gave precedence to the school of Shammai by quoting their views first. The Rabbis concluded that the privilege conferred on Bet Hillel taught that God raises up those who humble themselves, but lowers those who attempt to exalt their positions.

Shammai was described as an angry man with a sharp temper, the antithesis of Hillel. Indeed, as the Rabbis taught, "A man should always be gentle like Hillel, and not impatient like Shammai" (Shab. 30b). This is best illustrated in the classic story of the heathen who asked to be converted if he could be taught all of the principles of Judaism while he stood on one foot. Shammai summarily drove him away, whereas Hillel calmly spoke to the heathen and succeeded in converting him (Shab. 31a). Despite his often inflexible personality, Shammai also advocated friendliness: "Make your study of the Torah a matter of established regularity, say little and do much, and welcome all men with a friendly face" (Avot 1:15).

The difference in their leaders led the disciples of Shammai and Hillel to adopt diametrically opposite views toward the Romans. The school of Shammai was intensely patriotic, refusing to bow to foreign rule and even discouraging any contact with the occupying power. In contrast, the followers of Hillel adopted a more peaceful and conciliatory approach, urging the Jews to accept the fact that they were powerless to defeat the Romans and thus make the best of the situation. *See also* Hillel.

Shemaiah, *tanna* colleague of Avtalyon (first century B.C.E.).

They were paired as the fourth of the *zugot* and are always mentioned together in the Talmudic sources. Like Avtalyon, Shemaiah was said to have been descended from Sennacherib, the king of Assyria who destroyed the Northern Kingdom of Israel (Git. 57b). Shemaiah's dictum in Pirkei Avot (1:10)—"Love work, despise mastery, and keep your distance from [i.e., do not become overly familiar with] the ruling authorities"—probably reflected his and Avtalyon's attitude to the government of their time. It was an allusion either to Alexander Yannai, who forced their teachers, R. Judah ben Tabbai and R. Shimon ben Shetach, to flee, or to the Herodian persecution.

Once when a crowd was escorting the high priest home from the Temple after the conclusion of the Yom Kippur service, they suddenly deserted him in order to greet Shemaiah and Avtalyon, the celebrated teachers of Hillel. The high priest was overcome with envy at the honor the people had accorded these masters of the Law. When Shemaiah and Avtalyon later came to take their leave of him, the high priest sarcastically said, "May the descendants of the heathen depart in peace!" They retorted, "May the descendants of the heathen, who do the work of Aaron [to love peace and pursue it], indeed depart in peace—but not the descendant of Aaron, who does not do the work of Aaron [i.e., whose arrogance causes strife]" (Yoma 71b). *See also* Avtalyon; Hillel.

Sheshet, Babylonian *amora* (third/fourth century).

Although blind (Ber. 58a), Sheshet was blessed with a superb memory and knew by heart the Mishnah and the Tosefta (Shev. 41b). Sheshet would review all his studies every thirty days and then exclaim, "Rejoice, O my soul; for your sake have I read [the Bible], for you have I studied [the Mishnah]" (Pes. 68b). A disciple of R. Huna, Sheshet respected his teacher and never wanted to miss a word of his wisdom. It was written, "Sheshet became impotent because of his long discourses [i.e., not wanting to walk out in the middle of a lecture to relieve himself, he impaired his generative organs]" (Yev. 74a).

Sheshet was not impressed with the overly subtle hairsplitting in vogue at Rav's academy. As the Talmud relates, Rav and R. Samuel once debated whether, based on a "rumor" substantiated by only one witness, a man who had been captured should be considered dead and his children permitted to receive their inheritance. Citing the verse "My anger shall wax hot and I will kill you with the sword," R. Eliezer ben Hyrcanus questioned the purpose for the second half of the verse, "and your children will be orphans and your wives widows" (Exod. 22:23), which would appear to be self-evident. He concluded, "This teaches that their wives will seek to remarry and not be permitted to do, and their children will desire to inherit their father's property and not be allowed to do so [i.e., they would remain permanently widows and fatherless, in the sense that they cannot set up their own estate]." When a student presented this answer to Sheshet as a solution to the problem, the sage sarcastically retorted, "Perhaps you are from Pumbedita, where they draw an elephant through the eye of a needle?" (BM 38b). Shocked by what he considered a ridiculous ruling by Rav, that if a man was suspected of having intercourse with a married woman it must be confirmed by witnesses, Sheshet cried out: "It seems that Rav made this statement while he was sleepy and about to doze off" (Yev. 24b). Sheshet taught at the academies of Mechoza and Nehardea, later founding his own academy at Shilchi.

Deeply pious, Sheshet was said to have never walked four cubits (six feet) without wearing his *tefillin* (Shab. 118b). He considered "a woman's hair [to be] a sexual incitement," based on the verse from the Song of Songs (4:1), "Your hair is like a flock of goats" (Ber. 24a). Sheshet once was in a crowd waiting to see the entry of a king. When a heretic taunted the blind Sheshet that he certainly would not be able to "see" the king, Sheshet embarrassed the unbeliever by recognizing, despite his blindness, the moment of deep silence when the king appeared. When asked by the astonished heretic how he accomplished this feat, Sheshet alluded to the way in which Elijah recognized the presence of God's Majesty when He came to the cave where the prophet was hiding from the anger of Ahab and Jezebel: "Earthly royalty is like the heavenly," though God's appearance is in a "still small voice" (1 Kings 19:11–13). "What happened to that heretic? Some say that his companions put his eyes out; others say that Sheshet cast his eyes upon him and he became a heap of bones" (Ber. 58a).

In the name of Sheshet, R. Huna bar Joshua observed that when necessary to read two widely separated Torah portions on the same day, "it is not proper to roll the scroll because of respect for the community." Instead, it is necessary to read from a second scroll prepared in advance so as not to keep everyone waiting for the continuation of the service (Yoma 70a).

"When Sheshet bowed down during the recitation of the *Amidah*, he used to bend like a reed [sharply, in a single swift motion], but when he straightened up he used to raise himself like a snake [slowly and with effort, his head first and then his body]" (Ber. 12b). This was designed to show that, while eager to bow down before God, he was in no hurry to straighten himself. The Talmud adds that whoever does not bow during this blessing will be punished by having his spine twisted like a curled serpent (BK 16a).

"When Sheshet kept a fast, he concluded his prayer by reminding God that during Temple times, the fat and blood of a sacrificial offering was sufficient to secure atonement. With the Temple no longer standing, "I have fasted and my own fat and blood have been diminished." Consequently, he prayed that God consider this "as if I had offered them before You upon the Altar, and may You show me favor" (Ber. 17a).

In his teaching, Sheshet insisted on the authority of precedent, usually justifying a decision by saying, "You have learned it [in the Mishnah or in a *baraita*]" (BM 90a; Yoma 48b). R. Rami bar Hama applied to Sheshet the verse, "Wisdom is good with an inheritance" (Eccles. 7:2), meaning that the ideal was for a Rabbi to have, in addition to a clear understanding of the issue, a knowledge of the rulings of previous scholars (Bek. 52b).

Interpreting the verse from Proverbs (3:16) "Length of days is in her right hand, and in her left hand are riches and honor," Sheshet was quoted as comparing the right hand, generally the stronger one for work, to a person who deeply and intensively studied Torah or to those who studied the Torah for its own sake, with the left hand implying the opposite (Shab. 63a).

Sheshet was described as having a delicate stomach: "If he ate anything in the morning, his food would not benefit him in the evening [i.e., he would have no appetite in the evening]." Consequently, he fasted the entire day before the seder so that he would have an appetite to perform the ritual Passover obligation of eating *matzah* at night (Pes. 108a). Nevertheless, Sheshet used to carry heavy beams and, as a cure for chills, noted that "Work is a splendid thing to make one warm" (Git. 67b).

Sheshet was often invited to dine with the exilarch, but he always found some reason to decline. Once he used the excuse, "Your servants are not reliable, being suspected of [the prohibited practice of] serving meat torn from the flesh of a living animal" (Git. 67b). He considered both days of a festival to be of equal importance in the Diaspora. Unlike two of his esteemed colleagues, Sheshet once refused to eat the meat of a stag that had been caught by a non-Jew on the first day and slaughtered and served on the second (Er. 39b).

According to legend, when it was time for Sheshet to die, "he caught sight of the Angel of Death in the marketplace and asked, 'Do you [want to kill me] in the marketplace like a beast? [If you want to take my soul], come to my house!'" (MK 28a).

Sheshet bar Idi, Babylonian *amora* (fourth century).

In a discussion of where to place *tefillin* for safekeeping when not in use, it was related that Sheshet bar Idi "used to put them on a stool and spread a cloth over them" (Ber. 24a). Sheshet bar Idi ruled that when entering a *sukkah*, the prayer "*leishev ba'sukkah*" (to dwell in the *sukkah*) is recited before the *Shehecheyanu* prayer, which is said whenever one does something "new" in a given year (Suk. 56a).

Shila, Babylonian *amora* (third century).

A student of Rav and R. Hisda, Shila served as head of the academy at Nehardea and was succeeded by Samuel. When judging a case in which a Jew had intercourse with a non-Jewish woman, Shila ordered him to be flogged rather than executed based on the principle, "since we have been exiled from our land, we have no authority to put [anyone] to death" (Ber. 58a).

Shimi bar Ashi, Babylonian *amora* (fourth/fifth century).

Impressed when observing R. Abbaye teaching his son (Yoma 27a; Kid. 48b), Shimi bar Ashi asked the sage "to give him lessons [lit., 'let the Master allow me to sit for a while']." R. Abbaye refused on the grounds that "I use my time for my own studies." Shimi bar Ashi offered an alternative. "Would your honor teach me at night?" R. Abbaye remained resistant: "[At night] I have to do some irrigation." When Shimi bar Ashi volunteered to do R. Abbaye's irrigation during the day, so that the latter could teach him at night, R. Abbaye reluctantly agreed. Shimi bar Ashi told the people higher up that those lower down had the right to draw water first; then he informed those lower down that the people higher up had the right to draw water first. "Meanwhile, he had dammed the watercourse and irrigated R. Abbaye's fields." However, R. Abbaye was not pleased. "You have acted on my behalf according to two contradictory authorities [Rav and Samuel]." Consequently, R. Abbaye would not eat anything grown in his fields that year (Git. 60b). *See also* Papa.

Shimon bar Abba, Palestinian *amora* (third/fourth century).

Born in Babylonia, Shimon bar Abba moved to the Land of Israel, where he became the best student of R. Yochanan. He was so poor that his teacher applied to Shimon bar Abba the verse from Ecclesiastes (9:11), "Nor is bread won by the wise." According to one legend, Shimon bar Abba earned his meager living as a gravedigger. After collecting bones from old graves, Shimon bar Abba concluded that he could determine from the appearance of a bone what that person used to drink—black bones belonged to those who drank cold water, red bones to wine-drinkers, and white bones to those who drank warm water (Gen. R. 89:2).

On the advice of his other celebrated teacher, R. Hanina bar Hama, Shimon bar Abba successively wed the two daughters of Samuel, the head of the academy of Nehardea, but both died soon after their marriages (JT Ket. 2:6). These experiences may have prompted one of his sayings: "There are two kinds of acts of love, that of participation in a wedding ceremony, and that of participation in a funeral. When two happen at the same time, and you have an opportunity to attend only one and do not know which to choose, follow the advice of King Solomon: 'It is better to go to the house of mourning than to a house of feasting' (Eccles. 7:2)."

Despite the decreasing level of scholarship in the Land of Israel during this period, the few remaining eminent Rabbis retained pride in their illustrious heritage. They believed, "The small group of scholars in the Land of Israel are of greater significance than a large Sanhedrin in a foreign country" (JT Ned. 6:16). Consequently, they would not permit their students to move to Babylonia. As an example, R. Hanina bar Hama refused to write a letter of recommendation for Shimon bar Abba, not wanting to allow such a promising student to leave the country (JT MK 3:1). *See also* Hanina bar Hama.

Shimon bar Pazzi, Palestinian *amora* (third/fourth century).

Born in Tiberias, Shimon bar Pazzi was a student of R. Joshua ben Levi and the primary transmitter of his teachings. Most of Shimon bar Pazzi's own recorded teachings were *aggadic* and taken from lectures he gave in Babylonia. He envisioned a celestial debate between God and the ministering angels about the wisdom of creating man (Gen. R. 8:5). Mercy said, "Man should be created; for he will perform acts of mercy." But Truth disagreed: "He should not be created; for he will be full of deceit [or 'strife']." Benevolence argued for the creation of man, "for he will do good works," while Peace was in opposition, "for he will be filled with dissension." Then God took Truth and cast her down to the ground (Dan. 8:12). But the angels said, "Why, O Lord of the world, do You thus dishonor Truth? Cause her to spring out of the earth [Ps. 85:12]."

Explaining why the Hebrew word *va-yetzer* (He formed) is written in the text (Gen. 2:7) with two *yuds*, when one would be grammatically sufficient, Shimon bar Pazzi explained that one refers to *Yotzri* (my Creator) and the other to *yitzri* (my evil inclination), alluding to the inner struggle between them that takes place within every human being: "Woe is me if I follow my evil inclination rather than combat it and do the will of my Creator" (Ber. 61a; Er. 18a). Shimon bar Pazzi concluded: "Every story in Scripture that begins with the words, 'After the death of . . . it came to pass,' refers to a retrogression, to a discontinuance of something that the deceased had brought about. For example, after the death of Moses [Josh. 1:1], the manifestations of mercy [the well, the manna, and the protecting clouds] ceased; after the death of Joshua [Judg. 1:1], Israel was again attacked by the remnant of the native population; and after Saul's death [2 Sam. 1:1], the Philistines again entered the country" (Gen. R. 52:7).

Shimon bar Yochai, Palestinian *tanna* (second century).

Along with R. Meir the only scholars ordained by R. Akiva, Shimon bar Yochai remained devoted to his teacher throughout his life. When R. Akiva was imprisoned for teaching Torah in violation of Roman law, Shimon bar Yochai discovered a way to slip into his cell and study with his master (Pes. 112a). One of the five disciples of R. Akiva who survived the failure of the Bar Kochba revolt, Shimon bar Yochai led the revival of Torah learning after that catastrophe (Yev. 62b). He also served as an emissary of the Sanhedrin to Rome, pleading for the abolition of decrees against the observance of the commandments (Me'il. 17a–b).

A student of the spiritual leader of the revolt, Shimon bar Yochai bitterly opposed the Romans for the cruel martyrdom they inflicted on his teacher ("Even the best of gentiles should be killed"; Mech. B'shallach 2). After an informant revealed to authorities derogatory comments that Shimon bar Yochai had made about the Romans (Shab. 33b), the sage was condemned to death and forced to flee with his son Eleazar. For twelve years they hid in a cave studying Torah, sustained by a spring of water, dates, and the fruit of a large carob tree.

After the Roman emperor died, which annulled his decree against them, Shimon bar Yochai and Eleazar emerged from the cave. Seeing a man plowing and sowing, they exclaimed: "They forsake eternal life and [instead] engage in life that is transitory." Wherever they cast their eyes the land was immediately consumed by fire. So a heavenly voice cried out, "Have you emerged to destroy My world: Return to your cave!" (Shab. 33b). According to the Rabbis, excessive piety is not commensurate with life, and practical work is necessary for the world. Thus their return to the cave was depicted as a punishment, not a meritorious deed. Eventually, Shimon bar Yochai and his son were forced to admit the impracticality of all Jews engaging in full-time Torah study, but they continued to maintain that no human activity can truly compare to it.

In another legend, as Shimon bar Yochai emerged into the light, he saw a man hunting birds. As the man spread his net, a heavenly voice called out, "Pardoned," and the bird escaped. For the sage, this confirmed the scope of Divine providence: "Even as a bird does not perish without Heaven, how much more so a human being" (JT Shev. 9).

Shimon bar Yochai recuperated from his years in the cave in the public baths provided by the city of Tiberias. Because it was believed that Tiberias was located on the site of an old cemetery, many pious Jews and those of priestly descent refused to live there lest they be contaminated by the impurity of the dead. Determined to repay the kindness of the inhabitants of the city by purifying it, Shimon bar Yochai took lupines, cut them up, and threw them on the ground, causing all the unexposed corpses to miraculously rise to the surface. When a Samaritan decided to make fun of the sage by burying a corpse in an area that had been purified, Shimon bar Yochai made him disappear (Shab. 33b–34a; Gen. R. 79:6).

Emphasizing the primacy of study over prayer, Shimon bar Yochai noted that scholars constantly engaged in Torah study did not interrupt it even for recitation of the *Shema*. Had he been at Mount Sinai when the Torah was given to Israel, "I would have asked God to give man two mouths, one to talk of Torah and one to use for all other needs [including prayer, so that a person would not have to interrupt his study when reciting them]." Nevertheless, he maintained that "Engaging in the study of Scripture is not so important," meaning that it was less significant than the study of Mishnah (JT Ber. 1:2).

The Rabbis believed that appropriate dress was especially important when reciting the two major prayers of the liturgy: one must be clothed from the waist down to say the *Shema* and also cover the top of the body for the *Amidah* (Ber. 24b–25a). According to legend, during the twelve years in which Shimon bar Yochai and his son hid in the cave, "They would strip their garments and sit up to their necks in sand. The whole day they studied; when it was time for prayers they robed, covered themselves, prayed, and then put off their garments again, so that they should not wear out" (Shab. 33b).

Is the requirement to study Torah all-consuming, or can a Jew take time out to earn a living? Disagreeing with R. Ishmael ben Elisha, who believed that a Jew must combine Torah study with a worldly occupation or be forced to beg for charity and abandon learning altogether, Shimon bar Yochai adamantly argued that the Torah did not want Jews spending time plowing, sowing, reaping, or engaged in other mundane tasks. He believed that God meant them to be completely immersed in Torah and the Divine service, convinced that "When Israel performs the will of the Omnipresent, their work is performed by others [gentiles]." Commenting on this issue, one sage stressed the difference between the earlier and later generations: "The earlier generations, who made Torah study their primary concern and did not focus on ordinary work, were successful in both. The later generations, who made work their primary concern and Torah study only secondary, were not successful at either" (Ber. 35b). Shimon bar Yochai added, "If three have eaten at one table and have not spoken words of Torah, [it is] as if they have eaten sacrifices [offered] to the dead . . . but if three who have eaten at one table spend time discussing Torah, it is as if they had eaten at the table of God" (Avot 3:3). Related to this were his warnings: "No scholar may partake of a feast unless it is connected with a religious deed [i.e., to fulfill a commandment]" (Pes. 49a); and "Croup comes into the world as a punishment for the lack of study" (Shab. 33b).

When Shimon bar Yochai was walking with R. Judah and R. Jose before his years hiding in the cave, his companions remarked favorably about the contributions of the Romans, who had established markets, bathhouses, and bridges. Shimon bar Yochai dismissed these improvements as merely serving their decadent desires: "They established markets to place prostitutes within them; bathhouses to pamper themselves; and bridges to take tolls" (Shab. 33b–34a). But only in a cave where food and drink are miraculously provided and clothes not needed can one be devoted solely to the study of Torah. The Talmud stresses that a society cannot exist without markets, bathhouses, and agriculture, which provide such necessities as food, water, clothing, and basic hygiene.

Rather than relying exclusively on scholarly opinions from previous generations, Shimon bar Yochai based his views on logical reasoning, even if this required intentionally refuting ideas that he believed were in error. He frequently posed the question, "Why does the Torah command us to do this?" In explaining the biblical proscription against a creditor taking the garment of a widow as collateral (Deut. 24:17), the Mishnah states that this law applies equally to widows who were rich and poor. For Shimon bar Yochai, this was an illogical conclusion, for rich widows clearly would own several garments. As support for his view, he reasoned that the creditor of a poor widow with only a single garment would have to return it every evening, and these repeated visits by the creditor would bring her into disrepute among her neighbors (BM 115a).

Shimon bar Yochai taught that God gave Israel "three precious gifts [Torah, Land of Israel, World to Come], and all were given only through suffering" (Ber. 5a). He added, "See how beloved Israel is in the sight of God!" Citing a series of biblical verses, he noted that when they were exiled to Egypt and Babylonia, the *Shechinah* went with them. Moreover, when Israel will be redeemed in the future, the *Shechinah* will return with them (Meg. 29a).

Among moral maxims attributed to Shimon bar Yochai are: "It is better for a man to be cast into a fiery furnace than to shame his neighbor in public" (Ber. 43b); "Deceiving one's neighbor with words is worse than obtaining his money under false pretenses, because only of the first is it written, 'and you shall fear your God'" (BM 58b); and "A man should recite his virtues in a whisper and his faults in a shout" (Sot. 32b). In the rabbinic debate about the significance of dreams, he added: "Just as wheat cannot be without straw, so there cannot be a dream without some nonsense" (Ber. 55a). Shimon bar Yochai stressed, "There are three crowns—the crown of Torah, the crown of priesthood, and the crown of royalty—but the crown of a good name excels them all" (Avot 4:13). His prescription for hastening the coming of the Messiah was: "If Israel were to keep two Sabbaths according to its laws, they would be redeemed immediately" (Shab. 118b).

According to tradition, Shimon bar Yochai was the author of the *Zohar* (Book of Splendor), the principal kabbalistic book on which all subsequent Jewish mystical works are based. The *Zohar* is an immense mystical commentary on the Pentateuch and parts of the Writings, written in both Hebrew and Aramaic and consisting of twenty separate treatises. Its central tenet is that human actions such as good deeds, prayer, and mystical meditation can impact the Divine world, thus promoting a harmonious union between the "upper" and "lower" spheres that increases the flow of Divine energy to the human world. Conversely, sinful and unrighteous behavior impedes this life-giving flow. Modern scholars attribute the *Zohar* to the late thirteenth-century Moses de Leon, although some traditionalists argue that he simply discovered material that had remained unknown for centuries.

The gravesite of Shimon bar Yochai is in Meron, a village in the Upper Galilee near Safed. Today it is the site of a festive celebration where thousands of kabbalists and Hasidim in Israel hold a festive celebration on Lag ba'Omer, studying mystical texts and singing and dancing around large bonfires to mark the traditional date of the sage's death. *See also* Eleazar ben Jose; Judah ben Ilai.

Shimon ben Akashiah, Palestinian *tanna* (second century).

Shimon ben Akashiah's sole statement in the Mishnah is the observation, "As uneducated persons grow older, the more their intellect gets distracted," based on the biblical verse, "He deprives trusty men of speech and takes away the reason of elders" (Job 12:20). In contrast, "of aged scholars, the older they get the more their minds become composed [i.e., they gain intelligence]," based on the verse (Job 12:12), "With aged men there is wisdom, and understanding in length of days" (Kin. 3:6).

Shimon ben Eleazar, Palestinian *tanna* (second century).

Like his teacher, R. Meir, many of whose laws he transmitted, Shimon ben Eleazar attacked the Samaritans for denying that the bodies of the dead would be resurrected before the Day of Judgment. Although a personal friend of

Judah ha-Nasi, Shimon ben Eleazar often was his *halachic* adversary. Among his *aggadic* sayings are: "He who acts from love [to perform ethical and religious acts] is greater than he who is does so because of fear, because with the latter [the merit] remains effective for 1,000 generations but with the former it remains effective for 2,000 generations" (Sot. 31a); and "There are two kinds of friends: one who reproves you, and the other who praises you. Love him who reproves you, and hate him who praises you. The former leads you into the future life [World to Come], while the latter only removes you from this world" (ARN 29). Shimon ben Eleazar asked, "Have you ever seen a wild beast or a bird with a craft? Yet they are sustained without anxiety [i.e., earn a living with difficult work]. Animals were created for the purpose of serving me [a human being], while I was created to serve my Master. Should not I [a human being] support myself without toil? But [that is not the case] because I have acted evilly and destroyed my livelihood [i.e., much of human troubles are of their own making]" (Kid. 4:13).

In Pirkei Avot (4:23), Shimon ben Eleazar is quoted as saying: "Do not try to pacify your friend in his time of anger; do not console him while his dead lies before him; do not question him about his vow at the time he makes it; and do not attempt to see him at the time of his disgrace." Analyzing the conditions after the Hadrianic persecutions, Shimon ben Eleazar observed: "Every precept for which the Jews were willing to be martyrs [lit., 'submitted to death'] at the time of the royal decree, such as idolatry and circumcision, is still held firmly in their minds. However, those precepts for which the Jews were not prepared to die, such as *tefillin*, have become somewhat neglected" (Shab. 130a). When there was a need for punishment, Shimon ben Eleazar recommended a nuanced approach: "A child and a woman should always be pushed aside with the left hand and drawn closer with the right hand" (Sot. 47a).

Shimon ben Eleazar said, "If the young tell you to build and the old to destroy, heed the advice of the elders and do not listen to the young. For the building of youth is destruction, while [even] the destruction by the elders is building [constructive]." As an example of this principle that wisdom comes with age, the Talmud offers the bitter experience of Rehoboam (1 Kings 12), who refused to heed the advice of his elderly counselors to ease the burdens of the people, lest it appear to weaken his authority. Instead, he listened to the words of his rash young friends who urged him to strengthen his rule by rejecting their demands, which resulted in the division of his kingdom (Ned. 40a).

According to the Talmud, Shimon ben Eleazar was the author of the well-known aphorism "A man should always be as gentle as the reed and not unyielding as the cedar," which reflected an experience he had when returning home from the town in which his teacher lived. Happy and elated because he had studied much Torah, Shimon ben Eleazar was greeted by a man who was extremely ugly. When the sage mockingly asked, "Are all your fellow citizens as ugly as you are?" the man replied, "I do not know, but go and tell the Craftsman who made me how ugly is this vessel You have made." Realizing that he had deeply hurt the man by insulting him, Shimon ben Eleazar dismounted and prostrated himself before him saying, "Please forgive me for speaking badly against you." But the man refused, declaring that he would not forgive the sage until he confronted God about the ugly vessel He had made. Shimon ben Eleazar traveled behind the man seeking his forgiveness until he reached his home city, where the assembled people excitedly greeted "our Rabbi, our teacher." When the ugly man asked to whom the populace was addressing in such exalted terms, they replied, "The man who is traveling behind you." Then the ugly man exclaimed, "If this man is a teacher, may there not be many like him in Israel!" After hearing his story, they pleaded, "Forgive him, for he is a great Torah scholar." He replied, "For your sakes I forgive him, provided that he does not act in the same manner in the future." Soon afterward, "Shimon ben Eleazar entered the study hall and said, 'A man should always be as gentle as the reed and not as unyielding as the cedar' [as he had been to the ugly man]. And for this reason, the reed merited that from it should be made pens [used] to write Torah scrolls, *tefillin*, and *mezuzot*" (Taan. 20a–b).

Shimon ben Gamaliel I, Palestinian *tanna* (first century C.E.).

President of the Great Sanhedrin at Jerusalem during the last two decades before the destruction of the Temple, Shimon ben Gamaliel I was one of the leaders in the revolt against the Romans and is said to have been one of the executed Ten Martyrs. Although head of the Pharisees, he was willing to work with the Sadducees against their common enemy. Even Josephus, his political adversary, wrote that Shimon ben Gamaliel I would have successfully defeated the Romans had the Israelites followed his advice rather than warring among themselves.

The grandson of Hillel, Shimon ben Gamaliel I maintained that no rules and regulations should be imposed upon the people that they were unable to follow (Tosef. Sanh. 2:13). He also was willing to bend religious rules to save people from unscrupulous business practices. During the Second Temple period, women were required to bring sacrifices to the Temple after every birth. Since most were not able to travel to Jerusalem regularly, on those infrequent occasions when they visited the capital they had to offer several sacrifices. The typical offering was a pair of doves, and the demand and price for these birds increased substantially during the festivals. When the price of doves once rose to a golden dinar, Shimon ben Gamaliel I vowed not to sleep before the cost dropped to one silver dinar. He went to the *bet din* and decreed that a woman who ordinarily would be required to offer five pairs of doves need only bring one pair. Immediately after this ruling, the price declined to only one-quarter of a silver dinar (Ker. 1:7).

Shimon ben Gamaliel I could perform gymnastic feats that no other Rabbi could accomplish. At the joyous Festival of Water-Drawing on Sukkot, it was said that "He used to take eight flaming torches and throw them in the air, juggling them by catching each in turn. And none would touch each other or the ground. When he prostrated himself [bowed in prayer], he used to dig his two thumbs in the ground, bend down [while still leaning on them], kiss the ground, and raise himself up again [by these two fingers while doing a headstand], a feat which no other man could accomplish" (Suk. 53a).

Shimon ben Gamaliel I had an eye for beauty. The Talmud relates that, when standing on a step on the Temple Mount, he saw a heathen woman who was particularly attractive and exclaimed, "How great are Your works, O Lord [Ps. 104:24]" (Av. Zar. 20a).

The guiding principle of Shimon ben Gamaliel I was: "All my days I have been raised among sages, and I have found that there is nothing better for oneself than silence; not study, but practice is the main thing [i.e., the performance of the *mitzvot*, because the primary purpose of Torah knowledge is to regulate behavior]. And one who talks excessively brings on sin" (Avot 1:17). *See also* Imma Shalom.

Shimon ben Gamaliel II, Palestinian *tanna* and the father of Judah ha-Nasi, the compiler of the Mishnah (second century).

Forced into hiding as a youth in Betar when the Bar Kochba war broke out, Shimon ben Gamaliel II escaped the fortress before the Roman massacre (Git. 58a; Sot. 49b). When the Sanhedrin was reconvened in Usha, Shimon ben Gamaliel II was elected as *nasi* (president). Serving with him as leaders of the Sanhedrin were R. Nathan as the *av bet din* and R. Meir as the *hacham*. Although the three maintained a close relationship initially, R. Nathan and R. Meir felt personally offended when Shimon ben Gamaliel II decreed that everyone in the academy should rise when the *nasi* entered and remain standing until he gave them permission to sit, an honor not accorded to their positions. Consequently, R. Nathan and R. Meir developed a plan to depose Shimon ben Gamaliel II from his position of leadership. Knowing that Shimon ben Gamaliel II was not learned in tractate Uktsin, they decided to ask him to expound on regulations concerning the stems of fruit and their effect on its cleanliness. If unable to do so, R. Nathan and R. Meir would argue that the person leading the academic discussions should know the entire Torah, and that Shimon ben Gamaliel II did not meet that qualification. However, R. Jacob ben Korshai overheard their plans. Fearing that this would result in shame to the *nasi*, he informed Shimon ben Gamaliel II of the plot so that he could prepare himself for all possible questions. The next day, when R. Nathan and R. Meir posed their question to Shimon ben Gamaliel II, he knew the material perfectly. Seeing the shocked look on their faces, he said, "Had I not learned it, you would have shamed me," and he removed them from the academy.

Whenever R. Nathan and R. Meir disagreed with an explanation of Shimon ben Gamaliel II, or if there was a question that he could not solve, they wrote solutions on slips of paper and threw them into the academy. R. Jose said to his colleagues, "Torah is outside and we are inside," arguing that R. Nathan and R. Meir be permitted to return to the academy because of their vast knowledge. Shimon ben Gamaliel II agreed, but demanded to "penalize them so by not saying traditions in their names." So laws determined by R. Nathan were prefaced by "some say," while those of R. Meir were quoted as "others say," although this eradication of their names did not last. Both R. Meir and R. Nathan were told in dreams to appease Shimon ben Gamaliel II. R. Nathan agreed and bowed before the will of the *nasi* and submitted to punishment, but R. Meir remained adamant, declaring: "Dreams neither help nor hinder [i.e., they are vain]." This story had two major messages. First, attempting to claim the highest academic rank based on knowledge of more Torah than the *nasi* was fraught with hazard, since it might only result in banishment from the academy. Second, it was incumbent on the head of the academy never to fall behind the knowledge of his colleagues and to be more sensitive regarding displays of honor when there were other Rabbis more knowledgeable than he (Hor. 13b–14a). Another controversial stance taken by Shimon ben Gamaliel II was to make the Babylonian academies dependent on the Sanhedrin in the Land of Israel in all issues relating to the calendar.

Shimon ben Gamaliel II mourned the loss of Jerusalem and longed for the time when the Jews would be freed from Roman rule and reestablish their capital as a center where the surrounding nations would congregate to learn the true faith. He stressed the importance of Tisha b'Av, the date of the destruction of the First and Second Temples: "Anyone who eats or drinks on the ninth of Av is as if he ate and drank on the Day of Atonement" (Taan. 30b). Recalling stories his father told of the beauty of the Temple, Shimon ben Gamaliel II noted that no organ was permitted because it interfered with sweet harmonies of the singers (Ar. 10b).

In addition to his profound Torah knowledge, Shimon ben Gamaliel II apparently was trained in Greek philosophy. This led him to declare that the Bible could be written only in the original Hebrew and in Greek (Meg. 9b). Also versed in the natural sciences, his sayings demonstrate knowledge of plants and animals as well as the anatomy of the human body and how to avoid or cure disease (Ber. 25a, 40a; Shab. 78a, 128b; Yev. 80b; Ket. 59b, 110b). In his *halachic* decisions, Shimon ben Gamaliel II tended toward a lenient interpretation of the laws. He opposed prohibiting actions that were not breaches of Jewish law per se, but which had been forbidden only because of fear they might lead to a *halachic* violation. He took into account common tradition and personal habits. Shimon ben Gamaliel II protected the rights and dignity of wives with respect to their husbands and weighed the benefit of the overall community relative to the interests of specific individuals. He demanded justice for gentile slaves and ruled that there was an obligation to redeem slaves who had been kidnapped just as it was required to ransom free men. When the Rabbis vied with one another in championing their opposition to capital punishment, Shimon ben Gamaliel II caustically retorted, "[Yes] and they would also have multiplied the shedders of blood [murderers] in Israel! [i.e., they would eliminate the fear of retribution, which is a deterrent to murder]" (Mak. 1:10).

In the Hasmonean period, under Greek and Roman influence, the custom developed of erecting ornate monumental tombstones for the nobility, such as *Yad Avshalom* (Monument of Absalom) in Jerusalem. Decrying this ostentatious practice, Shimon ben Gamaliel II declared, "One does not erect *nefashot* [monuments] to the righteous, for their words are their memorial" (Gen. R. 82:10).

In all but three instances (BB 173b; Git. 74b; Sanh. 31a), "Whenever Shimon ben Gamaliel II gives a ruling in our Mishnah, the *halachah* follows him" (Git. 75a). The Jerusalem Talmud offers as the reason, "Because he gave fixed *halachot* according to his *bet din*" (JT BB 10:14). His most famous saying is: "On three things does the world endure—justice, truth, and peace" (Avot 1:18). Elsewhere, Shimon ben Gamaliel II observed: "Great is peace, for Aaron the priest became famous only because he sought peace"; "He who makes peace in his own house is like one who makes peace in Israel" (ARN 28); and "Great is peace, for even the ancestors of the tribes resorted to a fabrication in order to make peace" (Gen. R. 100:8). Remarking on the continued Divine love for Israel and God's way of fashioning the world, Shimon ben Gamaliel II observed: "In the past, bread sprang up from the ground and dew came down from heaven . . . but now the reverse occurred, bread [manna] began to come down from heaven and dew to ascend from the ground" (Mech. on Exod. 16).

Stressing the importance of learning, Shimon ben Gamaliel II maintained: "He who studies the Torah in his youth is like a young man who marries a virgin and both possess their youthful passion; she turns to him with love and he embraces her; but he who begins to study the Torah in his old age may be compared to an old man who marries a virgin; she lovingly caresses him but he avoids her" (ARN 23).

Other sayings of Shimon ben Gamaliel II include: "If a man has no food and he sells his daughter or a Torah scroll, he will never have any luck [from that money; lit., 'he will never see a sign of blessing']" (Meg. 27a); "It is permitted to violate the Sabbath for the sake of a living newborn child, but not for a dead King David" (Shab. 151b); and "A student who abandons the Torah is like a bird that cannot find its nest and is certain to fall to the ground when it is weary of its wanderings" (Eccles. R. 1).

Shimon ben Halafta, Palestinian *tanna* (second century).

A teacher during the transition period between the *tannaim* and the *amoraim*, Shimon ben Halafta studied with Judah ha-Nasi, who often assisted his impoverished pupil in a way not to embarrass him (Ruth R. 5:7). He was so highly esteemed that, once when he was taking leave of his teacher, Judah ha-Nasi ordered his son to ask Shimon ben Halafta for a blessing, which went as follows: "May God grant that you will neither cause shame to others nor be shamed by others" (MK 9b).

Once when two hungry lions roared at him and threatened to tear him apart as he walked along the road, Shimon ben Halafta quoted the verse, "The young lions roar after their prey" (Ps. 104:21), and immediately "two lumps of flesh descended [from heaven]. The lions ate one and left the other." Taking the remaining piece of meat to the schoolhouse, he asked whether it was clean [fit for food] or not. The students answered, 'Nothing unclean descends from heaven'" (Sanh. 59b).

Apparently interested in animal husbandry, it was said that Shimon ben Halafta saved the life of a hen by attaching a reed to her dislocated hip bone, and he made new feathers grow on a second hen that had lost them. In another tale, the sage treated one of his hens "who had lost all her feathers by warming the bird in an oven, after first wrapping her in a [warm] leather apron used by bronze workers; the hen then grew feathers even larger than her original ones" (Hul. 57b). As an example of the Talmudic statement that some animal behavior could serve as a model for proper human conduct, Shimon ben Halafta pointed to the honesty displayed by members of the ant species: "Once an ant dropped one grain of wheat. All the other ants passing by sniffed at it, yet none took it. It remained there until the ant to whom it belonged came and took it" (Sifre Deut. 5:2). Turning to botanical hyperbole, Shimon ben Halafta noted: "I had a single pepper stalk in my property [that grew so tall] that I climbed it to the height of a fig tree" (JT Pe'ah 7:3).

Known for his parables, Shimon ben Halafta employed one to explain the rule that only circumcised men could participate in the Passover seder (Exod. 12:43). "A king gave a banquet, commanding that only those guests who wore his badge should be admitted. So God instituted a banquet in celebration of the deliverance from Egyptian bondage, but required that only those who bore on their bodies the seal of Abraham could partake of it" (Exod. R. 19:6).

When asked by Judah the Prince why he no longer came to visit on the festivals, Shimon ben Halafta was forced to admit that he did not function as well as in the past: "The rocks have grown tall [I used to climb them easily when I was young], [what was] near has become distant [it is difficult to travel so far now that I am old], two have turned into three [I now need a cane in addition to two legs], and the peacemaker of the home has ceased [i.e., a reference to the male organ and consequent cessation of marital relations in old age; Rashi]" (Shab. 152a).

Among his best-known sayings are: "From the day the fist of flattery prevailed [i.e., hypocrisy has become all-powerful], justice became perverted, good deeds deteriorated, and thus no person may claim, 'My merits are better than yours'" (Sot. 41b); and "God found no vessel that could contain the blessing for Israel other than that of peace," based on the verse, "The Lord gives strength to his people; the Lord will bless His people with peace (Ps. 29:11)"—the final words in the Mishnah (Uk. 3:12).

Shimon ben Hillel, Palestinian *tanna* (first century B.C.E.).

The son of Hillel and the father of Rabban Gamaliel I (Shab. 15a), Shimon ben Hillel became *nasi* (head of the Sanhedrin) in 32 B.C.E.

Shimon ben Jehozadak, Palestinian *tanna* (third century).

Of priestly heritage, Shimon ben Jehozadak was the teacher of R. Yochanan, who related several of his *halachic* and *aggadic* statements: "A scholar who does not avenge insults, but retains anger like a serpent, is no [true] scholar" (Yoma 22b); "One should not appoint anyone administrator of a community unless he carries [on his back] a basket of reptiles [a family skeleton; a less-than-perfect ancestry], so that if he becomes arrogant, one could tell him: Turn around!" (Yoma 22b); and "Better that a letter of the Torah be put aside than that the Name of God be publicly profaned [lit., 'It is proper that a letter be rooted out of the Torah so that thereby the Heavenly Name will be publicly honored']" (Yev. 79a).

According to R. Yochanan, after a special meeting attended by the sages in Lydda, Shimon ben Jehozadak announced a resolution approved by the majority: if a person was commanded to transgress any of the laws of the Torah to escape being killed, he may do so in order to save himself, with the exception of "idolatry, incest [which includes adultery], and murder" (Sanh. 74a).

Shimon ben Judah ha-Nasi (second/third century).

A teacher in the Land of Israel during the transition period between the *tannaim* and the *amoraim*, the younger son of Judah ha-Nasi was appointed as the *hacham* (wise one) of the *yeshivah*. Shimon ben Judah ha-Nasi was far more learned than his elder brother, Gamaliel, who succeeded his father as *nasi* (Ket. 103b). One saying of Shimon ben Judah ha-Nasi is preserved in the Mishnah (Mak. 3:15): "If a man is rewarded for abstaining from the drinking of blood, for which he has a [natural] loathing, how much more so [should he be rewarded for abstaining from] robbery and incest, for which a man's soul has a craving and longing [inborn inclination]."

Shimon ben Lakish, Palestinian *amora* (third century).

Most commonly known as Resh Lakish, he was renowned for his strength and corpulence in addition to his scholarship. So impoverished that he was forced to give up his Torah study, Resh Lakish became, depending on the version of the story, a highwayman, a trainer of wild lions in a circus, or a gladiator who risked his life fighting wild beasts in the arena. According to legend, one day the brilliant sage R. Yochanan was bathing in the Jordan. Resh Lakish, who was then a highwayman, saw R. Yochanan and leapt in after him, mistaking R. Yochanan for a woman since he had no beard. R. Yochanan said, "Your strength should be devoted to the study of Torah." Resh Lakish retorted, "And your beauty should be for women." R. Yochanan proposed the following bargain: "If you repent and return to your studies, I will let you marry my sister, who is even more beautiful than I" (BM 84a).

Resh Lakish agreed, studied with R. Yochanan, and became a brilliant scholar. He was so eager to learn that he "made it his practice to repeat in systematic order his studies [each section of the Mishnah] forty times, corresponding to the forty days" during which the Torah was given on Mount Sinai (Exod. 24:28) (Taan. 8a). Resh Lakish and R. Yochanan, who engaged in debates on numerous *halachic* issues and whose discussions and arguments comprise much of the Jerusalem and even the Babylonian Talmud, were designated "the two great authorities" (JT Ber. 8:6). When R. Yochanan went to Tiberias to found an academy there, he invited Resh Lakish to be his primary assistant (BK 117a). R. Ulla was so impressed with Resh Lakish's incisive analysis that he exclaimed, "One who saw Resh Lakish [engaged in debate] would think that he was uprooting mountains and grinding them against each other!" (Sanh. 24a). Nevertheless, in all but three cases, when Resh Lakish and R. Yochanan expressed different opinions, the matter was always decided according to the view of R. Yochanan.

Resh Lakish stressed the importance of studying Torah, warning his students that "if you forsake me [the Torah] for one day, I shall forsake you for two days" (JT Ber. 9:8). He added, "The words of the Torah abide only with one who kills himself for them" (Git. 57b). Resh Lakish believed that a scholar should be exempt from paying taxes for the city wall (BB 7b) and "may not afflict himself by fasting because by doing so he lessens his heavenly work [i.e., by fasting he weakens himself and this causes his studies to suffer]" (Taan. 11b). Nevertheless, scholars were required to comport themselves in an appropriate manner, respecting the opinions of others and debating in an "amicable" way (Shab. 63a). "If a sage becomes angry, his wisdom departs from him; if he is a prophet, his prophecy departs from him" (Pes. 66b). Because the evil inclination "grows in strength from day to day and seeks to kill him" (Suk. 52b), each person (especially the scholar) should "always incite the good impulse [in his soul] and fight against the evil inclination" (Ber. 5a). Resh Lakish concluded, "A person does not commit a transgression unless a spirit of folly enters into him" (Sot. 3a).

With regard to converts, Resh Lakish maintained, "The proselyte is dearer to God than was Israel when it was gathered together at the foot of Mount Sinai. Without the miracles of Revelation [lightning, thunder, sound of the heavenly shofar], the Jews would not have accepted the Torah. But a proselyte, without seeing a single miracle, has embraced God and accepted the Kingdom of Heaven [of his own free will]. Could God love anyone more than him?" (Tanh. Lech Lecha).

Resh Lakish noted, "He who is merciful when he should be harsh will in the end be harsh when he should be merciful" (Eccles. R. 7:16). He used as a proof text that King Saul disobeyed the Divine decree and was merciful to Agag, king of the Amalekites (1 Sam. 15:8–9), but later ordered the utter destruction of the city of Nob and all its priests (1 Sam. 22:19). With respect to one who was needy, Resh Lakish stated, "He who lends [money] is greater than he who performs charity; and he who forms a partnership [helps by embarking on a business venture] is greater than all [for the poor man is relieved that he neither has to borrow nor accept charity]" (Shab. 63a).

Who is greater—the repentant sinner or the wholly righteous man who has not sinned? Shimon ben Lakish favored the repentant sinner, whose sins were considered as if they had been committed unintentionally or, in another version, even accounted as virtues. The Talmud reconciles these two descriptions by explaining that the first refers to repentance out of fear, while the second alludes to repentance out of love (Yoma 86b). R. Abbahu agreed: "In the place where penitents stand, even the wholly righteous cannot stand" (Ber. 34b). Even those who have been wicked all their days are pardoned if they repent for their sins at the end of their lives (Kid. 40b). The Talmudic dictum, "Repent one day before your death" (Shab. 153a), means that it is necessary to spend every day in repentance, for none knows which will be his last.

In their younger days, Shimon ben Lakish and two companions were robbers. Shimon ben Lakish repented and became a man of great piety and learning. His companions, however, kept to their evil ways. It happened that all three died on the same day. Shimon ben Lakish was taken to Paradise, while his former comrades were doomed to Gehinnom. When they complained before God that all three were robbers together, they were told that "he repented in his lifetime, but you did not." They replied, "Give us the opportunity and we will repent very sincerely." But God answered, "Repentance is only possible until one's death." A *midrash* offers a parable: "A man wishes to take a sea voyage. If he does not take with him bread and water from an inhabited land, he would not find anything to eat or to drink on the sea." The same applies to one who travels "to the end of the wilderness [on land]. Likewise, if a man does not repent in his lifetime, he cannot do so after death" (PdRE 43).

Nevertheless, the inclination toward evil can be a powerful positive force if channeled correctly. As a *midrash* observes, "Were it not for the *yetzer ha-ra* [used here as the sexual urge], no man would build a house, marry a wife, or father children" (Gen. R. 9:7). Moreover, it is only the existence of the *yetzer ha-ra* that gives humans the opportunity to become moral beings, for without an inclination toward evil the concept of "goodness" would have no meaning. As Resh Lakish observed, "Come, let us show gratitude to our forefathers [who worshiped the Golden Calf], for had they not sinned [i.e., been under the influence of the inclination toward evil], we would not have come into the world" (Av. Zar. 5a).

Why does the opening verse of the Song at the Sea describe God as "highly exalted" (Exod. 19:1), using the same word twice in the Hebrew? According to Resh Lakish, this was intended to teach that God was exalted above all the other exalted ones. As one sage remarked, "The king of wild animals is the lion; the king of cattle is the ox; the king of birds is the eagle; and man is exalted over them. The Holy One is exalted over all of them, as well as over the whole earth and the entire universe" (Hag. 13b).

Resh Lakish took a jaundiced view of the judicial process. Interpreting the biblical verse, "For your hands are defiled with blood and your fingers with sin; your lips have spoken lies and your tongue muttered wickedness" (Isa. 51:3), he observed: "'For your hands are defiled with blood'—this refers to a corrupt judge [who take bribes and rule in favor of his benefactor, thus wrongly taking money away from the other party, which is like killing him]; 'and your fingers with sin'—to the court scribes [who prepare false documents for a fee and record verdicts falsely]; 'your lips have spoken lies'—to the lawyers [who train their clients to lie when stating their claims]; and 'your tongue muttered wickedness'—to the litigants" (Shab. 139a).

Among the numerous sayings attributed to Resh Lakish are: "First adorn [improve] yourself and [only] then decorate [improve] others" (BM 107b); "He who responds 'Amen' with all his might, the gates of Paradise are opened for him" (Shab. 119b); "Man is given an additional soul on Friday [the eve of the Sabbath, to impart the proper spiritual dimension to the day], which is taken back from him when the Sabbath ends" (Taan. 27b); God "does not smite Israel unless He has previously created a means for healing them" (Meg. 13b); "When afflictions are visited on the world, the Jews are the first ones to suffer; when joy comes to the world, the Jews also are the first to feel it" (Lam. R. 2:3); "He who commits the sin of adultery, even if only with his eyes, is an adulterer" (Lev. R. 23:12); and "Whoever has a synagogue in his town and does not go there to pray is an evil neighbor" (Ber. 8a).

The relationship between Resh Lakish and R. Yochanan had a tragic ending, which illustrates the danger of dredging up the past. One day, there was a dispute in the house of study about whether certain utensils—a sword, knife, dagger, spear, handsaw, and scythe—can become ritually unclean. R. Yochanan ruled that this was possible "when they are tempered in a furnace." But Resh Lakish insisted, "When they have been scoured in water." Irritated by this challenge to his authority, R. Yochanan said: "A robber understands his trade" (referring to his colleague's use of these weapons in his former work as a gladiator). Resh Lakish angrily replied, "How have you helped me? There [at the Roman circus] I was called Master and here I am called Master!" Mortified by this remark, R. Yochanan retorted, "I benefited you by bringing you under the wings of the *Shechinah* (Divine Presence)." Seeing his old friend and teacher so deeply hurt, Resh Lakish fell seriously ill. His wife pleaded with her brother to forgive Resh Lakish, but R. Yochanan stubbornly refused. When Resh Lakish died, R. Yochanan was plunged into deep depression, tearing his clothes and weeping inconsolably until he lost his mind. Then the Rabbis prayed that R. Yochanan be freed of his misery, and he died (BM 84a).

The death of these two giants, Resh Lakish and R. Yochanan, effectively ended the period of creative Jewish rabbinic scholarship in the Land of Israel (Pearl, 336). *See also* Levi ben Lahma; Yochanan.

Shimon ben Menasia, Palestinian *tanna* (second/third century).

Shimon ben Menasia and R. Jose ben Meshulam formed a society of pious men called *Kehala Kaddisha* (Holy Congregation), whose members devoted one-third of the day to the study of the Torah, one-third to prayer, and the remaining third to work. Other members of the society divided the year into two parts, devoting the winter to study and the summer to their worldly occupations (JT Maas. Sheni 2:4). A disciple of R. Meir, Shimon ben Menasia always quoted his master in legal matters. Commenting on the verse, "You shall keep the Sabbath, because it is holy for you" (Exod. 31:14), Shimon ben Menasia noted that "the words 'for you' imply that the Sabbath is given to you [a Divine gift], rather than you being given to the Sabbath" (Mech.

Ki Tissa). This is consistent with the Talmudic dictum that it is permissible to violate one Sabbath, such as by saving a life, so that a person can observe many Sabbaths in the future (Yoma 85b). Shimon ben Menasia interpreted the verse, "Drop a dispute before you bare your teeth" (Prov. 17:14), as meaning that before hearing the testimony of two contending parties, a judge may set aside the law and call upon them to settle the issue amicably. However, "after the case has been laid bare" (i.e., once he has heard all the arguments and decided which party was correct), the judge no longer has the right to attempt to arrive at a compromise and must render a decision (Sanh. 6b). As Shimon ben Menasia observed, "It is not possible for one to be killed every day; but God reckons the life of the pious as though they daily died a martyr's death" (Sifre Deut. 32).

In a bizarre statement, Shimon ben Menasia stated, "Woe for the loss of a great servant." He based this on the biblical verse, "And over every living creature [translated as 'a wild animal that cannot be put to service and only caught and eaten'] that moves upon the earth," which he interpreted as referring to the snake. "For had not the snake been cursed, every Israelite would have had two valuable snakes [in his house], sending one to the north and one to the south to bring him costly gems, precious stones, and pearls." Moreover, the snake was originally intended to be put into service before it was cursed, so that it would have been used as a beast of burden instead of the donkey and the camel (Sanh. 59b).

Shimon ben Nethaniel, Palestinian *tanna* (first century C.E.).

One of R. Yochanan ben Zakkai's five primary disciples (Avot 2:10) and son-in-law of Rabban Gamaliel I, Shimon ben Nethaniel was praised by his teacher for his fear of sinning (Avot 2:11). In reply to the question, "What is the proper way to which a man should cling?" (in order to live meritoriously and inherit the life of the World to Come), Shimon ben Nethaniel replied, "To carefully consider the outcome [consequences] of his actions." Conversely, in response to the question "From which type of person should one distance himself?" Shimon ben Nethaniel answered, "One [who] borrows and does not pay back his debt" (Avot 2:13–14).

As an indication of his great piety, Shimon ben Nethaniel said: "Be meticulous in reading the *Shema* [twice daily at the appointed time] and the *Amidah* [lit., 'the prayer,' which is to be recited three times daily]; when you pray, do not make your prayer a set routine [pure rote], but rather [an appeal for] mercy and a supplication before the Omnipresent, as it is said, 'For He is gracious and compassionate, slow to anger, abounding in mercy, and forgiving of evil' [Joel 2:13]; and do not judge yourself to be a wicked person" (Avot 1:18). *See also* Yochanan ben Zakkai.

Shimon ben Shetach, outstanding scholar of the Second Temple period (first century B.C.E.).

During the reign of Alexander Yannai and Queen Salome Alexandra, who was Shimon ben Shetach's sister (Ber. 48b), he paired with Judah ben Tabbai as the third *zugot*. Shimon ben Shetach was the leader of the Pharisees, the majority party in Judea, who interpreted the law according to traditions handed down over generations. They were opposed by the aristocratic Sadducees, who insisted on a literal interpretation of biblical law. As head of the Sanhedrin, Shimon ben Shetach was determined to eradicate all Sadducee teachings. To this end, he enacted the law of the "dissenting elder," which imposed a death sentence on any member of the Sanhedrin who opposed a majority interpretation of the law, even if the dissenting view would result in a more strict interpretation or an addition to a Torah law.

A paragon of honesty and personal integrity, the *aggadah* relates that Shimon ben Shetach once received a donkey as a gift from his students. As he went to mount it, Shimon ben Shetach found a valuable jewel hung around its neck. When his students congratulated him on his good fortune, Shimon ben Shetach stated, "I bought a donkey, not a precious stone." So he ordered the jewel to be returned to the gentile from whom they had bought the animal. Thereupon the gentile exclaimed: "Praised be the Lord, the God of Shimon ben Shetach!" (Deut. R. 3:3).

Shimon ben Shetach was said to have "instituted the woman's marriage settlement [*ketubah*]" (Shab. 14b, 16b) as a measure to protect the economic condition of women and to discourage divorce. This stipulated the obligations of the husband to care for the needs of his wife, as well as providing that his property be pledged as security to pay to the wife the sum specified in the *ketubah* if she were divorced or widowed.

The relations between Shimon ben Shetach and King Yannai were always strained. When a slave or mercenary of the king killed a man, the Sanhedrin informed Yannai of the crime and the king sent the slave to appear before the court. However, the court demanded that the king appear, since at the time a slave was like any livestock for which the owner was ultimately responsible. When Yannai sat down before the Sanhedrin, Shimon ben Shetach ordered him to rise, "not to honor us but to honor the Creator of the universe." The king refused to do so unless the demand was made by all the other members of Sanhedrin, who fearfully remained silent. When Shimon ben Shetach turned toward his colleagues, they looked down and refused to meet his gaze. The sage looked at his colleagues with disgust, sarcastically questioning whether they really had any doubt that the law applied to the king. Instantly, the angel Gabriel came and killed them. So the law was enacted that a king (not of the House of David) may neither judge nor be judged. In addition, a king may not be called as a witness and no one may testify against him (Sanh. 19a–b).

Known for his strictness in legal matters, Shimon ben Shetach, in an attempt to eradicate witchcraft, once sentenced to death eighty women in Ashkelon who had been convicted of sorcery (Sanh. 45b–46a). In revenge, their relatives bribed false witnesses to testify against Shimon ben Shetach's son, whom they accused of a capital crime. Hearing their testimony, the Sanhedrin sentenced the young man to death. As he walked to the place of execution, the son protested his innocence so convincingly that even the witnesses were moved to admit their testimony was false. When the judges were about to free the condemned man, he called to their attention the legal rule that a witness must not be believed when he withdraws a former statement. Then he turned to his father, saying: "If you desire that the welfare of Israel shall be strengthened by your hand, then consider me as a beam on which you may tread without regret," and the execution was carried out (JT Sanh. 6:6). This tragedy was probably the reason why Shimon ben Shetach warned that witnesses must be carefully cross-examined: "Interrogate the witnesses extensively; and be cautious with your words, lest they learn to lie [by fabricating their testimony to comport with what they think you want them to say]" (Avot 1:9).

Shimon ben Shetach once saw a man with a knife in his hand pursuing another. The sage ran after him and saw the man, with sword in hand and blood dripping from it, looking down at a mortally wounded man dying on the floor. He exclaimed, "Wicked man, it is clear who murdered this man. But what can I do, for your blood [life] does not rest in my hands, for it is written in the Torah, 'At the mouth of two witnesses . . . shall he be put to death' [i.e., two witnesses are required to convict a criminal, but I am the only one who witnessed the crime] [Deut. 17:6]. 'May He [God] who knows one's thoughts exact vengeance from the one who murdered his fellow!' It is related that before they moved from the place, a snake came and bit him [the murderer] so that he died" (Sanh. 37b).

According to the Jerusalem Talmud, Shimon ben Shetach pioneered education for the young, introducing compulsory school attendance (JT Ket. 8:11). Previously, fathers who wanted their children to become educated sent them to the academies of great scholars. Those whose parents did not value education remained ignorant, coming in contact with religious training only on the infrequent occasions when they visited Jerusalem. *See also* Honi the Circle-Drawer; Judah ben Tabbai.

Shimon ha-Tzadik (Simeon the Just), high priest and teacher of the pre-*tannaitic* period (fourth/third century B.C.E.).

The precise identity of Shimon ha-Tzadik is unclear. The Talmud, Josephus, and Second Book of Maccabees contain accounts of him that combine fact and fiction. The appellation "the Just" reflected the piety of his life and the concern and benevolence that he displayed toward his fellow Israelites. Shimon ha-Tzadik was deeply interested in both the spiritual and material development of the nation. Consequently, he was said to have rebuilt the walls of Jerusalem and repaired the damage done to the Temple.

According to legend, when Alexander the Great marched through the Land of Israel in 333 B.C.E., Shimon ha-Tzadik, clad in the elaborate vestments that the high priest wore only when entering the Holy of Holies on Yom Kippur, went to Kfar Saba (Antipatris) to meet the conqueror. As soon as Alexander saw him, he descended from his chariot and bowed respectfully before him. When Alexander's courtiers criticized this obsequiousness to a Jew whose nation he had threatened to destroy, the Macedonian replied that he had seen a vision in which an old man who resembled the high priest had appeared and predicted his victory. Alexander demanded that a statue of himself be placed in the Temple. However, the high priest explained to him that this was impossible, promising him instead that all the sons born of priests in that year should be named Alexander (Yoma 69a).

Shimon ha-Tzadik held the position of high priest for forty years. After this time, the office was sold to the highest bidder. Therefore, his successors did not live long and their tenure in office was brief (Lev. R. 21:9). The Talmud relates a series of miraculous events that occurred in the Temple in Jerusalem while Shimon ha-Tzadik was high priest. On Yom Kippur, when the high priest cast lots to determine which of two goats would be sacrificed as a sin offering to God and which would be sent out to the wilderness for Azazel, the lot for the former "would always come up in the right hand" of the high priest rather than be random. After the goat assigned to Azazel was thrown from the top of the cliff to its death on the rocks below, the crimson string tied around its neck always turned white, indicating that God had forgiven the people of Israel for their sins. The western lamps of the Menorah, though lit first, always continued burning longer than the others, and the fire on the altar never burned out, even though only two pieces of wood were added at sundown. During this period, the *omer*, two breads, and showbread were blessed so that "every priest who obtained a piece as big as an olive would eat it and become satisfied, and there was even some left over" (Yoma 39a).

Shimon ha-Tzadik introduced major rituals that are still practiced today. Among them were the recitation of *Kiddush* and Havdalah; blessings over food; reading the *haftarah* on Sabbath and festival mornings; and the rule that even the poorest individual must drink at least four glasses of wine at the Passover seder. Described in Pirkei Avot (1:2) as "one of the last of the Men of the Great Assembly," Shimon ha-Tzadik's most famous maxim is: "The world depends on three things—on Torah study, on the service (of God), and on acts of lovingkindness [*al ha-Torah, al ha-avodah, v'al gemilut hasadim*]."

On one Yom Kippur, Shimon ha-Tzadik returned from the Holy of Holies in a melancholy mood. When asked the reason he was so forlorn, he replied that on every previous Day of Atonement a figure clothed in white had ushered him into the Holy of Holies and then escorted him out. This time, however, the apparition had been clothed in black and had taken him in but not led him out—a sign that this year was to be his last—and the sage died seven days later (Yoma 39b). *See also* Aha bar Bizna; Hana bar Bizna.

Shimon the Pakulite, Palestinian *tanna* (first/second century).

According to Rashi, "Pakulite" may mean "cotton dealer," presumably Shimon's occupation. The Talmud relates that Shimon the Pakulite "arranged [the sequence of] the eighteen blessings [*Shemoneh Esrei*, known as the *Amidah*] in the proper order in the presence of Rabban Gamaliel in Yavneh" (Meg. 17b). The Rabbis asked, "Seeing now that 120 elders, among whom were many prophets, drew up the prayers in the proper order, why did Shimon the Pakulite formulate them?" The answer: "They [the prayers] were forgotten, and he formulated them afresh." The Talmud adds, "Beyond this it is forbidden to declare the praise of the Holy One, blessed be He [i.e., it is forbidden to add any more blessings]."

Simlai, Palestinian *amora* (third century).

Simlai is best known as the first sage to observe that "613 commandments were communicated to Moses [on Mount Sinai]; 365 negative commandments, corresponding to the number of days in the solar year, and 248 positive commandments, corresponding to the number of parts of the human body" (Mak. 23b). In the name of one of his teachers, R. Eleazar ben Shimon, Simlai noted: "The son of David [Messiah] will not come until all the [corrupt] judges and officers are gone from Israel" (Sanh. 98a).

According to Simlai, the Torah begins and ends with God performing the supreme Jewish virtue of *gemilut chasadim* (Sot. 14a). As Adam and Eve were about to be banished from the Garden of Eden, God sewed the first couple their "garments of skin . . . and clothed them" (Gen. 3:21). When Moses died alone on Mount Nebo after viewing the Promised Land that he was forbidden from entering, the Bible states that God "buried him in the valley in the land of Moab" (Deut. 34:6).

When about to pray, Simlai urged, "One should always first recount the praises of the Omnipresent and then offer his supplications" (i.e., first give thanks for what one has before thinking of what one lacks) (Av. Zar. 7b; Ber. 32a). With reference to the command to both "Remember" and "Observe" the Sabbath, Simlai explained that one should remember the Sabbath before it comes and observe it once it has arrived. To accomplish this, whenever a person sees a new utensil or other beautiful object, he should reserve it for the Sabbath (Pes. Rab. 23).

Known primarily as an *aggadist*, Simlai "delivered the following discourse: What does an embryo resemble when it is in the bowels of its mother? Folded writing tablets. Its hands rest on its two temples, its two elbows on its two legs, and its two heels against its buttocks. Its head lies between its knees, its mouth is closed, and its navel is open; it eats what its mother eats and drinks what its mother drinks, but produces no excrement because otherwise it might kill its mother. However, as soon as it sees the light of day [lit., 'went out to the air space of the world'], the closed organ [its mouth] opens and the open one [its navel] closes, for otherwise the embryo could not live even one single hour. A light burns above its head and it looks and sees from one end of the world to the other. . . . It is also taught all the Torah from beginning to end. . . . As soon as it sees the light an angel approaches, slaps it on its mouth, and causes it to forget all the Torah completely" (Nid. 30b). *See also* Hamnuna II.

T

Tanhum ben Hanilai, Palestinian *amora* (third/fourth century).

A student and close friend of R. Joshua ben Levi (BK 55a), Tanhum ben Hanilai said: "One should never deviate from custom [local communal practice and tradition, which may eventually become binding with the force of *halachah*]." As an illustration of this principle, he noted: "When Moses ascended on high to receive the Torah, he ate no bread nor drank any water [for forty days and nights, like the angels; Exod. 34:28]. In contrast, when the ministering angels descended below [to visit Abraham and announce the birth of Isaac], they did [or at least appeared to] eat and drink like mortals [Gen. 18:8]" (BM 86b).

Tanhum ben Hanilai observed, "One who starves himself for the sake of Torah study in this world, the Holy One, blessed be He, will fully satisfy him in the next," based on the verse (Ps. 36:9), "They shall feast on the rich fare of Your house; You let them drink at Your refreshing stream" (Sanh. 100a). He believed that "No rain falls unless the sins of Israel have been forgiven" (Taan. 7b).

Expanding on Rava's dictum "Set a fixed [regular] time for the study of Torah" (Er. 54b), Tanhum ben Hanilai recommended that a third of this time should be allocated to the study of scripture, a third for Mishnah, and a third for Gemara (Av. Zar. 19b). He quoted his father as saying, "A man who has no wife lives without joy, without blessing, and without goodness" (Yev. 62b). Known for his high ethical and moral character, Tanhum ben Hanilai always reminded his family at meals "to set aside a portion for the poor" (Tanh. Mishpatim 8). He described God as saying to Israel, "My daughter [the Torah] is in your hands; your daughter [the soul] is in My hands. If you protect Mine, then I shall protect yours" (Tanh. Ki Tissa, 28).

A characteristic of the *aggadic* system of Tanhum ben Hanilai was to connect the last words of one biblical verse with the opening words of the next. Thus, by relating Leviticus 1:16 with 2:1, he deduced that the crop of a bird-offering was unworthy of being sacrificed on the altar and must be discarded: "The bird flies about and swoops throughout the world and eats indiscriminately of food obtained by robbery and violence [unlike domestic animals that are raised in the crib of their master . . . and therefore the entire animal is offered up]" (Lev. R. 3:4).

Tanhuma bar Abba, Palestinian *amora* (fourth century).

A student of R. Huna and prolific *aggadist*, Tanhuma bar Abba is reputed to be the author of *Midrash Tanhuma*, which comments on the entire Torah. The work is divided into the weekly readings, with each section introduced by the phrase, "Our teacher taught . . ." This is followed by a legal question leading to a long and complex answer, which ends with a proof text that is the beginning biblical verse of the Torah portion for that week.

Tanhuma bar Abba was a staunch defender of Jews and Judaism against the Romans and other non-Jews. The Talmud relates that the Roman emperor once proposed to him, "Come, let us all [Jews and non-Jews] become one people." The sage replied, "But we who are circumcised cannot possibly become like you; [however], you can become circumcised and be like us." The emperor retorted, "You have spoken well; nevertheless, anyone who gets the better of the king [in debate] must be thrown into the vivarium." So Tanhuma bar Abba was tossed into the enclosure where wild beasts were kept, but (like the biblical Daniel) the animals did not eat him. A "heretic" who had watched these events remarked, "The reason they did not eat him is that they are not hungry." Then "they threw him [the heretic] in, and he was eaten" (Sanh. 39a).

Tarfon, Palestinian *tanna* (first/second century C.E.).

A leading scholar in Yavneh after the destruction of the Temple in Jerusalem, Tarfon was a member of a priestly family. As such, it was reported that during a period of famine he betrothed several hundred poor women so that they might, as wives of a priest, be permitted to share in the tithes (*terumah*) (Tosef. Ket. 5:1). A wealthy man (Ned. 63a), in response to the question, "Who is rich?" Tarfon replied, "One who possesses one hundred vineyards, one hundred fields, and one hundred slaves working in them" (Avot 4:1).

Outside the academy, Tarfon kept a low profile lest he receive special benefits because of his Torah knowledge. After once saving himself from a beating by revealing his identity, Tarfon was forever distressed: "Woe is me that I made use of the crown of the Torah." On another occasion, while trying to take some figs from his own tree, a watchman failed to recognize the sage and struck him as a thief. When he discovered Tarfon's identity and asked forgiveness, the sage replied: "As each stick came down on me, I pardoned you for each successive blow" (JT Shev. 4:2).

The Haggadah mentions Tarfon as one of the five leading scholars who stayed up the entire night of Passover discussing the Exodus of the Israelites from Egypt. Living in Lydda, the Talmud records his friendship and many *halachic* discussions with R. Akiva. One subject on which they disagreed was the relative importance of study and practice (observing the commandments; good deeds). According to Tarfon, "Practice is greater." R. Akiva disagreed (and the other Rabbis concurred): "Study is greater, for it leads to practice" (Kid. 40b). Although generally a follower of the stricter school of Shammai, Tarfon and R. Akiva agreed, "Were we members of the Sanhedrin, no person would ever be put to death [i.e., their cross-examination of the witnesses would have been so exhaustive that some flaw would have appeared in their testimony, effectively abolishing capital punishment]" (Mak. 7a).

Tarfon was so devoted to his aged mother that he placed his hands beneath her feet when she had to cross the courtyard barefoot lest she experience any pain. Indeed, when his mother wanted to get on or off her bed, Tarfon would bend down and let her step on his back to make it easier for her (Kid. 31b). When the sages visited Tarfon as he was sick in bed, his mother asked them to pray for her son, "who treats me with more honor than is due to me." After hearing about her son's devotion, they exclaimed: "Even if he had performed a thousand thousand times as much, he still would not have fulfilled half of what the Torah commands regarding honoring parents" (JT Pe'ah 1:1). On festivals and holy days, Tarfon delighted his wife and children by preparing for them the finest fruits and dainties.

Tarfon had a deep antipathy for those Jews who had converted to Christianity, swearing on the head of his son that he would burn every book of these heretics that came into his hand, even though they contained the name of God. "Even if someone was running to slay me, or if a snake was pursuing me to bite me, I would enter a heathen Temple [for refuge], but not the houses of these [converted Jews], for the latter know [of God] yet deny [Him], whereas the former are ignorant and deny [Him]" (Shab. 116a).

In his best-known saying, Tarfon compares the relationship between human beings to that of laborers and their employer: "The day is short, the task is abundant, the laborers are lazy, the wage is great, and the Master of the house is insistent. You are not required to complete the work, yet you are not free to withdraw from it. If you have studied much Torah, they will give you great reward; and your Employer can be relied upon to pay you the wage for your labor, but remember that the reward of the righteous will be given in the World to Come" (Avot 2:20–21). Later he observed that God did not cause the Divine Presence to rest upon Israel until they completed the building of the Tabernacle (ARN 11). *See also* Yochanan ben Nuri.

Tavyomi. *See* Mar bar Rav Ashi.

U

Ukba. *See* Mar Ukba.

Ulla, Palestinian *amora* (third/fourth century).

A student of R. Eleazar ben Pedat and R. Yochanan, Ulla was a leading *halachic* authority who often quoted decisions in the names of his teachers. As a respected scholar, Ulla frequently visited Babylonia and was invited by the exilarch to deliver *halachic* lectures (Shab. 157b; Ket. 65b; Kid. 31a).

Ulla rendered important decisions regarding the benedictions to be recited over various foods (Ber. 38b) and at the Havdalah ceremony at the conclusion of the Sabbath (Pes. 53b, 104b), as well as the calculation of the new moon. Strict in his interpretation of religious laws, especially violations of the Sabbath (Shab. 147a), Ulla labeled a ruling of R. Huna with which he did not agree as being "like vinegar to the teeth, like smoke to the eyes" (Prov. 10:26) (Kid. 45b).

Returning to the Land of Israel from Babylonia, Ulla was in danger of being killed by a fellow traveler who had attacked another member of the group. When the murderer asked Ulla, "Did I do well," Ulla replied in the affirmative, fearful that disapproval would endanger his own life. To avoid prolonging the agony of the victim, Ulla added that the murderer "cut his throat [of his victim] clean across." Later Ulla came before R. Yochanan and asked, "Maybe, God forbid, I have strengthened the hands of transgressors?" The sage replied, "You have saved your life," meaning that the action was excusable as being in self-defense (Ned. 22a).

To demonstrate "how far the honor of a parent extends," Ulla cited the heathen Dama son of Nethina (an identical story is attributed to R. Eliezer ben Hyrcanus) (Kid. 31a). Maxims of Ulla quoted by R. Hiyya ben Ammi include: "Since the day that the Temple was destroyed, the Holy One, blessed be He, has nothing in His world except for the four cubits of *halachah*"; "A man who lives from the labor [of his hands] is greater than one who fears Heaven [i.e., who relies upon the support of other people for his living]"; and "A man should always live in the same town as his teacher" (Ber. 8a). He believed that "Jerusalem shall be redeemed only by righteousness [i.e., the performance of charity]" (Sanh. 98a).

When R. Eleazar ben Pedat learned that Ulla died in Babylonia during one of his visits there, he exclaimed, "That you, Ulla, should die in an unclean land!" Consequently, he arranged for Ulla to be buried in the Land of Israel (Ket. 111a). *See also* Helbo; Hiyya bar Ammi.

Ulla bar Rav, Babylonian *amora* (third/fourth century).

Ulla bar Rav was a disciple of R. Abbaye, to whom he addressed the question: "Is a child in rags [improperly clad] allowed to read from the Torah?" In response, his teacher replied: "You might as well ask about a naked one. Why is one without any clothes not allowed? Out of respect for the congregation [*k'vod ha-tzibbur*]. So [it is the same] here" (Meg. 24b). When "Ulla bar Rav visited Rava [head of the academy at Sura], he recited [*kiddush*] in accordance with [the customs of] the elders of Pumbedita, and he [Rava] said nothing to him [in protest]" (Pes. 117b).

Y

Yannai, Palestinian *amora* (second/third century).

Never called by his patronymic, Yannai was often referred to as "Rabbah" (the Great) to distinguish him from other *amoraim* of the same name. A wealthy descendant of a priestly family, Yannai was said to have planted 400 vineyards (BB 14a) and given an orchard to the public (MK 12b). Upon the death of his teacher, Judah ha-Nasi, Yannai ruled that even priests might attend the funeral of such a great master (JT Ber. 4:6), though ironically he ascribed no greater authority to the Mishnah (which his teacher had edited) than to collections of *halachot* and *beraitot* compiled by R. Hiyya and other students of Judah ha-Nasi. Indeed, when his major pupil R. Yochanan, who transmitted most of Yannai's *halachic* pronouncements, remarked that the Mishnah rendered a decision different from his, Yannai answered: "The Mishnah gives only the decision of a single *tanna* [Judah ha-Nasi]," implying that Yannai's conclusion reflected the consensus of the Rabbis (Shab. 140a).

Yannai established an important school in Upper Galilee. Unlike other academies, however, at Akbarah the students were treated as belonging to the master's family, living under his roof, working on Yannai's estate, and sharing in its revenue. His decisions were generally rigid regarding private persons, but liberal when the whole community was concerned. Responding to a comment of Rabbah bar Huna, "Every man who possesses learning without the fear of Heaven is like a treasurer who is entrusted with the inner keys but not with the outer—how is he to enter?" Yannai proclaimed: "Woe to him who has no courtyard yet erects a gate for it" (Shab. 30a–31b), thus comparing learning to a gate through which one enters the court of piety and implying that righteousness and awe of God must come first. Yannai advocated submission to recognized governmental authority (Men. 98a) and that students should sample multiple teachers: "He who learns the Law from one master will never achieve great success" (Av. Zar. 19a). In response to the *mishnah* dealing with fasting on Yom Kippur—"A sick person is fed at the word of experts" (Yoma 83a)—Yannai stated, "If the patient says, 'I need [food],' while the physician says he does not need it, we listen to the patient," based on the verse (Prov. 14:10) "The heart knows its own bitterness."

Yannai warned, "A man should never stand in a place of danger and declare, 'A miracle will befall me'; perhaps a miracle will not take place. And if a miracle does occur, it will be deducted from his merits [reward in the World to Come]" (Shab. 32a). Addressing the theodicy question, Yannai observed: "It is not in our power to explain either the tranquility of the wicked or the suffering of the righteous" (Avot 4:19). Nearing his death, Yannai instructed his children to "bury me neither in white shrouds [lest he not merit being among the righteous in Heaven and instead be destined for Gehinnom, where he would appear like a bridegroom among mourners], nor in black shrouds [in case he was destined for Paradise and would be like a mourner among bridegrooms]" (Shab. 114a).

When giving charity, it is essential that the recipient not be shamed in any way. "When Yannai saw a man give a *zuz* to a poor person publicly, he said: 'Better you had given him nothing rather than give him [publicly] and put him to shame'" (Hag. 5a). Kind words to the poor can be of more value than money (BB 9). If one gives a large amount glumly, it is as if he had given nothing; but if one gives with a cheerful countenance, even if very little, it is as if he had given him all the good gifts in the world (Lev. R. 34:15).

The Rabbis went to great length to avoid embarrassing a teacher. A disciple of Yannai, who frequently asked questions during his lectures, refrained from doing so on a Sabbath or festival because of the many strangers attending, lest his teacher be shamed if the questions were too difficult to answer (MK 5a).

When waking up from sleep, the school of Yannai declared that one must say: "Blessed are you, O Lord, who resurrects the dead. My Master, I have sinned before You. May it be Your will, Lord my God, that you give me a good heart, a good portion, a good inclination, a good associate, a good name, a good eye, and a good soul, and a humble soul and modest spirit. And do not allow Your Name to be profaned among us. And do not make us the subject of [evil] talk among Your creatures. And do not lead us in the end to destruction. And [do not turn] our hope to despair. And do not make our welfare depend on gifts from others. And do not make us depend for sustenance on other people. For the beneficence of others is small, and their hatred is great. And set our portion with Your Torah, and with those who do Your will. Rebuild Your house, Your [Temple] courtyard, and Your city, and Your Temple speedily in our days" (JT Ber. 4:2). *See also* Judah ben Hiyya.

Yeshebab the Scribe, Palestinian *tanna* (first century C.E.).

One of the Ten Martyrs executed by the Romans for defying the prohibition against the teaching of Torah, Yeshebab was the clerk of the Sanhedrin at Yavneh. His tasks were to copy books of the Torah and record the proceedings of the court. Extremely generous, Yeshebab is cited in the Talmud as one who attempted to give away all his property to the poor, despite the rabbinic ruling that "If a man desires to spend liberally [in charity] he should not spend more than a fifth, [since by spending more] he might himself become in need [of the help] of people [i.e., dependent on charity for his own needs]" (Ket. 50a).

Yochanan, Palestinian *amora* (third century).

Yochanan is almost always quoted without his patronymic, bar Nappacha (meaning "smith"). According to the Talmud, Yochanan's father died soon after he was conceived and his mother died while giving birth (Kid. 31b). Brought up by his grandfather, Yochanan spent some time with Judah ha-Nasi, who prophesied that the lad would someday become "a teacher in Israel" (Pes. 3b). Self-described as "the only one remaining of Jerusalem's men of outstanding beauty," his appearance was said to be like a silver goblet filled with the seeds of red pomegranate, with a brim encircled with a wreath of red roses, and set between the sun and the shade (BM 84a). After serving as the assistant to Judah II in Sepphoris, Yochanan became head of an academy in Tiberias. He attracted large numbers of gifted students from both the Land of Israel and Babylonia, many of whom became major scholars and related his teachings. Yochanan's authority was accepted throughout the Jewish world, and few contemporary scholars opposed him. He himself recognized no foreign authority except Rav, whom he addressed as "our master in Babylonia" (Hul. 95b).

Yochanan based his *halachic* teachings on an in-depth analysis of the Mishnah, which he considered the highest authority. He said, "I have nothing but the Mishnah" (JT Ter. 2:3; Kid. 1:2), and "Whatever is written in the Mishnah has been commanded to Moses from Mount Sinai" (JT Pe'ah 2:6). For Yochanan, the statements of earlier scholars were the epitome of wisdom: "The [least] fingernail of the earlier generations is better [of greater worth] than the whole body of the later ones" (Yoma 9b). He added, "The hearts [intellectual powers] of the ancients were like the larger outer door of the Temple [twenty cubits wide], but that of the last generations was like the smaller inner door [only ten cubits wide], while ours is like the eye of a fine needle" (Er. 53a).

Nevertheless, Yochanan had great respect for the *amoraim*, the scholars of his own day, whom he described as engaged in the "building of the world" (Shab. 114a). However, to qualify as a "master builder" a scholar had to be completely dedicated to devote all his efforts to Torah study, renouncing all worldly pursuits for the sake of spiritual concerns (JT MK 3:7) and not dishonoring the Torah by arrogant pride in his knowledge (Er. 55a). "When Jews devote themselves to the Torah and to charity, their evil natures are under their control, rather than their evil natures controlling them. Study is so important that one who engages it in this world is conducted into the academies of Shem and Eber, of Abraham, Isaac, and Jacob, and of Moses and Aaron, in the World to Come" (Song R. 7:8). Yet mere scholarship was not sufficient: "If one has learned much but does not observe the commandments, it would have been better had he not been born" (JT Ber. 1:3; Exod. R. 40:1).

Yochanan endeavored to reconcile contradictory decisions in the Mishnah, substituting for many *halachot* the *beraitot* taught by his former masters (R. Hiyya and R. Oshaia). He developed specific rules, most still operative today, for making a final decision in cases when *tannaim* expressed opposite opinions. Convinced that Jewish life had changed substantially since the compilation of the Mishnah, Yochanan resolved to accumulate the teachings of subsequent scholars related to this basic text. This became the foundation for the Jerusalem Talmud and, although some teachers made later additions, it remained unfinished much as compiled by Yochanan.

Yochanan stressed the central position of prayer as replacing the Temple sacrifices: "He who puts on *tefillin*, recites the *Shema*, and says the *Tefillah* [*Amidah*] . . . is like one who has built an altar and offered a sacrifice upon it" (Ber. 15a). Similarly, the person who acts as the *shaliach tzibbur* (prayer leader; lit., "messenger of the congregation") should be told to "go and offer a sacrifice for us, pray for our needs, and fight our battles!" (JT Ber. 4:4). Yochanan taught, "Whenever God comes into a synagogue and does not find ten persons, He immediately becomes angry [since in the absence of a *minyan* some important features in the service must be omitted]" (Ber. 6b). He stated, "If anyone prays for his needs in Aramaic, the ministering angels do not pay attention to him, because they do not understand that language [and thus cannot transmit these prayers to God]!" (Sot. 33a). However, this extreme view did not prevail, and prayer in other languages was permitted. In keeping with Yochanan's belief that the Bible should be read and studied with a pleasant melody (Meg. 32a), the *baal koreh* who chants the Torah reading uses a special *trope*—a series of musical notations used as early as Talmudic times. R. Jose of Tyre cited Yochanan's opinion (Ber. 9b) that before reciting the *Amidah*, one should say, "O Lord, open my lips, and let my mouth declare Your praise" (Ps. 51:17); after the prayer, one should say, "May the words of my mouth and the meditation of my heart be acceptable to You, O Lord, my Rock and my Redeemer" (Ps. 19:15), both of which remain the current practice.

In his religious decisions, Yochanan was comparatively liberal. Although extremely pious himself, he argued that the welfare of the individual or an entire community might require deviation from the strict letter of the law. "Jerusalem was destroyed only because they gave judgments in [strict] accordance with biblical law" (BM 30b). For example, it was permissible to violate the Sabbath to save the life of a sick person, who would later live to observe many Sabbaths (JT Yoma 8:8). Yochanan permitted the popular custom of painting decorative figures on walls, even though it had been considered contrary to the biblical injunction against making graven images (JT Av. Zar. 3:3). He also allowed the study of Greek—by men, to enable them to defend themselves against informers—and by women, because familiarity with that language was deemed an attractive accomplishment in their gender (JT Pe'ah 1:15).

Attempting to explain why the righteous often suffer, Yochanan offered the following parable: "When the potter checks his kiln, he does not use fragile vessels because when he strikes them they break. Instead he uses good vessels, which do not break even if he strikes them several times. Similarly, God does not test the wicked. Instead He tests the righteous, as it is written, 'God tests the righteous man' [Ps. 11:5]" (Song R. 2:16). Yochanan's favorite part of the Bible appeared to be the Book of Job. After each reading, he said: "The end of man is to die, and the end of a beast is to be slaughtered, and everything that exists is doomed to die. Happy is he who was raised in the Torah and who devoted his efforts to it. Such a person has given pleasure to his Creator . . . and has departed the world with a good name" (Ber. 17a). This may in part reflect the fact that he outlived all ten of his sons, finding comfort in his studies.

As an example of Divine compassion even when afflicting Israel, Yochanan noted: "God sent them back to their mother's house [i.e., Abraham had migrated to the Land of Israel from Ur of the Chaldees, which is in Babylonia]. This is like a man who becomes angry with his wife: Where does he send her? To her mother's house" (Meg. 13b). The comparison of Israel to an olive-tree is "to tell you that just as the olive produces its oil only after being crushed, so Israel returns to the right way only after suffering" (Men. 53b).

Yochanan observed that some animal behavior could serve as a model for proper human conduct. "If the Torah had not been given [to guide us], we could have learned modesty from the cat [which covers its excrement], honesty from the ant [which does not take the food of another], chastity from the dove [which is faithful to its mate], and good manners from the rooster [who first courts and then mates]" (Er. 100b). He asserted, "Three kinds of dreams are fulfilled: an early morning dream, a dream that a friend has about one, and a dream that is interpreted in the midst of a dream." Others added "a dream that is repeated" (Ber. 55b). A person should avoid situations conducive to such sins as adultery and envy. Yochanan remarked, "It is better for a man to walk behind a lion than behind a woman [an act that may engender lustful thoughts]." However, he did admit, "It is better to walk behind a woman than behind an idol" (Ber. 61a).

For an agrarian society like ancient Israel, nothing was more important than rain. Sufficient rainfall was perceived as demonstrating God's favor, whereas insufficient rainfall was considered Divine punishment for the sins of the people. According to Yochanan, "God keeps three keys under His control and does not entrust them to the hand of any messenger—the keys of rain, childbirth, and the revival of the dead" (Taan. 2a). He believed, "The day on which it rains is as great as the day of the Gathering of the Exiles [of Israel] . . . because on that day even warring armies stop fighting." However, "Rain is held back because of people who pledge charity publicly and then fail to pay" (Taan. 8b). Moreover, "Rain may fall even for the sake of a single individual, but general prosperity is granted only for the sake of the many" (Taan. 9a).

The Rabbis posited a situation in which a group of Jews walking along a road were stopped by heathens who demanded, "Give us one of you and we will kill him. If not, we will kill all of you." They ruled that all must suffer death rather than surrender one of their own. However, "If the heathens single out a specific person, as was the case with Sheba ben Bichri, that person may be surrendered to them, so that the others may be saved. Resh Lakish said, 'Only someone under sentence of death, as Sheba ben Bichri was, may be turned over.'" But Yochanan (and the subsequent tradition) disagreed, maintaining that any person who has been specifically named, whether under sentence of death or not, may be handed over to save others from death (JT Ter. 8:12).

The Talmud relates examples of Rabbis bringing about a cure by taking the hand of a sick person. When R. Hiyya bar Abba fell ill, Yochanan went in and asked the ailing sage, "Are your sufferings welcome to you?" From his sickbed, R. Hiyya bar Abba replied, "Neither they nor their reward [i.e., the implication that if one lovingly submits to his sufferings, he will receive a great reward in the World to Come]." Then Yochanan cured his colleague by the touch of his hand. When Yochanan later became ill, R. Hanina performed a similar service. The Talmud asks why, if he could cure R. Hiyya bar Abba, Yochanan could not heal himself? The answer: "The prisoner cannot free himself from jail [and similarly the patient cannot cure himself]" (Ber. 5b).

Yochanan emphasized that the Divine approach to the concept of "measure for measure" may be different from what would be expected by human beings. A mortal can put something into an empty vessel, but not into a full one. But for God, this is not so; God puts more into a full vessel (i.e., gives more wisdom to the wise) than into an empty one, as it is written, "He gives wisdom to the wise, and knowledge to those who have understanding [Dan. 2:21]" (Ber. 55a). According to the Talmud, the wise men of its day had almost prophetic powers. Indeed, R. Amemar said, "A wise man is even superior to a prophet" (BB 12a). Yochanan had a more cynical view: "Since the Temple was destroyed, prophecy has been taken from prophets and given to fools and children" (BB 12b).

Based on the *aggadic* description of the economic activities of Zebulun enabling his older brother Issachar to devote his life to study, it became an honored tradition in Judaism for wealthy individuals to support Torah scholars and for a rich man to select a brilliant student as a son-in-law, freeing him from the need to earn a living and allowing him to immerse himself completely in acquiring Torah knowledge. According to Yochanan, "Whoever puts the profits of business into the purse of a scholar [by contributing to his support] will be rewarded with the privilege of sitting in the Heavenly Academy" (Pes. 53b).

Yochanan explained that Jeroboam merited becoming king because he once had the courage to rebuke King Solomon for his misdeeds. However, although Jeroboam was rewarded for having reproved Solomon, he was later punished by God because he had rebuked Solomon in public, thus shaming him in front of the people (Sanh. 101b).

Among Yochanan's many sayings are: "There are six things, the fruit of which man eats in this world, while the principal remains for him in the World to Come—hospitality to strangers, visiting the sick, meditation in prayer, rising early to attend the academy, raising children to the study [knowledge] of Torah, and judging everyone in the scale of merit [i.e., seeking a favorable interpretation of his actions, even when they look suspicious]" (Shab. 127a); "The return of the Exiles [will be] as important as the day when [God] created heaven and earth" (Pes. 88a); "There are three persons whose piety God proclaims every day [for having earned His special favor]—a bachelor who lives in a large city and does not sin [despite his anonymity, he overcomes the temptations of many beautiful and wealthy women]; a poor man who returns lost property to its owner; and a wealthy man who tithes his produce in private [i.e., without ostentation]" (Pes. 113a); "One should not talk during a meal, lest the windpipe acts before the gullet [so that the food goes down the wrong pipe and endangers his life]" (Taan. 5b); and "There are three persons who have a share in the World to Come—he who dwells in the Land of Israel, he who raises his children to the study of Torah, and he who honors the Sabbath" (Pes. 113a).

Yochanan was so devastated at the death of his close friend and son-in-law R. Shimon ben Lakish that for more than three years he was unable to attend his academy. On his deathbed, Yochanan ordered that he be buried in a shroud that was neither white nor black, because at the time of resurrection, he would not feel out of place [ashamed] in the company of either the pious or the wicked (JT Kil. 9:3). When Yochanan died, R. Isaac ben Eleazar said in his eulogy: "This day is as hard for Israel as if the sun had suddenly set at noon" (MK 25b). *See also* Hanina bar Hama; Hiyya bar Abba; Honi the Circle-Drawer; Ilfa; Isaac bar Joseph; Isaac Nappacha; Judah bar Shila; Samuel bar Nachmani; Shimon ben Lakish; Ulla; Ze'iri.

Yochanan ben Beroka, Palestinian *tanna* (second century).

Yochanan ben Beroka is best known for his maxim in Pirkei Avot (4:5): "He who desecrates the Name of Heaven in secret will receive his punishment in public; unintentional or intentional, both are alike regarding desecration of the Name."

Yochanan ben Nuri, Palestinian *tanna* (first/second century).

A close colleague of R. Akiva and a disciple of Rabban Gamaliel II, Yochanan ben Nuri defended his late teacher against R. Joshua ben Hananiah, a fellow student, when he attempted to abolish some of Rabban Gamaliel's rulings. Rising to address the academy, Yochanan ben Nuri exclaimed: "I submit that the body should follow the head. Throughout the lifetime of Rabban Gamaliel, we established the *halachah* according to his opinion, and now you are attempting to invalidate his decisions? R. Joshua, we will not listen to you, for the *halachah* has been fixed in agreement with the views of Rabban Gamaliel [and everyone agreed]" (Er. 41a).

Yochanan ben Nuri became a renowned scholar, described as a "bundle of *halachot*" (ARN 18), a "basket of fancy goods" (Git. 67a), and one who "was able to calculate how many drops there are in the sea" (Hor. 10a). Yet he was so poor that he had "neither bread to eat nor clothes to wear" (Hor. 10a). He lived in extreme poverty, forced to join the last of the gleaners to bring home his living for the entire year" (JT Pe'ah 8:1).

Yochanan ben Nuri was willing to be lenient when the situation warranted. After R. Tarfon declared unequivocally, "One may light [the Sabbath lamp] with nothing but olive oil," Yochanan ben Nuri strenuously disagreed. "What shall the Babylonians do, who have only sesame oil? And what shall the Medeans do, who have only nut oil? And what shall the Alexandrians do, who have only radish oil? And what shall the people of Cappadocia [in Asia Minor] do . . . who have only naphtha?" (Shab. 26a). Yochanan ben Nuri was influential in developing the laws and customs of the Jews of Galilee, who followed his rulings, but not in Judea, where the inhabitants followed the opinions of R. Akiva (JT RH 4:6). *See also* Eleazar ben Hisma.

Yochanan ben Zakkai, youngest and most distinguished disciple of Hillel (first century C.E.).

Yochanan ben Zakkai was called the "father of wisdom and the father of generations (of scholars)" because he ensured the continuation of Jewish scholarship at Yavneh after Jerusalem fell to the Romans in 70 C.E. According to legend, during the Roman siege of Jerusalem, Yochanan ben Zakkai summoned his nephew, Abba Sikra, a zealot leader, and asked how long he would allow the people of Jerusalem to die of hunger before surrendering to the Romans. Abba Sikra replied that even suggesting peace to his fellow zealots would result in his death. When Yochanan ben Zakkai asked how he might leave the city to save himself and others, the two devised a plan. Pretending to be dead, Yochanan ben Zakkai escaped from the city in a coffin carried by trusted disciples, since the Romans respected the Jewish law that did not permit a body in the city of Jerusalem to remain unburied overnight. Making his way to the camp of the Roman general Vespasian, Yochanan ben Zakkai predicted that he would soon become emperor of Rome. When this transpired, Vespasian granted Yochanan ben Zakkai's request for permission to gather a small community of sages and organize a school at Yavneh. The Sanhedrin was reestablished, with Yochanan ben Zakkai as its head, and Yavneh remained the seat of Jewish scholarship and culture until the Bar Kochba revolt (132–135), when the Sanhedrin was disbanded and many of the inhabitants of the city fled.

"When Yochanan ben Zakkai saw that the Temple was destroyed, he stood and rent his garments, took off his *tefillin*, and sat weeping, as did his pupils with him" (ARN 7). The destruction of the Temple and the cessation of the sacrificial services led to a movement of excessive abstinence and despair of the possibility of atoning for sins. A disciple of Yochanan ben Zakkai, walking in Jerusalem with his teacher, viewed the ruined Temple and wailed about the place "where the sins of Israel found atonement." The master replied, "We have atonement equal to that other—deeds of lovingkindness [*gemilut chasadim*]" (ARN 4).

Yochanan ben Zakkai was an inspiration for his students. Though the head of the Sanhedrin, Yochanan ben Zakkai was friendly to all he met and "no man ever greeted him first, not even a heathen in the marketplace" (Ber. 17a). "During his whole life he never used profane speech, nor walked four cubits without [studying] Torah or without [wearing] *tefillin*; nor did any man arrive earlier than he at the house of study, nor did he sleep or [even] doze while there; nor when finding himself in a filthy alleyway did he meditate [on his studies or other sacred subjects]; nor did anyone ever find him sitting in silence, but only engaged in study; no one but himself ever opened the door to his disciples; never in his life did he say anything [i.e., give a legal decision in public] that he had not heard from his teacher; he never said, 'It is time to leave the house of study,' except on the eve of Passover [when it was necessary to rush home for the seder before the children would fall asleep] and on the eve of the Day of Atonement [when the final meal of the day had to be eaten early before the fast began]" (Suk. 28a).

As Yochanan ben Zakkai cautioned his students, "If you have learned much Torah, do not claim for yourself any special credit, because for such [purpose] you were created" (Avot 2:9). Yochanan ben Zakkai also taught the masses. Because his academy was so small and the number who wished to hear him teach the laws of the upcoming festivals so many, Yochanan ben Zakkai would teach all day in the open "in the shade afforded by the high walls of the Temple" (Pes. 26a). He once exclaimed, "How happy [fortunate] is Israel; for as long as they perform the will of God, no nation or people has any power over them. But when they fail to obey the Divine will, God delivers them into the hands of a low people [that oppress them]" (Ket. 66b). He also taught, "If you have a seedling in your hand and they say to you, 'Look, here comes the Messiah!'—go plant the seedling first and then come out to meet him" (ARN 31).

Yochanan ben Zakkai eliminated some biblical laws that he believed were no longer appropriate to the social conditions of the times. These included abolishing trial by the ordeal of bitter waters for a woman suspected of adultery (Num. 5:11–31) and the ritual of breaking the neck of a heifer when an unidentified man was murdered outside the limits of a town (Deut. 21:10).

In the Torah, there are special rules pertaining to the theft of a sheep or an ox (Exod. 21:37). A thief who sold or slaughtered the animal was required to make fourfold restitution for a sheep and fivefold restitution for an ox. This meant that, in addition to the value of the stolen animal, the thief must pay a fine of three times the value of a sheep and four times that of an ox. According to Yochanan ben Zakkai, the difference in penalties was related to "the importance attached to the dignity of man. An ox walks away on its own feet . . . while a sheep was usually carried on the thief's shoulder [i.e., the embarrassment suffered warranted less of a fine]" (BK 79b).

"When Yochanan ben Zakkai became ill, his disciples went in to visit him. Seeing them, the sage began to weep. His disciples said to him: 'Lamp of Israel, pillar of the right hand [of the side of the Temple], mighty hammer! Why do you weep?'" The sage replied that if a man would weep (i.e., be terrified) when summoned by a bribable human king who could imprison or even kill him, how much more should one weep at the end of life when "taken before the supreme King of kings, the Holy One, blessed be He, who lives and endures for ever and ever, whose anger, if He is angry with me, is an everlasting anger, who if He imprisons me imprisons me for ever, who if He puts me to death puts me to death for ever, and whom I cannot persuade with words or bribe with money—even more, when there are two ways before me, one leading to Paradise and the other to Gehinnom, and I do not know by which I will be taken" (Ber. 28b).

On his deathbed, Yochanan ben Zakkai prayed that the fear of Heaven would be upon his disciples like the fear of flesh and blood. When his disciples asked why the fear of God should not be even more, the sage responded: "When a man commits a transgression [in private], he says, 'I hope no person will see me' [i.e., if the fear of God is no more than this, it will keep his disciples from many sins]" (Ber. 28b). As the Talmud relates, "When Yochanan ben Zakkai [finally] died, [the luster of] wisdom ceased" (Sot. 49b).

Pirkei Avot (2:10–11) lists the praises of Yochanan ben Zakkai for five of his most noteworthy disciples—R. Eliezer ben Hyrcanus, R. Joshua ben Hananiah, R. Jose ha-Kohen, R. Shimon ben Nethaniel, and R. Eleazar ben Arach: "Eliezer ben Hyrcanus is like a cemented cistern that does not lose a drop; Joshua ben Hananiah, praiseworthy is the mother who bore him; Jose ha-Kohen is a scrupulously pious person; Shimon ben Nethaniel avoids sin; and Eleazar ben Arach is like a spring that flows ever stronger." He then added, "If all the sages of Israel were placed on one side of a scale, and Eliezer ben Hyrcanus on the other, he would outweigh them all." But Abba Saul said in his name, "If all the sages of Israel, with even Eliezer ben Hyrcanus among them, were on one side of the scale and Eleazar ben Arach on the other, he would outweigh them all." *See also* Abba Sikra; Eleazar ben Arach; Eliezer ben Hyrcanus; Hanina ben Dosa.

Yochanan the Sandalmaker, Palestinian *tanna* (second century).

His Hebrew appellation, *ha-Sandelar*, may either have reflected his occupation or indicated that he was a native of Alexandria. Although Yochanan's workshop was in the market of the harlots, for whom he made shoes, he never raised his eyes to look at them. Recognizing his piety, the harlots used to swear "by the lives of the holy rabbis of Israel." In response to a query about abolishing an accepted custom, Yochanan the Sandalmaker replied: "Since your ancestors were accustomed to forbid this, do not change their custom, so that they may rest in peace."

When R. Akiva was imprisoned, Yochanan the Sandalmaker disguised himself as a peddler and stood outside the window of his cell. Seeking the answer to a *halachic* question, Yochanan the Sandalmaker would insert it as part of the advertisement for his wares: "Who wants pins? Who wants needles? Is a *halitzah* (alternative to a levirate marriage) without witnesses valid?" Hearing these words, R. Akiva would call out the answer: "Do you sell weaver's pins, called *kushin*? Kasher . . . it is valid!" In this way, the guards never realized what was going on, and R. Akiva continued to decide important legal matters.

Yochanan the Sandalmaker's most famous maxim is: "Every assembly that is for the sake of Heaven will endure [will achieve success], but every assembly not conducted for the sake of Heaven will not last [will ultimately fail]" (Avot 4:14).

Yudan, Palestinian *amora* (fourth century).

A student of R. Abba and mentioned only in the Jerusalem Talmud, Yudan is best known as a transmitter of the *aggadic* literature. This includes exegetic and homiletic explanations of biblical passages and comments on biblical personages and narratives, as well as maxims of the most prominent *tannaim* and older *amoraim*. Speaking of the atoning power of suffering, Yudan observed that if a slave is liberated because of pain inflicted upon a single member of his body (Exod. 21:20), how much more entitled to liberty in the World to Come is a man who has been afflicted with sufferings in his whole body (Gen. R. 92:1)? He added, "Redemption will not come to this people all at once, but little by little. . . . Now they live in the midst of great troubles, and if redemption were to come all at once, they would be unable to bear such great salvation. . . . It will gradually grow larger. Therefore is redemption likened to the dawn, as it is written 'Then shall your light break forth as the dawn' (Isa. 58:8)" (Mid. Ps. 18:36).

Yudan observed, "A person who supplies the righteous with bread is considered as if he fulfilled the entire Torah" (Mid. Ps. 58:8). Commenting on the verse, "and man became a living [*hayah*] being" (Gen. 2:7), Yudan explained that man was originally created with a rudimentary tail, so that he resembled an animal (*hayah*); later, however, God removed this appendage lest man's dignity suffer (Gen. R. 14). A master of parables, Yudan said: "Everyone has a patron. When he is in need he may not suddenly enter into the presence of his benefactor to ask for aid, but must wait at the door while a slave or person living in the house carries his request before the master. God, however, is not such a patron; when a man faces trouble, he should not cry out to the angels Gabriel or Michael, but directly to God, who will hear him without any mediators and immediately answer him" (JT Ber. 9:1).

Yudan ben Ishmael, Palestinian *amora* (third century).

Addressing the issue of whether Torah instructors should be remunerated for their services, Yudan ben Ishmael declared that they should be paid for the time spent teaching. Otherwise, they could have used that time to earn money in some different type of work.

Z

Zadok ben Eleazar, Palestinian *tanna* of priestly descent (first century C.E.).

Although a pupil of the school of Shammai, Zadok ben Eleazar's *halachic* decisions always reflected the teachings of the school of Hillel (Yev. 15b). According to legend, "Zadok ben Eleazar observed fasts for forty years in order that Jerusalem might not be destroyed, [and he became so thin that] when he ate anything the food could be seen [as it passed through his throat]. When he wanted to restore himself, they brought him a fig; he would suck the juice and then throw the rest away" (Git. 56a). When Jerusalem finally fell, the seriously ill Zadok was captured by the Romans. However, he was freed by Titus in response to an appeal by Yochanan ben Zakkai, whom Zadok ben Eleazar joined at Yavneh.

The Talmud reports how the physicians healed Zadok ben Eleazar. "The first day they let him drink water in which bran had been soaked; on the next day water in which there had been coarse meal; and on the next day water in which there had been flour, so that his stomach expanded little by little" (Git. 56b). An influential member of the Sanhedrin under Rabban Gamaliel II, Zadok ben Eleazar always sat to the right of the sage. Together with Yochanan ben Zakkai and Rabban Gamaliel II, Zadok ben Eleazar rendered a decision on the conditions under which food might be eaten outside the Tabernacle during Sukkot (Suk. 26b).

Zadok ben Eleazar's most famous saying is: "Do not make the Torah [learning] a crown for self-glorification, nor a spade with which to dig [i.e., derive personal benefit from it]" (Avot 4:7).

Zebid, Babylonian *amora* (fourth century).

Zebid transmitted many of the *halachot* of his contemporary, R. Abbaye, but ironically his support for these opinions led directly to his death. "R. Hiyya Parva'ah visited the house of the exilarch and was asked, 'How is it when an egg is roasted [by a heathen]?' He replied, 'R. Hezekiah and R. Bar Kappara permit it, but R. Yochanan prohibits it, and the opinion of one authority cannot stand against that of two.' Zebid said to them, 'Pay no attention to him, because Abbaye declared that the legal decision agrees with R. Yochanan.'" The heathen servants of the exilarch were so infuriated by

Zebid's remark that they "gave him a cup of spiced vinegar [poison] from which he died" (Av. Zar. 38b).

Zebid was a central figure in a property dispute. The mother of Zutra bar Tobiah signed away her property to her son because she intended to marry Zebid, who otherwise would have acquired ownership of her property through their marriage. She then married Zebid, but he later divorced her. When she appeared before R. Bibi bar Abbaye to claim the return of her property, he ruled that she had made a gift of her property specifically because she desired to marry and in fact did so. Since she carried out the intention upon which the gift depended, she could no longer reclaim it. R Huna bar Joshua disagreed, indicating that the law only applied if the woman did not declare her reason for the gift. In this case, she had explicitly declared that she made the gift because she had not wanted it to go to Zebid. Now that she was divorced, the reason for making her gift had disappeared, and thus she was entitled to the return of her property (BB 151a).

In the name of Rava, Zebid declared: "The general principle in regard to a lost object is that once the owner has said, 'Woe is me for the monetary loss [I have sustained],' he has given up hope of [ever recovering] it [and whoever finds it now may keep it]" (BM 23a).

Zechariah ben ha-Katzav, Palestinian *tanna* (first century C.E.).

A butcher (*katzav*) by profession (like his father), Zechariah ben ha-Katzav was a priest in Jerusalem at the time of the Roman conquest and a colleague of R. Yochanan ben Zakkai. Zechariah ben ha-Katzav addressed the issue of a woman who was kept captive by non-Jews. If held for ransom, she was permitted to live with her husband after being released. However, if the captors had intended to kill her, after being released, she was forbidden to live with her husband, under the assumption that she submitted to the non-Jews to save her life. If a non-Jewish army had occupied a city, the wives of all the priests were prohibited from continuing to live with their husbands unless they brought witnesses (even women or slaves) who could attest to their purity; the word of the woman herself was not considered sufficient proof. Zechariah ben ha-Katzav declared: "I swear by the sanctity of the Temple that her hands did not move out of my hand [i.e., his wife was never out of his sight and thus he knew she remained pure] as long as the heathens [Roman soldiers] were in Jerusalem." However, other sages noted: "No one may testify concerning himself [i.e., in this matter, his testimony cannot be accepted]" (Ket. 27a–b).

Zeira, Palestinian *amora* (third/fourth century).

Born in Babylonia, where he studied in the great academies of Sura and Pumbedita, Zeira is one of the most cited sages in the Talmud. When Zeira emigrated to the Land of Israel, "He fasted one hundred fasts to forget the Babylonian teaching so that it would not trouble him [interfere with his new studies]" (BM 85a). The Palestinian method of study was far simpler than the Babylonian, and Zeira did not want the dialectic system he had diligently learned in Babylonia to interfere with the clearer, more direct approach used in the Land of Israel. Zeira reveled in his adopted country: "The very atmosphere of the Land of Israel makes one wise" (BB 158b), and "Even the ordinary conversation of the people of the Land of Israel requires study" (Lev. R. 34:7). Although a renowned scholar, Zeira modestly declared: "If the generations [of scholars] that preceded us were like angels, then we are like men; if they were like men, we are like donkeys" (Shab. 112b).

When Zeira moved to the Land of Israel, he could not find a ferry to take him across the Jordan. Therefore, he grabbed hold of a narrow rope bridge that stretched across the river and reached the other side. A heretic viewing this scene sneered, "You hasty people, who put your mouth before your ears [i.e., at Mount Sinai, when you said 'na-aseh v'nishma' (we will do and then understand), thus accepting the Divine commandments before even knowing what they contained], you still have no patience." Zeira calmly replied, "This is the spot where Moses and Aaron stood and they were not permitted to cross over into the Promised Land. Who could assure me that I would be worthy [of entering]?" (Ket. 112a). In another version, his love for the Land of Israel and eagerness to arrive there were so intense that he crossed the Jordan fully clothed (JT Shev. 4:9).

When asked by his students why he lived so long, Zeira replied: "In all my days, I have never shown anger [impatience] in my house; walked in front of one greater than I [in Torah knowledge]; meditated about Torah matters in filthy alleys; walked four cubits without musing over Torah matters or without wearing *tefillin*; fallen asleep in the study hall, neither a full night's sleep or even a nap; rejoiced at the disgrace [stumbling] of another; or called a colleague by a disparaging nickname" (Meg. 28a). Whenever Zeira had an argument with someone, he would repeatedly pass by the person's house in the hope that the other would see him and come out, thus restoring peace between them. "On concluding his prayer [Zeira] added the following: 'May it be Your will, O Lord our God, that we neither sin nor bring upon ourselves shame or disgrace more than our fathers'" (Ber. 16b).

Why was the Book of Ruth included in the biblical canon when it contains no mention of ritual laws? According to Zeira, it was "to teach us how great is the reward of those who do deeds of lovingkindness" (Ruth R. 2:14). After the death of her husband, the Moabite Ruth opted to devotedly accompany her grieving mother-in-law Naomi back to Israel. Boaz, a wealthy landowner, meticulously obeyed the Torah mandate to permit the poor to glean from the corners of his fields. Moreover, he commanded his workers to make certain that Ruth received enough food to support her and Naomi. For these acts of lovingkindness, Ruth and Boaz were rewarded as being the great-grandparents of King David.

In the description of how the eminent sages used to participate actively in preparations for the Sabbath, it was noted that Zeira "kindled the fire" (Shab. 119a). When "tired from studying" . . . [Zeira would] sit by the door of the school of R. Nathan bar Tavi, so that he could rise when a scholar passed and thus earn a reward in the World to Come (by showing respect to learned people)" (Ber. 28a). He deemed "worth all the rest of my learning" in the dictum: "If one sneezes in his prayer it is a good sign for him, that as they give him relief below [on earth] so they give him relief above [in heaven]" (Ber. 24b). Warning against sleeping during time allocated for study, Zeira said, "If one dozes in a house of study, his knowledge will be rent to pieces [i.e., he will forget most of it, retaining only scraps]" (Sanh. 71a). Among Zeira's famous statements are: "A man should not promise something to a child and not keep the promise because he will thereby teach him to lie" (Suk. 46b), and "For [performing a commandment in] an exemplary manner one should go up to a third of [the ordinary expense involved in] its observance" (BK 9b).

When Zeira died, the sage delivering the eulogy stated: "Babylonia [lit., 'the land of Shinar'] gave him birth; the Land of Glory [Israel] reared him as its darling; 'Woe is me,' laments Tiberias, for she mourns the loss of her most precious jewel [distinguished citizen]" (MK 25b). *See also* Jonah; Oshaia Rabbah; Rava.

Ze'iri, Babylonian *amora* (third century).

Ze'iri was a disciple of Rav in his native country and later of R. Yochanan in the Land of Israel. When R. Yochanan offered Ze'iri the hand of his daughter in marriage, Ze'iri refused because he was a Babylonian (and of purer birth) and R. Yochanan only a Palestinian. One day they "were traveling on a road and came to a pool of water. Ze'iri placed R. Yochanan on his shoulder and carried him across." R. Yochanan then observed, "Our learning is fit [appeals to you], but our daughters are not?!" (Kid. 71b).

The Rabbis rejected the concept of *caveat emptor* (let the buyer beware), instead placing the full responsibility for disclosing defects and other shortcomings on the seller, even in the absence of a written guarantee. The Talmud uses a story concerning Ze'iri to contrast this rabbinic view with the standard business practices employed in other areas at that time. Arriving in Alexandria, Ze'iri purchased a donkey without realizing that it was a magical animal produced by sorcery from a kind of wooden board that reverted to its original form when brought in contact with water. When he stopped at a stream to give the donkey a drink, the magical spell was broken and the animal dissolved before his eyes and became a board of wood. When he attempted to get his money back, the vendor replied: "Were you not [the esteemed] Ze'iri, we would not return [your money]; does anyone buy anything here [in Egypt, deemed the original home of magical arts] without first testing it with water?" (Sanh. 67b).

Ze'iri was so well respected as an explicator of *beraitot* that Rava observed, "Every *beraita* not explained by Ze'iri was not truly explained" (Zev. 43b). A saying of R. Hanina transmitted by Ze'iri was: "The son of David [Messiah] will not come until there are no conceited [arrogant] men in Israel" (Sanh. 98a).

Zerika, Palestinian *amora* (fourth century).

A disciple of numerous renowned masters, Zerika once remarked to R. Safra the difference between the approaches of the sages of Babylonia and the Land of Israel when faced with a severe drought. The sages of Babylonia boldly prayed for rain openly, while those in the Land of Israel did so modestly and in private. "When the world was in need of rain, the pious men of Babylonia (R. Huna and R. Hisda) said: 'Let us assemble and pray. Perhaps the Holy One, Blessed be He, may be reconciled and send rain.' But the great men of the Land of Israel, such as R. Jonah father of Mani, would go into his house when the world was in need of rain and say to his [family]: 'Get my haversack and I shall go and buy grain for a *zuz*.' Leaving his house, Zerika would go and stand in some low-lying spot—in accord with verse from Psalms (130:1), 'Out of the depths have I called You, O Lord'—and dressed in sackcloth he prayed and rain came. When he returned home [his family] asked him, 'Have you brought the grain?' He replied: 'Now that rain has come, the [entire] world will feel relieved'" (Taan. 23b).

Zerika agreed with the opinion of R. Jacob ben Korshai: "The *halachah* is always in agreement with R. Akiva when he differs from a colleague of his; with R. Jose ben Halafta even when he differs from several of his colleagues; and with Rabbi [Judah ha-Nasi] when he differs from a colleague of his" (Er. 46b). In the name of R. Eleazar ben Pedat, Zerika quoted the maxim: "Whoever makes light of washing his hands [before and after a meal] will be uprooted from the world" (Sot. 4b). In a discussion of the mishnaic phrase dealing with who is a "foolish pietist . . . [one] who brings destruction on the world" (Sot. 20a), Zerika cited the response of R. Huna: "One who is lenient with himself [in the interpretation of the Law] and strict with others" (Sot. 21b).

Zutra. *See* Mar Zutra.

Zutra bar Tobiah, Babylonian *amora* (third century).

In most of his Talmudic citations, Zutra bar Tobiah quoted his teacher, Rav. For example, "From where do we learn that a blessing should be said over sweet odors? Because it says, 'Let every soul [*neshamah*, lit., "breath"] praise the Lord' [Ps. 90:6]. What gives enjoyment to the soul and not to the body? A fragrant smell" (Ber. 43b). Another saying of Rav transmitted by Zutra bar Tobiah was: "Better a man throw himself into a fiery furnace than publicly put his neighbor to shame" (Ket. 67b).

Zutra bar Tobiah reported his teacher as stating, "By ten things was the world created: by wisdom, understanding, reason, [physical] strength, rebuke [limitation and restraint], might [moral power], righteousness, judgment [enforcement of justice], lovingkindness, and compassion." He then added the biblical proof texts for this assertion: "by wisdom and understanding, for it is written: 'The Lord founded the earth by wisdom; He established the heavens by understanding' [Prov. 3:19]; by reason, for it is written, 'by His knowledge the depths were burst apart' [Prov. 3:20]; by strength and might, for it is written, 'who by His strength fixed the mountains firmly, who is girded with might' [Ps. 65:7]; by rebuke, as it is written, 'The pillars of heaven were trembling, but they became astonished at His rebuke [stiffening the previously weak and shaky pillars of heaven]' [Job 26:11]; . . . by righteousness and judgment, for it is written, 'Righteousness and justice are the base of Your throne' [Ps. 89:15]; by lovingkindness and compassion, for it is written, 'O Lord, be mindful of Your compassions and Your mercies, they are as old as time' [Ps. 25:6]" (Hag. 12a). *See also* Zebid.

Appendix A
Chronological List of Rabbis

Fourth/third century B.C.E.	Shimon ha-Tzadik
Third century B.C.E.	Antigonus of Sokho
Second century B.C.E.	Jose ben Yochanan Jose ben Yo'ezer Joshua ben Perachyah Nittai of Arbela
First century B.C.E.	Admon ben Gaddai Avtalyon Ben Hei Hei Honi the Circle-Drawer Judah ben Tabbai Shemaiah Shimon ben Hillel Shimon ben Shetach
First century B.C.E./ first century C.E.	Hillel Jonathan ben Uzziel Shammai
First century C.E.	Abba Hilkiah Abba Sikra Bava ben Buta Ben Bag Bag Eleazar ben Arach Gamaliel I Hanan ha-Nechba Hanina ben Dosa Joshua ben Gamla

Judah ben Bathyra
Shimon ben Gamaliel I
Shimon ben Nethaniel
Yeshebab the Scribe
Yochanan ben Zakkai
Zadok ben Eleazar
Zechariah ben ha-Katzav

First/second century

Akabiah ben Mahalalel
Akiva
Dosa ben Harkinas
Eleazar ben Azariah
Eleazar of Modi'in
Eliezer ben Hyrcanus
Elisha ben Abuyah
Gamaliel II
Halafta
Hananiah ben Akashia
Hanina Segan ha-Kohnim
Imma Shalom
Ishmael ben Elisha
Jose ben Kisma
Jose ha-Kohen
Jose the Galilean
Joshua ben Hananiah
Joshua Hagarsi
Judah the Baker
Nahum of Gimzo
Nechunia ben Gudgada
Nechunia ben Hakanah
Pappus ben Judah
Samuel ha-Katan
Shimon the Pakulite
Tarfon
Yochanan ben Nuri

Second century

Abba Benjamin
Abba Gurion of Sidon
Abba Jose ben Simai
Abba Saul
Abtolmus ben Reuben
Ahai ben Josiah

Aquila
Ben Azzai
Ben Bava
Ben Dama
Ben Peturah
Ben Zoma
Beruriah
Dostai ben Yannai
Eleazar ben Harsom
Eleazar ben Hisma
Eleazar ben Jose
Eleazar ben Judah of
    Bartota
Eleazar ben Mattai
Eleazar ben Parta
Eleazar ben Shammua
Eleazar ben Shimon
Eliezer ben Jacob
Eliezer ben Jose
    ha-Galili
Hanan I
Hananiah
Hananiah ben Hakinai
Hananiah ben Teradion
Hidka
Hiyya
Hutzpit the Interpreter
Ilai I
Ishmael ben Jose ben
    Halafta
Ishmael ben Yochanan
    ben Beroka
Jonathan
Jose ben Halafta
Jose ben Judah
Jose ben Judah of Kefar
    Habavli
Joshua ben Korcha
Josiah
Judah ben Bathyra
Judah ben Ilai
Judah ben Tema

Levitas of Yavneh
Mathia ben Heresh
Meir
Nathan
Nehemiah
Nehorai
Onkelos
Pinchas ben Yair
Reuben ben Estrobile
Shimon bar Yochai
Shimon ben Akashiah
Shimon ben Eleazar
Shimon ben Gamaliel II
Shimon ben Halafta
Yochanan ben Beroka
Yochanan the Sandle-
    maker

Second/third century	Palestine	Babylonia
	Gamaliel III	Abba bar Abba
	Halafta ben Dosa	Assi
	Hama bar Bissa	Rav
	Hanina bar Hama	Samuel
	Judah ha-Nasi	Samuel bar Isaac
	Shimon ben Judah	Samuel bar Shilath
	ha-Nasi	
	Shimon ben Menasia	
	Yannai	

Third century	Palestine	Babylonia
	Abbahu of Caesarea	Abba bar Kahana
	Adda of Jaffa	Adda bar Ahava
	Alexandri	Anan
	Bana'ah	Dimi bar Joseph
	Bar Kappara	Hamnuna II
	Eleazar ben Pedat	Hanan bar Abba
	Eleazar Hakapar	Hinena bar Idi
	Gamaliel IV	Hisda
	Hama ben Hanina	Hiyya bar Rav
	Hanan II	Huna
	Hezekiah ben Hiyya	Jeremiah bar Abba
	Hiyya bar Abba	Judah bar Ezekiel

Hiyya bar Ashi
Ilfa
Jeremiah ben Eleazar
Jonathan ben Eleazar
Jose ben Hanina
Joshua ben Levi
Judah II
Judah ben Hiyya
Levi
Levi ben Lahma
Levi ben Sisi
Mani bar Pattish
Shimon ben Jehozadak
Shimon ben Lakish
Simlai
Yochanan
Yudan ben Ishmael

Judah bar Samuel bar
  Shilath
Mar Ukba
Nathan bar Asia
Oshaia
Oshaia Rabbah
Rabbah bar Abbuha
Rabbah bar Bar Hana
Rabbah bar Hana
Rava bar Hinena the
  Elder
Samuel bar Nachmani
Shila
Ze'iri
Zutra bar Tobiah

Third/fourth century

Palestine
Ammi
Avdimi of Haifa
Dimi
Hanina ben Papa
Helbo
Ilai II
Isaac Nappacha
Judah III
Judah bar Shila
Rami bar Ezekiel
Rava
Samuel bar Ika
Shimon bar Abba
Shimon bar Pazzi
Tanhum ben Hanilai
Ulla
Ulla bar Rav
Zeira

Babylonia
Abba bar Zavda
Abbaye
Aha bar Bizna
Aha bar Jacob
Assi
Hamnuna I
Hana bar Bizna
Joseph
Kahana
Nachman bar Jacob
Rabbah bar Huna
Rabbah bar Mari
Rabbah bar Nachmani
Rabbah bar Rav
  Hanan

Fourth century

Palestine
Avdimi bar Hama
Bar Hedya
Berechiah

Babylonia
Aha ben Adda
Amram Hasida
Aviya

Gamaliel V
Hanin
Hanina ben Abbahu
Hezekiah
Hillel II
Isaac bar Joseph
Jonah
Judah ben Shimon
Mani
Mar bar Ravina
Mari bar Rachel
Menasia bar Tachlifa
Nachman bar Hisda
Nachman bar Isaac
Papa
Rabbah bar Shila
Rabin bar Adda
Rafram bar Papa
Rami bar Hama
Safra
Sheshet bar Idi
Tanhuma bar Abba
Yudan
Zebid

Bebai
Dimi bar Hinena
Dimi of Nehardea
Dimi the brother of R.
    Safra
Hama
Hananel bar Papa
Hiyya bar Ammi
Huna bar Hinena
Huna bar Joshua
Huna bar Nathan
Jeremiah

Fourth/fifth century

Palestine
Ashi
Gamaliel VI
Isaac bar Mesharsheya
Mar Zutra
Mesharsheya
Ravina I
Samuel of Difti
Shimi bar Ashi

Babylonia
Amemar

Fifth century

Palestine
Hama ben Papa
Hanina of Sepphoris
Ravina II

Babylonia
Mar bar Rav Ashi
Rabbah Tosfa'ah

Appendix B
Maps of Talmudic Academies

Talmudic Academies in Babylonia

Talmudic Academies in the Land of Israel

Glossary

Abba. Familiar form of the Hebrew word for "father."

Aggadah. Nonlegal rabbinic writings in the Talmud and Midrash that include statements of major moral and ethical principles (often elucidated by the use of parables and anecdotes), stories about biblical heroes and the great Rabbis, and Jewish folklore. Unlike *halachah*, *aggadah* is not legally binding. It serves to explain and clarify Jewish laws and customs and accentuate the ethical ideas of the Torah.

Agunah (chained woman). One whose marriage has in fact ended, but who legally remains a married woman (bound to a husband who no longer lives with her) and thus is unable to remarry. The *halachah* prescribes that a marriage can only be dissolved by divorce, with a valid divorce document (*get*) delivered by the husband to the wife, or the death of either spouse.

Akedah (binding of Isaac). Hebrew term for the biblical account of the Divine command to Abraham to offer his son Isaac as a sacrifice to test the patriarch's loyalty and faith (Gen. 22).

Aleinu (It is our duty). Opening word and name for a prayer proclaiming the sovereignty and unity of God, which is found near the end of every prayer service.

Aliyah. Literally meaning "ascent," the Hebrew word used to describe the honor of being called up to read a portion from the Torah.

Am ha'aretz. Literally "people of the land," a Hebrew phrase used in the Bible to refer to the Jewish masses. In Talmudic times, this term was applied to the common people who did not observe rabbinic ordinances.

Amidah (standing [prayer]). Referred to in the Talmud as simply *Ha-Tefillah* (The Prayer) and now known popularly as the *Shemoneh Esrei* (18 [blessings], though there actually are 19), the *Amidah* has been the core of the prayer service since the destruction of the Second Temple.

Amora (explainer). Teacher of Jewish law in the Land of Israel and Babylonia after the redaction of Mishnah by Judah the Prince (c. 200 C.E.). The discussions of the *amora'im* (200–500 C.E.), who interpreted the Mishnah and applied it to case law, form the Gemara, which together with the Mishnah constitute the Babylonian Talmud and the Palestinian Talmud.

Apocrypha. Literally meaning "hidden books," the collective name for Jewish books written in the Hellenistic and Roman periods that were included in the Septuagint (Greek translation of the Bible) but not accepted into the normative Hebrew canon.

Arachin (Ar.). Fifth tractate of Kodashim (holy things) in the Mishnah, it deals with the laws of valuations of people, houses, fields, and objects vowed to the Sanctuary.

Aramaic. Ancient Semitic tongue that was the official language of the Persian Empire and became the vernacular of the Israelites who were exiled to Babylonia after the destruction of Jerusalem in 586 B.C.E.

Ark of the Covenant. Oblong portable cabinet of acacia wood, inlaid with pure gold both inside and outside, which contained both the shattered first tablets and the intact second tablets of the Ten Commandments. It was carried by the Levites during the Israelites' trek through the wilderness as a visible reminder of the covenant between God and the people, providing assurance that the Divine Presence was always with them on their journey.

Av bet din. Literally "father of the law court," the Hebrew title of the vice president of the Supreme Court (Sanhedrin) in Jerusalem during the Second Temple period.

Avodah Zarah (Av. Zar.). Eighth tractate of Nezikin (damages) in the Mishnah, it deals with laws concerning the prohibition of idolatry.

Avot. *See* Pirkei Avot.

Avot de-Rabbi Natan (ARN). Minor tractate of the Talmud, a commentary on the Mishnah tractate Avot. It has traditionally been ascribed to R. Nathan, the second-century son of a Babylonian exilarch, who moved to Palestine and was the chief *halachic* adversary of Judah the Prince.

Babylonian Talmud. Compendium of the wide-ranging discussions and elaborate interpretations of the Mishnah by scholars known as *amora'im* in the great academies of learning in Babylonia.

Bar. Hebrew term meaning "son of" used in Babylonia during the Talmudic period.

Baraita. Aramaic word meaning "outside," a piece of legal, historic, or *aggadic* tradition that was not included in the Mishnah of Judah the Prince. *Baraitot* are attributed to rabbinic teachers who lived in the Land of Israel at or before the time of the Mishnah.

Bat kol. Literally "daughter of the voice," this Hebrew expression was commonly used in the Talmud to denote a heavenly voice or the voice of God, which was heard by individuals or groups of people. Distinct from a prophetic communication, it often functioned in the context of giving approval to a *halachic* decision.

Bava Batra (BB). Third section of the first tractate of Nezikin (damages) in the Mishnah, it deals with property law (real estate, inheritance, sales, and partnerships) and such issues as beautification and protection of the environment and honest business practices.

Bava Kamma (BK). First section of the first tractate of Nezikin (damages) in the Mishnah, it deals with torts (damages to person and property). It requires wrongdoers to ask for forgiveness and injured parties to grant it.

Bava Metzia (BM). Second section of the first tractate of Nezikin (damages) in the Mishnah, it deals with civil law (lost and found property, fraud, usury, bailments, relations with workers).

B.C.E. (acronym for "Before the Common Era"). This neutral term is used by Jews and biblical scholars to denote the period traditionally labeled "B.C." (before [the birth of] Christ) by Christians.

Bechorot (Bek.). Fourth tractate of Kodashim (holy things) in the Mishnah. Literally meaning "firstlings," it deals with the laws relating to firstborn children and animals.

Beitzah (Betz.). Seventh tractate of Mo'ed (festivals) in the Mishnah, it deals with general laws regarding the festivals.

Ben. Hebrew term meaning "son of" used in the Land of Israel during the Talmudic period.

Berachot (Ber.). First tractate in Zera'im (seeds) and the initial tractate in the entire Mishnah, it deals with blessings and prayers, illustrating the central role these play in Jewish life.

Bet Midrash. Literally "house of study," in Talmudic times this Hebrew term was used to describe an academy for the study of Jewish religious texts that was presided over by a legal scholar. Today, it refers to an independent religious school or one located in a synagogue.

Bikurim (Bik.). Eleventh and final tractate of Zera'im (seeds) in the Mishnah, it deals with the ceremony and laws relating to the offering of the first fruits at the Temple.

Birthright. Privilege of the firstborn son in ancient Israel to lead the family and receive a double share of the inheritance.

C.E. (acronym for "Common Era"). This neutral term is used by Jews and scholars to denote the period traditionally labeled "A.D." (*anno Domini*; in the year of the Lord [i.e., Jesus]) by Christians.

Cubit. Biblical measurement of length, based on the distance between the elbow and the tip of the middle finger, which in an average man equals about 18 inches (1.5 feet or 45 cm).

Demai (Dem.). Third tractate in Zera'im (seeds) in the Mishnah, it deals with the requirements for tithing produce when there is doubt whether proper tithes have been given.

Deuteronomy Rabbah (Deut. R.). *See* Midrash Rabbah.

Ecclesiastes Rabbah (Eccles. R.). *See* Midrash Rabbah.

Eduyot (Eduy.). Seventh tractate of Nezikin (damages) in the Mishnah, it primarily deals with various rabbinic teachings (testimonies, *eduyot* in Hebrew) of later sages on the legal controversies and rulings of earlier authorities, such as those between Bet Hillel and Bet Shammai.

Ephod. Ornamented long vest worn by the high priest over the blue robe. Attached to the ephod was the breastplate containing the *Urim* and *Thumim*.

Eruv. Literally meaning "blending" or "intermingling," a rabbinically permitted way to overcome the restrictions on carrying and travel on the Sabbath while preserving the sanctity of the day. The establishment of an *eruv* takes advantage of the legally mandated permission to carry inside a private domain by converting a large public area into a huge "private domain."

Eruvin (Er.). Second tractate of Mo'ed (festivals) in the Mishnah, it deals with the permissible limits for carrying on the Sabbath.

Esther Rabbah (Esth. R.). *See* Midrash Rabbah.

Exilarch. Political head of the Jewish community in Babylonia from the first through the thirteenth centuries.

Exodus Rabbah (Exod. R.). *See* Midrash Rabbah.

Gehenna. Greek form of the Aramaic "*Gehinnom*" (the Valley of [the sons of] Hinnom), the ravine in the southern part of ancient Jerusalem. Although translated as "Hell," the traditional rabbinic view of *Gehenna* was a purgatory, where even the worst of sinners would spend only a year.

Gehinnom. *See Gehenna.*

Gematria. Interpretive device whereby words are understood through the numerical value of their letters (numerology).

Genesis Rabbah (Gen. R.). *See* Midrash Rabbah.

Get. Talmudic term for a formal divorce document that is signed by the husband and then delivered to his wife. Just as a Jewish marriage is entered into by a contract between husband and wife (see *ketubah*), it can be terminated only by a legal document nullifying the original contract.

Gittin (Git.). Sixth tractate of Nashim (women) in the Mishnah, it deals with the laws of divorce.

Golem. Legendary creature made of dust and clay by human hands in a magical, artificial way to serve its creator. The most famous *golem* legend involved the sixteenth-century Rabbi Judah Loew of Prague, who created one to protect the Jews of his city against a false charge of blood libel.

Haftarah. Literally meaning "concluding portion," a selection from the Hebrew prophets that is read after the Torah reading on Sabbaths, major festivals, and fast days.

Haggadah. Literally meaning "telling" (of the Exodus), a collection of prayers and blessings, stories, legends, commentaries, psalms, and songs that are traditionally recited at the Passover seder.

Hagigah (Hag.). Twelfth tractate in Mo'ed (festivals) in the Mishnah, it deals with the special sacrifices for the three pilgrimage festivals.

Halachah. Literally meaning "walking," the all-inclusive term for the body of law (rules, prohibitions, requirements) that governs every aspect of Jewish life and constitutes the essence of Jewish religious and civil practice.

Hallah (Hal.). Ninth tractate of Zera'im (seeds) in the Mishnah, it deals with the dough offering to the priests.

Hametz. Hebrew term for leavened products, which are explicitly prohibited on Passover. The Rabbis deemed that this characteristic applied to the five species of grain indigenous to the Land of Israel—wheat, barley, oats, rye, and spelt.

Hanukah. Eight-day festival, beginning on the twenty-fifth of Kislev (December), which commemorates the victory of Judah Maccabee and his followers over the army of the Syrian ruler, Antiochus Epiphanes, and the rededication of the defiled Temple (165 B.C.E.).

Hanukiah. Eight-branched candelabrum, also called a "Hanukah menorah," which is lit as the major ritual associated with the festival.

Havdalah. Literally meaning "separation," an ancient ritual ceremony that marks the conclusion of the Sabbath (or a festival).

Hazzan. Synagogue official who leads the congregation in prayer and song.

Hermeneutics. Method of biblical interpretation developed by the Rabbis of the Talmudic period.

Holy of Holies. Innermost portion of the Temple, which housed the Ark of the Covenant. A windowless ten-meter cube, the Holy of Holies was entered only once a year, by the high priest on Yom Kippur.

Horayot (Hor.). Tenth tractate of Nezikin (damages) in the Mishnah, it deals with erroneous decisions (*horayot*) made by the court on matters of religious law (and how to correct them).

Hullin (Hul.). Third tractate of Kodashim (holy things) in the Mishnah, it deals with the ritual slaughter of animals and the dietary laws.

Intercalation. Addition of an extra month seven times in every nineteen years. This was necessary because the Jewish lunar calendar is approximately eleven days shorter than the solar year. Without any adjustments, the festivals would "wander" and shift from their appointed seasons of the year.

Judge. Title for the twelve leaders of the Israelites after the death of Joshua until the beginning of the monarchy. Well-known judges include Deborah, Gideon, Jephthah, and Samson.

Kavanah. Hebrew word meaning "devotion, intent, or conscious purpose," which describes the state of mind required for praying or performing a *mitzvah*.

Keriah. Ritual tearing of a garment as a sign of grief, which is a traditional Jewish mourning custom.

Keritot (Ker.). Seventh tractate of Kodashim (holy things) in the Mishnah, it deals with the biblical punishment of *karet* (punishment "at the hands of Heaven") and lists the offenses to which it was applied.

Ketubah. Literally meaning "written document," the Jewish marriage contract. Written in Aramaic, it stipulates the obligations of the husband toward his wife, including his duty to "maintain, honor, and support her as it is fitting for a Jewish husband to do."

Ketubot (Ket.). Second tractate in Nashim (women) in the Mishnah, it deals with the mutual rights between husband and wife as detailed in the marriage contract (*ketubah*).

Kiddushin (Kid.). Seventh tractate in Nashim (women) in the Mishnah, it deals with the laws of betrothal and marriage (including prohibited marriages).

Kilayim (Kil.). Fourth tractate in Zera'im (seeds) in the Mishnah, it deals with prohibitions against "diverse kinds"—crossbreeding and mingling of varied species of plants, animals, and clothing. *See also Sha'atnez*.

Kippah. Head covering worn by Jews in modern times. Also known by its Yiddish equivalent *yarmulke* (skullcap), it has become a universally recognized symbol of Jewish identity.

Kohen. Member of the hereditary priestly caste (*kohanim*), the male descendants of Aaron. They were to be shown honor and deference because they were consecrated to God and offered the sacrifices to the Lord.

Lag ba'Omer. Thirty-third day of the counting of the *omer*. According to tradition, the terrible "plague" that afflicted the students of R. Akiva ceased on that day.

Lamentations Rabbah (Lam. R.). *See* Midrash Rabbah.

Lashon ha-ra. Literally "evil speech" but translated as "gossip," the term refers to any derogatory or damaging statements against an individual, even when the slanderous or defaming remarks are true, which if publicized to others would cause the subject physical or monetary damage, anguish, or fear.

Levirate marriage (*yibbum*). Obligation of a surviving brother to marry the widow of his brother, if he died without having sired children.

Levites (*levi'im*). Descendants of the tribe of Levi (third son of Jacob and Leah), who were consecrated by Moses to serve in the Tabernacle and Temple as gatekeepers, musicians, teachers, and assistants to the priests (*kohanim*).

Leviticus Rabbah (Lev. R.). *See* Midrash Rabbah.

Lulav. Branch of the date palm that is part of the four species used on Sukkot. The four species are often collectively called *lulav*, since it is their largest member.

Machoza. Town in Babylonia, on the shores of the Tigris, which was an important Jewish center and site of a major talmudic academy after the destruction of Nehardea in 259. In the early fourth century, many scholars from the academy of Pumbedita moved to Machoza, but this center of learning was destroyed in 363.

Major prophets. The three prophets—Isaiah, Jeremiah, and Ezekiel—whose writings are substantially longer than the combined output of the twelve so-called "minor" prophets.

Makot (Mak.). Fifth tractate in Nezikin (damages) in the Mishnah, it deals with the rules governing flogging, false witnesses, and the cities of refuge.

Mamzer. Often mistranslated as "bastard," this Hebrew word does not refer to someone born out of wedlock. Instead, a *mamzer* is the child of a sexual relationship between a man and woman whose marriage could never be valid under Jewish law. Examples include a child born to a married woman by some man other than her lawful husband; a child born of a woman who had remarried without having obtained a valid divorce (*get*) from her first husband; a child of an incestuous relationship. According to the Bible, a *mamzer* and all of his or her descendants may never marry a Jew, though a marriage between two *mamzerim* is permitted.

Manna. Food that nourished the Israelites during their forty years of wandering in the wilderness.

Masoretes. Textual scholars of the sixth through ninth centuries who determined and preserved the authentic (masoretic) text of the Torah.

Matzah. Unleavened bread that is made from flour and water and is the quintessential symbol of Passover.

Mechilta. *Halachic midrash* on the Book of Exodus.

Megillah. Hebrew word for "scroll," usually used for the Book of Esther (*Megillat Esther*), the reading of which is the main feature of the festival of Purim.

Megillah (Meg.). Tenth tractate of Mo'ed (festivals) in the Mishnah, it deals with the reading of the Scroll of Esther on Purim.

Menahot (Men.). Second tractate in Kodashim (holy things) in the Mishnah, it deals with the preparation of meal offerings, *tzitzit*, and *tefillin*.

Menorah. Seven-branched candelabrum that once stood in the Jerusalem Temple. One of the most beloved and enduring symbols of Judaism, the menorah is the emblem of the modern State of Israel.

Mezuzah. The distinctive mark of a Jewish home and a reminder of the Divine Presence, it consists of a piece of parchment with biblical verses that is affixed at an angle to the upper third of the doorpost on the right side of the outside door, as well as to the doorpost of every living room in the house (excluding bathrooms, storerooms, and kitchen).

Midrash. Deriving from a Hebrew root meaning "to search out," the word can refer to either the process of interpreting the Bible or to the genre of rabbinic literature that has collected these interpretations. Midrash fills in the gaps of the terse biblical narrative, which provides little information as to the thoughts and feelings of the characters or the motivations behind their actions.

Midrash Rabbah. Literally "The Great Midrash," a ten-part collection of *aggadic midrashim* on the Five Books of Moses and the five *megillot* (Song of Songs, Ruth, Lamentations, Ecclesiastes, Esther), which were written by different authors, in different locales, and in different historical eras (from the fifth to the twelfth centuries).

Mikva'ot (Mik.). Sixth tractate in Tohorot (purity) in the Mishnah, it deals with the regulations concerning the *mikveh*.

Mikveh. Literally a "collection [of water]," the Hebrew term for a ritual bath. Immersion in the *mikveh* is indispensable in the conversion of both male and female non-Jews to Judaism.

Minor prophets. Collective term for twelve prophets—Hosea, Joel, Amos, Obadiah, Jonah, Micah, Nahum, Habakkuk, Haggai, Zephaniah, Zechariah, and Malachi. The popular epithet "minor" has solely a quantitative connotation and is not necessarily an indication of relative importance.

Minyan. Literally "number," the term for the quorum of ten necessary for congregational worship and certain other religious ceremonies.

Mishnah. Literally meaning "repetition" or "teaching" in Hebrew, the earliest major rabbinic book and the basis for the Talmud. It was compiled in the early third century by Judah ha-Nasi, who sifted through, evaluated, and edited the vast number of legal opinions constituting the Oral Law that had been expressed over the centuries in the academies of learning, primarily in the Land of Israel.

Mishneh Torah. Massive fourteen-volume legal code compiled by Maimonides in the twelfth century.

Mitzvah (pl., *mitzvot*). Derived from a Hebrew root meaning "to command," the term is applied to a religious obligation. In common usage, *mitzvah* has also come to mean a "good deed." The 613 *mitzvot* in the Torah are traditionally divided into 248 positive requirements and 365 negative prohibitions.

Mo'ed Katan (MK). Literally meaning "little festival," this eleventh tractate of Mo'ed (festivals) in the Mishnah deals with the nature of work permitted during the intermediate days of Passover and Sukkot, as well as mourning on holy days.

Molech. Canaanite fire deity to whom pagans offered their young children as sacrifices.

Musaf. Literally "additional," the service added after the morning service on those days when an additional sacrifice was offered in the Temple—Sabbath, New Moon, the three pilgrimage festivals (Passover, Shavuot, Sukkot), New Year (Rosh Hashanah), and the Day of Atonement (Yom Kippur).

Nasi (prince). Talmudic title for the president of the Sanhedrin, who served as the spiritual head of the Jewish people and later was also recognized as their political leader (patriarch) by the Roman government.

Nazir. Fourth tractate of Nashim (women) in the Mishnah, it deals with the vows of the Nazirite.

Nazirite. Literally meaning either one who was "separated" (from the temptations of the environment) or "consecrated" (to God), a person who voluntarily assumed restrictions beyond the obligatory commandments in order to reach an elevated state of holiness. The Nazirite vowed to allow the hair to remain uncut during the period of the vow; abstain from grapes or grape products such as wine; and avoid any contact with a human corpse. The most famous Nazirite was Samson.

Nedarim (Ned.). Third tractate in Nashim (women) in the Mishnah, it deals with the making and annulling of vows.

Nehardea. City in Babylonia and site of a famous talmudic academy, which was destroyed in 259.

Niddah (Nid.). Seventh tractate in Tohorot (purity) in the Mishnah, it deals with family purity (menstruation and the monthly period of separation between husband and wife) and the ritual uncleanness related to childbirth.

Numbers Rabbah (Num. R.). *See* Midrash Rabbah.

Omer period. Seven weeks from the second day of Passover until the festival of Shavuot. For the ancient Israelites, the Omer period was the critical time when the success of the harvest was determined. Except for the thirty-third day of the Omer (*Lag ba-Omer*), the Omer period is observed as a time of semi-mourning, during which traditional Jews do not get haircuts, celebrate weddings, or attend concerts.

Oral Law. Body of rabbinic discussions, expositions, and commentaries on the Torah (Written Law) that deals with all aspects of existence from the most trivial to the sublime. According to tradition, it was part of the Revelation given to Moses and subsequently transmitted faithfully by the leaders of each generation to their successors. The Oral Law consists of two major divisions: *halachah* and *aggadah*.

Passover. Spring pilgrimage festival, also known as the "Feast of Unleavened Bread," which commemorates the redemption of the Jewish people from bondage and the Exodus from Egypt.

Patriarchate. Administration under the Sanhedrin, whose president (*nasi*, or "patriarch" as he was called in the outside world) became officially recognized as the representative of the Jewish people in its relations with the Roman authorities. The most famous patriarch was Judah the Prince, who compiled the Mishnah.

Pe'ah. Second tractate in Zera'im (seeds) in the Mishnah, it deals with the setting aside of the corners of the field for the poor, as well as other duties owed them.

Pesachim (Pes.). Third tractate in Mo'ed (festivals) in the Mishnah, it deals with regulations regarding Passover (*hametz*, *matzah*, paschal sacrifice).

Pesikta de-Rav Kahana (PdRK). Collection of *midrashic* homilies on the scriptural readings in synagogues for special Sabbaths and holidays, written in the fifth century in the Land of Israel.

Pesikta Rabbati (Pes. Rab.). Medieval *midrash* on the Scriptural readings in synagogues for special Sabbaths and holidays.

Pharisees. One of the three major sects in Israel before the destruction of the Second Temple in 70 C.E., its teachings formed the basis of rabbinic Judaism.

Pirkei Avot (Ethics of the Fathers). Portion of the Mishnah that has no legal content and consists of the moral and practical teachings of some sixty sages whose lives spanned nearly five centuries.

Pirkei de-Rabbi Eliezer (PdRE). *Aggadic midrash* on the biblical narrative, written in the eighth century and named for the Talmudic sage, Eliezer ben Hyrcanus.

Pumbedita. Site of one of the two major Talmudic academies in Babylonia. Founded in the third century after the destruction of Nehardea and rivaled only by the academy at Sura, Pumbedita remained a center of Jewish learning for almost 800 years.

Purim. Hebrew word literally meaning "lots," the joyous festival on the fourteenth of Adar that celebrates the deliverance of the Jews from the plot of the Persian villain Haman to kill them. The main feature of Purim is the synagogue reading of the Book of Esther.

Rabban. Variant of the title "rabbi." During the Mishnaic period, it was used as an honorary title, especially for heads of the Sanhedrin.

Rabbi. Literally "my master" or "my teacher" in Hebrew, this title was originally used during the first century C.E. to identify those Torah scholars who had been properly ordained as graduates of the Talmudic academies in the Land of Israel. (The alternative title in Babylonia was *rav*.)

Rav. Literally "great" or "teacher," an alternative title in Babylonia for "rabbi."

Rosh Hashanah. Literally "head of the year," the first and second days of the month of Tishrei (September) that are celebrated as the beginning of the Jewish New Year and the anniversary of the Creation of the world.

Rosh Hashanah (RH). Eighth tractate of Mo'ed (festivals) in the Mishnah, it deals with the laws concerning the sanctification of the New Moon, fixing the months and years, the blowing of the shofar, and the order of prayers on Rosh Hashanah.

Rosh Hodesh. Literally "head of the month," the first day of the month that correlates with the sighting of the crescent of the new moon.

Ruth Rabbah (Ruth R.). *See* Midrash Rabbah.

Sabbath. The seventh day of the week and a time of rest and spiritual renewal, which begins at sunset on Friday evening and ends on Saturday evening when three stars are visible in the sky.

Sabbatical year. In Hebrew *shemitah* (lit., "release"), every seventh year in which all the land of Israel was to lie fallow and it was forbidden to cultivate the soil, water, and prune trees. Owner, servants, gentile laborers, the poor, the stranger, and even wild and domesticated animals had equal rights to the produce.

Sadducees. One of the three major sects of Judaism in the late Second Temple period, a predominantly aristocratic group, many of whom were priests officiating in the Temple.

Sages. Collective term for the *tanna'im* and *amora'im*, the Rabbis of the Talmudic era cited in the Mishnah and Gemara.

Sanhedrin. Supreme judicial, religious, and political body in the Land of Israel during the Roman and Byzantine periods.

Sanhedrin (Sanh.). Fourth tractate in Nezikin (damages) in the Mishnah, it deals with courts of justice, judicial procedure, and criminal law.

Satan. Rather than a demonic creature who is the personification of evil and the enemy of God, the biblical word *satan* is merely a common noun that means "adversary," "accuser," or "hinderer." The role of Satan is to make things difficult for human beings, so that they can overcome temptations and their evil inclinations.

Savora'im. Literally "reasoners" and the disciples of the last *amora'im*, the *savora'im* probably completed the final editing of the Babylonian Talmud in the mid-sixth century (after the work of Rav Ashi and Ravina).

Se'ah. Biblical measurement of volume, thought to be equal to about five gallons.

Seder. Literally "order," the home celebration held on the first night of Passover (also the second in the Diaspora) that fulfills the biblical injunction that parents tell their children about the miraculous deliverance of their ancestors from Egypt.

Sefer Yetzirah. Literally "Book of Creation/Formation," widely regarded as the first classic text of Kabbalah.

Semichah. Literally meaning "laying (of hands)," the traditional ordination required before a rabbi can decide practical questions of Jewish law.

Sha'atnez. Literally meaning "mixture," this Hebrew term refers specifically to a fabric made of a mixture of wool and linen (flax) that is explicitly forbidden in the Torah.

Shabbat (Shab.). First tractate in Mo'ed (festivals) in the Mishnah, it deals with the rules governing the observance of the Sabbath, including the thirty-nine categories of prohibited work.

Shavuot. The second of the pilgrimage festivals, it occurs fifty days after Passover. Initially a harvest festival, during the Talmudic period Shavuot was transformed into the anniversary of the giving of the Torah on Mount Sinai.

Shechinah. Translated as "Divine Presence," one of the rabbinic names for God.

Shekalim (Shek.). Fourth tractate in Mo'ed (festivals) in the Mishnah, it deals with the half-shekel tax that was used to maintain the worship services during the Second Temple period.

Shema. Declaration of faith of the Jewish people in the Unity and Oneness of God and their acceptance of the yoke of the Kingdom of Heaven (Deut. 6:4).

She'ol. Dwelling place of the dead according to the Bible.

Sheva Brachot. Literally "seven blessings," the seven benedictions recited at the wedding ceremony under the *huppah* after the bridegroom places the ring on the finger of his bride.

Shevarim. One of the three sounds of the shofar, a series of three short broken notes that resemble a sobbing sound, in recognition of the sins we have committed.

Shevu'ot (Shev.). Sixth tractate of Nezikin (damages) in the Mishnah, it deals with different types of oaths.

Shiloh. Capital of Israel during the time of the judges, situated north of Bethel in the mountains of the territory of Ephraim.

Shirat ha-Yam (Song at the Sea). Victory hymn using powerful poetic metaphors and celebrating the mighty acts of God, which Moses and the Israelites sang after crossing the Sea of Reeds to escape the pursuing Egyptians (Exod. 15:1–18).

Shivah. Literally "seven," the most intense period of mourning, which is observed for father, mother, wife, husband, son, daughter, brother, and sister (including half-brother and half-sister).

Shofar (ram's horn). Ancient musical instrument that is the most recognizable symbol of Rosh Hashanah.

Showbread. Twelve large flat, oblong loaves of wheat flour (corresponding to the number of the tribes of Israel) that were placed on the Table in the Sanctuary each Sabbath. They were left there until the next Sabbath, when they were removed (miraculously still fresh) and eaten by the priests.

Sifra. *Halachic midrash* on the Book of Leviticus, probably written in the second or third century.

Sifrei. *Halachic midrash* on the Books of Numbers and Deuteronomy (third century).

Song of Songs Rabbah (Song R.). *See* Midrash Rabbah.

Sotah (Sot.). Fifth tractate in Nashim (women) in the Mishnah, it deals with the woman suspected of adultery.

Sukkah. Hastily constructed, insubstantial structure that Jews erect as part of the observance of the fall Festival of Sukkot.

Sukkah (Suk.). Sixth tractate of Mo'ed (festivals) in the Mishnah, it deals with the laws concerning the Festival of Sukkot and the four species.

Sukkot. Last of the three agricultural pilgrimage festivals. Also known as Tabernacles, this fall festival of thanksgiving celebrates the joy of the harvest and commemorates the temporary shelters (*sukkot*) in which the Israelites dwelled as they wandered through the wilderness.

Sura. Ancient city in southern Babylonia and the site of one of the two major Talmudic academies, which was founded in the early third century by Rav. In the fourth and fifth centuries, the Talmud was edited by Rav Ashi and Ravina in Sura, which remained a center of Jewish learning for 700 years.

Ta'anit (Taan.). Ninth tractate in Mo'ed (festivals) in the Mishnah, it deals with the fast days other than Yom Kippur.

Tallit. Traditional prayer shawl worn during daily morning prayers and all services on Yom Kippur. Ritual fringes (*tzitzit*) are attached to each of the four corners of the *tallit* in accordance with biblical law.

Talmud. In general use, the term "Talmud" refers to the Babylonian Talmud, though there is also a much smaller Jerusalem Talmud. The Babylonian Talmud is a compendium of the extensive discussions and interpretations of the Mishnah in the great academies of learning, by scholars known as *amora'im*, from the first half of the third century (Rav and Samuel) to the editing by Rav Ashi and Ravina around 500.

Tamid (Tam.). Ninth tractate in Kodashim (holy things) in the Mishnah, it deals with the regulations for the daily burnt offerings in the Temple as well as the general organization of that institution.

Tanach. Hebrew term for the Bible, the acronym *Ta-Na-Kh* (or *Tanach*) is derived from the initial letters of the names of its three major divisions— Torah; *Nevi'im* (Prophets); and *Ketuvim* (Writings).

Tanhuma. *Aggadic midrash* on each section of the Torah, attributed to Tanhuma bar Abba, a fourth-century *amora* and prolific *aggadist* in the Land of Israel.

Tanna. Literally "repeater" in Aramaic, the initial teachers of the Mishnah in the first and second centuries. Because of the prohibition against writing down the Oral Law, the *tanna'im* acted as "living books" in transmitting the teachings of the Mishnah to their disciples. The classical period of the *tanna'im* began with the death of Hillel and Shammai and ended with the generation after Judah ha-Nasi, the editor of the Mishnah.

Targum Onkelos. Official Aramaic translation of the Bible (second century), which is printed next to the Torah text in most rabbinic Bibles.

Tashlich (You will cast). From the verse in Micah (7:19), "You will cast (*v'tashlich*) all our sins into the depths of the sea," the ceremony on the afternoon of the first day of Rosh Hashanah in which Jews recite special penitential prayers and psalms and throw crumbs or small pieces of bread into a body of water (river, lake, or ocean) to symbolically cast away their sins.

Techeilet. Thread of blue put with seven white ones on each corner of the *tallit*. This blue was made from a rare dye that was extracted from a sea snail (*hilazon*) by a few families on the Mediterranean coast.

Tefillah. Talmudic word for the *Amidah*, the core of the prayer service since the destruction of the Second Temple.

Tefillin. Two small black leather boxes that are bound by black leather straps to the forehead and arm. Also known as phylacteries, they contain parchments on which are written the four sets of biblical verses that mention the commandment to wear them as "a sign upon your hand and as frontlets between your eyes."

Tekiah. One of the three sounds of the shofar, a long sustained blast.

Ten Lost Tribes of Israel. The tribes of the North Kingdom of Israel that, after the Assyrian conquest in 721 B.C.E., were scattered throughout the empire, assimilated, and lost to history. Over the centuries, various groups have claimed that they are the descendants of these lost tribes.

Ten Martyrs. Renowned sages executed by the Romans following the unsuccessful Bar Kochba revolt (132–135 C. E.) for defying Emperor Hadrian's prohibition, under penalty of death, against the observance and study of Jewish law. Although their identity is uncertain, they probably were among these eleven rabbis: Akiva ben Joseph, Ishmael ben Elisha, Elazar ben Dama, Hanina ben Teradyon, Judah ben Bava, Hutzpit the Interpreter, Yeshevav the Scribe, Eleazar ben Shammua, Hanina ben Hakhinai, Shimon ben Gamaliel I, and Ishmael the high priest.

Ten Plagues. Afflictions suffered by the Egyptians because of Pharaoh's refusal to allow the enslaved Israelites to leave Egypt. The ten plagues were: (1) blood; (2) frogs; (3) vermin (lice); (4) wild beasts; (5) pestilence (disease of the flocks); (6) boils; (7) hail; (8) locusts; (9) darkness; and (10) slaying of the firstborn.

Teruah. One of the three sounds of the shofar, a blast of at least nine staccato notes that has been interpreted as symbolic of wailing.

Terumah. From a Hebrew root meaning "life up from," a generic term for the various offerings given to the *kohanim*. The *terumah* could be eaten only by a ritually clean *kohen* and members of his household, including his Israelite wife and gentile slaves.

Tetragrammaton. Greek for "four-letter word," the holiest name of God and the one that is most distinctly Jewish.

Tisha b'Av. Ninth day of the month of Av (July/August), the saddest day in the Jewish calendar. This major fast day marks the anniversary of the destruction of the First Temple by the Babylonians in 586 B.C.E. and the Second Temple by the Romans in 70 C.E.

Torah (1). The first five books of the Bible. Also known as the Pentateuch, the Torah begins with Creation and ends with the death of Moses, as the Israelites are poised to cross the Jordan River into the Promised Land.

Torah (2). Inclusive term used for all of Jewish law and learning—both the Written Law and the Oral Law, as well as all the commentaries and *responsa* produced during the subsequent centuries to the present day.

Tosefta. In Hebrew *tosafah*, a collection of *beraitot* arranged according to the order of the Mishnah. About four times larger than the Mishnah itself, the Tosefta (meaning "supplement") is an independent work that contains versions of *halachot* that supplement but sometimes contradict the Mishnah.

Tractate (*masechet*). Individual volumes into which each order of the Mishnah is divided.

Twelve Tribes of Israel. Founders of the Jewish people, listed in two ways in the Bible. Jacob had twelve sons with his wives, Leah and Rachel, and his concubines, Bilhah and Zilpah—Reuben, Shimon, Levi, Judah, Dan, Naphtali, Gad, Asher, Issachar, Zebulun, Joseph, and Benjamin. However, for purposes of settling the Promised Land, Joseph received a double share that was passed on to his sons, Ephraim and Menasseh. The postsettlement listing of the Twelve Tribes of Israel excludes Levi, because this tribe inherited the priesthood rather than any of the tribal lands and was scattered among the people. Jews today are the descendants of the two southern tribes (Judah and Benjamin) plus the Levites, since the ten northern tribes were lost after the Assyrian conquest.

Tzara'at. Although often translated as "leprosy," the signs described in the Torah and the reversibility of this skin condition make it doubtful that it refers to that incurable disease. The Rabbis regarded *tzara'at* as Divine punishment for slander or tale-bearing (see *lashon ha-ra*), indicating that such a person is a "moral leper" who must be excluded from the camp of Israel.

Tzitzit. Ritual fringes that are attached to each of the four corners of the *tallit* in accordance with biblical law.

Urim and *Thumim*. Typically translated as "lights and perfections" or "revelation and truth," an oracular device sanctioned by the Bible for determining the will of God on specific issues that were beyond human ability to decide.

Written Law. The Five Books of Moses.

Yeshivah. From a Hebrew root meaning "to sit," an academy of intensive higher learning in Babylonia and the Land of Israel during the Talmudic period and beyond.

Yetzer ha-ra and *Yetzer ha-tov*. Literally the "inclination toward evil" and the "inclination toward good," these Hebrew terms reflect the rabbinic concept that within each person there are opposing natural drives continually in conflict.

Yevamot (Yev.). First tractate in Nashim (women) in the Mishnah, it deals with levirate marriage and prohibited marriages.

Yom Kippur (Day of Atonement). Major fast day, ten days after Rosh Hashanah, which is devoted to individual and communal repentance and is the most solemn day in the Jewish calendar.

Yoma. Fifth tractate in Mo'ed (festivals) in the Mishnah, it deals with the Temple service on the Day of Atonement as well as the regulations concerning the Yom Kippur fast and the significance of atonement and repentance.

Zevachim (Zev.). First tractate in Kodashim (holy things) in the Mishnah, it deals with the sacrificial system in the Temple.

Zohar. Known as the "Book of Splendor," the principal *kabbalistic* book that is the basis for all subsequent Jewish mystical works. Although attributed to the second-century rabbinic authority Shimon bar Yochai and his colleagues and disciples, scholars now believe that the Zohar was written in the late thirteenth century by Moses de Leon.

Zugot. Literally "pairs," the Hebrew term for the pairs of sages in the Land of Israel who for five generations (second century B.C.E. to first century C.E.) were the leaders of rabbinic Judaism. In each pair, one was the *nasi* (president of the Sanhedrin) and the other was designated as the *av bet din* (head of the religious court). The *zugot* were: Jose ben Yo'ezer and Jose ben Yochanam; Joshua ben Perachyah and Nittai of Arbela; Judah ben Tabbai and Shimon ben Shetach; Shemaiah and Avtalyon; and Hillel and Shammai.

Bibliography

ArtScroll Siddur. Brooklyn: Mesorah Publications, 1986.

Bader, Gershom. *The Encyclopedia of Talmudic Sages*. Northvale, NJ: Jason Aronson, 1996.

Berlin, Adele, and Marc Zvi Brettler, eds. *The Jewish Study Bible*. Oxford: Oxford University Press, 2004.

Bialik H. N., and Y. H. Ravnitzky, eds. *The Book of Legends: Sefer Ha-Aggadah*. Trans. William G. Braude. New York: Schocken, 1992.

Etz Hayim. Philadelphia: Jewish Publication Society, 2001.

Ginzberg, Louis. *The Legends of the Jews*. Baltimore: Johns Hopkins University Press, 1998.

Holtz, Barry. *Back to the Sources*. New York, Summit Books, 1984.

Jewish Encyclopedia. Jewishencyclopedia.com.

JPS Hebrew-English Tanakh. Philadelphia: Jewish Publication Society, 2001.

Kolatch, Alfred J. *Masters of the Talmud: Their Lives and Views*. Jonathan David, 2003.

Mandel, David. *Who's Who in Tanakh*. Savyon (Israel): Ariel, 2004.

Millgram, Abraham. *Jewish Worship*. Philadelphia: Jewish Publication Society, 1971

Millgram, Abraham. *Sabbath, the Day of Delight*. Philadelphia: Jewish Publication Society, 1959.

Naidich, Judah. *Jewish Legends of the Second Commonwealth*. Philadelphia: Jewish Publication Society, 1983.

Pearl, Chaim. *Stories of the Sages*. Trans. from *Sefer ha-Aggadah*, by H. N. Bialik and Y. H. Rawnitzky. Tel Aviv: Dvir, 1991.

Schottenstein Edition of the Babylonian Talmud. Brooklyn: Mesorah Publications, 2005.

Schottenstein Edition of the Jerusalem Talmud. Brooklyn: Mesorah Publications, 2005.

Soncino Talmud (CD-ROM). Davka Corporation and Judaica Press, 1991–1995.

Steinsaltz, Adin. *The Essential Talmud*. New York: Bantam Books, 1976.

Stone Chumash. Brooklyn: Mesorah Publications, 1994.

The Talmud of the Land of Israel. Trans. Tzvee Zahavy. Chicago: University of Chicago Press, 1989.

About the Author

Ronald L. Eisenberg is a professor of radiology at Harvard Medical School and on the faculty at Beth Israel Medical Center in Boston. Dr. Eisenberg has been awarded master's and doctoral degrees in Jewish studies from Spertus Institute in Chicago and has published six critically acclaimed books on Jewish topics, including *The Jewish World in Stamps* (Schreiber, 2003), *The JPS Guide to Jewish Traditions* (Jewish Publication Society, 2004), *The 613 Mitzvot* (Schreiber, 2005), *Dictionary of Jewish Terms* (Schreiber, 2008), and *What the Rabbis Said* (Praeger, 2010). He has authored more than twenty books in his medical specialty and is also a nonpracticing attorney.